leisure and
spirituality

Engaging Culture

WILLIAM A. DYRNESS
AND ROBERT K. JOHNSTON,
SERIES EDITORS

The Engaging Culture series is designed to help Christians respond with theological discernment to our contemporary culture. Each volume explores particular cultural expressions, seeking to discover God's presence in the world and to involve readers in sympathetic dialogue and active discipleship. These books encourage neither an uninformed rejection nor an uncritical embrace of culture, but active engagement informed by theological reflection.

leisure and
spirituality

biblical, historical, and contemporary perspectives

paul heintzman

Baker Academic
a division of Baker Publishing Group
Grand Rapids, Michigan

Published by Baker Academic
a division of Baker Publishing Group
P.O. Box 6287, Grand Rapids, MI 49516-6287
www.bakeracademic.com

Printed in the United States of America

Library of Congress Cataloging-in-Publication Data
Heintzman, Paul.
    Leisure and spirituality : biblical, historical, and contemporary perspectives / Paul
Heintzman.
        pages cm. — (Engaging culture)
    Includes bibliographical references and index.
    ISBN 978-0-8010-4872-2 (pbk.)
    1. Leisure—Religious aspects—Christianity. I. Title.
BV4597.55.H45 2014
248—dc23   2014034558

15 16 17 18 19 20 21   7 6 5 4 3 2 1

For my wife Monique
and my daughter Jessie

In loving memory of my parents,
Margaret and Garnet Heintzman

contents

illustrations

Figures

Tables

acknowledgments

The majority of this book (introduction through chapter 11) is a revised and expanded version of my master's thesis titled *A Christian Perspective on the Philosophy of Leisure* completed under the supervision of Dr. Loren Wilkinson at Regent College in Vancouver. I am profoundly grateful to Loren who is a model of how to think and live Christianly in today's world, which he demonstrated through his classes, directed readings courses, informal discussion groups, and a multitude of extracurricular activities. In addition, I appreciated his encouragement at key points in the thesis writing process. I am also thankful for all of my professors at Regent College in the areas of biblical studies, biblical languages, theology, spirituality, and interdisciplinary studies, all of whom to some extent informed my thesis. Particularly related to this book, I am deeply indebted to Dr. James Houston who through his courses enriched and expanded my awareness and appreciation of the classics of Christian spirituality, thereby deepening my spiritual life.

Chapters 12 and 13 arise from the social scientific research I have been conducting on leisure and spiritual well-being since completing my PhD thesis titled *Leisure and Spiritual Well-Being: A Social Scientific Exploration* at the Department of Recreation and Leisure Studies, University of Waterloo. My supervisor, Dr. Roger Mannell, helped me refine and fine-tune my social scientific research skills and pushed me to go beyond exploring the relationship between leisure and spiritual well-being to investigate the processes that link these two phenomena. I'm also appreciative of all the professors in the Department of Recreation and Leisure Studies at the University of Waterloo who enhanced and expanded my understanding of leisure and related phenomena.

There are a number of other people who directly or indirectly influenced my writing of this book. First of all, I am extremely grateful to my parents who nurtured me in the Christian faith. My decision to enroll in Recreology as an undergraduate student at the University of Ottawa was a direct result of attending Inter-Varsity Christian Fellowship's Urbana Missions Conference during my last year of high school. Throughout my undergraduate education and in various ways since then, Inter-Varsity Christian Fellowship's emphasis upon "all truth is in Christ" has led me to try and understand leisure from a Christian perspective.

As an undergraduate student at the University of Ottawa I had an excellent introduction to leisure studies through the teaching of Tom Goodale, Claude Cousineau, Peter Witt, Cor Westland, Ted Storey, Jack Wright, Roger Dion, Francis Bregha, Irene Spry, Claude Moulin, and Andrée Charbonneau. In relation to this book, the course Leisure Concepts and Values taught by Roger Dion was of considerable influence. The textbook for this course was James Murphy's *Concepts of Leisure: Philosophical Implications*, which provided an excellent introduction to the understandings of leisure at that time. One assignment in this course was to write a review of a journal article or a book related to the philosophy of leisure. This assignment provided me with the opportunity to read my first book on leisure from a Christian perspective: Gordon Dahl's *Work, Play and Worship in a Leisure-Oriented Society*. For the past decade as a professor of leisure studies at the University of Ottawa, I have had the privilege of teaching this same Leisure Concepts and Values course, which has provided me with the opportunity to regularly reflect on leisure concepts and to keep up-to-date on the latest writing on this topic.

I am deeply grateful for Dr. Glen Van Andel, Professor Emeritus of Recreation at Calvin College, who has been a faithful mentor and encourager for over 25 years. Beginning in 1989 Glen organized the annual Christianity and Leisure conferences, which have been wonderful forums to share and receive feedback on some of the chapters in this book. At the first two conferences I had the privilege of meeting the authors of books on Christianity and leisure that I had previously read: Gordon Dahl (*Work, Play and Worship in a Leisure-Oriented Society*), Robert K. Johnston (*The Christian at Play*), and Leland Ryken (*Work and Leisure in Christian Perspective*). Also, through these conferences I have developed friendships with several Christian professors of recreation and leisure studies at Christian colleges or public universities who have encouraged me in this and other writing projects.

Much of the content of this book were covered in Spring School courses I taught at Regent College, Vancouver, in 2004 and again in 2008 and also a course at Tyndale Seminary, Toronto, in the summer of 2012. I appreciate the feedback and insights of the graduate students in these courses.

I'm extremely grateful to Robert K. Johnston, the coeditor of the Engaging Culture book series, who has been very supportive of this book since I first introduced the idea to him in the summer of 2005. Robert shared the idea of the book with his coeditor William Dyrness and Baker Academic's Executive Editor Robert Hosack whose support of this book project I also greatly appreciate.

I'm very thankful for those who took time out of their busy schedules to provide me with feedback on earlier versions of some of the chapters: Karl Johnson (chapters 3, 4, and 8); Peggy Hothem (chapter 10); and Mark Harris (chapter 12). Given that I have used the American Psychological Association's Style Manual for close to 30 years, I have greatly appreciated the assistance of Lisa Ann Cockrel, Susan Matheson, and the other editors at Baker Academic to ensure that I followed *The Chicago Manual of Style*.

Thanks to Ray Corrin for his hospitality in making his apartment near the university available on those occasions when I worked late into the night. Most of all I am thankful for my wife Monique's and my daughter Jessie's patience with me, and loving care for me, as I worked many evenings and Saturdays on this book.

introduction

"Leisure" is the most misunderstood word in our vocabulary.[1]

We are "free," it seems, to have anything but a nurturing leisure. "I have so little time," goes the frequently heard lament.[2]

As the church continues to be interested in the total person, that person's total life experience, and helping each person toward meaningful, quality leisure experiences in life, an increasing concern for leisure education can be expected. . . . It should be kept in mind that the church has many thousands of years' experience in helping people from all social strata find life and find it more abundantly.[3]

The first quotation, from Witold Rybczynski's book *Waiting for the Weekend*, suggests that there is conceptual confusion in our society about what leisure is. The second quotation, from author Kathleen Norris, reflects that the practice of leisure in our society is less than ideal, in terms of both quality and quantity. The third quotation, from a textbook on leisure education, implies that the Christian church with its many years of experience has much to offer in regard to leisure. This book is an exploration of how Christians and the church can address the phenomenon of leisure in contemporary society. In this introduction, after outlining societal changes related to leisure, I present four reasons why Christians should explore this topic—possible problems with current leisure practice, potential benefits of leisure, leisure as a spiritual need, and the lack of theological reflection on leisure—and then provide the methodological approach that will be used to explore the topic, along with an overview of the book.

Societal Changes Related to Leisure

While leisure is not a unique phenomenon of contemporary society, modern social scientists have observed that leisure presents Western society with a situation that is historically unique. As a result, the last few decades have witnessed a tremendous growth in the field of leisure studies and leisure research.

This growing interest in the subject of leisure has been generated by *structural* changes in industrial society that have influenced the number of hours devoted to work. While there is a debate, which we will explore in more detail in chapter 2, as to whether work hours have been increasing or decreasing over the past few decades, over the long term the number of hours devoted to work during a week, a year, and a lifetime has decreased substantially. In the United States, the number of hours of work per employed person decreased 46 percent from 1870 to 1992.[4] Based on approximately the same time period, it has been estimated that during the 120 years from 1870 to 1990, the "waking leisure" hours of U.S. citizens increased threefold.[5] Likewise, in the United Kingdom, a study of lifetime hours discovered that the amount of time devoted to work has decreased from approximately 50 percent to 20 percent in the past 150 years.[6] Turning to Canada, in 1850 most Canadians spent approximately sixty-four hours per week on the job, whereas over a hundred years later, in 1981, Canadians worked about 38.5 hours per week.[7] In addition, the amount of work in one's lifetime reflected a growing trend toward nonwork due to later entry into the labor force, earlier retirement, greater unemployment, and longer paid holidays. These changing patterns of work in Canadian society were influenced by a number of factors, including labor-saving technology, the influence of the labor movement, and government intervention to protect workers from inadequate conditions. Thus residents of North America and Britain enjoy many more hours of time free from work than their nineteenth-century predecessors.

While we enjoy more hours of free time than those living in the mid-nineteenth century, it needs to be pointed out that the nineteenth century was somewhat of an aberration. Sebastian de Grazia observed that, compared to ancient Rome and medieval Europe, "free time today suffers by comparison, and leisure even more."[8] In classical antiquity and the Middle Ages there were approximately 115 holidays, or "holy days," a year. While some people worked long hours in those eras, this was usually only during certain seasons of the year. Winter months were not as busy and unfavorable weather often provided a break from work. The workday for most urban citizens was short. For example, in ancient Rome afternoons were usually devoted to social and recreational activities, and almost no one worked at night. Our assumption of how much more free time we have compared to earlier societies is distorted by the influence of the Industrial Revolution. As we will see in more detail in chapter 8, industrialization dramatically increased the length of the working day for most people. Undoubtedly we have much more free time than those who worked in nineteenth-century factories, but from the longer perspective, much of this increase in free time over the past one hundred years has only rectified the abnormal situation brought about by the Industrial Revolution.

The structural changes in society since the mid-nineteenth century have been accompanied by shifts in *values* and *attitudes*. A leading American leisure studies scholar, Geoffrey Godbey, wrote, "Leisure has become an increasingly expected and important part of people's lives in modern nations."[9] Theologian J. I. Packer came to a similar conclusion: "As it appears, leisure and luxury are becoming the main interests of the Western world."[10]

In a chapter titled "The Increasingly Central Role of Free Time in Modern Nations," Godbey explained,

> While the "work ethic" is supported almost everywhere and, in particular, held up as a way to get ahead economically, leisure and its use is increasingly replacing work as the center of social arrangements. Monetary spending for leisure increases, the use of federal land increasingly is for leisure purposes, resorts fill up, major professional sports events routinely sell out, participation in avocational organizations shows overall increases, gardening surges, sports bars are crowded, and the leisure use of libraries, museums, and botanical gardens increases.[11]

Chris Rojek, Susan Shaw, and Anthony James Veal have put forward a number of indicators that together coalesce to "magnify the centrality of leisure in contemporary Western lifestyle."[12] First are increased academic programs and students in leisure studies. Second, more governmental, market, vocational, and professional resources are devoted to leisure forms and practice. Third, there is greater appreciation of leisure's relationship to quality of life issues, such as the connections between popular eating and drinking leisure activities and illness and mortality, as well as the role of leisure activities in reducing stress and tension and the place of physical leisure activities in facilitating health. Fourth is the spreading of consumer culture. The fifth indicator showing that leisure is central to our lifestyle is changes in working patterns, including the casualization of work, the increase in flexible working hours, and fixed term and part-time work. Rojek, Shaw, and Veal concluded that "paid labour is now commonly viewed as the means to finance leisure choice and practice rather than" the central life interest.[13] However, they noted that leisure is not, nor will become, life's primary activity as work remains a very important source of value.[14] Writing within the Canadian context, Margo Hilbrecht suggested that it is inconclusive as to whether leisure has replaced work as people's central life interest.

> What about leisure replacing work as a central life interest? Certainly, this is the case for some, particularly those who enjoy a serious leisure pursuit. . . . It may also be true for people who find themselves in monotonous, dead-end jobs and who have adopted the compensatory approach to leisure. Even though this may be the situation for some workers, there are others whose jobs remain satisfying and engaging and who may even become completely absorbed by their work.[15]

More recently, Hilbrecht wrote that "work continues to dominate most people's lives and remains a central life interest and necessity for much of the population" for a variety of reasons, including extrinsic monetary rewards, the opportunity for self-esteem and identity development, and the character of the work itself.[16] Nevertheless, there is much evidence to suggest that the value and desirability of leisure has increased in recent decades.

After noting the increased significance of leisure in people's lives, Godbey argued that there needs to be a more organized effort to prepare people, and especially children and youth, for leisure. He sees this as the responsibility of families, educational institutions, and other social institutions. Of particular relevance for this study is his mention of religious organizations playing a role in leisure education. In addition to preparing people for leisure, he emphasized that there "needs to be a more general recognition of the importance of leisure as a powerful force for good or evil."[17] As we will see later in this introduction, leisure outcomes are not always beneficial; they can also be detrimental.

Possible Problems of Leisure Practice

Christians who seek to be salt and light in contemporary culture cannot remain silent about the changing structural and attitudinal realities but must articulate an understanding of the meaning of leisure and its relationship to work in today's society. Packer wrote,

> All around the world, as capitalist consumerism and the market economy grind on, . . . leisure and lifestyle are becoming areas of entrapment for Christian people. Failure to see this is a fact, to perceive it as a problem, to think about it in biblical antithesis to the ruling secular notions, and to plan to operate as God's counter-culture in these areas would indicate that we are already falling into the traps.[18]

Defining leisure as discretionary time, Packer went on to identify three problems in relation to contemporary leisure practice. First is the problem of idolatry or the worshiping of false gods. He suggested that some people worship their work, while others worship their leisure activities, whether they be gardening, reading, music, hobbies, sports, or vacations. Thus rather than serving God, people are serving and worshiping created things (Rom. 1:25). Second is the problem of hedonism, where pleasure is pursued as life's supreme value and goal. Packer suggested that many professing Christians do not question the assumption that leisure is wholly for increasing one's pleasure. Elsewhere he has written, "Today the love of luxury and the pull of pleasure are more intensely felt than at any time in Christendom. . . . The quest for pleasure—intellectual, sensual, aesthetic, gastronomic, alcoholic, narcissistic—is one aspect of . . . Western decadence."[19] Third is the problem of utilitarianism, where the value of an activity is determined by the degree to which the activity is productive and useful, rather than seeing the intrinsic value of the activity. From a utilitarian perspective, leisure is to "re-create" a person to work more productively. Packer explained that while leisure activities should have intrinsic value for Christians, the Christian work ethic is sometimes presented as a form of workaholism that overlooks the biblical teaching that God "richly provides us with everything for our enjoyment" (1 Tim. 6:17). Leisure time is necessary for this enjoyment.

This third problem of utilitarianism identified by Packer is supported by the findings of a PhD thesis by Margaret Hothem, who interviewed ten theologians at an evangelical Protestant seminary on the relationship between their Christian faith and leisure.[20] Leisure for these participants often had a utilitarian role, although not necessarily in regard to work. Rather, the functions of leisure were related to reward, exercise, family obligations, and change of activity. Leisure was not an end in itself or an ideal state of being, but rather it was primarily viewed for its utilitarian value.

In the past, of the three leisure-related problems identified by Packer, utilitarianism was probably the one most prevalent among Christians and Christianity. Protestant Christianity has traditionally identified itself with the work ethic. Packer noted that evangelical Christians have emphasized work over leisure, activity over rest, and life commitments over lifestyle choices, with little theological reflection on leisure.[21] Likewise, Paul Stevens wrote, "Good Christians are active in the church, and are known for their sacrificial activity rather than their experience of rest."[22]

Thus contemporary Christians have inherited a set of moral and religious values in which work is frequently conferred universal and unqualified value. Not only is work often considered the foundation of our economic system, but it is offered as a solution to personal and social problems. Activity, industry, individualism, thrift, ambition, and success have been regarded as important virtues, with work considered to be the criterion for measuring human worth. In this value system there is a diminishment of the leisure experience. This emphasis on work is consistent with my experience of teaching courses at Christian educational institutions or giving workshops at churches on a Christian view of leisure. Usually I begin these sessions by asking the students or participants why they are taking the course or participating in the workshop. In most cases the responses include concerns about working too much and being burned out and stressed but at the same time feeling guilty for taking time for rest and leisure activities. These responses personify the title of Tim Hansel's very helpful book, *When I Relax I Feel Guilty*.[23]

In present society the possibility exists that for some Christians, as suggested by Gordon Dahl,[24] the pendulum might swing from an overvaluing of the work ethic to an overvaluing of a leisure ethic, where the concern is now with the first two problems identified by Packer—idolatry and hedonism. Although acknowledging that commitment to Christian service, achievement, and work is strong in most churches, Leland Ryken pointed out the opposite problem where some Christians are so preoccupied with pursuing leisure activities that they are not available to serve in the church, and sports and television have made the Sunday evening service obsolete.[25] A similar observation is made by Karl

Johnson in the concluding sentence of his PhD thesis, titled "From Sabbath to Weekend": "On Sunday many Christians are watching football or, as Shulevitz puts it, charting the shortest distance between their megachurch's ATM and the mall."[26] The challenge to contemporary Christians is to establish a biblical understanding of work and leisure and their relationship that is appropriate for twenty-first-century society. Alternatives to both the traditional work ethic that has dominated Christian life and to the hedonism and narcissism characteristic of some contemporary approaches to leisure need to be considered. A Christian perspective that acknowledges the creational mandate of work and yet finds value in leisure needs to be articulated.

The Potential Benefits of Leisure

After identifying the problems with contemporary leisure practice, Packer went on, quoting Ryken, to state that leisure is something that should be valued by Christians.

> All leisure . . . is a gift from God that, when used wisely, "provides rest, relaxation, enjoyment, and physical and psychic health. It allows people to recover the distinctly human values, to build relationships, to strengthen family ties, and to put themselves in touch with the world and nature. Leisure can lead to wholeness, gratitude, self-expression, self-fulfillment, creativity, personal growth, and a sense of achievement." So leisure should be valued and not despised.[27]

Many of the reasons given in the above quotation of why leisure is to be valued by Christians are consistent with the notion of leisure benefits. Within the leisure and recreation field, during the last two decades much effort has been devoted to identifying and documenting the benefits of leisure activities, programs, and services. A benefit may be defined as "a *change* that is viewed to be advantageous—an improvement in condition, or a gain to an individual, a group, a society, or to another entity."[28] The substantial textbook *Benefits of Leisure*, published in 1991, sought to provide an exhaustive list of leisure benefits along with a thorough assessment of the research that documents these benefits.[29] The following year *The Benefits of Parks and Recreation* documented four types of leisure benefits—personal, social, economic, and environmental.[30] This book was updated in 1997 and again in 2009 in a digital format called the Benefits Databank. One of the criticisms of the leisure benefits approach is that it tends to emphasize only the positive outcomes of leisure. While this is the case, in a retrospective chapter included in the 1991 *Benefits of Leisure* textbook, Roger Mannell and Daniel Stynes noted,

> A full understanding of the beneficial consequences of leisure also requires knowledge about the detrimental consequences. Leisure choices involve both benefits

and costs to individuals and society. What may be seen as a benefit to one individual or social group may be a cost to another. One level of exercise may be a benefit, too much a cost.[31]

Rather than the "benefits of leisure," it is probably more appropriate to use the terminology "outcomes of leisure," which includes both beneficial and detrimental outcomes. Such an approach was taken in the World Leisure Organization's 2006 *Hangzhou Consensus* that summarized a number of the empirically documented outcomes of leisure.[32] Table 1.1 summarizes some of the outcomes enumerated in this report. As can be seen, both beneficial and detrimental outcomes are recognized. Nevertheless there are numerous empirically documented beneficial outcomes in the following areas: social functioning; physical, psychological, and spiritual health and well-being; youth development; aging; family and community; the economy; and the environment. These outcomes support Packer's claim, noted earlier, that leisure should be something that Christians value. Of particular interest for readers of this book may be the spiritual outcomes of leisure, which we will consider now.

Table 1.1

Selected Outcomes of Leisure from the *Hangzhou Consensus*

Social Benefits

- Leisure provides opportunities for family development, relationship building, and community bonding.
- Leisure provides opportunities for shared experiences, intimacy, and emotional closeness.
- Leisure provides opportunities for cooperation and collaboration.
- Leisure can create meaningful contributions to community.
- Places for leisure can develop connections with community and culture.
- Leisure spaces can encourage cultural resistance and resistance to stereotypes and other forms of social control.

Health and Well-Being

- Leisure, viewed as discretionary behavior outside of work and other obligations, positively influences physical, psychological, and spiritual health and well-being through opportunities for making meaningful choices and through the benefits provided by specific activities.

- Leisure is not automatically good for health and well-being. Leisure choices and activities can have neutral or negative impacts, and displace behaviours that contribute to health and well-being.
- The benefits of physically active leisure for physical health are scientifically well documented, and the evidence for the psychological health and well-being benefits of other forms of leisure is still emerging, ranging from reasonably well established to highly speculative.
- Some evidence exists that leisure involvements contribute to individual health and well-being by structuring free time and replacing idleness with constructive behavioral alternatives.
- Research suggests that fun and pleasurable leisure experiences not only enhance the quality of the present moment but cumulatively contribute to long-term psychological well-being.
- Leisure contributes to identity formation and affirmation, and the evidence suggests that

Continued

- under some circumstances it may contribute to personal psychological growth.
- Good evidence is emerging that leisure can promote coping and personal growth in response to the stress of daily hassles and negative life events that include disability and illness.
- Leisure involvements have been found to contribute to health and well-being by positively influencing other domains of life, such as work, family, and interpersonal relationships. However, some types of leisure can negatively affect the quality of experience in these domains.

Youth Development

- For youth, leisure can be a powerful context for human development, but at the same time it can be a context for risky behaviour; these may not be mutually exclusive.

Ageing

- Leisure is a context within which individuals can distance themselves and resist ageist stereotypes but is also a context within which these stereotypes can be perpetuated.
- Although the relationships between leisure and ageing well are complex, leisure can provide meaningful opportunities for continued engagement in life—for being, becoming, and belonging—and is essential for ageing well.

- A growing body of research demonstrates that leisure is positively and significantly related to the physical, cognitive, emotional, psychological, and social well-being of older adults and can play an important role in coping with the stresses associated with life changes and transitions experienced in later life.

Family and Community

- Leisure is a prominent component of family life and a primary context for the development of individuals' leisure aspirations, experiences, and competencies.
- Community leisure opportunities may contribute positively or negatively by challenging or reinforcing divides and inequalities.

The Economy

- Leisure is a significant component of developed economies, accounting for around a quarter of consumer expenditure and a significant quantity of public sector resources.

The Environment

- Leisure, recreation, and tourism contribute to the development of pro-environmental attitudes, values, ethics, and behaviours.
- Leisure, recreation, and tourism is an important basis (as economic and political justification and social mobilization) for the protection of natural, historical, and cultural resources and landscapes.

Source: Edgar L. Jackson, ed., *Leisure and the Quality of Life: Impacts on Social, Economic and Cultural Development: Hangzhou Consensus* (Hangzhou, China: Zheijiang University Press, 2006), 5, 13, 14, 15.

Leisure as a Spiritual Need

Contemporary leisure scholars have made connections between leisure and spirituality. In discussing the spiritual orientation of leisure, James Murphy wrote, "Leisure may be viewed as that part of life which comes closest to freeing us. . . . It enables [people] to pursue self-expression, enlightenment, and [their] inner soul."[33] Stanley Parker noted, "Separated from . . . [a] spiritual view, the idea of recreation has the aimless circularity of simply restoring us to a state in which we can best continue our work."[34] Godbey stated that "recreation and leisure behaviour is ultimately infinite, nonrational, and full of meaning which is, or can be, spiritual."[35] "Leisure worthy of the name," Thomas Goodale wrote, "must be filled with purpose, compelled by love, and wrapped in the cosmic and spiritual."[36]

Not only have leisure studies scholars recognized the connection between leisure and spirituality, but religious writers have also acknowledged the role of leisure in spiritual development and wellness. For example, in his book *Religion and Leisure in America*, Robert Lee wrote, "Leisure is the growing time of the human spirit."[37] Gwen Wright stated that "creative leisure is viewed as a necessary component of a spirituality which provides the basis for wholeness in humans."[38]

In his book *Leisure: A Spiritual Need*, Leonard Doohan, who defined leisure as "a mental and spiritual attitude, a condition of mind and soul," made a very thorough case that leisure needs to be integrated into all dimensions of spirituality, because the crucial components of Christian spirituality require leisure.[39] A healthy spiritual life needs the healing dimension of leisure. For physical, psychic, social, and intellectual development we need to spend time with God in order to experience God in our life and in creation. Doohan stated, "To fail to see the value of simply being with God and 'doing nothing' is to miss the heart of Christianity. We need leisure to be with God."[40] Leisure provides opportunities for the reflection, meditation, and interiorization needed to have a true rather than a distorted image of God. Leisure is also necessary for contemplation and prayer because preparation for growth in prayer is through leisure. Leisure develops our sense of mystery, awe, wonder, and appreciation so that we are open to the creative and ever new action of God. In addition to personal reflection and meditation, leisure provides opportunities for sharing with others that enables the church to grow in creative ways. Furthermore, social action and social justice require a leisure component, as authentic prophetic engagement results from reflection and contemplation, not just activity.

Doohan explained that it is in leisure that a person is prepared for encounters with God.[41] Faith overtly expresses itself in the relaxed focus of leisure. Not only is leisure necessary for the affirmation of faith, but it is also needed to experience what we believe and to nourish our faith.[42] In leisure circumstances, Jesus calls people to himself.[43] Doohan wrote,

> Hurriedly moving in no direction, many people are numb to spiritual values. A leisurely approach to life is a basic element in the first stages of spiritual growth. Conversion is not possible without pause, rest, openness, appreciation of who the Lord Jesus is, reflection on the cross, awe and wonder at the resurrection.[44]

Leisure can be a preparatory step toward conversion, which begins a journey into God's rest.

Leisure, argued Doohan, is not an optional component of spirituality but rather an essential component that needs to be reintegrated into contemporary Christianity to facilitate human maturity and counterbalance the pressures of contemporary life.[45] Authentic leisure, claimed Doohan, inspires spiritual growth, re-creative self-enrichment, relaxation and rest. "No authentic spirituality exists without leisure."[46] Drawing on the writings of Teresa of Avila, Doohan pointed out that the recognition of the importance of leisure for spiritual growth and development is an insight that is not new.[47]

Doohan suggested that a leisured approach to life, characterized by reflection, a sense of wonder, openness, appreciation of the works of God, and the acceptance of life as a gift, is essential to both the early and later stages of spiritual growth, and this is especially the case for those who are busy.[48] Twentieth-century Christianity has tended to stress pietistic practices, apostolic action, the work ethic, and human effort, while neglecting the more contemplative, leisurely, and passive dimensions of life. Christian spirituality has overemphasized work and action. However, leisure unmasks our exaggerated efforts at religious and personal growth and exposes our false spiritual attitudes that do not give sufficient emphasis to the activity of God within us. Given the character of God's grace, leisure is the main form of preparing for one's initial and continuing encounters with God.[49] In sum, "spirituality requires a leisured approach to life."[50]

In the twenty years since Doohan's book was published, there has been increasing empirical literature on leisure and spirituality. Although only a few studies in this body of literature are specifically on Christian spirituality, these few studies document the benefits of leisure for Christian spiritual growth. For example, in a qualitative study on the role of leisure in the spirituality of New Paradigm Christians (defined as those who go to New Paradigm churches—seeker churches that have a contemporary style of service geared especially to those who are not members of the church), Jennifer Livengood found the following: solitary and quiet leisure activities provided opportunities to pray and focus on God; social leisure activities with both Christians and non-Christians were considered spiritual experiences; interactions with Christian friends provided the opportunity to grow spiritually; and leisure in natural settings provided opportunities to encounter God and to experience God's creation.[51] My study on the spiritual impact of a wilderness canoe trip by a men's church group found that the main impact of the trip was spiritual friendships among the men, which were facilitated by conversations on the trip, an openness among the group members because it was a men's-only group, being in the wilderness that was viewed as God's creation, and the opportunity to get away from the distractions of everyday life to focus on spirituality.[52] Likewise, in a study of new Christians in Holland, leisure activities were seen as opportunities to focus on developing relationships with God and other Christians.[53] These relatively recent empirical studies seem to confirm Doohan's emphasis on the importance of leisure to spiritual growth and development.

Need for Theological Reflection on Leisure

While Christians, particularly since the Reformation, have produced a large body of theological literature to provide ethical guidance with respect to work, there is a paucity of theological and ethical guidance on leisure. We are confronted with what Lee called a "theological lag," in that theological and ethical thinking lags behind social and technological change.[54] The evangelical theologians interviewed in Hothem's PhD thesis on Christian faith and leisure acknowledged that the church and Christian educational institutions have generally been silent on topics related to the theology and ethics of leisure.[55] A number of the theologians in the study explained that they had not previously thought very much about leisure ethics and that churches have not provided much education on leisure. As recently as 2012, Ben Witherington III observed that there was hardly any ethical and theological discussion from a biblical perspective on topics such as rest and play and their importance in Christian life.[56]

Why is it important to consider a theology of leisure? Drawing on Edward Fitzgerald's comment that the little theological attention that has been given to leisure has led to an incomplete theology of the other dimensions of Christian living,[57] Doohan stated that theological reflection on leisure is vital for an adequate theological foundation for Christian living, including Christian spirituality, in today's contemporary society.[58] Without a theology of leisure, Christian understandings of leisure may merely reflect secular understandings of leisure. In a study of Australians, John Schulz and Chris Auld found that "agreement with the orthodox beliefs of Christianity did not affect the meanings individuals associated with leisure,"[59] and thus leisure meanings for Christians were not that much different from the rest of the population. (This lack of difference might also be explained by methodological reasons related to how the study was designed and implemented, as well as the use in the study of leisure meanings—for example, leisure as exercising choice or escaping pressure—rather than traditional leisure concepts—for example, leisure time, leisure activity.) James Houston pointed out that far too often the Christian conception of leisure, as a pause between work and more work, is a secular notion of leisure.[60] Similarly, Dahl, who was a Lutheran campus minister, believed that the problem with most attempts to develop a Christian understanding of leisure is that they have generally begun with conventional notions of leisure, such as leisure as free time.[61] Christians have frequently understood leisure principally in terms of its juxtaposition to work—as rest or reward from work.

Dahl believed that since there is not a clear Christian understanding of leisure, the first step must be one of conceptual reconstruction.[62] In recent decades Christians have begun to develop a more thorough philosophy of leisure. Foundational work was done in the mid-twentieth century by Roman Catholic theologian and philosopher Josef Pieper in *Leisure: The Basis of Culture*, which described leisure as an attitude of mind and a condition of the soul that is rooted in divine worship.[63] The 1960s witnessed two books written by American Protestants. Lee, in *Religion and Leisure in America*,[64] illustrated how human time and God's eternity are connected in the Christian use of leisure, while Rudolf Norden's book *The Christian Encounters the New Leisure* argued that Christian vocation encompasses both God's call to leisure and to work.[65]

Christian reflections on leisure were more prevalent in the 1970s and the 1980s perhaps because of the prediction at that time of a leisure society that has not really materialized. Dahl, author of *Work, Play and Worship in a Leisure-Oriented Society*, conceived of leisure as a *qualitative* aspect of human life: a Christian experiences leisure when he or she comes into complete awareness of the freedom found in Christ.[66] David Spence, in *Towards a Theology of Leisure with Special Reference to Creativity*, suggested that "leisure is the opportunity and capacity to experience the eternal, to sense the grace and peace which lifts us beyond our daily schedules."[67] Harold Lehman, a Mennonite scholar who wrote *In Praise of Leisure*, saw leisure as God's gift that takes on many different dimensions.[68] Writing on the related topic of play in his book *The Christian at Play*, theologian of culture Robert Johnston stated that the style of life God intended for us includes both work and play in a crucial balance and creative rhythm.[69] John Oswalt, an Old Testament scholar, explored leisure through the themes of creation, grace, freedom, worship, and the Christian's calling in his book *The Leisure Crisis: A Biblical Perspective on Guilt-Free Leisure*.[70] Jeanne Sherrow, a leisure studies scholar, in her book *It's About Time: A Look at Leisure, Lifestyle, and Christianity*, maintained that leisure is time that God has given Christians to make a difference in themselves, in day-to-day living, in relationships, and in the world.[71] Ryken, in *Work and Leisure in Christian Perspective*, emphasized leisure primarily in terms of recreation or activity and within a rhythm to life that involves a balance of work and leisure.[72] Roman Catholic theologian Doohan, in *Leisure: A Spiritual Need*, argued that leisure is a spiritual attitude that must be integrated into every aspect of our lives in order to make us more fully human and more fully Christian.[73] Not only are most of these books out of print but much of the social scientific data on leisure trends and issues included in them are now dated.

Since 1990 fewer books have been written on Christian perspectives of leisure, although there have been a few excellent essays on the topic, such as those by Packer[74] and Douglas Joblin.[75] Ryken's 1987 book was revised and republished in 1995.[76] A collection of academic essays on a range of leisure topics, presented at the annual conference of what is now called the Christian Society for Kinesiology and Leisure Studies, was published in 1994 and republished in 2006.[77] In 2004 British churchman Graham Neville published *Free Time: Towards a Theology of Leisure*, composed of eight essays that offer a theological reassessment of leisure based on the expansion of free time in contemporary society.[78] Most recently, in 2012 New Testament scholar Witherington wrote *The Rest of Life: Rest, Play, Eating, Studying, Sex from a Kingdom Perspective*. As suggested by the title, Witherington's book includes chapters on rest and play but does not directly address the topic of leisure.[79]

This book builds on these previous books and in particular unites Roman Catholic and Protestant traditions of leisure through a holistic approach that also brings a Christian perspective to the leisure studies literature and research. For example, this book interacts with the most recent ideas and issues in the leisure studies field, such as the psychological state-of-mind view of leisure, feminist perspectives on leisure, serious leisure, casual leisure, and project-based leisure. Furthermore, the book makes connections between leisure and spirituality that are not a significant focus of previous books, other than Doohan's.[80]

At least seven understandings of leisure have been identified by contemporary scholars in the field of leisure studies: (1) the classical view of leisure as a state of being; (2) leisure as non-work activity; (3) leisure as free time; (4) leisure as a symbol of social class; (5) leisure as a psychological experience or state of mind; (6) feminist understandings of leisure as enjoyment; and (7) the holistic view of leisure. This book, in an attempt to continue to clarify and to develop a fuller understanding of the concept of leisure from a Christian perspective for our time, will take the position that none of these seven concepts is essentially or exclusively a Christian concept. Rather, more than one of these concepts may be descriptive of a Christian understanding of leisure. In particular, based on Christianity's biblical and theological heritage, a holistic concept of leisure will be argued for: one that combines the classical state-of-being concept of Augustine, Aquinas, medieval monasticism, and more recent Roman Catholic scholars, with the Protestant understanding of leisure as non-work activity.

Methodology and Overview of Book

Methodologically this book will proceed from the premise that the theological task "consists of an ongoing dialogue between biblical, traditional and contemporary sources."[81] While this process will be submitted to the authority of Scripture, it is necessary to interact with the realities and ideas of contemporary culture, and also to learn from the twenty centuries of Christian history and tradition. Thus this book will begin with an examination of the contemporary leisure situation and moves on to a survey of the concept of leisure throughout history before discussing possible biblical background to the leisure concept.

The book consists of six parts and an epilogue. Part 1 examines leisure within the contemporary cultural context of Western industrial society in general and North American society in particular. First, the major concepts currently used to define leisure will be outlined. The seven concepts of leisure, identified above, will be presented as a useful guide for our thinking. These concepts will then provide a framework in which we can both analyze the approaches to leisure throughout history and discuss the biblical backgrounds to the concept of leisure. Second, current issues and trends in leisure practice will be summarized.

Part 2 focuses on the historical background to the concept of leisure. The contemporary meanings of leisure can be better understood when placed in historical perspective. Within the scope of this book, it will be impossible to review comprehensively the history of the leisure concept, and thus only a brief historical survey of leisure will be given with particular focus on two historical conceptions of leisure that have been predominant throughout Christian history: (1) the state-of-being view of leisure as developed in Greek culture and adapted in the contemplative life of medieval monasticism; and (2) the Protestant view of leisure as non-work time and activity that was often conceived as reward for past work or recreation that refreshes for future work.

In order to interact Christianly with both contemporary and historical concepts of leisure, and to develop an adequate Christian perspective on the philosophy of leisure, it is necessary to enter into "the systematic hermeneutical task of appropriating the meaning of the biblical message for today's world."[82] Thus part 3 consists of a review of the biblical record in the hope of uncovering insights into a biblical understanding of leisure. Although there is not a fully developed theology of leisure in the Bible, various writers have identified a number of biblical elements that may guide us in our understanding of leisure today. This part of the book will primarily focus on two of these elements that are essential to the development of a Christian understanding of leisure: (1) the principle of Sabbath rest reflective of the Old Testament idea of rhythm to life; and (2) the concept of rest that is characteristic of the quality of life available in Jesus Christ. However, other biblical words and themes related to leisure will also be explored.

A Christian philosophy of leisure cannot be arrived at in isolation but must include a treatment of the biblical doctrine of work. Therefore part 4 looks at the concept of work with particular reference to the concept of leisure. The place of work in contemporary society will be discussed, the history of work reviewed, and the biblical doctrine of work examined.

Part 5 is a Christian perspective on the philosophy of leisure, arising from the synthesis of biblical, historical, and contemporary sources in parts 1–4, and will be developed through a four-stage process. First, beginning with the biblical material, it will be argued that the biblical idea of rhythm in life supports the Protestant view of leisure as non-work time or activity that refreshes and restores, while the concept of rest reflective of the quality of life offered in Jesus Christ provides support for what has historically been called the classical state-of-being view of leisure. Second, it will be argued that the classical and Protestant views of leisure are not mutually exclusive but together provide a comprehensive, holistic view of leisure. Third, an identity approach to the relationship between work and leisure, consistent with the holistic view of leisure, will be argued for. Fourth, the ethics of leisure will be examined.

Given that the classical understanding of leisure as a state of being and a spiritual attitude is central to the concept of leisure developed in part 5, part 6 explores the relationship between leisure and spirituality, in particular the leisure-spiritual processes that link leisure with spiritual well-being and a model that explores leisure-spiritual coping (that is, spiritual coping that exists within the context of one's leisure). I will illustrate the leisure-spiritual coping model using a case study that describes my own experience of cancer. Finally, the epilogue provides a brief summary of the theology of leisure presented in the book.

part 1

leisure in contemporary society

concepts of leisure

To develop a Christian understanding of leisure for today it is necessary to understand the philosophical ideas about leisure and leisure-related practices in contemporary culture. This chapter will first briefly discuss current issues in the philosophy of leisure, and then explain the major concepts currently used to define leisure. The next chapter will review current trends and issues related to leisure.

Issues in the Philosophy of Leisure

In present society to some degree, and especially among certain subcultures, there has been a swing of the pendulum from the work ethic to a leisure ethic. Dahl identified the possible danger "that the generation which has shattered the idols of work will be tempted to bow down before the gods of play—sacrificing their new freedom and dignity upon the altars of pleasure in liturgies of distraction and frivolous pursuits."[1] More recently Neville wrote that "leisure is in danger of being taken over by what has been called a 'fun morality.'"[2] Although work may still be the central life interest of most people, the work ethic is being replaced to some extent, or at least augmented or altered, by a new leisure ethic: people who do not receive satisfaction from their work search for a deeper meaning in other activities.

Within this context it is important to consider how we go about understanding leisure. Francis Bregha, in a thought-provoking article titled "Philosophy of Leisure: Unanswered Questions," wrote,

> More and more people are occupying their leisure with a bewildering variety of acts and deeds that leave their trace on their neighbours and communities. . . . As our society is undergoing multiple transformations, the very pace of change

creating tension and confusion, the ethics of leisure acquires also a developmental importance. Where are we heading? In a deliberately jaundiced view, one can offer a disturbing diagnosis: Resources are vanishing. Education fails to educate. Religions are being replaced by narcissistic cults. Bureaucracies keep cloning themselves. Culture and pornography grow indistinguishable. Wealth coagulates in ever fewer hands. Creativity and productivity are declining. Contraception undercuts the will to perpetuate. . . . No need to go on. Even if half of such statements were true, there would be enough reason to be concerned. Leisure, caught in a web of these mutually reinforcing trends, risks then to become an exercise in collective hedonism. Much of it can be swept with the growing current of general corruption.[3]

Thus alternatives to the hedonism and narcissism characteristic of many contemporary approaches to leisure need to be considered. Again we turn to Bregha, who wrote, "It is therefore quite evident that leisure, in addition to its individual and collective morality, is inviting us to a philosophical discussion of its destination. What is its meaning within the complexity of the historical changes surrounding us? What is it that leisure should protect and improve? What should leisure resist and avoid?"[4]

The crucial question is: Where do we start in our philosophical discussion of leisure? Bregha again: "Once more we are facing the initial philosophical difficulty. Mankind can possibly be understood biologically, physically, even chemically. When the task is to explain it philosophically, we must call in an outside principle, such as God, Reason, historical determinism or nature."[5] What is to be our starting point or principle? Bregha viewed this as "the basic difficulty in the formulation of leisure's philosophy."[6] In the past, leisure was seen within the context of the divine. In another essay Bregha wrote,

Leisure's link to religion has been gradually weakened as religious festivities, rites and feasts occupy less and less of a place in our lives. Instead, modern technology has multiplied the means available for the pursuit of secular leisure while saying very little about their value or moral direction. It should be clear that we are possibly the first generation that faces a peculiar problem in regard to our leisure. As long as leisure found its origin in God and its expression in partaking in worship, its morality was beyond reproach. Now that a divorce has taken place and leisure is linked to freedom rather than God, a vast question mark as to its ultimate purpose is before us. Who is to guide us through the maze of good and evil now that God is absent and freedom is perceived in many ways?[7]

Bregha concluded his essay,

Leisure itself still depends as much on the knowledge and wisdom entering into our options, on our ability to choose goals that will bring us happiness, on our inner strength and independence that affirm our unique character, and finally on an environment that is conducive to leisure because it offers peace, per chance beauty and quiet enjoyment.[8]

This approach to discussing leisure is thoroughly humanistic in that it places humans at the center: leisure depends on human "knowledge and wisdom," a human's "ability to choose goals," and a human's "inner strength and independence." However, for a Christian, as Doohan pointed out, "a humanistic approach to life is not enough to ensure the fruits of leisure."[9] Rather, any philosophical discussion of leisure must naturally be carried out within the context of the divine. While society has divorced leisure from God, the Christian asserts that the ultimate purpose of leisure can be found only when it is again linked to God, for God is Creator and Lord of our lives. If God is not therefore acknowledged as the Lord of leisure, then we cannot develop an adequate and meaningful philosophy of leisure.

However, Bregha saw the attempt to develop a philosophy of leisure in association with something else (in our case, God) as having two specific dangers. First, it "leads to the paradox of subordinating leisure, once isolated as a state or an activity, to other, presumably higher ends—i.e., God, happiness."[10] Then leisure becomes simply an instrument or a technique. The second danger in formulating a philosophy of leisure by connecting it to some other solitary value or phenomenon lies in "forgetting that if there is to be a philosophy of leisure, it must of necessity be part of a general philosophy of life and coherent with it."[11]

These two dangers outlined by Bregha, if they really are dangers at all, can be resolved only when leisure is brought under the sovereignty of God, for if leisure is not brought under the sovereignty of God, it will then be brought under the sovereignty of humans and become subservient to human purposes. When leisure is linked to God, then the second danger will also be overcome, for God is sovereign over all life, and when leisure is linked to God, it will then be seen within the whole totality of life under the sovereignty of God.

Therefore it is essential for Christians to begin any consideration of the philosophy of leisure with the recognition that leisure must be God-centered and God-directed. How do we proceed from this starting point? If leisure is to be God-centered, then our philosophy of leisure must be informed by God's revelation to humanity through his Word; thus Scripture is our final authority in developing a Christian philosophy of leisure. However, as we saw in the introduction, since the theological task "consists of an ongoing dialogue between biblical, traditional and contemporary sources,"[12] it is necessary to interact with the realities and ideas of contemporary culture and also learn from twenty centuries of Christian history and tradition. Thus the remainder of this chapter will be a review of the main leisure concepts.

Concepts of Leisure

Imagine . . . the bewilderment a naïve researcher suffers when discovering leisure may be free time, freedom, an activity, a state of mind, or a license of some sort.

> Grasping the meaning of leisure is sufficiently frustrating that our innocent colleague might prudently move onto a seemingly simpler concept. . . . [L]eisure studies is plagued by conceptual confusion.[13]

Much time is spent in leisure sciences and leisure studies trying to define leisure. Theorists puzzle over the meaning of leisure, but no single conceptualization emerges for it or for the related terms "recreation" and "play." Definitions of leisure abound. In this chapter I will not eliminate all the confusion, but hopefully by the end of the chapter you will be able to understand the major ways that leisure has been defined in the Western world. Since North American society is increasingly multicultural, I will very briefly introduce "non-Western" examples of the leisure concepts discussed, keeping in mind that we need to be cautious when equating non-Western views and words with Western views. My approach in this chapter will be historical in that I will start with earlier understandings of leisure, then illustrate how the concept of leisure has evolved over time. A historical perspective helps us to understand how past ideas and events have shaped current ideas about leisure.

In the third edition of his textbook *Recreation and Leisure in Modern Society*, Richard Kraus identified five concepts of leisure: the classical view of leisure, leisure as non-work activity, leisure as free time, leisure as a symbol of social class, and the holistic view of leisure.[14] In *Concepts of Leisure: Philosophical Implications*, James Murphy thoroughly elaborated on these five concepts of leisure along with one other, the anti-utilitarian concept of leisure.[15] A more recent chapter, titled "Defining Leisure," does not include the anti-utilitarian concept but includes two recent leisure concepts: leisure as a state-of-mind or psychological experience and feminist leisure as meaningful experience.[16] This section will briefly review these seven concepts of leisure, which are summarized as follows:

Concept	Key Idea(s)
Classical Leisure	A state of being; an attitude
Leisure as Activity	Non-work activity
Leisure as Free Time	Time after work and existence tasks
Leisure as a Symbol of Social Class	Conspicuous consumption
Leisure as a State of Mind	An optimal psychological experience
Feminist Leisure	Meaningful experience; enjoyment
Holistic Leisure	Leisure in all of life

The Classical View of Leisure: Leisure as a State of Being

The classical view emphasizes "contemplation, enjoyment of self in search of knowledge, debate, politics, and cultural enlightenment."[17] According to Kraus, it is "a spiritual and mental attitude, a state of inward calm, contemplation, serenity, and openness."[18] David Gray summarized the classical view of leisure as "pursuit of truth and self-understanding. It is an act of aesthetic, psychological, religious and philosophical contemplation."[19] As such, leisure is engaged in for its own sake and not for another purpose. Understood in this sense, leisure involves a certain state of being, blessedness, or attitude. In contrast to contemporary Western society that often relates leisure to mechanical or clock time, leisure is a qualitative state of being; it is, like love, a condition of being, unrelated to time.

"Classical" refers to ancient civilizations, and in the Western world it refers to the view of leisure in ancient societies, such as Greece and Rome. The classical view of leisure associated with the "cultivation of self" notion arose in ancient Greece where leisure was regarded as the highest value of life and work was disdained. The ancient Greek word *scholē*, which means "leisure," was a state of being that implied freedom or the absence of the necessity of being occupied. In ancient Greece there were clear distinctions between work, recreation, and leisure: work was a means to provide for life's needs; recreation was rest from work; and leisure was the noblest pursuit in life. The ideal lifestyle consisted of leisure, but this lifestyle depended on a society where slaves, who made up 80 percent of the population, did most of the work. Since the upper classes in Greek society were not required to work, they were free to engage in such pursuits as art, politics, the business of government, law, debate, philosophical discussion, contemplation, and the enjoyment of self in search of knowledge—in general, the opportunity for spiritual, intellectual, and cultural learning and enlightenment. Thus in the ancient Greek view leisure was the basis of culture. Much of this understanding of leisure is based on the writings of Aristotle, which we will look at in more detail in chapter 3. Although Aristotle's view of leisure has received much attention, his view reflected that of aristocratic philosophers; a variety of other perspectives on leisure probably existed in ancient Greek society.[20]

While a criticism of the Greek ideal of leisure was that it was based on a society supported by slavery, the classical view, as it developed and evolved over time, did not necessarily continue to be associated with slavery. In Roman society *otium*, the Latin word for "leisure," was linked to contemplation and freedom. The Greek ideal was modified in early Christianity, where leisure became associated with the contemplative or spiritual life. As we will see in chapter 3, this Christianized understanding of the classical view is evident in medieval monasticism, as well as in the writings of Augustine (354–440), Thomas Aquinas (1225–1274), and more recently of Pieper, a twentieth-century Roman Catholic theologian and philosopher who defined leisure as "a mental and spiritual attitude . . . a condition of the soul . . . a receptive attitude of mind, a contemplative attitude" in his book *Leisure: The Basis of Culture*.[21]

Like Pieper, de Grazia, in his book *Of Time, Work, and Leisure*, brought attention to the classical view in the twentieth century.[22] Both viewed leisure as "a condition or state of being, a condition of the soul, which is divorced from time."[23] De Grazia also emphasized that leisure should not necessarily be equated with free time, since anyone may have free time, but not everyone has leisure. For de Grazia leisure was an ideal: "Leisure refers to a state of being, a condition of man, which few desire and fewer achieve."[24]

Today, the classical view of leisure is advocated by many in the Roman Catholic tradition—which is not surprising since the classical view is consistent with Roman Catholic teaching[25]—such as Doohan,[26] Dennis Billy,[27] Thomas DuBay,[28] James O'Rourke,[29] Joseph Teaff,[30] and by some (such as Douglas Steere[31]) in other Christian traditions who, like Pieper, see leisure as a spiritual attitude. The classical view is also espoused by leisure scholars who see value in Aristotelian philosophy. For example, Charles Sylvester emphasized that classical leisure, unlike some more recent concepts of leisure, involves the virtue of moral judgment; it is important to use leisure rightly.[32] John Hemingway highlighted that Aristotle viewed leisure as the arena through which an individual developed character and participated in the affairs of the community.[33]

The classical Western view of leisure has some similarities with the classical Hindu view of leisure.[34] In Hinduism a distinction is made between *Pravritti*, the active life, and *Nivritti*, the contemplative life, which is associated with leisure. *Nishkam-karma-yoga*, or inner leisure, is characterized by a relaxing peace and a mind free from turmoil.

Leisure as Activity

The leisure as activity view may be defined as "non-work activity in which people engage during their free time—apart from their obligations of work, family and society."[35] Historically, the activity view of leisure was usually a utilitarian view; that is, the activity was engaged in to achieve a benefit, such as physical health. An example that illustrates this view's utilitarian nature is this definition of leisure from the International Study Group on Leisure and Social Sciences: "Leisure consists of a number of occupations in which the individual may indulge of his own free will—either to rest, to amuse himself, to add to his knowledge and improve his skills disinterestedly and to increase his voluntary participation in the life of the community after discharging his professional, family and social duties."[36] As indicated by the last phrase of this definition, leisure has often been considered subservient to work and associated with a rhythm to life of work and recreation that is often based around the organization of work. The opportunity to engage in leisure activities is scheduled around the dominant and primary element in the rhythm—that is, work. Kenneth Roberts wrote, "Enjoying leisure in modern society is conditional upon having a job because, without work, a person's normal rhythm of life and his approach to the daily routine is undermined, and participation in normal forms of recreation and social relationships becomes impossible."[37] More recently the leisure as activity concept has not necessarily been a utilitarian view, as we will see shortly when we discuss the more recent concept of casual leisure.

Historically, a change began to take place in Western society with the shift from Greece to Rome. In Roman society *otium* (leisure) began to be seen as for *negotium's* (work's) sake. Cicero (106–43 BCE) viewed leisure as "virtuous activities" by which a person "grows morally, intellectually, and spiritually."[38] Typical of Roman writers, he suggested a person is occupied in the work of the military, politics, or business and then re-creates.[39] The classical view of leisure was gradually forgotten, work became the noblest activity, and leisure took the form of activity, or recreation, to re-create oneself to go back to work. As we will see in chapter 4, this view was reinforced during the Renaissance (fourteenth through sixteenth centuries) and the Reformation (sixteenth century).

A modern proponent of the activity view of leisure was the French sociologist Joffre Dumazedier, who wrote, "Leisure is activity—apart from the obligations of work, family and society—to which the individual turns at will, for relaxation, diversion, or broadening his knowledge and his spontaneous social participation, the free exercise of his creative capacity."[40] Thus for Dumazedier leisure has three functions: relaxation, entertainment, and personal development. Relaxation "provides recovery from fatigue," entertainment "spells deliverance from boredom," and personal development "serves to liberate the individual from the daily automatism of thought and action."[41] This view of leisure is reflected in the Province of Quebec, and other French societies, where it is typical to have municipal departments of *loisirs* (leisure), which are equivalent to parks and recreation departments throughout the rest of North America. Dumazedier also wrote of semi-leisure as "a mixed activity in which leisure mingles with an institutional obligation."[42] Within a Christian context Packer categorizes weekly worship as semi-leisure.[43]

Serious Leisure. Recently Robert Stebbins developed the concepts of serious leisure, casual leisure, and project-based leisure based on an activity understanding of leisure. He defined "serious leisure" as "the systematic pursuit of . . . an activity that participants find so substantial and interesting that . . . they launch themselves on a career centered on acquiring and expressing its special skills, knowledge, and experience."[44] He identified three types of serious leisure: amateurs (e.g., amateur artists), hobbyists (e.g., collectors), and volunteers (e.g., social-welfare volunteers). The distinctive qualities of serious leisure are

- needing to persevere in the activity;
- finding a career of achievement or involvement in the activity;
- making a significant personal effort in the activity;
- obtaining long-lasting tangible or intangible benefits or rewards through the activity;

- having a strong identification with the chosen activity; and
- participating in a unique ethos or social world with others who engage in the activity.[45]

While Stebbins, in his definition of serious leisure, described it as an activity, and therefore I discuss it under the activity concept of leisure, he also noted that serious leisure can be a form of leisure experience as well as a type of leisure activity.[46] Recently, Karen Gallant, Susan Arai, and Bryan Smale suggested shifting the focus of serious leisure from an activity that has individual outcomes to an experience within community and social processes.[47]

In contrast to serious leisure, Stebbins defined "casual leisure" as "an immediately, intrinsically rewarding, relatively short-lived pleasurable activity requiring little or no special training to enjoy it."[48] Casual leisure may involve play, relaxation, passive or active entertainment, conversation, sensory stimulation, or casual volunteering. The central characteristic of casual leisure is pleasure.

Casual Leisure. Casual leisure overlaps with what was previously known as the anti-utilitarian concept of leisure, which is best expressed by the phrase "doing your own thing."[49] Gray wrote that this concept dismisses the view that all human life must produce a useful outcome: "It rejects the work ethic as the only source of value and permits the investment of self in pursuits that promise no more than the expression of self."[50] The anti-utilitarian concept of leisure is a reaction to the philosophy of utility, which prevents people from experiencing joy and participating in activities that have no purposeful end. The anti-utilitarian concept implies that leisure is a valuable end in itself. Humans need to cultivate the dimension of pleasure in their life. This concept of leisure is associated with what Charles Reich described as a "personal liberation and the primacy of pleasurable, natural, humanistic, and sensory experiences."[51] Walter Kerr articulated an understanding of leisure that embraces Reich's basic ideas: "It accents joy, encourages self-expression, and rejects the work-ethic and utilitarianism as the only sources of value in our society."[52]

Project-Based Leisure. "Project-based leisure" is "a short-term, moderately complicated, . . . though infrequent, creative undertaking carried out in free time"[53] that involves considerable effort and planning, and sometimes knowledge and skill. These may be one-shot projects, such as investigating one's genealogy, or occasional projects, such as decorating one's home for Christmas every year. Using the concepts of serious, casual, and project-based leisure, Stebbins defined "optimal leisure style" as "the deeply rewarding and interesting pursuit during free time of one or more substantial, absorbing forms of serious leisure, complemented by judicious amounts of casual leisure or project-based leisure if not both."[54] Optimal leisure lifestyles (OLLs) are realized by participation in leisure activities that individually and in combination help a person enhance one's human potential, self-fulfillment, well-being, and quality of life.

Defined as activity, leisure may have political or social purposes. Leisure may be seen as a form of political practice where everyday leisure activities can challenge or weaken dominant belief systems, thereby serving as a form of resistance.[55] Heather Mair used the term "civil leisure" to describe people who use their non-work time for social activism concerning important societal issues.[56]

The activity view of leisure has relevance in Islam.[57] The prophet Mohammed (570–633 CE) wrote: "Recreate your hearts hour after hour, for the tired hearts go blind," and "Teach your children swimming, shooting, and horseback riding."[58] In Islam, leisure activities fulfill three desires: (a) amusement, relaxation, and laughter; (b) rhythmic tunes and the experience of objects through the senses; and (c) the desire to wonder, learn, and gain knowledge.

What Is Recreation?

Before we move on to the next concept of leisure let us consider the concept of recreation, which is very similar to the leisure as activity concept. There is generally more consensus about the meaning of recreation than the meaning of leisure. The English word "recreation" is derived from the Latin word *recreatio*, which means restoration or recovery. The notion implies the re-creation of energy or the restoration of the ability to perform a specific function and therefore presupposes that some other activity has depleted one's energy or has negatively affected the ability to function.

Sebastian de Grazia defined recreation as "activity that rests men from work, often by giving them a change (distraction, diversion), and restores (re-creates) them for work."[59] Recreation may also be used to restore a person for volunteer, family, education, or health purposes. Unlike some understandings of leisure, such as the classical view where leisure is an end in itself, recreation is not engaged in "for its own sake," but represents a means to an end. For example, John Kelly defined recreation as "voluntary non-work activity that is organized for the attainment of personal and social benefits including restoration and social cohesion."[60]

Leisure as Free Time

A prevalent conceptualization of leisure in our society is the discretionary or nonobligated-time view that reflects a quantitative perspective: "that portion of time which remains when time for work and the basic requirements for subsistence have been satisfied."[61] Leisure as discretionary or nonobligatory time parallels the economic concept of discretionary money. From this perspective, time may be divided into three categories: existence (time devoted to the meeting of biological requirements and essential life-maintenance activities, such as sleeping, eating, and personal care); subsistence (time spent in work or work-related responsibilities, such as travel, study, or social involvements based on work); and leisure (time remaining after one's existence and subsistence needs have been met). These categories are not completely watertight. For example, time devoted to eating may be for pleasure and/or existence. Nevertheless, leisure is seen as discretionary time. Its most important characteristic is that it lacks a sense of obligation or compulsion and is available for use according to one's desires.

In preindustrial societies, time was viewed cyclically; that is, time was rooted in the rhythms of the natural world. People's lives revolved around sunrise and sunset, the change of seasons, and the planting and harvesting of crops. They were unlikely to separate work and leisure within their daily life, and the demands of work were often lightened by songs and storytelling. Traditional gatherings, like a barn-raising or a quilting bee, possessed both leisure and work-like components. As a result, notions of work and leisure blended together.

The Industrial Revolution (1760–1830), however, changed everything. Unlike previous eras, the work of the industrial age was focused not on the farm but in the factory. People began to move to the cities to tend to the machines. Work was situated *in space* at the factory and structured *in time* as the worker had to be at the work place at a certain time to perform work duties. Facilitated by the development of clocks, work could be assigned to specific times, and work time could be measured precisely. Time began to be viewed mechanically, and this linear notion of time began to influence and change people's understanding of leisure. Time away from work was free of the often unpleasant demands of the workspace, so it was called "free time." This free time became synonymous with leisure.

Not only is this concept common among the general population, but this approach to conceptualizing leisure is also prevalent among economists and sociologists who are especially interested in economic and sociological trends. Hence the *Dictionary of Sociology* supplies the following definition of leisure: "Free time after the practical necessities of life have been attended to; . . . Conceptions of leisure vary from the arithmetical one of time devoted to work, sleep, and other necessities, subtracted from 24 hours—which gives the surplus time—to the general notion of leisure as the time which one uses as he pleases."[62] When leisure is viewed as free time, the amount of leisure a person has depends on factors such as how long a person lives; when a person retires; the length of a person's work week; whether a person has a full-time job, a part-time job, or a second job; and the length of holidays and other paid time off. Furthermore, the size and timing of the units of free time are as important as the total amount of free time. For example, free time is different for a person who works eight hours a day for five days a week from a person who works ten hours a day for four days a week.

If one accepts this view of leisure, then leisure for the contemporary person is fragmented, as Gray described:

Currently our daily leisure is broken up into rather small segments—perhaps a little before work and a little at lunch time, but most is available in the late afternoon or early evening, after work and before bed. The total number of leisure hours per day—usually four—is broken up into small increments. This limits its uses. Our weekly leisure is weekend leisure . . . the longer period of time and more flexible schedule which mark the weekend permit activities which would be impossible during the remainder of the week.[63]

The Jewish concept of Sabbath has some similarities to the notion of leisure as free time. As we will see in chapter 5, the Jewish Scriptures command the Jewish people not to work on the Sabbath. For example, Exodus 20:8–10a reads, "Remember the Sabbath day by keeping it holy. Six days you shall labor and do all your work, but the seventh day is a sabbath to the LORD your God. On it you shall not do any work." The Sabbath is a time of no work but, as Heschel explained, also a time of celebration: "not a date but an atmosphere."[64] Thus it does not completely fit within a quantitative free-time understanding of leisure but also includes a qualitative dimension, as we will see in more detail in chapter 5. Sabbath was not only the foundation of Jewish life but it also provided a more democratic form of leisure than what was seen in Greek society. Aristotle's leisure was based on the ancient Greek institution of slavery, whereas the Jewish Torah declared that everyone, including male and female servants, had an inalienable right to Sabbath.[65] The Jewish Sabbath was adopted and modified in the Christian Sunday and Islamic Friday. As we will see in more detail in chapter 5, while it is often suggested that the roots of the Western concept of leisure are in ancient Greek society, some argue that it is equally rooted in the ancient Jewish tradition of the Sabbath with its organization of life into seven days and a valuing of leisure.[66]

Leisure as a Symbol of Social Class: Conspicuous Consumption

The concept of leisure as a symbol of social class undertands "leisure as a way of life for the rich elite."[67] In 1899, the American sociologist Thorstein Veblen wrote a classic book, titled *The Theory of the Leisure Class*, in which he questioned the intrinsic character of leisure activities and suggested that leisure behavior was influenced by the desire to impress others and distinguish oneself from other people. He defined leisure as "non-productive consumption of time. Time is consumed non-productively (1) from a sense of the unworthiness of productive work, and (2) as an evidence of pecuniary ability to afford a life of idleness."[68] He used the terms "conspicuous leisure" and "conspicuous consumption" to suggest that the visible display of leisure and consuming was more important than engaging in the leisure activity for its own sake or for personal development motivations. Thus leisure had a symbolic nature. Veblen illustrated how people in the wealthy ruling classes, throughout history, have been identified by their possession and use of leisure, while people in the lower classes emulate or imitate those in the wealthy classes so that society becomes increasingly consumptive. In previous, less-industrialized societies, more leisure opportunities were available to the privileged aristocratic members of the ruling classes who were free from labor. Veblen showed that in the feudal, Renaissance, and industrial periods of Europe's history, the possession and visible use of leisure (along with the abstention from labor) was the characteristic feature of those in the wealthy upper classes. Veblen was critical of the "idle rich" who exploited and lived on the toil of others while totally engaging themselves in a life of "conspicuous consumption." He described the way of life of the privileged class as follows:

> The . . . gentleman of leisure . . . consumes freely and of the best, in food, drink, narcotics, shelter, services, ornaments, apparel, weapons and accroutrements. . . . He must also cultivate his tastes. . . . He becomes a connoisseur . . . and the demands made upon the gentleman in this direction therefore tend to change his life of leisure into a more or less arduous application to the business of . . . conspicuous leisure and conspicuous consumption.[69]

Veblen's description of the lifestyle of the "idle rich" profoundly affected social scientists and led to the conceptualization of a leisure class. This concept views leisure as a way of life for the wealthy elite.

Veblen's analysis may be less applicable to contemporary Western life as it was in the previous eras, since working-class people today tend to have more opportunities for leisure due to a variety of factors: the diffusion of culture, increased affluence along with the spread of wealth, the increased influence of the mass media, increases in mobility, and increases in free time. These factors have led to greater opportunities for the ordinary citizen to obtain material possessions, to participate in various forms of recreation and entertainment, and hence to diminish the socioeconomic dimension of leisure. In other words, there has been a democratization of the leisure class.

While Veblen's analysis may be outdated, Kraus pointed out that it is still applicable to a small group of "jet setters."[70] Although the wealthy and privileged members of today's society may not have a great amount of free time, they still continue to participate in a wide range of expensive and prestigious leisure activities. They tend to travel extensively, to entertain, to patronize the arts, and to participate in exclusive and high-status activities. This class, whether called "jet-setters" or "leisure-class," defines itself through its use of leisure. As an example, a 2003 article in the *Financial Post*, titled "Ridiculously, Deliciously Conspicuous Consumption," reflects Veblen's theory.[71] The subtitle of the article illustrates the emulation principle: "Imagine that money's no object, that you're one of the elite making ultra-luxury goods the hot trend of the season. Now go ahead and drool." The items included an $85,000 designer piano and bejewelled underwear worth $11 million.

Although Veblen's analysis may be less relevant today, social scientific research has attempted to classify leisure behaviors and lifestyles according to social class, race, occupation, and other determinants. Murphy concluded: "Studies indicate that social class may no longer be so significant to leisure interests and behaviors, and that certain social indicators, including race, economics, education, and environment, may be more important factors in determining leisure orientation and preference."[72]

Current examples of leisure as a symbol of social class can be seen elsewhere in the world. In an ethnographic study titled *The Native Leisure Class: Consumption and Cultural Creativity in the Andes*, Rudi Colloredo-Mansfeld documented how the sale of textiles gave rise to an indigenous leisure class in Otavalo, a market town in northern Ecuador.[73] The merchant elite has become a leisure class characterized by the consumption of products, both local (e.g., fajas [sashes]) and global (e.g., televisions, cars). Wealthy Otavalena women show off their wealth by wearing a new faja for every social occasion, thereby creating an overt symbolic division. Consumption has become culturally important and a primary way to obtain stature in that the wealthy display their identity through their conspicuous consumption rather than through their work.

Leisure as a State of Mind: A Psychological Experience

The state-of-mind view of leisure, also known as subjective leisure, or leisure as psychological experience, became prominent in the 1980s. As stated by Beverly Driver and S. Ross Tocher, it may be defined as "an experience that results from recreation engagements"[74]; however, it often focuses on the optimal leisure experience. This psychological approach to leisure experiences can include properties such as

- emotions and moods that vary along a positive-negative dimension;
- feelings of relaxation, arousal, or activation that vary in intensity;
- cognitive components, such as thoughts, ideas, beliefs, and images;
- time duration—perceptions of how quickly time is passing during an experience or activity;
- levels of absorption, attention, and concentration in an activity;
- self-consciousness, self-awareness, and ego loss;
- feelings of competence in regard to knowledge or skill;
- a sense of freedom; and
- a sense of interpersonal relatedness.[75]

The state-of-mind view of leisure sees leisure as an overriding experience that is not defined in contrast to work, but rather one for which certain conditions are necessary to experience it.

The state-of-mind view is founded on psychology. The psychologist William James introduced the term "stream of consciousness" in 1890 to refer to mental experiences or conscious states perceived as ever-changing and continuous. Another psychologist, Abraham Maslow, suggested that self-actualizers experienced peak experiences, which he defined as "moments of highest happiness and fulfillment."[76] Building on the work of psychologists, an early leisure scholar, John Neulinger, defined pure leisure as "a state of mind brought about by an activity freely engaged in and done for its own sake."[77] The two criteria for this experience are perceived freedom (the perception that a person is engaging in the activity because he or she has the choice to do so and desires to do it) and intrinsic motivation (the individual gains satisfaction from the activity itself and not from an external reward).

Another psychological concept frequently associated with the state-of-mind view of leisure is the theory of "flow." The social psychologist Mihaly Csikszentmihalyi proposed that flow experiences were intensely absorbing experiences where the challenge of an activity matched the skill level of the individual so that the person lost track of both time and awareness of self (A and C on fig. 1.1).[78] If a person's skills were much higher than the challenges of the activity, the person would experience boredom (B), while if the challenges were much higher than the skills, the person would experience anxiety (D).

Figure 1.1

Csikszentmihalyi's Diagram of the Flow State

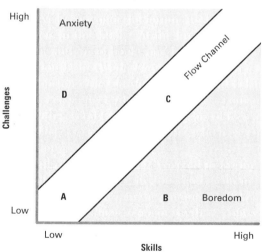

Source: Adapted from Mihaly Csikszentmihalyi, *Flow: The Psychology of Optimal Experience* (Toronto: Harper & Row, 1990), 74.

Jing Jie, the highest goal in life and the highest pursuit of Chinese Taoist leisure, has been suggested to be similar to flow.[79] In Taoism, *Jing Jie*, an essence characterized by happiness and joyfulness that underlies all organic life, cannot be pursued but is a benefit of participation in activities such as martial arts, creative arts, or meditation. The Chinese experience of *rùmí*, a fascinating, enchanting, and absorbing experience, has also been shown to be similar to leisure as a psychological experience.[80] The word *rùmí* is composed of two characters: *rù*, which means "to enter," and *mí*, which means "to be lost." Together they mean "entering into something and becoming lost in it."

What Is Play?

Although play is not the topic of this book, leisure as a state of mind shares many traits with play: intrinsic motivation, free choice, suspension of reality, and positive affect. Johan Huizinga, in his classic book *Homo Ludens*, defined play as "a free activity standing quite consciously outside 'ordinary life' as being not 'serious' but at the same time absorbing the player intensely and utterly."[81]

Feminist Leisure: Meaningful Experience

The contemporary women's movement emerged in the 1960s, but it was not until the late 1980s that much attention was devoted to women's leisure.[82] While there are a variety of feminist perspectives, all views stress that women are exploited and oppressed, and that women have a universal right to leisure. Feminists are concerned with the distortion and invisibility of female experience; the right of every woman to dignity, equity, and freedom of choice; and the removal of all forms of oppression and inequality within society.[83] Feminist theory is critical of the traditional views of leisure (i.e., free time, activity) because they are built on premises that in many cases do not apply to women. For example, the free-time view of leisure is based on a duality of paid work and leisure that is not always applicable to many women, as much of their work is at home (and unpaid), even for those who work outside the home.[84] Also, some women feel they are not entitled to or have time for leisure. Feminist theory also critiques the activity concept of leisure because women often have obligations intertwined with "recreational activities" (e.g., caring for children while swimming). Thus work and leisure may occur simultaneously, while leisure activities are frequently fragmented by the carrying out of responsibilities. Furthermore, there are unique constraints on women's participation in leisure activities.[85] Intrapersonal constraints include an ethic of care where women feel responsibility to care for others—children, parents, spouse—sometimes to the point of feeling they have no right to leisure, ultimately limiting their leisure access. Interpersonal constraints, such as social control by others, and structural constraints, such as lack of provided opportunities to participate, also place limits on women's activity participation. Meanwhile, leisure as psychological experience is criticized as being focused too much on the individual with not enough recognition of situational and social factors.[86]

The result of much feminist research on leisure has led to an enhanced understanding of leisure as meaningful experience characterized by enjoyment.[87] These meaningful experiences may be found in many aspects of life. Often meaningful experience is associated with time for self to relax and do nothing, affiliative leisure that involves relationships with other people (such as friends and family), and agentic leisure characterized by autonomy where one can express oneself through self-determined (as opposed to determined by other people) activities or experiences. Because the emphasis is on meaningful experience, the activity, social setting, or physical location is seen as a leisure container in which the experience of leisure may take place. Feminists also speak of leisure enablers, the opposite of leisure constraints, that allow and facilitate leisure experiences. An example of a leisure enabler is a sense of entitlement to leisure. Leisure may also provide women with the opportunity to engage in acts of resistance that challenge the dominant values of society and thereby lead to women's empowerment.

Feminist observations about intrapersonal (e.g., ethic of care) and interpersonal (e.g., social control by others) constraints on women's leisure also exist in non-Western cultures. For example, Chiang-Tzu Lucetta Tsai used the feminist perspective to examine the leisure practices of Taiwanese women.[88] Confucian teachings, prevalent in Taiwan, support a patriarchal society where a women's leisure is constrained by perceptions of women as passive and submissive, responsible for child rearing and domestic labor, and inherently and biologically inferior to men. Detailed regulations exist for women's leisure (e.g., women are discouraged from going out alone during leisure time), and leisure revolves around children and family. Thus gender inequality in contemporary Taiwanese leisure settings is primarily due more to premodern patriarchy and gender relations than lack of opportunity or individual obstacles. Despite the influence of Western feminism, Taiwanese women experience social pressure to conform to traditional roles in regard to leisure participation.

The Holistic Concept of Leisure

The articulation of the holistic concept of leisure emerged in the mid-twentieth century in connection with an emphasis on understanding phenomena from a holistic perspective, although in practice it has existed throughout human history. Holism, according to Murphy, "recognizes interrelationships among all things and implies that no part is meaningful outside of the whole, that no part can be identified or understood except in relation to the whole."[89]

This concept of leisure suggests a lifestyle that is holistic, in that one's life is not seriously fragmented into a number of spheres, such as work, free time, religion, and family activities. Rather, all involvements are viewed as part of a whole. According to Max Kaplan, when leisure is viewed from a holistic perspective, it is a total way of life.[90] Almost any element may be viewed as leisure, since leisure may be experienced within the context of work, family, religion, and education. Thus, as suggested by Anthony W. Bacon, leisure is a multidimensional concept consisting of a variety of elements that interact to generate specific lifestyles.[91] Therefore the holistic approach would create the possibility of experiencing leisure in a variety of situations. Kaplan wrote,

> Leisure, then, can be said to consist of relatively self-determined activities and experiences that are seen as leisure by participants, that are psychologically pleasant in anticipation and recollection, that potentially cover the whole range of commitment and intensity, that contain characteristic norms and constraints, and provide opportunities for recreation, personal growth and service to others.[92]

Work and leisure are inextricably related in this holistic concept of leisure. Thus the holistic concept eliminates the dichotomy between work and leisure that has been a serious obstacle for many people's experiencing of leisure. Leisure is no longer viewed as discretionary time and work as the supreme activity in life. This perspective calls for a value reorientation, to confer value on leisure as value has been conferred on work. Kaplan wrote, "As we seek to establish the post-industrial—hopefully, the 'Cultivated' society, a major direction has apparently become discernible—a general return to the fusions of work and nonwork which characterized the first part of the social model."[93] The aim is not only to maximize leisure but also to fuse it with satisfying work. In addition, work time would be distributed according to the rhythm of one's life. Leisure is seen as continuous time, not chopped up time, as in work life.

According to Kaplan, the holistic concept of leisure tends to fuse the two traditions of leisure as an end (the classical view of leisure) and leisure as a means of restoration and revitalization (leisure as a form of non-work activity). This conception combines leisure as a manifestation of one's essence with one's motivation to create tools and symbols to master oneself and one's environment.[94]

The basis of holistic leisure has existed for centuries, but it was conceptualized during the 1960s and 1970s in response to a variety of social influences that Murphy documented,[95] such as the counterculture (e.g., the hippie movement); an increasing emphasis on holistic understandings, where the whole is seen as more than the sum of the parts; a crisis of identity and meaning, where people were trying to find meaning in their work and in society; feelings of despair resulting from the Vietnam war; the fragmentation of life; and rapid change as documented in Alvin Toffler's book *Future Shock*.[96] Historically societies tended to be holistic, but in the feudal and preindustrial period social roles and elements of culture began to become distinguished, and then in the industrial era, work and leisure were clearly delineated. In many ways, holistic leisure returns to the preindustrial period in which work and leisure were simply different facets of everyday life.

A number of factors in the past few decades (most relating to the changing nature of work) have led to the possible development of a holistic integration of work and leisure. These factors include

- a search for authentic experiences at work and elsewhere;
- the humanization of work;
- a shift from the manufacturing to the service sector;
- a rise in professionalism;
- a broadening of the labor force with more women and more part-time workers; and
- removing work from the workplace through technology, such as computers, which reverses the trend of the industrial revolution when work was moved from the home to the factory.[97]

All these factors make it more likely to experience elements of leisure in work and to integrate work and leisure into a holistic lifestyle. Thus recently Joy Beatty and William Torbert have used the Yin-Yang symbol to describe the intertwining fusion of work and leisure.[98]

Holistic expressions of leisure may be seen in preindustrial societies, such as ancient Israel (as we will see in more detail in chapter 5), when leisure involved components of time (Sabbath), activity (festivals), place (the Promised Land), attitude (faith), and state of being (physical and spiritual rest);[99] in the monastic life where there is unity of work and leisure as monks integrate both manual and intellectual work with the contemplative life of leisure (*otium*);[100] and in the lives of many women, especially those working at home for whom work and leisure coexist.[101] Another example is Native Americans and First Nations (a Canadian term for North American tribal groups) who developed a culture based on a close association with the land and a cyclical, holistic worldview. For these peoples leisure is not a separate segment of life but is linked to all life situations, such as birth and death,[102] and is reflected in cultural ceremonies, celebrations, and festivals.[103]

Conclusion

This chapter began with a discussion of the fundamental difficulty in the formulation of leisure's philosophy and determined that for the Christian, the philosophy of leisure must begin with the sovereignty of God. Next we reviewed the major concepts of leisure found in contemporary leisure literature: the classical state-of-being view of leisure; leisure as activity; leisure as free time;

leisure as a symbol of social class; the psychological understanding of leisure as a subjective experience or state of mind; feminist perspectives on leisure as meaningful enjoyment; and the holistic view of leisure. We will return to these concepts in chapter 10 when I critique them from a Christian perspective based on historical material that is reviewed in chapters 3 and 4 and biblical material that is presented in chapters 5, 6, and 7. But first, to complete the first part of the theological task or dialogue, we will learn about current leisure trends and issues in the next chapter.

contemporary leisure
trends and issues

In order to develop a Christian understanding of leisure for today it is necessary to understand the trends and issues related to leisure in contemporary society. This chapter will review seven contemporary issues related to leisure—one issue corresponding to each of the seven concepts of leisure discussed in the last chapter. We will discuss

patterns of time use (related to the view of leisure as free time);

leisure consumption and related social and environmental justice issues (related to the view of leisure as a symbol of social class);

boredom (related to the view of leisure as state of mind);

inequality of leisure opportunities (related to feminist views of leisure);

the quality of leisure activity (related to the view of leisure as non-work activity);

the lack of a spiritual dimension to leisure (related to the classical view of leisure as a state of being); and

the work-leisure relationship (related to the holistic view of leisure).

Patterns of Time Use

If leisure is considered free time, then it is important to look at patterns in working hours and free time. Information on trends is of more value in social analysis than a snapshot of one particular year or decade. In the 1990s, two rival viewpoints appeared regarding patterns of time use related to work and leisure time.[1] Economist Juliet Schor, in her book *The Overworked American*, contested predictions of increasing leisure time and reported that leisure time has been decreasing and work hours have been increasing since World War II.[2] Taking the opposite view, John Robinson and Geoffrey Godbey argued that leisure time has increased.[3] Due to issues of measurement and the varied subgroups within the workforce, it is difficult to determine which viewpoint is correct. Several explanations for the two viewpoints have been proposed: increased work time could be due to decreasing vacation time among Americans; variations among life-cycle groups (e.g., employed parents work longer hours); and subjective measures, such as perceived time pressure.[4] We will examine both the pessimistic and optimistic views, the view that work hours have remained stable, and some explanations that may explain differences in the viewpoints.

Pessimistic View

In her chapter titled "The (Even More) Overworked American," Schor labeled the United States as "the world's standout workaholic nation." Compared to other industrial nations, it has the highest proportion of employed citizens and the greatest number of days on the job per year and hours worked each day.[5] Based on data from the U.S. Current Population Survey, Schor concluded that work hours per year increased 199 hours (based on a forty hour workweek), or approximately five weeks, from 1973 to 2000. Furthermore, for married-couple households, with household heads aged twenty-five to fifty-four, total yearly hours of paid employment by both spouses increased 12 percent, or 388 hours, between 1979 and 2000. Schor explained that while productivity improvements from 1850 to 1950 resulted in a dramatic decrease in work hours, the last three decades of the twentieth century were characterized by a constant increase in work hours. Labor productivity increased about 80 percent from 1969 to 2000, suggesting that the average worker at the turn of the millennium could produce almost two times as much as in 1969. However, instead of using that extra productivity to reduce the workweek, people used the extra money to purchase more goods produced by the consumer economy. A "powerful cycle of 'work-and-spend'" led to "an orgy of consumer" spending as per capita real consumption expenditures doubled over a thirty-year period. For example, the average physical house size increased by 50 percent.[6]

In 2006 Schor observed that within Organisation for Economic Co-operation and Development countries, average work hours for working-age persons (those considered to be able and likely to work, typically between the ages of twenty and sixty-five) decreased only 2 percent over the previous two decades, and 7 percent for all employees, which is dramatically different from the 18 percent decrease during the 1950–1980 period.[7] Despite predictions of social scientists in the 1960s that advanced industrialized societies would be societies of leisure with citizens focused on leisure not work, a lack of "free" time and high stress levels are widespread in Western societies. These subjective measures of time poverty and stress levels, argued Schor, reflect changes in actual hours of work, especially from previous trends of work time decreases. In the United States work time per employee increased 3 percent from 1980 to 2000 and an incredible 16 percent for working-age persons. The U.S. data is significant as it led the way in working hour and leisure time trends during the twentieth century. Similar trends exist in Western Europe, suggesting that in the most affluent countries in the world, the majority of the working population has experienced increased hours of work.[8]

In a chapter titled "Overemployment: The Growth of Work and the Loss of Leisure," Christian economist John Stapleford identified six major U.S. labor market trends during the past three decades.[9] First, inflation-adjusted median family and household income was highest in 1973, decreased through the 1970s, and has increased very slightly since then. Second, there was an unprecedented increase in women entering the labor force, partially due to the desire to maintain the household standard of living. Third, while acknowledging that the data is mixed, Stapleford concluded Americans are working longer hours. For example, during the past two decades of the twentieth century, for Americans working a minimum of twenty hours a week, the mean workweek increased one to four hours, although the average increase for women was as high as six hours; this works out to an additional month per year. Stapleford observed, consistent with Schor's explanation, that this increase in work hours reflects a desire to maintain a higher standard of living. Corresponding to increased work hours, Americans have increasingly felt pressure as they balance home, work, and leisure time. The percentage of Americans who claim they never have excess time increased from 48 percent in 1965 to 61 percent in 1995.

Fourth, the number of employed workers with multiple jobs in the United States nearly doubled from four million in 1970 to eight million in 2007. Approximately 41 percent of those who hold multiple jobs do so to earn income to pay off debts and meet household expenses, while only 15 percent engage in an extra job for the enjoyment of it (about one-quarter are married women who live with their spouses). Many people who hold multiple jobs are engaged in a part-time home-based business to supplement income from a primary job. When unpaid domestic work is added to the mix, men are doing more housework and less paid work, but women who have entered the paid work force are doing substantially more housework and paid work combined, even though their housework time has decreased. Stapleford concluded: "Everyone's working more, especially women, and there's still more work to do."[10] Fifth, income inequality in the United States has increased. When households are divided into fifths based on their income, the share of total income for all but the highest fifth decreased from 1975 to 2005. Sixth, about one-third of the increase in household income inequality is the result of changing household composition, especially the dramatic increase of female-headed families as a result of separation, divorce, and out-of-wedlock births. Stapleford summarized these trends as follows:

> The trend in the United States has been falling real wages, accompanied by falling real average household and family income. In response, people are working longer hours or more jobs, and women have entered the labor force in unprecedented proportions. The result is more total hours devoted, especially by women, to paid and unpaid (domestic) work and a rise in the proportion of persons under age fifty-five who feel more stress.[11]

More recently Benjamin Hunnicut, in his book *Free Time: The Forgotten American Dream*, noted that U.S. workers now work longer than workers in any other modern industrial nation, except for South Korea.[12]

Optimistic View

Godbey took a more optimistic view of Americans' free time based on a time-use study conducted by the U.S. Census Bureau and published by the Bureau of Labor Statistics in 2005 that found, on average, Americans have forty hours of free time per week.[13] Furthermore, Godbey pointed out that the 2003 Americans' Time Use Survey (ATUS), which uses a time-diary methodology, found that Americans had an average of six hours of free time a day, and 96 percent of the survey participants engaged in some form of leisure activity on the survey day.[14] Godbey suggested these findings seem to contradict American's perceptions of their frantic and overworked lives. Americans estimate their free time as fewer than twenty hours per week—half of what the above studies found. As Godbey put it, "One is tempted to say that Americans don't know what they're doing."[15]

This contradiction between the amount of free time Americans actually have and the amount they think they have may be explained by the observation, "Of course I don't have any free time because I spend so much of my time watching TV."[16] Another explanation is provided by Al Gini, who believes that although people have more free time than they think they do, many people find it very difficult to relax, and many actually boast about their belief that they are busy and overworked.[17]

One of the sections of Godbey's book is titled "Increasing Free Time across the Life Span." He explained that work hours are increasingly taking a smaller percentage of one's total life, while free time is increasing as a percentage of one's total life.[18] Three factors contribute to the increased percentage of free time during one's life: later labor force entry, earlier retirement, and increased life expectancy. The average American worker retires in his or her late fifties or early sixties. For those who reach age sixty-five, life expectancy is eighty years for men and eighty-four years for women. On average, these people will be relatively healthy until they are seventy-seven years old. Furthermore, compared to the past, older people are not disproportionately poor but compose one of the wealthiest groups (measured in terms of financial assets). Thus free time increases dramatically over the lifespan, but it tends to be hoarded so that large amounts occur during the last fifteen to twenty years of life. To paraphrase a saying about life expectancy: the good news is that free time has increased; the bad news is it's tacked on to the end of life.[19] However, Godbey's second factor of earlier retirement may no longer be as significant, as labor force participation by Americans older than sixty-five has increased in recent years.[20] Children are the other group to have more free time, as school-age children go to school for approximately 180 days of the year in the United States, and it is thought that both time spent in homework and household chores has declined.

Stable View

While some believe that free time is decreasing and others believe that it is increasing, there is some data to suggest that the amount of free time is remaining relatively stable. Mark Aguiar and Erik Hurst, using data from U.S. time-diary surveys (the 1965–1966 and the 1985 American Use of Time surveys, and the 2003, 2004, and 2005 American Time Use Surveys), investigated time-use trends in the lives of Americans from 1965 to 2005.[21] They found that average leisure time increased during this forty-year period. Their definition of leisure includes what is commonly referred to as existence activities (eating, sleeping, and personal care) in addition to leisure activities (entertainment, hobbies, reading, exercising, playing sports, socializing with family and friends, and watching television). They found that leisure time for men increased during this period by nearly five hours per week for a total of 106.2 hours per week, while for women there was an increase of three hours per week for a total of 105.1 hours per week. It is important to note that almost all this increase took place before 1985, and since then leisure time has been stable for men but has declined for women.

A paper published in 2011 assessed trends in national time-use data collected since the 1960s in Canada, the United Kingdom, and the United States, and found little support that there have been dramatic increases in leisure time in these countries. However there is also no solid evidence that leisure time has dramatically declined in Canada and the United Kingdom, although there has been a recent decrease in average leisure time in the United States.[22] Overall, Canada and the United States have seen small net increases in leisure time, while in the United Kingdom leisure time has remained stable at a higher net level. Furthermore there are lower levels of leisure time in the United States compared to the other two countries, and the leisure time of Americans and Canadians is more constrained by full-time employment than that of the U.K. population.

Evidence that work hours and leisure time is relatively stable is also provided by the Time Use Domain of the 2012 Canadian Index of Wellbeing. This domain of the index examines time use, how people experience time, what influences time, and how time use impacts well-being.[23] Analysis of the time-use data is based on the idea of balance; there is a finite amount of time each day, so most activities are beneficial if done in moderation but are detrimental if done excessively, as this means less time is devoted to other necessary activities. The 2012 report states that the percentage of Canadians who worked fifty hours or more a week decreased from 14.7 percent in 1994 to 10.8 percent in 2010, which is an overall decline of 29.6 percent over the seventeen years.[24] Overall, as illustrated by the indicators in figure 2.1, there has been a slight improvement in the time-use domain of well-being over this seventeen-year period.

Figure 2.1

Trends in Time Use, Canadian Index of Wellbeing (CIW), and Gross Domestic Product (GDP) (per capita) from 1994 to 2010

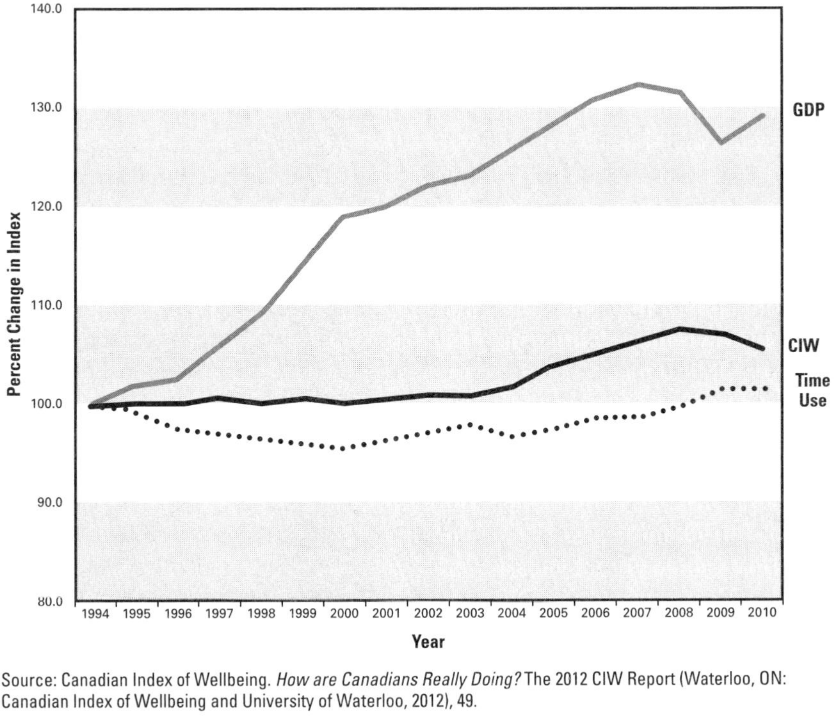

Source: Canadian Index of Wellbeing. *How are Canadians Really Doing?* The 2012 CIW Report (Waterloo, ON: Canadian Index of Wellbeing and University of Waterloo, 2012), 49.

Possible Explanations for Differing Views

Vacation Length. A possible reason to explain longer hours of work in the United States is shorter vacation periods. On average, citizens of developed countries have between thirty and forty hours of free time per week.[25] While Americans have approximately the same amount of free time as Europeans, the American configuration of free time contains fewer large blocks of free time.

Europeans average five weeks of vacation while Americans average two to two and a half weeks.[26]

The United States is unique among developed countries in that the federal government's Fair Labor Standards Act does not require that employees be given paid vacation by their employers.[27] In contrast, 137 countries, including all industrialized nations, legislate holidays.[28] As a result the vacations of Americans are shorter than those in other developed countries, and 31 percent of Americans have no paid vacation.[29] On average Americans have twelve days of vacation, but 30 percent of workers do not use all these vacation days. Three days of vacation on average are not used even though almost 50 percent of employees who do take vacations indicate that they return to work feeling rejuvenated and refreshed.[30] A recent survey indicated that only 14 percent of American workers take a two-week vacation—the average vacation length in the 1960s.[31] Furthermore, family vacations have decreased 28 percent since the 1970s, with the average length being a long weekend.[32] Among other developed countries, the French average thirty-nine days of vacation a year, Germans twenty-seven days, the Dutch twenty-five, the British twenty-three, and Canadians twenty days, although Canadians on average do not use three days of their vacation time.[33]

The amount of leisure time available determines, in part, the type of leisure activity engaged in. For example, small units of leisure time may allow for surfing the internet or watching television; however, longer periods of free time, such as vacations, are necessary to relax and slow down.[34] Documented health benefits of taking vacations or extended breaks from work include the following:

- During a nine-year period, older adults who took vacations, compared to those who did not, were less likely to die during the study period.
- Taking a one-week vacation from work led to fewer physical problems and better sleep.
- People who take very infrequent vacations had eight times the risk of a heart attack or the chance of dying from heart disease.

Other benefits of vacations include a higher quality of life, emotional well-being, better immune system functioning, cardiovascular health, and stress reduction.[35] Although it is difficult to measure the impact of lack of vacations on health costs, the consensus is that it is huge. In terms of life expectancy, United States is forty-eighth out of the fifty most developed countries in the world and in 2001 was easily the largest spender per capita on health care.[36]

Variation Based on Sociodemographics. Glenn Stalker found that employment contexts, family, and social characteristics representative of different states in the life-course accounted for significant variations in leisure time.[37] For example, leisure time is increasingly constrained for working parents of young children whose time is highly focused on both child-raising and paid work activities. Aguiar and Hurst investigated differences in leisure time according to different levels of education.[38] In 1985 leisure time was approximately the same for people of different education levels. After 1985 a significant leisure-time gap developed among men of differing education levels. From 1985 to 2005 there was an eight-hour weekly increase in the leisure time of men who had not completed high school and a six-hour decrease for men who were college graduates. In examining the differences in leisure time between less- and more-educated men for the 2003–2005 period, only 30 percent of the difference is because of differences in employment status, while 70 percent is due to more-educated people engaging in more non-job-related work (this applies to all employment-status categories—employed and unemployed). Less-educated employed males engage in less nonmarket work (e.g., maintaining the home, doing yard work, doing laundry, shopping for groceries, cooking, and cleaning the house), less child care of one's own children, and fewer civic and religious activities.

Time Crunch. Robinson and Godbey have identified the paradox that while people today may have more free time than in the past, subjectively they feel more "time-crunched" than ten to twenty years ago.[39] Recent Canadian data (published in the 2012 Canadian Index of Wellbeing's Time Use Domain) illustrates the problem of time crunch. Although, as we have seen, the percentage of Canadians who worked fifty hours or more a week decreased 29.6 percent from 1994 to 2010, there is a greater perception of time crunch due to increased commuting times; working conditions in the service sector where many services are provided twenty-four hours a day, seven days a week; fewer families with an at-home parent to manage the household and take care of eldercare and childcare responsibilities; and a larger need for care for Canada's aging population.[40] There was a 9.9 percent increase of Canadians aged twenty to sixty-four experiencing a high level of "time crunch," from 16.4 percent in 1994 to 18.2 percent in 2010. Time crunch was greatest among single parents with young children and lowest among single persons over the age of sixty-five. In 2010, a greater percentage of females (20 percent) than males (16.5 percent) experienced time pressure. Daily commuting time for Canadians increased 19.9 percent, from an average of 42.6 minutes in 1994 to a high of 53.2 minutes in 2010, which means that approximately a week of free time per year has been lost to commuting since 1994. Greater commuting times are associated with poorer health and add to decreased contentment with work-life balance. The percentage of working-age adults giving care to seniors increased 10.8 percent, from 17.4 percent in 1994 to 19.5 percent in 2008. In 2006, more females (22.5 percent) than males (16.3 percent) gave unpaid care to seniors, and females devoted more hours to this activity than males. Approximately one-quarter (27.8 percent) of employed Canadians had care responsibilities for an elderly dependent, while about one-sixth (16.8 percent) had both eldercare and childcare responsibilities in 2009.

Related to time crunch, in his book *The Tyranny of Time*, Robert Banks documented how the feverish pace of our society contributes to the erosion of thought and leisure. He observed that "there are a large number of people who are capable of creative achievement but never get around to doing anything."[41] Banks explained how the oppressive effects that result from a scarcity of time include: the threat to physical and psychological health; the decline in social life, including the weakening of interpersonal relationships; the decline in political life; the erosion of thought and leisure; and the undermining of religious sensitivity and the subversion of spiritual life. He pointed out that Christians are much worse off than many others in regard to time, especially if they live in urban areas, come from the middle class, hold managerial or professional jobs, or combine paid employment with significant household responsibilities. Banks suggested that Christians often take their jobs more seriously than others, assign great value to family obligations, and often provide leadership in community and voluntary associations. Beyond these job, home, and community responsibilities, Christians have responsibilities to fulfill in their local churches and in Christian organizations.[42] Packer wrote: "Modern Christians tend to make busyness their religion. We admire and imitate, and so become Christian workaholics, supposing that the busiest believers are always best."[43] The consequence of this activism is that "Christians are like trains—always on the move, always in a rush, and always late."[44]

With the prevalence of time crunch, the Take Back Your Time movement in the United States has been organized to create a national dialogue about overwork and time poverty.[45] Among other things, the Take Back Your Time organization (which has been supported by Christian groups such as the Lord's Day Alliance and the Massachusetts Council of Churches), lobbied for a Minimum Leave Protection, Family Bonding and Personal Well-Being Act of 2007 that would have amended the Fair Labor Standards Act.[46] It also organizes the annual Take Back Your Time day held every October as a consciousness-raising event.

Leisure Consumption, and Social and Environmental Justice Issues

Leisure as a symbol of social class is characterized by conspicuous consumption. Since Veblen's writing of *The Theory of the Leisure Class*, consumption has become democratized and is not limited to the wealthy class. Dahl wrote, "Leisure . . . has come to mean little more than an ever more furious orgy of consumption. . . . This 'virtuous materialism' . . . offers men the choice of either working themselves to death or consuming themselves to death—or both."[47] Thus a contemporary issue is leisure consumption and its implications for social and environmental justice issues. Roberts, a British leisure studies scholar, noted that in recent decades in the consumerist culture of the Western world people's leisure time has increased much more slowly than their spending power.[48] Thus the most sensitive indicators of leisure trends are spending data rather than time-budget surveys. Within Britain, the main growth areas of consumer spending have been home entertainment equipment and overseas holidays, and the amount of time devoted to shopping has increased by approximately 50 percent since the 1960s. More leisure time is being devoted to purchasing more and more goods, services, and even experiences that are packaged as commodities to be bought. Roberts concluded that our use of leisure time revolves around purchases. Shopping is often the main leisure activity on a non-workday, while other possible leisure occasions, such as family celebrations and holidays, are "orgies of spending and consumption."[49] With the introduction of Sunday shopping in the 1990s, the "Sabbath" in Britain became another important day of shopping. Consumption has been reinforced by another dominant form of leisure activity: television viewing. The major impact of television watching, argued Ellis Cashmore, has been to encourage people to consume more.[50]

In relation to leisure, the consumerist culture of the Western world is described both positively and negatively.[51] On the positive side, traditional economists suggest that an increased supply of leisure goods and services increases people's opportunities to engage in leisure activities as they please and therefore increases their freedom. Thus these goods and services are thought to provide peak leisure experiences for the people living in consumerist cultures. On the negative side,

> consumer capitalism blurs the distinction between human needs and artificially created wants, thereby locking people into a work-and-spend regime, creating ever-expanding markets for profit-seeking businesses that sell goods and services, which spread superficial contentment or, when people remain unhappy, persuade them that this may be their own fault.[52]

In this critique, the use of leisure time is considered to be influenced by commercial interests rather than a person's authentic needs so that leisure time is used in less than optimal ways.

As Roberts summarized, within the leisure studies literature there are numerous criticisms of the negative impact of consumerism and commercialization on leisure as it: transforms people into passive receivers of entertainment that does not require a critical response; is not conducive to classical contemplative leisure; creates unquenchable desires that leave people restless and unsatisfied; fills people's leisure time with simple diversions and amusements; and undermines authentic individuality.[53] Commercialism is also claimed to undercut and repress other forms of leisure as well as detract from community. Bonds between people are thought to be stronger among people who create their own leisure activity than among people who happen to buy the same types of goods and services. For example, in former communist countries people without money for leisure commodities retained the art of leisure time together through afternoons and evenings devoted to socializing with friends in local parks, the streets, or one another's homes.[54]

Defenders of consumerism argue that despite increased commercial leisure provision and consumption, plenty of leisure time is still organized by groups of friends, families, and individuals.[55] Furthermore, it is maintained that people are not gullible in buying whatever leisure suppliers provide but use their own judgment to purchase things to achieve their own leisure priorities that reflect their own context and sociodemographic characteristics.[56] People are able to make their own choices because there is such a wide range of goods and services from which to select.[57]

Two recent books by leisure scholars take differing views on leisure and consumption. In *Leisure and Consumption*, Stebbins, who holds an activity view of leisure, claimed that all leisure cannot be equated with consumption: "Leisure and consumption are not always an identity. . . . The end of consumption is to *have* something, to possess it, whereas the end of leisure is to *do* something, to engage in a positive activity."[58] Stebbins acknowledged that in some forms of leisure activity, such as coin collecting, consumption and leisure are more likely to be intertwined. However, he claimed that leisure and consumption exist in separate worlds and that the relationship between the two is of a practical nature. In most cases a leisure activity participant needs to purchase a specific good or service in order to participate in the activity, but the core experience of the leisure activity is separate from the practical expenditure. To emphasize the distinction between the consumption and the activity, he divided leisure-related consumption into the phase of shopping and the phase of consuming the purchase. Thus leisure and consumption exist in separate worlds but are natural partners because in most cases in the Western world people need to purchase a good or service to participate in an activity. However, this argument doesn't recognize the many extra goods and services people purchase that are not essential to the activity in which they participate.

In the book *Reclaiming Leisure*, Hayden Ramsay, who holds a classical view of leisure, presented a totally different view of consumption and leisure.[59] Ramsay claimed that consumerist leisure has decreased choice and disguised the attractiveness of inexpensive leisure activities, which offer few immediate pleasures but provide long-term engagement, a gradual development of contentment and understanding, as well as sustained personal rejuvenation. Before the development of consumerism, leisure generally did not require many external resources and was based on the development and use of people's inner resources, such as love, humor, intelligence, will, and imagination. Ramsay summarized the transformation of leisure as follows:

> The commercialisation of leisure has meant an ideological move from simple play and sound reflection; that is, from inner resources, wise use of personal time, investment in knowledge, and delight and wonder in our daily lives. The move has been towards love and fashion, pampering rather than developing, lifestyle rather than living, buying into activities that are more isolating, though easily repeatable. In short we have commodified leisure.[60]

While the commodification of leisure has greatly increased the possibilities for purchasing from leisure suppliers, Ramsay argued there has been a decrease in social engagement that meets personal needs for renewal, rest, growth, and understanding but that does not have a financial cost.[61] He claimed that consumerism encourages hedonism, egotism, personal ownership, acquisitiveness, possessiveness, the craving for more than one's fair share, and the disregard of existential questions unless they have commercial value.[62] It encourages greater freedom and individual choice in the purchase of goods and services[63] but does not facilitate the seeking of our true selves, or any truth beyond purchasing and advertising. The result is that visiting shopping malls and watching television are the most popular leisure activities today in the United States. Leisure activities focused on consumption provide escape from work but at the same time make more work.[64]

Ramsay quoted Gini: "Simply put, we have become addicted to the fruits of our production. . . . We have deconstructed Aristotle's adage 'the purpose of work is the attainment of leisure' to the far baser notion 'I work in order to consume and possess.'"[65] Due to the pervasiveness of consumerism, free time becomes obligated through exhortations to purchase more entertainment, trips, and holidays. Although there is no lack of leisure opportunities, research shows that Americans feel rushed, tired, and stressed.[66] Drawing on the ideas of Gerald Fain,[67] Ramsay wrote, "Instead of offering an ideal for life, leisure is just enjoying what industry sells us. . . . [C]an we really afford to reduce the noble idea of freedom to live as one chooses to spending time and money on commercialised pleasure?"[68] Ramsay suggested that consumptive leisure has brought mixed results as it has undermined human well-being and diminished leisure, and thus it is necessary to reject the ideology of consumerism in order to attain a radically different understanding of leisure.[69]

Neville identified passive consumerism, exploitation, and standardization as three negative effects of commercialized leisure.[70] The repetitive nature of television programs encourages passivity that fails to encourage human development but rather leads to the couch-potato syndrome. Standardization of leisure behaviors reduces creativity and variation while leading to huge profits for commercial providers. Ongoing promotion and advertising of equipment and clothing for specific leisure activities exploits vulnerable groups, such as children, without any benefit to them.

Neville wrote that "it is irresponsible to keep out of mind the framework within which the individual enjoys freedom of choice."[71] Such a framework includes the employment conditions of those who provide the facilities and equipment for each specific leisure activity. For example, what are the hours of work required and the wages provided in the provision of commercial leisure? Such questions become even more important in the global context of many leisure activities. For example, one might ask how the soccer balls used in the World Cup are manufactured.

In a more recent chapter titled "What about the 'Rest of the Story'? Recreation on the Backs of 'Others,'" Mair raised some of the same questions that Neville previously raised about the invisible relationships involved in the production and consumption of leisure goods and services, as well as their social environmental implications: "Where did they come from? Who made them? How did they get to us? What are they made from? Under what working conditions were they made? What happens to them when we throw them out or recycle them?"[72] In other words, do our leisure choices have a positive or negative impact on others and on the environment? What social alienation and environmental destruction do we bring about through our holidays and through the production and disposal of leisure products that we purchase and use? Due to "the seemingly endless desire for cheap, leisure-related goods to satisfy our wants and fill our free time," we may not consider these questions.[73] As Mair pointed out, we do not have a relationship with the people who produce our leisure products. And even when people are aware of the social and environmental impacts of their leisure activities, they may not act on this knowledge. A recent British study on attitudes about sustainable tourism and leisure concluded that the "respondents were not necessarily unaware of sustainability concerns; it was just that these concerns did not extend to their leisure lives outside the home."[74] Participants commented that being on holidays meant that they were free from thinking about social and environmental implications of their leisure and tourism activities. Nevertheless, the environmental impacts of leisure activities, such as long-distance travel, trekking, and outdoor recreation are immense.[75]

According to Daniel Scott, a research chair in global change and tourism at the University of Waterloo in Canada, most leisure activities create emissions.[76] Tourism creates 5 percent of global emissions, which is equivalent to Canada's and Germany's emissions combined. Travel, Scott suggested, is the new tobacco, and our addiction to "binge flying" is killing the planet.

In regard to outdoor recreation, there is considerable evidence that current motorized outdoor leisure activities, involving watercraft, dirt bikes, dune buggies, snowmobiles, and all-terrain vehicles, not only dominate water and landscapes by their operation, but also have negative impacts on ecosystems and the quality of other recreational experiences. In addition, they threaten wildlife, contribute to a loss of open space and habitat fragmentation, introduce invasive species, and increase fossil fuel consumption with its resultant impact on climate change.[77]

Even the impact of nonmotorized outdoor recreation can be substantial. In an investigation of consumption-based impacts of outdoor recreation, Jennifer Fresque and Ryan Plummer used ecological footprint analysis to examine four scenarios of backpacking.[78] The ecological footprint of a particular human population is an estimate of the total area of land and water (ecosystems) needed to produce resources consumed and assimilate wastes discharged. The backpacking scenarios differed in the distance and type of travel to the backpacking site, the equipment used, and the food consumed. The ecological footprints of the different scenarios were affected by the amount and type of food consumed (e.g., whether meat products were included) and in particular by the mode and distance of travel to the recreation site. Comparisons between the amount of land necessary to produce the necessary resources for the outdoor recreation scenarios that were one week in length, and the amount of land necessary for the livelihood of an "average" person for a whole year in some countries, were startling. For example, one of the scenarios required 126.7 percent more land than that required during one year by an average person in the Republic of Congo. The results underscore the high level of consumption in outdoor recreation, even in activities such as backpacking and when Leave No Trace principles are followed.

Arne Naess, a founder of Deep Ecology, has written about "outfitting pressure," where new, so-called improvements to outdoor recreation clothing and equipment are continuously developed and marketed even though they are unnecessary and frivolous for outdoor recreation participation.

> People swallow the equipment, hook, line and sinker, and lengthen their working day and increase stress in the city to be able to afford the "latest." Worn out, and with only a little time to spare, they dash off to the outdoor areas, for a short respite before rushing back to the cities. Still starved, they keep right on biting![79]

Boredom

When we consider leisure as a state-of-mind or a subjective psychological experience, one issue to consider is the prevalence of boredom in our society. While technology, material wealth, and affluence have been thought to be essential components of the "good life," Csikszentmihalyi explained they have not proven to be so.

> Despite the fact that we are now healthier and grow to be older, despite the fact that even the least affluent among us are surrounded by material luxuries undreamed of even a few decades ago . . . , and regardless of all the stupendous scientific knowledge we can summon at will, people often end up feeling that their lives have been wasted, instead of being filled with happiness their years were spent in anxiety and boredom.[80]

Several other authors have identified boredom as a problem related to the contemporary use of leisure time. Elie Cohen-Gewerc and Robert Stebbins suggested that boredom in free time is a common indicator of mentally unhealthy lifestyles that exist outside of work and other personal obligations.[81] Boredom, claimed Neville, is a touchstone of the negative and uncreative use of leisure time that may result from idleness.[82] This boredom may be a restless searching for novel gratifications and experiences that alternate with moods of disillusionment in which nothing appears worth participating. As such boredom is in contrast with leisure activity engaged in with a thankful and restful attitude. Although people may not openly complain about boredom, they experience it as they restlessly move from one type of entertainment to another, seeking new stimulation and something beyond what they already have.[83]

In his book *Still Bored in a Culture of Entertainment*, psychiatrist Richard Winter wrote that Western culture is struggling with an epidemic of boredom despite hundreds of entertainment opportunities, such as robotic toys, movie theaters, megamalls, sports events, MP3 and CD players, home entertainment centers, the internet, and video games.[84] Even with all the amusements, diversions, and distractions of our society, many people are bored. A survey of 2,500 consumers found that 71 percent desired more novelty in their life, which was 4 percent higher than the previous year.[85] The survey concluded that there was a boom in boredom despite a culture of entertainment. A comparison was made to drug users who need larger drug doses to experience the same effect. Likewise people in our society have developed a tolerance to the many entertainment options. Other writers have come to similar conclusions. A *Reader's Digest* article titled "How to Cope with Boredom" stated: "Despite its extraordinary variety of diversions and resources, its frenzy for spectacles and its feverish pursuit of entertainment, America is bored. The abundance of efforts made in the United States to counter boredom have defeated themselves, and boredom has become the disease of our time."[86] In Britain, Rowan Williams, the former archbishop of Canterbury, stated: "We are a deeply, dangerously bored society. And we're reluctant to look for the root of that. Why do we want to escape from the glories and difficulties of everyday life? Why do we want to escape into gambling or drugs or any other kind of fantasy?"[87]

Instead of searching for the root of boredom, many switch to something else. A survey discovered that the most frequent response to the experience of boredom was switching to a different television channel, while 44 percent indicated they ate when bored, and 27 percent stated they went for a drive.[88] Orrin Klapp explained that many people may not even be aware of their boredom since placebo activities, including the media, drugs, sports, gambling, and entertainment, mask and palliate boredom so that inner needs are not recognized.[89]

According to Patricia Spacks in her book *Boredom: The Literary History of a State of Mind*, the word boredom was not used in the English language until 1768, after which there was an incredible increase in the use of the word in culture and literature until the present time when it has become "a metaphor for the postmodern condition."[90] Likewise, in a study of ennui in literature, Reinhard Kuhn noted that this condition is "not one theme among others; it is the dominant theme . . . a modern plague."[91] Similarly in a review of cinema, theater, art, and literature, Klapp concluded that a strange cloud hangs over modern life. At first it was not noticed; now it is thicker than ever. It embarrasses claims that the quality of life is getting better. It reduces commitment to work. It is thickest in cities where there are the most varieties, pleasure, and opportunities. Like smog, it spreads to all sorts of places it is not supposed to be. The most common name for this cloud is boredom.[92]

Winter documented how boredom and chronic restlessness are common themes in movies, theater, music, and literature. For example, the contemporary novelist Walker Percy's characters are described by one reviewer as follows: "For Percy, the typical alienated man is not some half-starving, half-crazed student out of a novel by Dostoyevsky or Sartre, but precisely the well-fed, successful, middle-class man or woman who seemingly 'has it all' and yet feels totally bored and empty."[93]

Of particular interest is the link Winter made between increased leisure time and boredom.[94] Prior to the Industrial Revolution, work and leisure activities were intermingled; families worked long hours together accompanied by entertainment through shared stories and songs. Life after work might involve sitting together, making music, and talking with friends, all of which involved personal communication and contact with real people without escaping into a movie or television show. Even at the beginning of the twentieth century most leisure activities were participatory and interactive. However, by the end of the twentieth century 72 percent of Americans did not know who their neighbors were.[95] Today it is rare for families to eat together, play games, or make music. Family activities often revolve around the television. As Godbey and Robinson documented, extra time gained through increases in leisure time have mostly been used to view television.[96] Winter concluded that increased leisure time can be beneficial if one has many interests to pursue, but if one does not, then it provides more time to be bored, especially if a person is unable to entertain oneself and is reliant on the entertainment industry. He suggested that some boredom may be due to overstimulation, as it is difficult to determine what is important and relevant and where to find meaning.

Overstimulation's impact is greatest through the advertising and entertaining industries. Instead of entertaining ourselves, we depend on movies, television, and the internet. We are stimulated by the infinite possibilities to surf television channels and websites with the hope of finding larger and better optimal experiences. But the resulting experience doesn't necessarily satisfy. Winter quoted Gene Veith: "Boredom is a chronic symptom of a pleasure-obsessed age. When pleasure becomes one's number one priority, the result, ironically, is boredom."[97]

Inequality of Leisure Opportunities

When we consider feminist perspectives on leisure, one of the prevalent issues is that of leisure inequality. As Susan Shaw and Karla Henderson noted, in recent decades a growing body of empirical literature on women's leisure has developed in response to the conflicts women experience between various demands and responsibilities, and their leisure, as well as the gap between men's and women's leisure (both leisure activities and leisure time).[98] This gap has been documented by research that indicates women have less leisure time than men. For example, in the United States, on average women have less free time than men due to hours of paid work increasing more than the decrease of housework hours.[99] Men have about four hours more of free time a week than women, although the majority of this difference is accounted for by larger amounts of grooming and sleep time for women.[100] Women who are not employed tend to have greater amounts of free time than men who are employed, while women in the paid workforce have a little less free time so that the two groups of women balance each other out. The gap between men's and women's leisure is affected by various factors that limit women's leisure activity participation, such as societal expectations about women's responsibilities, roles, and lives; lack of resources needed for leisure; and women's position in society.

Although research on women's leisure does not usually use a constraints framework, Shaw and Henderson showed that women experience more constraints to leisure than men due to culturally based gender role expectations.[101] These constraints may be structural, intrapersonal, or interpersonal.

Structural Constraints. Constraints that prevent people from participating in leisure activities, even if they wish to, are called "structural constraints." They are intervening factors not linked to relationships with others that come between the interest in an activity and the participation in the activity. Structural constraints include lack of leisure programs and opportunities;[102] lack of facilities or inferior facilities; and lack of money, transportation, and time. Structural constraints also cause less than optimal participation and therefore lower levels of satisfaction and enjoyment.[103] Although the situation has improved in recent years, there are still fewer opportunities for girls and women, in comparison to boys and men, to participate in sports activities and leagues. For example, adolescent and adult women have fewer opportunities than men to participate in sports such as hockey and soccer.

In both the United States and Canada women earn lower wages compared to men. Furthermore, some women, especially older women living by themselves and single mothers, are often economically impoverished. Women's financial dependency may lead to a lack of available spending money for leisure participation that then leads to other constraints, such as a lack of transportation.

A significant structural constraint on women's leisure is a lack of time for self and time stress. Household responsibilities, unpaid work, and paid work combine to result in little time for personal leisure activities, relaxation, and rest. While paid work leads to a more positive situation in regard to increased leisure activity opportunities away from home, increased leisure choices, as well as financial resources and independence, the negative side is more time stress and decreased time for leisure. This lack of time for leisure activities is primarily because women continue to do the majority of housework even if they are employed. For example, a British study found that although many couples thought that domestic work ought to be shared when both partners work outside the home, women were doing the majority of the household labor.[104] In 1989, Arlie Hochschild invented the term "second shift" to describe the child care and housework women perform after returning home from full-time paid employment.[105] This second shift, still prevalent today, creates a significant gap between women's and men's experience of leisure.[106] For example, in Canada, a greater percentage of females (20 percent) than males (16.5 percent) experienced time pressure in 2010,[107] and earlier data indicated that working mothers experienced the greatest stress among all sociodemographic groups.[108]

The notion that leisure is earned through paid employment continues in later life.[109] While men tend to make a definite transition from work to retirement, one researcher found that women do not have a similar rite of passage in that there is no specific time when they receive a symbolic reward for completing their life of labor.[110]

Time devoted to family responsibilities also influences a woman's opportunity for leisure.[111] Care for children and older relatives are family responsibilities that are disproportionately performed by women. For example, the birth of a woman's first child has a dramatic influence on a woman's leisure. Often women will organize their leisure around their family tasks and duties, while men are much less likely to allow family to interfere with their leisure. As a result, women's own leisure experiences may be constrained. Research studies have documented that women put much time and effort into guaranteeing that family leisure activities are positive experiences for their family to the detriment of their own leisure desires and interests. Therefore these family leisure activities may appear to be leisure but may be experienced as unpaid work by women.

Intrapersonal Constraints. Factors that limit a person's preference for a specific leisure activity or cause a lack of interest in an activity are called "intrapersonal constraints." For example, a person's lack of self-confidence or family influences can affect his or her leisure activity preferences.[112] A significant intrapersonal constraint on women's leisure is "ethic of care" or women's caring behavior, which is especially the case for married women who have children or women who take care of aging relatives.[113] In other words, women limit their leisure because they feel their time should be devoted to taking care of the needs of their family.[114] However, ethic-of-care behaviors are not limited to women who are mothers; teenage girls appear more likely than boys to participate in activities to please others, while college-age women have been found to constrain their own leisure to please their male dating partners.[115] As women age and their children grow up, become independent, and leave home, some evidence exists that their ethic of care may lessen.

Related to ethic of care is some women's lack of a sense of entitlement to leisure.[116] If women through their ethic of care attend to the needs of others, they may not perceive they have a right to their own leisure and may not develop a sense of their own need for leisure. Both an ethic of care and a sense of the lack of entitlement to leisure are associated with a women's role in the family, where the needs of others are often put before a woman's own needs. Together ethic of care and a lack of entitlement to leisure are fundamental influences on a women's leisure that provide greater leisure time and opportunities for males.[117]

Lack of self-esteem is another intrapersonal constraint that limits women's leisure activities. Teenage girls' self-esteem and confidence decrease at the same time obsession with appearance and body image increases since adolescent females are especially vulnerable to social pressures to fit an ideal body image. Participation in leisure activities may be constrained by fear of embarrassment related to not looking right or not fitting in, or concerns about skill level or appearance. As a result, concerns related to body weight and appearance are more constraining for all ages of women in comparison with men.

Participation in leisure activities that others think are inappropriate for women is another intrapersonal constraint. For example, participation by girls and women in outdoor recreation, as well as activities perceived to be male, such as wrestling, boxing, rugby, football, and ice hockey, have been found to be constrained by expectations concerning gender roles that were communicated by others, including peers and family.

Another intrapersonal constraint for women is fear of violence, which is consistently found to be higher among women than men. Higher levels of fear may inhibit women from participating in activities that involve traveling alone in areas where they may feel unsafe, such as walking in the forest, cycling, or hiking, as well as going out on their own to nighttime leisure activities in the dark.

Interpersonal Constraints. Intervening factors linked to relationships with other people are called "interpersonal constraints." Some dimension of a person's relations with other people may influence the level or quality of desired activity participation.[118] Little research exists on women's interpersonal constraints, possibly because women tend to have more social relationships than men do, and therefore are unlikely to lack leisure partners.[119] For women, leisure often occurs in the context of friendships that may be seen as a leisure enabler. The little research on interpersonal constraints to women's leisure may reflect the major constraint of lack of time to be alone for self. Interpersonal constraints on women's leisure include the social disapproval of participating in activities that family members, friends, or others see as inappropriate.[120] Another example is the social control by husbands when they discourage or make it difficult for their wives to engage in desired leisure activities.

There is a lack of research on the gendered dimension of men's leisure constraints.[121] Higher levels of leisure participation by men and a stronger sense of leisure entitlement among men in comparison to women might suggest that gender is an enabling rather than a constraining factor for men. Nevertheless, there may be some gender-related leisure constraints among men, such as employment pressures and social pressures to succeed, and time constraints related to a father's role as financial provider.[122] For example, in Canada in 2009, almost triple the percentage of males (15.8 percent) worked over fifty hours a week compared to females (5.7 percent).[123] In addition, men who are not competitive or tough, or who do not match the masculine ideal, may encounter a variety of problems in their leisure activities, such as repressing needs and emotions (e.g., empathy) that do not correspond to prevailing ideas of masculinity; avoiding leisure activities they may enjoy in order to appear masculine; or feeling obligated to participate in sports they do not enjoy.[124] Some research indicates that men may encounter more restrictions than women on leisure activity choices as society may be more likely to accept women's participation in leisure activities that traditionally have not been considered female, in comparison to men participating in activities that traditionally have not been considered male.[125] Thus there may be interpersonal and intrapersonal constraints related to societal expectations of appropriate male leisure behaviors.

In summary, Shaw and Henderson concluded that women's opportunities for, and participation in leisure are powerfully influenced by structural constraints, especially lack of time for leisure activities; intrapersonal constraints, such as body attitudes, self attitudes, and ethic of care; as well as interpersonal constraints.[126] Preliminary research also illustrates that men's leisure may be constrained due to gender considerations.

As equality issues are not limited to gender issues, and feminist leisure scholars are interested in all forms of oppression, not just oppression against women, we will take a quick look at other types of leisure inequality. Access to leisure varies depending on physical environment, culture, socioeconomic characteristics (e.g., education, income), and personal characteristics (e.g., age, [dis]ability, race, gender).[127] For example, in his book *Black Recreation*, Jearold Holland explained that blacks often do not feel welcome in some leisure activities, and thus they participate instead in other leisure activities that a large number of blacks participate in, thereby reinforcing these activities as part of black psyche.[128] In her book *Race, Riots and Roller Coasters: The Struggle over Segregated Recreation in America*, Victoria Wolcott documented the racial incidents in recreational spaces during the last century. She concluded,

> Decades of white hostility and violence aimed at blacks who attempted to use recreational facilities have largely been forgotten. This violence took a variety of forms, from the young toughs who beat blacks attempting to swim at a city beach to the hidden violence of shutting down recreational facilities rather than desegregating them. But much of the blame for the wholesale decline of urban amusements lies in white abandonment of recreational facilities. And this abandonment, rooted in the refusal to share public space, had devastating consequences for the daily lives of urban dwellers.[129]

In the 1990s a body of empirical literature began to be developed that investigated and documented the current prevalence of discrimination related to race and ethnicity in a person's experience of regular, everyday recreation and leisure, their participation in planned and organized recreation activities, and the policy and programming consequences of these recreation activities. In a summary of numerous studies conducted in the 1990s and 2000s, Valerie Freysinger and Othello Harris noted that consistent findings in this field of research identified leisure constraints related to perceptions and experiences of unwelcomeness, discrimination, and racism that influence opportunities for recreation and leisure participation, enjoyment of and comfort in participation, leisure attitudes, participation style, and participation outcomes.[130] More recent research in the last ten years has uncovered the complexity of race in that there is evidence for the role of sociodemographic and other characteristics that may influence the experience of discrimination in recreation and leisure participation so that the experience of race is not necessarily homogeneous or universal.[131]

The Quality of Leisure Activity

If leisure is defined as activity, then we need to consider the quality of these activities. Churches, explained Neville, have had an ongoing concern in regard to the quality of leisure activities.[132] A number of indicators suggest that the quality of contemporary leisure is less than ideal. Roberts, a British leisure studies scholar, wrote, "Many people's leisure behaviour is sub-optimal for their own well-being."[133] He went on to explain that although most people in the affluent West know that their physical well-being would benefit from greater amounts of regular exercise, most people remain inactive. Roberts's assessment is supported by Cohen-Gewerc and Stebbins: "Some people do indeed smoke, eat, and drink alcohol too much; live a sedentary existence in their free time; and watch television to the point of dulling their wits; all in the name of leisure."[134]

In a chapter titled "Deviant Leisure: The Dark Side of Free-Time Activity," Chris Rojek, a sociologist of leisure, suggested that popular culture, as expressed through documentaries, fiction, television, and film, is obsessed with deviant leisure, such as theft, double dealing, property destruction, drug use, murder, and casual violence.[135] Millions devote their leisure time watching or reading these forms of popular culture that results in "mind voyaging about these worlds where there are no moral limits on free-time behavior. . . . The consumption of deviant leisure is conventionally enjoyed, albeit vicariously, as a 'normal' part of leisure in Western society."[136] Furthermore, he claimed that casual leisure in contemporary society often includes "desultory, time-filling, time-killing activities."[137]

The quality of some forms of contemporary leisure is reflected in the recent *Routledge Handbook of Leisure Studies*, which claims that twenty-first-century leisure ought to be understood as focusing on the new "Big Seven" activities: shopping, television viewing, gambling, sex, drugs, drink, and holidays.[138] A chapter is devoted to each of these activities, and while some of these activities (e.g., sex, drink, holidays) may, to use Packer's words, "be good or bad, holy or unholy, depending on how it is handled,"[139] others (e.g., gambling, drugs) may be considered less than desirable from the standpoints of ethics, health, and edification. For example, much of television viewing is passive consumerism, while shopping is associated with consumption and related environmental impacts.

Mike Martin suggested that an imbalance in leisure activities, such as too much time at a bar or watching television, can lead to family problems.[140] Other leisure activities, such as gambling, pathological spending, and drug and alcohol abuse, may lead to physical and mental health problems.[141] For many Americans, leisure time is not rejuvenating but is as stressful as work since it often involves a high level of organization to participate in expensive events in crowded settings that lead to frayed nerves and depleted savings accounts.[142] As a result many white-collar workers indicate they would prefer to go to their jobs than to engage in leisure with their families. Holidays and weekends are crammed with leisure activities that are regimented according to the clock that "tells us when to play, when to eat, when to shop, and . . . artificially compels us towards speed, punctuality and being 'on time.'"[143] Furthermore, with electronic devices, such as cell phones, smart phones, email, and the internet, leisure time is never far from the demands of work.

If we look at the amount of time devoted to various leisure activities from the American Time Use Survey, it is readily apparent that not only does television viewing account for more than half of daily leisure time, but also the time devoted to it (more than ninety minutes) is much greater than the next closest activity of socializing and talking (see figs. 2.2 and 2.3).[144] Television viewing has been the dominant form of leisure time activity in the United States since the 1960s due to its convenience and low cost.[145] Television viewing was the most common leisure activity at fifteen hours a week in 2005, which was an increase of five hours since 1965.[146] Approximately 80 percent of Americans view television on any given day.[147] In Canada, the percentage of teenagers who exceeded the recommended two-hour maximum of video games and television per day increased 14.2 percent, from 27.2 percent in 1994 to 31.7 percent in 2008.[148] When all screen time (video games, computer use, television) was considered, the percentage who exceeded two hours per day of screen time increased from 54.5 percent to 63.7 percent, with more boys (70 percent) than girls (57 percent) exceeding the two-hour maximum.[149] A comparative Adolescent Time Use study, involving youth from ten industrialized countries, found declining levels of both reading and physically active leisure participation in most of the countries.[150] The amount of reading decreased 50 percent or more from the 1980s to the late 1990s/early 2000s.

James Kunstler described the American family's focus on the television as follows:

> The American house has been TV-centred for three generations. It is the focus of family life, and the life of the house correspondingly turns inward, away from whatever occurs beyond its four walls. (TV rooms are called "family rooms" in builders' lingo. A friend who is an architect explained to me: "People don't want to admit that what the family does together is watch TV.") At the same time, the television is the family's chief connection with the outside world. The physical envelope of the house itself no longer connects their lives to the outside in any active way; rather it seals them off from it. The outside world has become an abstraction filtered through television.[151]

Television content is primarily focused on escaping reality and on consumption promoted through commercials sponsored by large corporations.[152] Television viewing has also been linked to obesity due to its passive nature. There is some evidence that television viewing is decreasing with the increased use of computer-based activities. However, according to Godbey, as television has become less dominant, television networks have produced more violent, sexual, and shocking content to try to maintain their viewership.[153]

Increased television viewing, with a corresponding decline in physical activity, may be responsible for the declining health of persons living in modern nations.[154] Leisure behaviors are likely to be passive and related to addictive behavior if there are low levels of self or community efficacy.[155] For example, children's television watching is positively related to childhood obesity as it decreases calorie burning that takes place during active forms of recreation. Similar to drug taking or excessive drinking or eating, television viewing is a passive, consumer-oriented type of entertainment. Furthermore, television viewing decreases a child's capacity for direct experiences and involvement with the environment in preference of vicarious experiences and engagements. Godbey noted that in addition to television being linked to obesity, television programs are increasingly vulgar. He went on to observe that television viewing, like drugs, prevents the mind from dealing with depressing thoughts but does not process them in a healthy way: "What such activities do is focus attention naturally and pleasurably but what they fail to do is to develop attentional habits that might lead to greater complexity of consciousness. Addictive behavior, then, is undertaken to relieve the pain that may creep into the unfocused mind."[156]

While a number of these comments may be simply observations by scholars and others, the Canadian Index of Wellbeing has attempted to systematically study trends in leisure and culture. This index has documented a number of trends for the period from 1994 to 2010.[157] The average percentage of time devoted to social leisure activities on the previous day that a participant was surveyed decreased every year for a total decline of 19.7 percent from 1994 (14.4 percent) to 2010 (12.4 percent). The average percentage of total time devoted to cultural activities and arts participation decreased from 1994 to 2005 but has remained stable since

Figure 2.2
Americans Daily Leisure Time Use

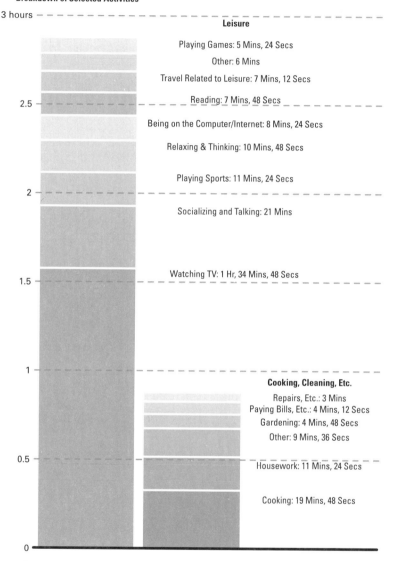

Breakdown of Selected Activities

3 hours –

Leisure

Playing Games: 5 Mins, 24 Secs

Other: 6 Mins

Travel Related to Leisure: 7 Mins, 12 Secs

2.5 – – – – – – – – – – Reading: 7 Mins, 48 Secs – – – – – – – –

Being on the Computer/Internet: 8 Mins, 24 Secs

Relaxing & Thinking: 10 Mins, 48 Secs

Playing Sports: 11 Mins, 24 Secs

2 –

Socializing and Talking: 21 Mins

Watching TV: 1 Hr, 34 Mins, 48 Secs

1.5 –

1 –

Cooking, Cleaning, Etc.

Repairs, Etc.: 3 Mins
Paying Bills, Etc.: 4 Mins, 12 Secs
Gardening: 4 Mins, 48 Secs
Other: 9 Mins, 36 Secs

0.5 – – – – – – – – – – – – – – – – – – – Housework: 11 Mins, 24 Secs

Cooking: 19 Mins, 48 Secs

0

Source: Bureau of Labor Statistics

Credit: Lam Thuy Vo/NPR, "What Americans Actually Do All Day Long, in 2 Graphics," National Public Radio, August 29, 2012, accessed October 15, 2012, http://www.npr.org/blogs/money/2012/08/29/160244277 /what-americans-actually-do-all-day-long-in-2-graphics?utm_source=NPR&utm_medium=facebook&utm _campaign=20120829.

Figure 2.3

Americans Daily Time Use

What Americans Do on an Average Workday

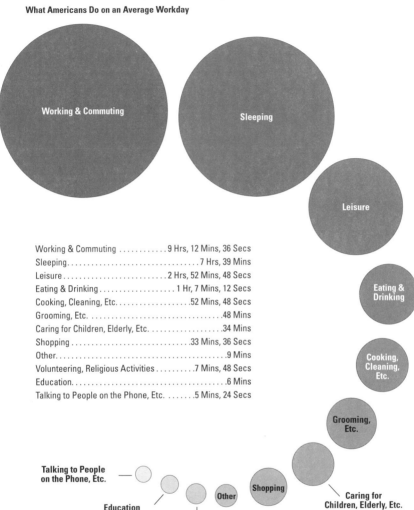

Working & Commuting .... 9 Hrs, 12 Mins, 36 Secs
Sleeping................................ 7 Hrs, 39 Mins
Leisure......................... 2 Hrs, 52 Mins, 48 Secs
Eating & Drinking .... 1 Hr, 7 Mins, 12 Secs
Cooking, Cleaning, Etc. .... .52 Mins, 48 Secs
Grooming, Etc. .... .48 Mins
Caring for Children, Elderly, Etc. .... .34 Mins
Shopping .... .33 Mins, 36 Secs
Other.. .9 Mins
Volunteering, Religious Activities .... .7 Mins, 48 Secs
Education...................................... .6 Mins
Talking to People on the Phone, Etc. .... .5 Mins, 24 Secs

Source: Bureau of Labor Statistics

Credit: Lam Thuy Vo/NPR, "What Americans Actually Do All Day Long, in 2 Graphics," National Public Radio, August 29, 2012, (accessed October 15, 2012) http://www.npr.org/blogs/money/2012/08/29/160244277/what-americans-actually-do-all-day-long-in-2-graphics?utm_source=NPR&utm_medium=facebook&utm_campaign=20120829.

then at less than 5 percent of total time. Women devoted a greater proportion of time to cultural activities, arts, and social leisure participation; however, the decrease in social leisure activities on the previous day from 1998 (17.1 percent) to 2010 (13 percent) was greater for women. In the early 2000s there was fluctuation in performing arts attendance, but it has declined dramatically every year since 2006 for a total decrease of 10.7 percent from 1994 to 2010.

The percentage of time devoted to volunteering with culture and recreation agencies decreased substantially (21.9 percent) from 1994 (48 percent) to 2010 (37.5 percent). Compared to women, men devoted much more of their volunteering time to culture and recreation agencies. Physical activity participation increased 24.0 percent from twenty-one times per month in 1994 to twenty-six times per month in 2010. However, older adults had much lower levels of physical activity than all other age groups. The number of visits to national parks and historic sites was steady throughout the 1990s but dropped dramatically after 2001, for a decrease of 28.7 percent from 1994 to 2010. In regard to vacation travel, vacations are now slightly longer with a 7.2 percent increase of trip length from 1994 to 2010. Women spent more nights away than men, and compared to other age groups, adults over age sixty-five were away significantly more nights. The percentage of income spent on recreation and culture increased 4.2 percent from 1998 to 2008 however the amount spent on culture and recreation dropped substantially in 2009 and 2010. Persons aged thirty-five to forty-nine spent the most on recreation and culture while

Table 2.1
Change in Canadians' Leisure and Culture from 1994 to 2010

Positive Changes

Average monthly frequency of participation in physical activity over fifteen minutes	+24%
Average number of nights away per trip in the past year on vacations over 80 km from home	+7.2%

Negative Changes

Average visitation per site in past year to all national parks and national historic sites	28.7%
Average number of hours in the past year volunteering for culture and recreation organizations	−21.9%
Average percentage of time spent on the previous day in social leisure activities	−19.7%
Average attendance per performance in past year at all performing arts	−10.7%
Average percent of time spent on the previous day in arts and culture activities	−8.5%
Expenditures in past year on culture and recreation as percent of total expenditures	−4.1%

Overall Change

Overall percentage change in leisure and culture	−7.8%

Source: Canadian Index of Wellbeing. *How Are Canadians Really Doing? The 2012 CIW Report* (Waterloo, ON: Canadian Index of Wellbeing and University of Waterloo, 2012), 41.

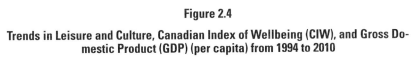

Figure 2.4

Trends in Leisure and Culture, Canadian Index of Wellbeing (CIW), and Gross Domestic Product (GDP) (per capita) from 1994 to 2010

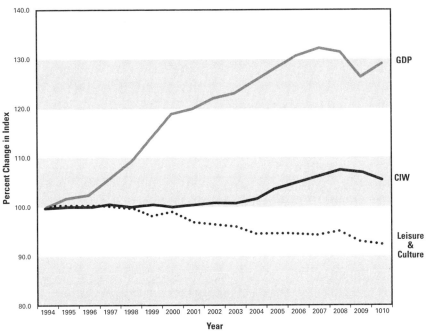

Source: Canadian Index of Wellbeing. *How are Canadians Really Doing?* The 2012 CIW Report. (Waterloo, ON: Canadian Index of Wellbeing and University of Waterloo, 2012), 40.

persons sixty-five and older spent significantly less on recreation and culture. Based on these findings, the Canadian Index of Wellbeing concluded that there has been an overall decline in Canadians' leisure and cultural engagement (see table 2.1 and fig. 2.4).

Lack of a Spiritual Dimension to Leisure

Given that leisure, in the classical understanding of it, is a spiritual attitude, then we need to consider the spiritual dimension of leisure. In 2000 Christian social-psychologist David Myers published a book titled *The American Paradox: Spiritual Hunger in an Age of Plenty*. The essence of his book and of the paradox, as stated in his preface, is,

> We now have, as average Americans, doubled real incomes and double what money buys. We have espresso coffee, the World Wide Web, sport utility vehicles, and caller ID. And we have less happiness, more depression, more fragile relationships,

less communal commitment, less vocational security, more crime (even after the recent decline), and more demoralized children.[158]

The result, Myers concluded, is that American society is characterized by a loss of meaning, a spiritual vacuum, and a growing spiritual hunger. Recently Hunnicutt has demonstrated that the original American dream of quality and spiritual values has been obscured by a growing economy as the one and only determinant of progress.[159] Similar conclusions have been reached by others. Martin Davies, in an essay in the book *The Philosophy of Leisure*, wrote that "in contemporary society the private realm is a dismal sphere of frustration, boredom, and neurosis."[160] Novelist Percy observed that "in spite of an ever heightened self-consciousness, increased leisure, ever more access to cultural and recreation facilities, ever more instruction on self-help, self-growth, self-enrichment, the self feels ever more imprisoned in itself."[161]

A number of contemporary authors claim that spirituality needs to be a more significant dimension of leisure in today's society as there is a lack of spiritual depth to contemporary leisure. For example, Joblin claimed that one of the reasons leisure has been relegated to a place of little importance in contemporary society is because it frequently is not connected to people's spirituality.[162] He explained that many leisure research studies take a holistic perspective but do not reference worship, sacred beliefs, prayer, meditation, contemplation, rituals, Sabbaths, retreats, and pilgrimages related to the spiritual dimension of life.[163] Within the therapeutic recreation field, C. Forrest MacDowell wrote, "Leisure wellness must include the awareness and expression of one's sense of spirit. . . . The greatest challenge of the leisure profession . . . is to know this spirit well."[164] Quoting Csikszentmihalyi, Godbey[165] noted that spirituality needs to become more important in leisure expression as spirituality plays a crucial role in decreasing entropy, which is a characteristic of contemporary American society.

> The United States, in the midst of unprecedented material affluence, is suffering from symptoms of increasing individual and societal entropy: rising rates of suicide, violent crime, sexually transmitted disease, unwanted pregnancy—not to mention a growing economic instability fueled by the irresponsible selfish behavior of many politicians and businessmen.[166]

Godbey went on to state that spiritual development is not acquired through the vast amounts of time devoted to television that North Americans watch but rather through inner processes that require disciplined habits that are attained slowly. The quest for spirituality, Godbey claimed, has significant implications for leisure, that "as the search for spiritual benefits intensifies, leisure activity may be less based around consumption and more around affirmation—affirming that life is good."[167] Robinson and Godbey suggested that Americans need to consume less, appreciate more, become aware of the good things in life, and ponder leisurely on life.[168] Thus leisure, according to Kelly and Godbey, must involve spiritual reflection and not only consumption of inconsequential experiences. Leisure "must also produce and reflect the spiritual impulse. The transition to a society of leisure . . . is today not so much a matter of techno-logical advance but of understanding the basis upon which the universe, all life within it, and even our very selves can be celebrated and are therefore sacred."[169]

One of the most scathing critiques of the lack of a spiritual dimension in contemporary leisure is by Ramsay, who contrasted contemplative, reflective leisure with the consumerist, commercial leisure prevalent in Western society.

> The story of leisure in the twentieth century turns upon the rejection of eternal realities and spiritual truths. With no God, cosmic answers, or first principles there is nothing worthy of contemplation; leisure, then, quietly drops the contemplative ideal and dedicates itself not to other reflective experiences that divert us from our daily burdens, but instead to securing interesting and enjoyable experiences that are within our price range or, preferably, just above it. . . . If we do not believe in God, ultimate values, or an afterlife, then naturally we will hope for heaven here and now, and commercial leisure provides the simplest sort of heaven—the opportunity amidst cares and uncertainties for comfort and excitement without having to set aside our everyday props of transactions and commodities.[170]

Ramsay argued that people need time alone with themselves that has no external obligations and pressures but rather time to think reflectively about truth. Noting that Pieper's approach to leisure is empowering, reasonable, and realistic, not idealistic, Ramsay claimed that a quiet, thoughtful, reflection on our situation allows us to be responsible for our affairs, reminds us of how good life is, how blessed we are, and readies us to progress through life. In response to people who have more leisure time but are feeling more rushed and stressed, Ramsay argued for a spiritually uplifting leisure that is realistic, reflective, and contemplative. Drawing on Aquinas, he stated the need to "rediscover the con-templative depths of our lives: to appreciate more what makes life meaningful, and to invest the time and energy that is most truly ours in a serious encounter with this source of meaning."[171] For tension control and stress relief to be effective and long-term, Ramsay believes that leisure must be reclaimed from overwork, frivolous and meaningless amusements, and commodification.

Staffan Linder, in his classic book titled *The Harried Leisure Class*, suggested two reasons why the cultivation of mind and spirit has not been enhanced by the economic progress in our society. First, the pace of life in our society is not conducive to intellectual and spiritual pursuits: "The mental energy and internal concentration required to cultivate the mind and spirit adequately are not easily mobilized after a hectic day." Second, "economic growth not only frees man from the requirement to work, but creates attractions other than spiritual cultivation, all of which compete for time available."[172] Linder argued that a leisure problem exists because people occupy their time with "nothingness"; they use the steady income provided by a job to purchase consumption goods. The enjoyment of these consumption goods takes time. If people are not consuming, they spend their time in complete passivity. Although Linder did not believe that people are necessarily idle, neither do they experience leisure, he stated. Rather, people are not prepared for leisure and therefore do not know how to utilize their time for spiritual development. Yet, as Walter Rauschenbusch wrote a hundred years ago, if "we had more leisure for the higher pursuits of the mind and the soul, then there might be a chance to live such a life of gentleness and brotherly kindness and tranquillity of heart as Jesus desired for men."[173]

Issues related to the Work-Leisure Relationship

If leisure is understood as a holistic lifestyle, then we need to consider the relationship of work and leisure and how they fit with other life dimensions. While there is conflicting evidence that free time has increased, we can safely conclude that free time in the United States has a fragmented distribution, as most (twenty-five of forty weekly hours) occurs in small chunks on weekdays rather than the weekend.[174] Thus free time and work time are intertwined, which is perhaps why people feel they have so little free time. Weekday free time provides less opportunity for many leisure activities compared to longer periods of free time, such as a whole day on a weekend. It has been found that people would prefer more free time in larger time periods, such as three-day weekends. Nevertheless, with newer forms of technology, such as the internet and email, work seems to be intruding into the weekend, while increases in free time tend to be during weekdays. The increase in free time during weekdays might explain increased time devoted to television watching in recent decades.[175] As work extends into the weekend and free time increases on weekdays, people's use of free time becomes less satisfying, as short units of free time do not provide a break and rest from tasks to be done at home and work. There is no opportunity to transition from a demanding work environment to a relaxed and peaceful leisure time. Godbey concluded that our free time is maldistributed and "configured in dysfunctional ways."[176]

In a recent chapter on "Leisure and the Changing Workplace" Hilbrecht[177] expanded on the ideas presented by Godbey. Workplace trends influence daily and weekly patterns of leisure. Many work schedules no longer reflect a Monday-to-Friday daytime pattern. Other patterns, including evening and weekend work, shift work, flexible hours, and telework, have become more common. Many workplaces have increased their hours of business. For example, many retail stores are now open on Sundays. Evening and weekend shifts, known as "anti-social" work hours, can mean that one's work schedules are different from those of family and friends, limiting the choice of leisure companions, as well as the range of available leisure activities. This creates challenges for leisure participation. Some employers expect their staff to be "unconditional workers" by being constantly accessible through email, cell phones, and other technology, as well as beginning early, staying late, and taking work home. Furthermore, self-employment, contract work, and part-time work has been increasing. With less-structured (and at times unpredictable) work hours, it is difficult for people to plan for leisure activities and thus feel less "free" in their non-work hours. Although there is not much research on the impact of irregular schedules on leisure participation, individuals with highly variable work hours tend to have lower levels of self-assessed health, higher levels of stress, and lower job quality than individuals with the traditional Monday-to-Friday daytime work schedules.[178]

As mentioned, newer technologies can blur the boundaries between work and leisure and impact the nature and quality of both. Work intrudes into one's leisure if one is expected to be constantly available. This raises the question of how best to integrate different life spheres including work and leisure. Hilbrecht explained how the concept of work-life integration has begun to be used instead of work-life balance to describe how people can see the connection between their employment and the remainder of their life.[179] "Balance" is not seen as the best metaphor to use because it may be fleeting and not easily attained; it is a two-sided model that tends to focus on work and family (and, specifically, women) with little attention to other activities, such as leisure, religion, and volunteering. Work-life integration takes a broader view than work-life balance; it is a holistic approach applicable to people at all stages of life while work-life balance tends to be focused on those who have families.

Conclusion

Using the framework of the seven concepts of leisure, I have discussed seven leisure issues and trends in contemporary society. First, although there are differing perspectives, leisure time has tended to remain stable over the past few decades, although people continue to experience time stress. Second, for the past several decades, television viewing has been the most prevalent leisure activity. Along with other observations about leisure activity participation, we can conclude that the quality of leisure activity participation is often less than ideal. Third, leisure consumption has become democratized, in that for large segments of the population leisure is consumerist and commodified, which can have negative social and environmental consequences. Fourth, although most contemporary Western people have extensive leisure and entertainment possibilities, boredom is a common experience in our society. Fifth, leisure inequalities exist as demonstrated by the gap between women's and men's leisure. Sixth, the spiritual dimension of leisure is impoverished. And seventh, work-leisure integration presents a number of challenges due to a number of work-related trends. Perhaps the content in this chapter is overly pessimistic. Along with these concerns, we need to keep in mind the positive outcomes or benefits of leisure that I outlined much more briefly in the book's introduction.

This chapter on leisure issues, along with the previous chapter on the main concepts of leisure, has fulfilled the first part of the theological task or dialogue— that is, to identify the contemporary information relevant to our discussion of leisure. The issues presented in this chapter primarily relate to leisure practice, although they are fundamentally linked to how we understand leisure. Thus the fundamental question to be asked is, "What is leisure?" This question is the primary focus of this book, and therefore I will now turn to a historical overview of some of the main understandings of leisure in the next two chapters, before presenting biblical material relevant to leisure in chapters 5, 6, and 7.

part 2

the history
of the leisure
concept

the history of classical leisure

Having explored the current "leisure situation" in part 1, we will now focus our attention on the historical background pertinent to the concept of leisure. Chapters 3 and 4 will focus on the history of the concept of leisure (but not on the practice of leisure) throughout history. Since leisure is not a unique phenomenon of this century, the contemporary meaning of leisure can be better understood when placed in historical perspective. In addition, through understanding previous Christian approaches to leisure we can gain insight for a Christian perspective of leisure today. Within the scope of this book it is impossible to review comprehensively the history of the leisure concept, and thus only a brief and somewhat simplified historical survey will be presented in which two historical concepts of leisure, pertinent to this book, are highlighted: chapter 3 will trace the classical view of leisure as developed in Greek culture, particularly by Aristotle, and adapted by Augustine, Aquinas, and in the contemplative life of monastic culture; and chapter 4 will review the activity view of leisure that became predominant after the Reformation, especially through the application of John Calvin's theology, and was clearly articulated in Puritanism and later secularized through various influences. First though, we will look at the etymology of the word "leisure."

Etymological Background of "Leisure"

Etymology is concerned with where a word came from and the development of its meaning. The English word "leisure" derives from the Latin *licere* by way of the French *leisere*. The root word *licere*, which means to be permitted or allowed, implies freedom from restraint, and also evolved into the word "license."[1] Literally, leisure meant exemption or permission in regard to the opportunity provided when one was free from legal occupation. Most Roman writers employed *otium* to denote the idea of leisure. *Otium* was linked with contemplation and opportunity for freedom from both time and occupation.[2]

The Greek equivalent of Latin's *licere* and *otium* is *scholē*, which can be traced to the same root as that of the Greek verb that means "to have."[3] De Grazia elaborated: "The etymological root of *scholē* meant to halt or cease, hence to have quiet or peace. Later it meant to have time to spare or, specially, time for oneself."[4] Contemplation or reflection could occur only when a condition of leisure was experienced. Leisure could not be forced, but as Serena Arnold explained, could take place only under servitude: "It was a non-materialistic and non-business-like condition and it was opportunity for knowledge and learning."[5] The notion of leisure was expressed positively, signifying that it was normally experienced, while work was viewed negatively as *ascholia*. Likewise, in Latin "business" is *negotium*, the negative of *otium*.

Latin and Greek notions of leisure were closely associated with education or learning as is suggested by the history of the word: in Greek leisure is *scholē*, and in Latin *schola*, the roots of the English word "school." Later *schola* was associated with a group of scholars or disciples, and hence the word "discipline" referred to a *schola*. In this meaning, learning and scholarship were characteristic of leisure in addition to the absence of any legal occupation. Much later, *schola* came to represent a place where scholarly lectures and discussions were held and where disciplines were studied. Therefore the English word "school," used to indicate the place where education and teaching takes place, comes from a word that means leisure. Furthermore, the Greek concept of leisure is the origin of the division between the liberal arts and servile work. *Artes liberals*, with the liberality of having their end in themselves, has the meaning of leisure in the best sense. Therefore the classical ideal of leisure has had an enormous influence. One strand of the ideal passes through the Stoics to Cicero and Seneca and from there northward, reaching as far as the English schools and to a lesser degree influencing the North American character as well. The other strand, which we are more concerned with in this study, extends through Plotinus and into Christianity and monasticism.

Classical Leisure

Leisure in Greek Culture

In Greek culture a clear distinction was made between work, recreation, and leisure. Ernest Barker explained this distinction as follows: work is something done as a means to something else, such as affluence or subsistence, rather than for its own sake; recreation is rest from work, which took the form of play and restored the health of body and mind, exhausted and deteriorated by work; and leisure, the noblest thing in life, is participation in some activity desirable for its own sake.[6] Thus the ideal Greek lifestyle was centered on leisure, not work. The possibility of such a lifestyle in Greek society was based on the existence of slave workers who accounted for 80 percent of the Greek city states' population. Leisure, not work, was the ultimate form of human activity. The dichotomy was not work and nonwork, but instead leisure (*scholē*) and nonleisure (*ascholia*).

Aristotle on Leisure

Numerous present-day writers acknowledge the Aristotelian position as fundamental in one way or another to an understanding of leisure. The association between leisure and Aristotle is so prevalent that in 1968 Pierre Berton could write: "A true age of leisure is on the horizon. It is not the second coming of Christ that we await but the second coming of Aristotle."[7] However, as Joseph Owens pointed out, very few writers on leisure provide an adequate review of Aristotle's understanding of leisure.[8] Rarely are the complexity and subtlety of his writings considered. The result, according to Goodale, is that "with few exceptions, our encounters with Aristotle's thought, as interpreted by many of those writing about leisure, are not very satisfying."[9]

Understanding Aristotle's writings on leisure is difficult for at least two reasons. First, there are differences in the translations, notes, and interpretations of his writings. Benjamin Jowett observed that leisure is one of the Aristotelian ideas that we have difficulty "in translating into English words and modes of thought."[10] Second, Aristotle lived in a society so different from ours as to seriously limit our ability to comprehend his thought. Therefore it is erroneous to take small segments of his writings from their context, and apply them over twenty-three centuries later.

Due to both the numerous references made to Aristotle in present day leisure literature and also the subtlety of his thought, it is necessary to examine in some detail his concept of leisure. Furthermore, and of particular relevance for our study, Pieper pointed out that it is important to study Aristotle on this topic since one of the foundations of Western culture is leisure: "The Christian and Western conception of the contemplative life is closely linked to the Aristotelian notion of leisure."[11]

The largest discussion of leisure by Aristotle is given in his *Politics* where he discusses education.[12] Although in *Politics* Aristotle referred to his concept of leisure frequently, the other passages that discuss it are neither long nor numerous in comparison with those on many important Aristotelian themes.[13] But his teaching on it throughout, according to Owens, is consistent and is deeply related to his major ethical issues.[14] My review of Aristotle's writings on leisure is structured around four topics: (1) the relationship between work and leisure; (2) rest and recreation; (3) the meaning of leisure; and (4) the ethical and divine element in leisure.

Work and Leisure. In literature on leisure one short passage from Aristotle's *Politics,* Book VII, is frequently quoted: "Nature herself . . . requires that we should be able not only to work well, but to use leisure; for as I must repeat once again the first principle of all action is leisure. Both are required but leisure is better than occupation and is its end."[15] Another translation of the same passage reads: "Nature requires not only that we should be properly employed, but that we should be able to enjoy our leisure in an honourable way."[16]

At the outset we note with Goodale "that being able to work well, or to be properly employed is so evident as to be a foregone conclusion. . . . That part of the passage is often neglected."[17] Yet leisure is valued above the toil and struggle of work. Work is not engaged in for its own sake; rather, as Aristotle wrote, "We do business in order that we may have leisure."[18] Elsewhere he wrote, "It is true that both occupation and leisure are necessary; but it is also true that leisure is higher than occupation, and is the end to which occupation is directed." Indeed, leisure "is the basis of all our life."[19]

Rest and Recreation. In *The Nicomachean Ethics* 10, Aristotle suggested that rest and recreation are good but not the highest good.

> Happiness, then, cannot consist in mere recreative pastime; for it is absurd to think that all our serious exertions and strenuous labors should terminate in so frivolous an end. We do not labor that we may be idle, but as Anarchis justly said, we are idle that we may labor with more effect; . . . The weakness of human nature requires frequent remissions of energy; but these rests and pauses are only the better to prepare us for enjoying the pleasures of activity. The amusements of life, therefore, are but preludes to its business, consisting of the exercise of those virtuous energies which constitute the worth and dignity of our nature.[20]

Another translation of this passage reads,

> Happiness is not to be found in amusements. . . . Indeed it would be strange that amusement should be our End—that we should toil and moil all our life long in order that we may amuse ourselves. . . . [T]o make amusement the object of our serious pursuits and our work seems foolish and childish to excess: Anarcharsis' motto, Play in order that you may work is felt to be the right rule. For amusement is a form of rest; but we need rest because we are not able to go on working without a break, and therefore it is not an end, since we take it as a means to further activity.[21]

For Aristotle the goal of labor is leisure, not amusements or pastimes. The function of recreation, amusement, and entertainment, in his opinion, is as a restorative to make possible further and other activity.

We can hardly fill our leisure with play. To do so would be to make play the be-all and end-all of life. That is an impossibility. Play is a thing to be chiefly used in connexion with one side of life—the side of occupation. (A simple argument shows that this is the case. Occupation is the companion of work and exertion: the worker needs relaxation: play is intended to provide relaxation.) We may therefore conclude that play and games should only be admitted into our state at the proper times and seasons, and should be applied as restoratives. The feelings which play produces in the mind are feelings of relief from relaxation. Leisure is a different matter.[22]

Furthermore, Aristotle stressed that the pursuit of entertainment and pleasures indulged in for their own sakes, and not brought under control, lead to ruin: "Agreeable amusements . . . are more often harmful than beneficial, causing men to neglect their health and their estates."[23] Allowed to proceed unchecked these pleasures may be destructive. To give one's free time to entertainment after the restoration of one's energy has been achieved is an abuse of leisure.

Leisure is valued above entertainment and recreation, as much as it is valued above toil and struggle. From Aristotle's viewpoint, people abuse pleasure just as they abuse work when they choose either as the ultimate goal in life.[24] Both the necessary drudgery of work and the relaxation of recreation function as preparation for the ultimate function of leisure. Neither is engaged in only for its own sake. But each, wrote Owens, "is in its own way meant to bring about the leisure in which human activity may be undertaken."[25] Owens commented: "What is . . . striking in Aristotle's conception . . . is that leisure opens out on a panorama more positive and more self-sufficient than relaxation or recreation or entertainment. Only after the pleasures of recreation have been enjoyed and have accomplished their purpose does the full role of leisure ever enter upon the scene."[26]

The Meaning of Leisure. What does leisure mean to Aristotle? De Grazia pointed out that Aristotle used the word "leisure" in at least two ways: as available time, and as absence of the necessity of being occupied.[27] Sometimes leisure seems to be another word for free time. For example, the affluent, Aristotle wrote, if they were to take care of their private affairs, would have little leisure for politics and would be unable to attend the assembly and the courts.[28] But there is also an ethical tone in Aristotle that suggests spare time when misused is not leisure. The strongest of Aristotle's criticisms of Sparta was that of Spartan women, whom he criticized for using free time for license not leisure.[29] Obviously for Aristotle, free time was not to be equated with leisure.

In one instance Aristotle provided a rough equivalent of leisure. He wrote of leisure and then continued, "or in other words freedom from the necessity of labour."[30] At first glance this seems similar to the modern notion of free time—time off the job. But in Aristotle's definition time has no role. According to de Grazia, leisure for Aristotle "is a condition or a state—the state of being free from the necessity to labor."[31] In origin, the word here for labor (*ascholia*) actually signifies the absence of leisure, unleisure, or the condition of being busy or occupied. Therefore leisure is freedom from the necessity of being occupied in the sense of being busy. This includes freedom from the necessity to labor, but it could also include any activity one is obligated to perform but would desire to be free from. The goal of being occupied is only to attain leisure for "leisure [is] the final end of occupation."[32] Thus de Grazia concluded that for Aristotle "leisure is a state of being in which activity is performed for its own sake or as its own end."[33]

This definition of leisure, as Spence documented, is closely associated with freedom and peace.[34] First, in terms of freedom, leisure depends on the absence of pressing duties and external demands. It requires a state of full freedom of which the opposite extreme is slavery. This freedom has no connection with free time—that is, time left over from a job or occupational activity. Rather, it is the state of being free from the necessity of labor, possible in Greek society because of the prevalence of slavery, which allowed the wealthy to claim leisure for themselves.

A second fundamental feature of leisure is its close association with peace in opposition to war. The words "peace" and "leisure" occur together frequently in Aristotle, the occurrence reinforcing his thesis that wars are fought to have peace and peace is needed for leisure. Spence wrote, "War symbolizes unleisure because it is essentially a threat to life, and preoccupation with the struggle for survival eliminates any possibility of leisure."[35] Similarly, poverty that threatens life and health is unleisure. The person of leisure was a man of means who was freed from the necessity of securing the fundamental conditions of life and was therefore able to turn his attention to higher things.

The ability to use leisure properly was the foundation of the freeman's whole life.[36] Therefore, for Aristotle, education is important and its purpose is to prepare people to occupy their leisure.

> It is clear, therefore, that there are some branches of learning and education which ought to be studied with a view to the proper use of leisure in the cultivation of the mind. It is clear, too, that these studies should be regarded as ends in themselves, while studies pursued with a view to occupation should be regarded merely as means and matters of necessity.[37]

What is one to do in leisure? Aristotle mentioned two activities as being worthy of the name leisure: music and contemplation. Both activities are not as limited as we might expect. For the Greeks music was almost a synonym for culture; it had value for the cultivation of the mind. Thus leisure, according to John Newman's understanding of Aristotle, "meant being occupied in something desirable for its own sake—the hearing of noble music and noble poetry, intercourse with friends chosen for their own worth, and above all the exercise, alone or in company, of the speculative faculty."[38] *Diagōgē*, or cultivation of mind, is the word that Aristotle sometimes used to describe the activities of leisure.[39] It is uncertain, however, whether in speaking of *diagōgē* he is implying that "in leisure you should cultivate your mind or that in the true state of leisure you cannot do anything but cultivate your mind."[40] Owens expanded on this idea of cultivation of mind as follows:

> The intellectual life to which Aristotle directs human activity requires all the moral or practical virtues. It demands moderate wealth, good fortune, friends to entertain and associate with, mature years, well-organized civil environment—in a word, everything that goes with full living. It does indeed consist essentially in the intellectual activity, but that is the activity by which the soul becomes and is all things with which it makes intellectual contact. It excludes nothing that is good and that contributes to one's happiness. Consequently it is not exclusive of things according to a man's capabilities. In this secondary way practical life plays its full part in human happiness. It is demanded for the habituation and control that are necessary for intellectual contemplation. It exhibits in itself the beauty and order that accord with the intellect's longings. In a corresponding way the useful arts, the fine arts, and all the doings of every day life fit into the picture of happiness that consists essentially in intellectual contemplation, in which deep understanding catalyzes toil as well as pleasure. The intellectual life envisaged by Aristotle as the supreme destiny of man is open to everything that promotes a man's well-being.[41]

The Ethical and Divine Element in Leisure. We have already noted that Aristotle's concept of leisure is related to his major ethical themes. Goodale, noting that most contemporary discussions of Aristotle's concept of leisure mention little "about virtue and less about the divine," concluded that "the omissions destroy the meaning."[42] Yet morality, virtue, contemplation, and happiness are linked in complex ways in Aristotle's thought. This passage from Harold Joachim's commentary on Aristotle's *Nicomachean Ethics* illustrates this complexity.

> The life of good conduct—of morally good action—is the best human life, the completest expression of human nature. . . . But there is in man an element which is either itself divine or the most godlike of elements in man: *vous*, or whatever that should be called whose nature it is to rule us, and to take thought of things noble and divine. And in the activity of this element—in contemplation—man experiences the completest felicity.[43]

This life of good conduct is related to leisure, for as Aristotle wrote, "Leisure is a necessity . . . for growth in goodness."[44] Elsewhere he wrote, "We need . . . restraint and a sense of justice . . . particularly in times of leisure and peace."[45] Regarding the connection between leisure and ethics in Aristotle, Sylvester explained that in Aristotle's *Politics*, "the cultivated ability to use leisure rightly establishes the basis of a person's entire life. Choice and conduct thus imbue leisure with moral substance, making leisure behavior and moral conduct virtually synonymous."[46]

Let us try to uncover some of the connections between Aristotle's themes. In *Nicomachean Ethics* Aristotle "identifies happiness as the highest good, it being an end itself."[47] Furthermore, "happiness is thought to involve leisure"[48]; indeed Aristotle believed happiness proceeds from leisure: "We think of it [leisure] as having intrinsic pleasure, intrinsic happiness, intrinsic felicity."[49] In addition, contemplation—which as we will see in a moment is like leisure, or is itself leisure—brings felicity.[50] Aristotle, in *The Nicomachean Ethics*, contended that happiness continues only as long as contemplation does: "Happiness therefore is co-extensive in its range with contemplation: the more a class of beings possesses the faculty of contemplation, the more it enjoys happiness."[51] Hence there are connections between goodness, happiness, leisure, and contemplation.

From a study of the first chapter of Aristotle's *Metaphysics*, Arnold concluded that the word "contemplation" is an important referent for leisure (*scholē*). Contemplation in the Greek sense is so similar to leisure that the two terms are almost interchangeable. Contemplation does not imply inactivity in the sense of placing oneself in the position of the Thinker, but instead means to observe, view, and behold. Etymologically, "contemplation" is closely linked with the Greek words *theōria* and *theōrein*, which meant to behold and look upon. Arnold wrote, "The *theōrikos* were those who travelled to see men and things and then reflect upon them as one would speculate or postulate an explanation of a phenomenon."[52] De Grazia noted, "Contemplation for . . . Aristotle was the best way of truthfinding."[53] It was valued above all other activities. But contemplation was more than reflecting on phenomena and discerning a person's place in the world; it was a very religious experience, the only activity in which to picture the gods.

For Aristotle, "contemplation was inextricably" connected "to the divine in man; to the somehow transcendent soul." He linked contemplation "to his notion of God and God's own sense of pleasure."[54] Contemplation, according to John Ferguson's interpretation of Aristotle, "is possible only by virtue of the divine element in man. We ought then not to confine our thoughts to the ephemeral, but so far as possible we ought to seek immortality."[55]

In conclusion, Aristotle saw leisure as the ultimate function of humans; work and recreation were simply preparation for leisure. Leisure was closely linked to contemplation and cultivation of the mind. It was also linked to virtue and the divine. Owens made this observation about Aristotle's thoughts on leisure:

> It [leisure] does not offer us any detailed blueprint. It requires us to do our own thinking. But it does furnish the guidance and inspiration for developing a fully rounded conception of leisure, as something highly purposeful and personal, something based upon and characterized by free choice, something that lies at the very core of genuine human living and that conditions the deepest moral fiber of moral conduct.[56]

Leisure in Roman Society

Roman culture—including literature, religion, and language—was greatly influenced by Greek philosophers and teachers who perpetuated their system of education in Roman society. Thus the Greek ideal of leisure continued in Rome, transmitted there largely through the writings of Plato, Aristotle, and Epicurus. Most Roman writers, however, used *otium* to render the idea of leisure. *Otium* was linked with contemplation and the opportunity for freedom from both time and occupation. As in Greece, its verbal opposite was constructed by adding a negative prefix, to make *negotium*. Most Roman writers discussed leisure in terms of the oscillation between *otium* and *negotium*. *Otium* attracted them; they extolled its benefits primarily in terms of the *beata solitude*, blessed solitude in the country.

Marcus Tullius Cicero (106–43 BCE), who was typical of most Roman writers on leisure, rarely goes beyond speaking of the alternation of *otium* and *negotium*. Cicero believed *otium* existed for the sake of *negotium*, and not for its own sake, as Aristotle would have argued. According to Cicero, a person is to be occupied in the affairs of the army, commerce, or state and then rests and recreates for further occupation. "Old age" is a peaceful, well-earned rest from the busyness of *negotium*. He wrote, "If the soul has food for study and learning, nothing is more delightful than an old age of leisure. . . . Leisure consists in all those virtuous activities by which a man grows morally, intellectually, and spiritually. It is that which makes a life worth living."[57] Aristotle would not have called Cicero's understanding of *otium* "leisure," since *otium* understood in this way is not for its own sake but for the sake of *negotium*. *Otium*, unlike the Greek *scholē*, was not an end in itself.

Pliny's (61–113 CE) conception of leisure resembles that of Cicero. His letters indicate that for most Romans leisure was something desired instead of something enjoyed. For him leisure was pleasurable stimulation from the external world—the calm retreat in the country for reflection, study, distraction, and freedom from the city's demands. He sought *otium* not for itself but because he was tired of *negotium*. Similarly, he instructed others to alternate between *otium* and *negotium*: when tired of one, turn to the other.

Of the Romans, Seneca (4 BCE–65 CE) came closest to Aristotle's notion of leisure. Seneca believed men like Cicero and Pliny did not experience leisure but were merely busy idlers. They merely had idle occupations, not leisure. He suggested that men of leisure were only those who took time for philosophy.

Seneca also contended that leisure was necessary for the perfect state. "That other *res publica*, the universal one that embraces gods and men alike, that houses all corners of the world, that defines citizenship by the path of the sun—that one we can serve even in leisure, actually serve it even better in leisure."[58] The goal of leisure is freedom as Seneca expresses it in one of his letters: "I am free, Lucilius, free, and wherever I am I am myself."[59]

Seneca drew together and fused Stoic thought with Greek writings on leisure and contemplation. This convergence of thought in the Greco-Roman world had a tremendous influence from the second to the sixth century. In contrast to this Stoic influence, Rome was also characterized by "Epicurianism," an attitude of self-indulgence, so *otium* was not necessarily a dominant characteristic of Roman society.

The Romans transformed leisure into a break from work, a time to rest from work and re-create oneself so that one could become rejuvenated and ready to return to work.[60] Leisure was now seen as entertainment and recreation rather than the contemplation and the pursuit of truth. With this transformation, leisure was no longer only for the elite but accessible to people of all social classes. Leisure was now understood as recreation or voluntary non-work activities that had personal and social benefits.

Leisure in Early and Medieval Christianity

The classical ideal of leisure and contemplation, reaching back to Aristotle and converging in Seneca, now continues through Plotinus and into Christianity, especially in monasticism where the contemplative element was singled out. It was only after the Greek and Roman civilizations plunged into the abyss of destruction that *otium* was cautiously considered by Christians. Christians had witnessed license within leisure and condemned festivals and spectacles during the waning years of Roman civilization. However, *otium* came to be "fused with the contemplative life within monasteries and continued to have an association with learning."[61]

Augustine. Augustine (354–440) made a distinction between an "active life" (*vita activa*) and a "contemplative life" (*vita contemplativa*). The contemplative life was similar to Aristotle's *Life of Contemplation* and was primarily taken from Greek and Roman thought. The *vita activa* encompassed almost every type of work, including studying, preaching, and teaching, whereas the *vita contemplativa* consisted of reflection and meditation on God and his truth.

> The charm of leisure must not be indolent vacancy of mind, but the investigation or discovery of truth, that thus every man may make solid attainments without grudging that others do the same. . . . Accordingly no one is prohibited from the search after truth, for in this leisure may most laudably be spent. . . . And therefore holy leisure is longed for by the lover of truth.[62]

With the exception of gardening, Augustine did not comment on pursuits that are considered leisure activities today.[63] Leisure was the serious pursuit of truth.

Both the active and the contemplative lives were good, but the later life was given higher status. At certain times the active life is unavoidable, but, whenever possible, one should choose the contemplative life: "The one life is loved, the other endured." For Augustine, "The obligations of charity make us undertake righteous business (*negotium*)," yet "if no one lays the burden upon us, we

should give ourselves up to leisure (*otium*) to the perception and contemplation of truth."[64] Augustine also recognized the mixed life of action and leisure
that consisted of an alteration between the diligent search for truth and active
benevolence.[65] All these lives were worthwhile and deserved an everlasting
reward as long as the life of leisure did not ignore the needs of one's neighbor
and the life of action did not ignore the contemplation of God. However the
good life did not allow for occupations that were neither serious nor charitable.
Augustine also wrote of heaven being characterized by leisure: "There we shall
be at leisure (*vacabimus*) and we shall see, we shall see and we shall love, we
shall love and we shall praise."[66]

Aquinas. Thomas Aquinas (1225–1274) also used Augustine's distinction of
the *vita contemplativa* and the *vita activa*. Aquinas, who devoted his life to the
reconciliation of Aristotle's thought and the Christian faith, brought together the
classical view of leisure and the contemplative life. He located Aristotle's notion
of leisure and contemplation in the beatific vision of God.[67] For Aquinas, the
vita contemplativa was "oriented to the eternal," while the *vita activa* existed due
to the "necessities of the present life." The active life was necessary because of
the body's needs and thus it was approved, but it was better if one could live
without such work. Both lives were accepted, but the contemplative life was
truly free, while the active life was restricted by necessity. In summary, "The life
of contemplation" was "simply better than the life of action."[68]

Monasticism. Jean Leclercq noted that an important theme of monastic culture was that of leisure.[69] He pointed out that this theme of leisure is of biblical
origin, although there is, no doubt, a classical tradition of *otium*. But when
William of St. Thierry (ca. 1085–1148), for example, took from Seneca and
Pliny the expression *otium pingue*, he gave it a totally new meaning. In Pliny,
the word *pingue* is associated with *otium* and *secessus*, which gives the meaning,
"comfortable leisure." However, William refers to the same meaning as used
in Ecclesiasticus in an expression frequently repeated by the monastic writers:
sapientia scribae in tempore otii ("Leisure is what gives the scribe the opportunity to acquire wisdom; the man with few business affairs grows wise," Ecclus.
38:25). William is describing "leisure fruitful and well-filled" by exercises of
contemplation.[70]

Since monastic life in the "cloistered paradise" anticipates eternal rest, it is a
life of leisure. In the monastic life, the symbol of the bed, and even of the "little
bed," is joined to the theme of leisure, creating *lectulus noster florius*. The bed
(*lectulo*) is monastic life, while *lectulus* is contemplation. This life of leisure is
expressed in terms such as *otium* (leisure), *quies* (quiet), *vacatio* (freedom), and
sabbattum (rest), which are sometimes used to reinforce each other as in *otium
quietis*, *vacation sabbati*. These terms describe an active leisure very different
from quietism. John Preston Dever noted, "St. Augustine established an active
leisure based on the tranquility of action in Christ. Through this active rest love
became the transcending power of one's life and one experienced the eternal

Sabbath or the heavenly existence on earth."[71] The term *otium* lies halfway between the two dangers of *otiositas* (idleness) and *negotium* (business), which is the very denial of *otium*. *Otium*, the predominant occupation of the monk, was a very busy leisure, *negotiosissimum otium*, as St. Bernard and many others have described it.

Although leisure was an important element of monastic life, it was strictly controlled, and work became associated with the cleansing of the spirit. The concept of leisure in the Middle Ages was influenced by the divine sanction that the church ascribed to work. In practical terms, good works were to fill free time so that one could escape the natural desires of one's body. As long as monasticism prevailed, idleness was strongly condemned. In monasticism, work was almost considered conducive to piety. Monasteries became hives of industry. Therefore monasticism was industrious in contrast to Aristotle's idea that labor was for slaves and not for freemen. Monasticism lifted work to an honored position similar to that accorded to leisure in Greek society by those who lived a life of contemplation at the expense of slaves. Although work came to have greater dignity, leisure and contemplation were still regarded as preferable to physical work.

The distinction between the active life and the contemplative life formed the basic pattern of medieval Christianity. It resulted in the notion that the only true, or at least the highest, Christian calling was a priestly or monastic one that focused on the contemplative life. The creational mandate of work was minimized.

4

the history of leisure as activity

The classical understanding of leisure began to decline with the rise of the Renaissance and the Reformation. Rather than leisure being regarded as the noblest activity of humanity, work came to hold that position. The shift away from the classical view of leisure is reflected in the linguistic convention of using the term "recreation" instead of "leisure." Leisure came to be considered in terms of recreation—time off work to re-create oneself to go back to work. The monastic practice of *otium* was gradually forgotten.

The Renaissance

The Renaissance, a humanitarian outpouring of intellectual endeavor that sought to model itself on the classical remnants of the ancient world, began before the mid-fourteenth century but reached its climax in the fifteenth to seventeenth centuries. The Renaissance "was multiform and was more a state of mind and a climate of opinion than a single, concrete movement."[1] Therefore it is difficult to make broad generalizations about the Renaissance. Furthermore, there wasn't necessarily a great discontinuity or contrast between the Renaissance and what came before.[2] For example, the increased emphasis on autonomous human reason often occurred within a framework of theism.

One of the features of the Renaissance was a humanism in which "a person is the measure of all things." The thinkers of the Renaissance were self-confident, believing in themselves and in humanity. Human nature and human history were regarded as realms of unmeasured possibilities, and it was felt that medieval religion failed to do justice to human freedom and human history. Therefore Renaissance thinkers tended to recover Neoplatonic conceptions of the dignity and liberty of humans and integrate them with the Christian conception of the freedom of the human spirit. They put more stress on the idea of humans in "the image of God" over and above humans as "creature and sinner," and thus the Renaissance was "a spiritual movement affirming the limitless possibilities of human existence."[3] This humanism of the Renaissance found expression in a wide variety of recreational activities, both utilitarian and enjoyable, that provided for the sound body in which a sound mind could exist.

Another feature of this humanism was that it put more emphasis on an exuberant appreciation of life in this present world and less on life beyond the grave. The Renaissance emphasized the enjoyment of life that had been somewhat challenged by the insecurities and otherworldliness that characterized the medieval world. About the Renaissance, Johan Huizinga wrote, "The whole mental attitude of the Renaissance was one of play. The splendors of the Renaissance are nothing but a gorgeous and solemn masquerade in the accoutrements of an idealized past."[4] Renaissance figures altered medieval conceptions of the duality of the *vita activa* and the *vita contemplativa* in favor of the ancient Stoic-humanist combination of the two. For example, Paul Marshall illustrated how the writings of the English Renaissance humanists are marked by an emphasis on leisure and peace. According to St. Thomas More's *Utopia*, "The main purpose of [the Utopian's] whole economy is to give persons . . . free time from physical drudgery . . . so that they can cultivate the mind—which they regard as the secret of a happy life."[5] Thomas Lupset, More's colleague and lecturer in rhetoric at Oxford, held a stoic view and sought the "rest that angels in heaven have." He thought that "our spirit and our mind only hath things that truly be called goods."[6] Thomas Starkey, chaplain to Henry VIII and another colleague of More, believed that "high philosophy and contemplation of nature be of itself a greater perfection of man's mind."[7]

Notwithstanding this praise for rest, philosophy, and contemplation, the Renaissance humanists did not disdain an active life. Work was given greater dignity than previously. De Grazia suggested that the Renaissance introduced a new philosophy of work emphasizing *praxis* more than *theōria*, moving away from *scienta contemplative* to *scienta operative*.[8] Lupset strongly urged participation in the affairs of the commonwealth, for "the meddling with the causes of the commonweal is more necessary and even rather and first to be chosen, as the principal mean whereby we may attain to the other [i.e., contemplation]."[9] The educated should be politically responsible and involved. Yet this work was still viewed as necessary only to facilitate the more valued life of freedom and contemplation. While this combination of contemplation and action was not substantially different from that of Augustine and Aquinas, greater value was placed on action and work than previously.

The Reformation

The Reformers further altered the medieval conception of the duality of the *vita activa* and the *vita contemplativa* and came to emphasize the active life, the life of work. This is most clearly expressed in the Calvinistic expression of Protestantism, but first we need to examine Martin Luther's view of work and leisure.

Martin Luther

Two aspects of Luther's theology had implications for leisure. First, Lehman pointed out that Luther's doctrine of vocation created a definite break from the dualistic view of work (spiritual and secular) found in the Middle Ages.[10] Luther rejected any piety associated with especially "holy" works.[11] He extended equality before God to the working person as well as to the monk in the monastery. His view that all life, not just religious life, was sacred had significant implications for the understanding of leisure. Every honorable activity of humans, including those outside of working time, "could be used creatively to the glory of God."[12]

Second, Paul Althaus documented that although Luther saw work as very honorable, "a most holy thing and, as the means through which God blesses us," the high value he put on rest prevented him from idolizing work.[13] Luther's evaluation of work was based on the Sabbath commandment that not only commands us to work but also establishes the limits to work by commanding us to rest. In Luther's hymn on the Ten Commandments, he interpreted the Sabbath commandment in this sense. "From thine own work thou must be free, that God his work have in thee."[14] In a letter of May 12, 1530, Luther exhorted Melanchthon: "We worship God when we rest; indeed there is no greater worship of God than this."[15] This exhortation reflects the center of Luther's theology, as stated by Althaus.

> God is God and he alone is the creator. We can worship God by resting; indeed in resting we can worship him better than in any other way because it is when we really relax our body and soul that we cast our care on God. We thus honor God as the one whose blessing rests upon and surrounds all our work, and who keeps on working for us even when we rest and sleep. The capacity truly to rest from our cares with our body and soul is a special confirmation of our faith and is related to justifying faith.[16]

John Calvin

Although Luther's theology played a major role in the Reformation by creating the break from the Roman church, Calvin's theology had a greater influence on the Protestant work ethic and the corresponding understanding of leisure.[17] Because Calvin's theology was not colored by nationalism, as was Luther's, it was better able to extend across international borders. As a result the Calvinistic doctrine spread throughout Europe and eventually to North America. Because of its prevalence during the past four hundred years and its influence in shaping the Protestant work ethic, it is worthy of our attention.

At this point we should note that while there is some truth to Max Weber's thesis that the Protestant work ethic was influenced by Calvinism, this work ethic is a result of the total sociocultural evolution of modernity. Christianity is only one of many forces that influenced the work ethic, and then only indirectly. Weber greatly overstated his argument by tracing the work ethic back to Calvin. Edward Vanderkloet pointed out that Calvin's view of work and leisure was heavily dependent on God's promise of shalom to his people through Christ.[18] For example, the Heidleberg Catechism, authored by some of Calvin's immediate followers, interprets the fourth commandment in terms of the true Sabbath rest that extends for the whole of one's lifetime.

Although leisure scholar Jay Shivers, consistent with some historians and writers, summarized Calvin's view of leisure as "an inordinate emphasis upon leisure being idleness, which is equated with mischief and the devil's work,"[19] Calvin, according to Lehman, actually advocated a realistic attitude concerning leisure and urged the moderate use of all time.[20] He opposed all excesses but approved of participation in the arts, games, and social parties of the day as long as it was kept under control and contributed to the rhythm of life.

The caricature of Calvin as being against entertainment and pleasure, so often created by uninformed critics, is simply not accurate.[21] He did not teach that one should deny oneself the ordinary pleasures of life or live so frugally as to harm bodily health. In Calvin's *Institutes* we read,

> Ivory and gold and riches of all kinds are certainly blessings of Divine Providence, not only permitted, but expressly designed for the use of man; nor are we any where prohibited to laugh, or to be satiated with food, or to annex new possessions to those already enjoyed by ourselves or by our ancestors, or to be delighted with musical harmony, or to drink wine.[22]

Thus I agree with Georgia Harkness that Calvin was not an ascetic. He believed that many gifts are bestowed on us by God, not for our necessity, but for our enjoyment.[23] The beauty of the created world is given to delight the senses. In the chapter of the *Institutes* titled "How We Should Use This Present Life and Its Helps," he explained that it is a person's privilege and responsibility to use them in moderation for enjoyment, avoiding both austerity and indulgence. Calvin affirmed that to not use creation's gifts for pleasure is ingratitude to God, although Christians are not to become attached to them.[24] But his followers often missed his emphasis on moderation and turned his teaching into a "basis for worldly asceticism and a distrust of all impulsive pleasures."[25]

In Calvin's view, recreational activity was rationalized on the basis that it enabled people to restore their physical and mental capacities so that they would be capable of returning to work. This was totally consistent with Calvin's view of work. Building on Luther's argument that it is God's work, not the work of humans, that achieves salvation, Calvin proclaimed that God had already determined the destinies of all people. Neither works, sacraments, holy days, priests, power of the church, nor anything else could change the destiny of a person. Yet Calvin taught that Christians are called neither to spiritual exercises nor to quiet acceptance of grace but actively to glorify God in their work, which is seen as the stewardship of God's creation.

To maintain the physical and mental capacity for work, there had to be some time for rejuvenation through recreation. But recreational activity was not to be confused with idleness; idleness was the one intolerable thing. Recreational activity was a necessity to enhance the primary activity of work.

Puritanism

The Puritans, who were ardent Calvinists, began with the Calvinist doctrine of calling and added their own brand of individual responsibility and hard work. Many Puritans believed it was one's responsibility to try to live in perfect obedience to God's will as a sign of one's election. All of life—work, worship, personal conduct, family life, government—entailed an opportunity to do what was right, which meant to lead a useful and responsible life in this world so that one might be suitable for election into one's real home in the next world. A useful and responsible life included work because work was understood as one way in which the Christian makes one's response to God. Thus for the Puritans secular work took on profound spiritual significance.

The Puritan's attitude to leisure, which was two-sided, was conditioned by the significance they gave to work. The negative side was captured by the popular saying of the time: "The man who doesn't work doesn't eat" (from 2 Thess. 3:10). Since a Puritan felt responsible for using one's God-given abilities in the work to which one was called, such qualities as contributed to that end were encouraged—sobriety, self-discipline, honesty, thrift, industry, frugality, and punctuality. Idleness and destructive forms of recreation, activities that would hinder one's life as a working member of society, were looked down upon, especially during the settlement of the New England colonies in North America, when the environment was decidedly unfavorable for leisure and recreational participation. The task of carving out an existence in the wilderness meant that survival was predominant in people's minds. If a person did not work, he or she was a severe burden on others.

Thus the Puritan ethic was the program of an active, not a monastic or contemplative, life.[26] The Puritan felt a responsibility to waste as little time as possible. The greatest criticism the Puritans had of recreation was based on it being a waste of time. The idea of "redeeming the time" was a prominent part of Puritan thought. Comparing time to money, Richard Baxter (1650–1691) exhorted his readers: "Use every minute of it as a most precious thing, and spend it wholly in the way of duty. . . . Remember how gainful the Redeeming of Time is . . . in Merchandise or in trading, in husbandry or any gaining course."[27] Banks, noting that we must be careful not to read our modern notion of busyness into such statements, quoted the diary of another Puritan, Richard Rodgers, to illustrate that Rodgers set aside "as much time for 'eating, recreating, idle talk and journeys' as for direct involvement in the Lord's work."[28] However, Puritans, in such actions as prohibiting holidays that did not coincide with Sunday, were preparing the way for a work-oriented lifestyle.

Yet for some Puritans there was another more positive side to their attitude toward leisure. The Puritan, like the person of the Renaissance, emphasized the celebrating of life but within the context of the divine. James T. Dennison Jr. pointed out that the popular impression of the Puritan as "kill-joys, dour and somber to the point of morbidity is absurd." Rather, "the Puritan worldview was one of rejoicing in the goodness of God's creation."[29] Richard Sibbes (1577–1635) wrote, "Worldly things, are good in themselves, and given to sweeten our passage to Heaven, [even to sweeten our] profession of Religion. . . . This world and the things therefore are all good, and were all made of God, for the benefit of his creature."[30] From a similar point of view, Nicholas Bownd (d. 1613) wrote, "I am not of that minde . . . to think that men should never take their delight, and, that all recreation was sinful."[31]

While the Puritans loved and enjoyed God's gifts in this life, they did not view them as ultimate. They were concerned about the excesses to which people might become enslaved through pleasurable recreations. Sibbes warned that the world is our servant, not our master. Christians are to take comfort in the world but are not to set their hearts on it or to let themselves be made "drunke with the cares below."[32] Convinced that the Christian's true home is in the next world, the Puritans believed that pleasurable experiences and enjoyment of earthly things were of little importance in themselves, and to the extent that such attachments could make a person forget God altogether, they felt called to overcome them. Overindulgence was an abuse of God's creation that served only to gratify the senses and deter people from their service to God. What the Puritans condemned and sought to regulate was not the recreational activities themselves but what they saw as the immoral excesses of the activities.

Yet the Puritans were realists who recognized the place of recreation in a useful and responsible life. The need for recreation was acknowledged as a basic part of human nature and was taken into account in the day's activities, but their recreation had to be utilitarian. According to Dennison, the Puritans defined recreation "as anything that gave refreshment to the body or spirit."[33] Honest or lawful recreations, consistent with New Testament teaching, furthered the kingdom of God in people, enabled the body to be better suited for divine service, and brought life and cheerfulness to the mind.[34] Illustrative of this attitude concerning recreation is advice from the New England Puritan Benjamin Colman.

> We daily need some respite & diversion, without which we dull our Powers; a little intermission sharpens 'em again. . . . Mirth is some loose or relaxation to the labouring Mind or Body, it lifts up the hands that hang down in weariness, and strengthens the feeble knees that could stand no longer to work: it renews our strength, and we resume our labours again with vigour. Tis designed by nature to chear and revive us thro' all the toils and troubles of life.[35]

Such diversion was encouraged as healthful and helpful, but for it to remain so, the activity had to be done in moderation. The Puritans often used the phrase "seasonable merriment" to describe the kind of recreation that was appropriate—merriment limited to the appropriate occasion. People should receive refreshment from their recreation, and if instead the activity made them more tired, it was wrong to do. Furthermore, the time and the effort required by the activity should yield results that made the effort worthwhile: "No Puritan objected to recreation as such; indeed it was necessary for a man to indulge in frivolous pleasures from time to time, in order that he might return to his work refreshed. But to serve the purpose, recreation had to be fun and not exhaust a man physically or bore him or frustrate him."[36] Thus recreation "was not an end in itself but a means to a greater end—devotion to a sovereign God through work."[37] The use of leisure for instrumental purposes happily coexisted with enjoyment in the Puritan view.[38] In regard to enjoying leisure, Packer pointed out that Isaac Watts, the leading Puritan songwriter, wrote, "Religion never was designed / To make our pleasures less."[39]

In a recent paper, Karl Johnson effectively documented the Puritan view as a middle ground between leisure as a means to an end and leisure as an end itself.[40] This middle-ground position reflected a time when there was much more interpenetrability of labor and leisure than is prevalent today. Johnson suggested that the Puritans' view of leisure is not too different from the view of leisure articulated by leisure scholars today who recognize both expressivist leisure and the benefits of leisure. He also noted that Puritans attempted to think critically about leisure as is evidenced by their opposition to blood sports, which were a form of cruelty to animals.[41] Johnson's summary on the Puritans' perspective on leisure is generally consistent with Ryken's rebuttals of common fallacies associated with the Puritan leisure ethic.[42]

In summary, the Puritans were not opposed to recreation, as long as it was truly refreshing, was not a waste of time, was not done in excess, and was not immoral, sensual, or glorifying the flesh. As with all other activities, this seasonable recreation must contribute to the main goal of life—acting in obedience to God. Instead of divorcing work and pleasure, the admonition not to waste time gave the Puritans a unity to the activities of their life. Barn raisings, quilting parties, weddings, corn huskings, and similar activities of daily life became occasions for recreation and merrymaking as well as time spent in cooperative effort toward a useful end. Because work was their dominant necessity, they did not see the other dimensions of life as separate within the total scheme of purpose and meaning in life. Thus "Puritanism was rooted in a view of life as a unified whole under the sovereignty of God."[43]

The Modern Era

The Renaissance notion of the autonomous individual and the Reformational emphasis on individual responsibility contributed to an even greater emphasis on work than leisure in the modern era. De Grazia characterized work in this modern period as follows:

> It was a kind of work they [the workers] had not bargained for—tied to other men as in galleys, tied to machines by the clock, and paced by an unseen boss. This was the new order of things. The classical economists and democrats took over the idea, the anarchists found it just right, the socialists embraced it—all varieties of socialists: the communists, the Christian, utopian, and scientific. Of course, each used a different emphasis, but for all work was good or would become so, was the right of every man, and a duty as well. The philosophic doctrine they held in common was that through work and work alone does man produce and know. The doctrine was that of the Renaissance, the actual time was that of the nineteenth century; the ideal of leisure had long before taken its exit.[44]

Work became a person's highest ideal in which all should participate. Leisure, considered only in terms of idleness, was regarded as unhealthy, something not to be encouraged. As the Christian worldview began to disintegrate, work was no longer seen in relation to the divine. A variety of influences, including the development of capitalism, the Enlightenment, the Industrial Revolution, and the philosophy of utilitarianism, contributed to this modern, exalted view of work.

With the rise of capitalism a new attitude condemnatory of leisure appeared. In capitalism, the social and economic values of both time and money were considered from a new perspective. Money was to be used to make more money and not to be enjoyed, used to support contemplation, or even be given to the poor. Historian Pardon E. Tillinghast noted that the whole organization of a person's life came to be based on maximum efficiency and not contemplation or enjoyment of creation.[45]

The Enlightenment of the eighteenth century was characterized by a secularizing of life. Belief in a supernatural world and in life after death declined. People viewed their life in a finite rather than an eternal context and thus their values and goals were confined to the temporal and material horizons of this world. As people narrowed their gaze to what they could gain from their brief span of life on this earth, a more intensive use of everyday time, a belief in human progress through work and the denigration of leisure, defined in terms of idleness, followed.

The influence of the Industrial Revolution (c. 1760–1830) on the social and economic realms of life further contributed to the development of a strongly dogmatic attitude toward work. The rationalization of time became more pronounced: leisure was time wasted. Work was no longer understood as a task from God, the Creator. The ideal of work for its own sake was adopted as a healthful, uplifting, and moral exercise. According to Tillinghast, work became "a redemptive activity in itself."[46]

In the nineteenth century the philosophy of utilitarianism emerged in which utility was the primary value in personal and social life. Utilitarian beliefs influenced people's attitude toward their free time. The view that only useful activity was valuable, moral, and meaningful predominated. Thus relaxation as an end itself, pure play, and idleness were all censured and viewed with suspicion. Competitive games and purposeful recreation activities were considered more important. People felt guilty unless their rest and recreation accomplished something worthwhile. Utilitarian notions continued in both capitalist and communist countries in the twentieth century; "work and leisure came under great regulation and stricter account of their profitability."[47] In a satirical but realistic description, Kerr illustrated how the utilitarian perspective of leisure, the desire for achievement, and the individual development through recreational activity has become all-pervasive.

> We are all of us compelled to read for profit, party for contacts, lunch for contracts, bowl for unity, drive for mileage, gamble for charity, go out for the evening for the greater glory of the municipality, and stay home for the weekend to rebuild the house. Minutes, hours, and days have been spared us. The prospect of filling them with the pleasures for which they were spared us has somehow come to seem meaningless, meaningless enough to drive some of us to drink and some of us to doctors and all of us to the satisfactions of an insatiate industry.[48]

As work became a human's highest ideal, leisure was defined as free time and regarded as subservient to work. England's Ten-Hour Bill (passed in 1847) crystallized the workday so that ten-hour workers had free time, a unit of concentrated nonworking time that they never had before. Work time and free time were now split, which has continued into the present. With the passing of the bill, the modern notion of leisure as free time was given significant legislative support.[49]

In the late nineteenth century, Veblen grafted to leisure the notions of free time and economic advantage characteristic of what he labeled the leisure class. Through his book *The Theory of the Leisure Class* (published in 1899), considered a classic among sociologists, Veblen greatly influenced modern thinking. Henceforth notions of leisure became associated with "free time, unproductiveness and absence of necessity to work, in fact an unwillingness to work."[50] Veblen's influence may be seen in the definition of leisure in the

Dictionary of Sociology as "the free-time after the practical necessities of life have been attended to"; thus the notion of leisure is defined in quantitative terms.[51] But as Arnold pointed out, "Semantic faithfulness to leisure as a term has been abrogated."[52]

Conclusion

In this chapter and the previous one I have highlighted two historical concepts of leisure: (1) the classical view of leisure as developed in Greek culture, particularly by Aristotle, and adapted in the contemplative life of monastic culture; and (2) the activity view of leisure as recreation—time off work to re-create oneself before going back to work. We saw how the classical view of leisure emphasized a person's being. For Aristotle, "Leisure is a condition of being or a state of being free from the necessity of labor," which is closely linked to contemplation, virtue, and the divine. Aristotle's conception of leisure did not offer a detailed blueprint but was open to being embodied in different ways. Thus in the medieval monastic culture this classical view of leisure was adapted and biblical content was added to it. Although leisure in terms of the contemplative life was given intrinsic value during the Middle Ages, spiritual works along with the priestly and monastic callings were overly emphasized at the expense of the life of action and work.

After the Reformation there was a movement toward the other extreme: the life of action and doing. Work in all its forms came to be the central activity in life. Leisure came to be subservient to work in that it was considered as time off work to re-create, restore, and refresh a person to go back to work. One positive aspect of this view of leisure was its recognition of a rhythm to life; life consists of both periods of work and nonwork. However, the problem was that this rhythm to life was organized around work. Leisure had no intrinsic value but was to serve work. During the past few hundred years, with the development of capitalism, the Enlightenment, the Industrial Revolution, and the philosophy of utilitarianism, work was removed from the context of a Christian worldview and exalted even more. Leisure, if not serving the purposes of work, was considered idleness.

Significant changes have been taking place in the past one hundred years. Leisure has become associated with free time when one can do as one pleases. More recently the being dimension of humans has been emphasized again as leisure has been associated with self-discovery and self-actualization. Presently, there is some movement away from the traditional work ethic to a new leisure ethic. To a certain extent, but not entirely, the present tension between the traditional work ethic and a leisure ethic mirrors the two major extremes that have existed in history: the emphasis on leisure and being during the classical and medieval monastic periods, and the emphasis on work and doing during the Reformational and industrial periods.

It is necessary at this point to look at the biblical account to see what it has to say about leisure and its relationship to work, to see if there is a middle way between the two historical extremes of being and doing, leisure and work. Thus in the next part of the book we will review the biblical materials that will be of assistance in developing a philosophy of leisure, and then in part 4 we will look at what the Bible teaches about work and its relationship to leisure.

part 3

the biblical background to leisure

the sabbath

In his book on a biblical understanding of work, Alan Richardson made the following observations about leisure in biblical times:

> The Bible knows nothing of "a problem of leisure." No such problem had in fact arisen in the stage of social evolution which had been reached in biblical times. The hours of daylight were the hours of labour for all workers (cf. Ps. 104:22f; John 9:4), whose only leisure-time was during the hours of darkness. The general standpoint of the Bible is that it is "folly" (i.e., sinful) to be idle between daybreak and sunset. A six- or an eight-hour day was not envisaged. Hence we must not expect to derive from the Bible any explicit guidance upon the right use of leisure.[1]

Although Richardson was correct in stating that the Bible does not provide us with explicit guidance concerning leisure, he was wrong in depicting the life of the person living in the biblical world as one preoccupied with work. The Hebraic lifestyle that included Sabbath observance and the celebration of festivals and holy days suggests that there was more to life than work. Also, although there are few biblical words related to leisure and there is not a fully developed theology of leisure in the Bible, various modern-day writers have identified a number of biblical elements that may guide us in our understanding of leisure: the creation model;[2] creativity in the Old Testament;[3] the principle of Sabbath rest;[4] the image of God in play;[5] the advice of Qoheleth in Ecclesiastes;[6] the Hebraic way of life including festivals, dance, feasting, and hospitality;[7] the quality of life found in Jesus Christ;[8] and the kingdom of God.[9] This part of the book will focus on two of the biblical elements that are essential to the development of the book: the principle of the Sabbath (which we will examine in this chapter) and the concept of rest (which we will explore in the next chapter). These elements will be developed to illustrate that a biblical understanding of leisure encompasses both a rhythm to life (a quantitative dimension) and the kind of life we have in Jesus Christ (a qualitative dimension). While the discussion of the biblical notions of Sabbath and rest will be the central focus of this part of the book, chapter 7 will examine biblical words related to leisure and biblical themes that can inform our understanding of leisure as activity. First though, I will briefly examine the biblical contribution to the Western understanding of leisure and then provide a concise overview of leisure in ancient Israel.

Judeo-Christian Contributions to Western Understandings of Leisure

Not only have a number of biblical elements been identified that contribute to a Christian understanding of leisure, but there is also evidence that the Judeo-Christian heritage has in turn contributed to Western understandings of leisure. Chapter 3 of this book began with significant attention to the ancient Greek understanding of leisure, partly because this tradition has been highlighted within leisure studies literature. Karen Fox and Elizabeth Klaiber suggested that the leisure studies field has emphasized one Greek tradition of leisure to the neglect of other Mediterranean traditions, such as the Judeo-Christian tradition.[10] In a study of leisure in ancient Israel, Robert Crabtree raised similar issues and concerns regarding the importance of research on ancient societies other than Greece. He questioned "the credit that was given to Aristotle and the Greek empire . . . as the sole originator of the concept of leisure."[11] Crabtree believed that Israel was an ancient society of special importance since it was the foundation for Christianity, which has had a significant influence on the Western world. Although Christianity has waned in the West, religious teachings still tend to be more familiar and relevant than Greek philosophy for the average Westerner. Furthermore, Christianity has grown elsewhere in the world to total over two billion adherents, and for these people the biblical record as a sacred text and not just history is more instructive for living than is Greek philosophy.

Like Crabtree, Dain Trafton noted that the concept of leisure grew from roots in ancient Hebrew, Greek, and Roman civilizations and went so far as to say that leisure "is primarily Hebrew and Christian."[12] Trafton's argument is based on the Genesis account of God's rest on the seventh day of the Judeo-Christian account of creation, life in the garden of Eden, and the Sabbath commandment to do no work on the seventh day. He claimed that these ancient traditions have contributed to the organization of life into seven days and a valuing of leisure. For Robert Gordis, Sabbath was not only the cornerstone and capstone of Jewish life, but also provided a more democratic form of leisure than in Greek society.[13] Aristotle's leisure was based on the ancient Greek institution of slavery, while the Jewish Torah declared that everyone, including male and female servants, had an inalienable right to Sabbath rest. As Fox and Klaiber noted, Sabbath is connected to justice.[14]

Leisure in Ancient Israel

Crabtree documented that the ideal concept of rest in ancient Israel supported a holistic view of leisure that involved components of time, activity, place, attitude, and state of being.[15] The time component involved several periods of time observed by the Israelites (i.e., Sabbath day, Sabbath year, year of Jubilee). As the Sabbath day will be investigated in much more detail later in this chapter, it will not be considered here. The purpose of the Sabbath year was to ensure social equality within Israel and to enhance the society's quality. Unlike the Sabbath day, total abstinence from work was not required. The Sabbath year allowed the land to rest and widows and the needy to harvest from the fields (Exod. 23:10–11) because the sixth year of bounty would provide for the landowners during the Sabbath year (Lev. 25:1–7), as well as the following year (Lev. 25:18–22). Also during the sabbatical year, Israelite slaves were to be given freedom (Exod. 21:2–6), and there was to be a remission of debts (Deut. 15:1–8). In the fiftieth year, the Year of Jubilee, all the Sabbath year observances were to be practiced and, in addition, all property was to revert back to the original family owner of the land.

Activities associated with Israel's holistic view of leisure included feasts, national holidays, and festivals, all of which focused on Israel's relationship with God and were associated with rest. The Mosaic Law prescribed seven feasts: Passover (Exod. 12:1–13:10); Unleavened Bread (Exod. 12:14–20); Harvest of Firstfruits (Exod. 23:16); Weeks of Ingathering (Exod. 23:16); Booths or Tents (Deut. 16:13); Trumpets (Lev. 23:23–25); and Atonement (Num. 29:7–11; Lev. 16:1–34). Rituals that symbolized what God had done in the past and would do in the future were associated with all these feasts.

National holidays and festivals included four mentioned in the Old Testament: Tisha B'Av (Jer. 52:12–13); Shiva Asar B'Tammuz (Jer. 39:2); Asarah B'Tevet (Zech. 8:19); and zom Gedaliah (Zech. 8:19). These events had historical significance and served to remind the Israelites of the covenants they had with their God. In addition they commemorated the continuation of their relationship with God, which was directly related to their experience of rest.

These feasts, festivals, and holidays provided the Israelites with the opportunity to reflect on the significant events of their history as a nation, in addition to looking ahead to the future fulfillment of God's covenants. Through celebrating these activities, the people realized the benefits of rest previously promised. The major significance of these events was that they commemorated the continuation of Israel's relationship with God, that was directly associated with the impact of rest.

In terms of geographical place, rest was associated with the Promised Land of Canaan (and was directly related to the time and activity components of leisure). Rest was also characterized by the experience of settlement, a great name, the presence of God in the Promised Land (2 Sam. 7), and peace or rest from war (1 Kings 5:4; 2 Sam. 7:1, 11). In the prophetic writings, rest was described in terms of the people returning to a place like Eden where every living thing would be in harmony and at peace (e.g., Hosea 2:20; Isa. 65:25; 11:6).

The experiences of time, activity, and place gave rise to an attitude of rest. This attitude of rest depended on two prerequisite attitudes: a fear of the Lord, which is a respect and reverence for the qualities of God, and faith, which is an unwavering confidence in God and the blessings that God has promised. Both attitudes were cultivated through meditation on Scripture (Josh. 1:8). The central notion of this attitudinal rest was that a situation would not be able to enslave an Israelite no matter what the circumstances were.

The attitude of rest that depends on the concepts of time, activity, and place enhanced a physical and spiritual rest or state of being manifested at the individual, family, and societal levels. With the proper perspective, many of the elements of life for one individual could become interrelated, integrated, and also dependent on one another. In addition this ideal state of being characterized by rest was realized in society through the family, in that individual families influenced the atmosphere of the society. Crabtree observed that this rest was a utopian ideal, which although attainable was not always actualized, especially at the family and societal levels. He concluded,

> It is important to realize that leisure of society is not a genuine Greek concept, but an assimilation of the Israeli rest (or Scriptural perspective of leisure) and the Aristotelian concept of leisure (humanistic perspective). These two lines of thought are part of the heritage of leisure, and the history of leisure should be presented with the two distinct arms of thought.[16]

While Crabtree's research provides helpful insights into leisure in ancient Israel before the time of Christ, the focus of this part of the book is how all of Scripture, including both Old and New Testaments, can inform a Christian understanding of leisure today. While Crabtree used a framework of five components of leisure (time, activity, place, attitude, and state of being) to describe leisure in ancient Israel, the approach in this chapter will touch on most of these five components but will primarily focus on biblical elements related to the time, activity, and state-of-being components.

Introduction to the Sabbath

The Sabbath commandment is more central to Israelite life than any other of the Old Testament instructions. Not only is the Sabbath commandment longer than any other of the commandments in the Decalogue, but the principle of the Sabbath is also reformulated and discussed throughout Scripture. However, a number of complex hermeneutical questions, cataloged below by Andrew Lincoln, are involved in the present-day interpretation of the commandment.

> The interpretation of the creation narrative in Genesis 1 and 2; the question of the relationship between the Old and New Testament, and, in particular, of the Christian attitude to the Old Testament law; the historical Jesus' attitude to the Sabbath; whether, and if so how, the practice of the New Testament church is normative; and the relationship between the New Testament material and the often clearer evidence of the second-century church.[17]

Lincoln wrote, "To do justice to the issues involved would require competence in a number of fields."[18] Nevertheless, without solving all these issues I will attempt to extract some general principles that are applicable and relevant to my discussion of leisure. My discussion of the Sabbath will start with the creation account and then trace through Scripture the teaching on this principle.

The Creation Account

The Genesis account of creation illustrates that history has been given a sabbatical structure by God upon which the weekly rhythm of life has been modeled. The work of creation took six days, and then God rested from his labor on the seventh day. Leland Ryken, Jim Wilhoit, and Tremper Longman III claimed that God's resting on the seventh day is the original biblical image of leisure.[19]

In this creation account there is a distinction between six days of labor and the seventh day of rest. This holds true even if the days of creation are considered to be time periods greater than twenty-four hours. This arrangement of the creation account into six days of labor, followed by a seventh day of rest, appears to have been organized so as to institute a weekly day of rest. As will be seen shortly, later scriptural teaching on the Sabbath in Exodus 20:11 appears to confirm this.

In the creation account, the word "Sabbath" (*shabbat*) does not occur, but the root (*shbt*) from which the word is derived is found at the end of the creation account in Genesis 2:2–3: "By the seventh day God had finished the work he had been doing; so on the seventh day he rested from all his work. Then God blessed the seventh day and made it holy, because on it he rested from all the work of creating that he had done." With William Dumbrell we observe that "the creation account . . . does not conclude with man and his mandate, for man is not the consummation of the account."[20] Rather, the creation account ends with a focus on God. Abraham Heschel concluded from this passage that "three acts of God denoted the seventh day (Gen. 2:2–3). To the prohibition of labor is, therefore, added the blessing of delight and the accent of sanctity."[21]

Thus the significant words in these verses for our study are "rested," "blessed," and "hallowed." I will first examine at length the word "rested" and then proceed to a discussion of "blessed" and "hallowed."

What is the significance of God resting? The Hebrew root, *shbt*, used here has traditionally been translated as "to cease, desist, or rest."[22] Support for this interpretation of God's resting in Genesis 2:2–3 is supplied by Exodus 31:17: "For in six days the LORD made the heavens and the earth, and on the seventh day he abstained from work and rested." In this verse the word *wayyinnaphash* is added to the word *shbt*. From this verse Hans Walter Wolff noted that there is a double significance to God's rest.

> (1) Now he is able to rest, for his entire work, all that a man needs, is completed. (2) Besides this, the additional word, "he took a deep breath," or "he refreshed himself" subtly suggests that he must rest; he had become exhausted from his work of creation. We are able to comprehend this fully only in the light of Jesus Christ's exhaustion in his work of redemption, as it is expressed in his cry "It is finished." In offering up himself, God gave us everything.[23]

Edward Young differed from Wolff over what it means for God to rest. Young believed the word "rest" is used in an anthropomorphic sense: "For God is not a weary workman in need of rest."[24] However, the important point, as Johnston noted, "is not that God found renewed strength for his labor but rather that he stopped working." God is a God whose very nature is one of rest.[25]

The creation account suggests that not only is God a God whose nature is one of rest, but rest is also an essential component of human nature. Young claimed that the language describing God's rest in Exodus 20:11 (God "rested"—Heb. *wayyanakh*—on the seventh day) and Exodus 31:17 (he ceased from his work and "was refreshed"—Heb. *wayyinnaphash*) is intentionally strong so that humans recognize the need to keep the Sabbath as a day on which one is to rest from one's daily work.[26] So what "God rested" in Genesis 2:2 implies, when read with the explanation given by Exodus 20:11 and 31:17, is that at creation God provided humans with a model of working six days and resting on the seventh. Human work was to subdue and rule creation, to work it, and take care of it (Gen. 1:27–28; 2:15). And after his work, rest was to follow. I agree with Richardson, who wrote, "Our human rhythm of work and rest is a refraction of that image of God, in which we were made, however obscured and distorted it may be; a human's work like the Creator's, is crowned with rest, and one's chief end is not to labour but to enjoy God for ever."[27]

Wolff pointed out that the creation account depicts the first complete day of human life as a day of rest.[28] God had just finished six days of work. But humans on their first full day of their life could rest with God and reflect on God's work of salvation. As Stevens put it, "Adam and Eve woke up to experience Sabbath, not to get on with their work. Sabbath was their first experience in the world."[29]

Only after this first full day of rest do humans turn to their work. Claus Wester-mann wrote: "The work that has been laid upon man is not his goal. His goal is the eternal rest which has been suggested by the rest of the seventh day."[30] Not only does the divine rest on the seventh day indicate the goal of creation, but, as Karl Barth suggested, it also is the summons to humanity to enter upon history and to enter life participating in this rest.

> The goal of creation, and at the same time the beginning of all that follows, is the event of God's Sabbath rest and Sabbath joy, in which man, too, has been summoned to participate. It is the event of divine rest in the face of the cosmos completed with the creation of man—a rest which takes precedence over all of man's eagerness and zeal to enter upon his task. Man is created to participate in this rest.[31]

Thus from God's resting on the seventh day we see not only a rhythm to life in which there is one day's break in seven, but also a quality of life characterized by freedom, rest, and joy.

We can perhaps interpret this notion of God resting in a slightly different way. Based on a study of the verbal root *shbt*, Gnana Robinson argued that the idea of "rest from labor" is not basic to this root but rather it has the meaning of "coming to an end or of completion."[32] Thus the seventh day is seen as a day of completion and perfection, and in accordance with its mystic character it brings the work of the preceding six days to a completion. This idea bears resemblance to that of the ancient rabbis who believed the universe was completed on the seventh day by an act of creation that brought *menukhah*—tranquility, serenity, peace, and repose.[33] For Robinson, that the root can mean "to stop" in Genesis 2:2–3 was only secondary: "one seven-day rhythm comes to an end, it is perfected, . . . and therefore the work is stopped until the next seven-day rhythm begins."[34]

Building on this meaning of *shbt*, Dumbrell understood God's resting in Genesis 2:2–3 to be that which brings creation to an end, that which completes creation and brings the creation cycle or sequence to an end.[35] Thus he concluded that the seventh day is what provides a theological explanation of creation. The seventh day comes to signify God's lordship over creation. It is a time for humans to pause and recognize that their time is in God's hand.

Even if the basic meaning of *shbt* in Genesis 2:2–3 is "coming to an end or of completion" and not of "rest from labor," we still have the idea of a sequence or rhythm in which the seventh day brings the work of the preceding six days to a completion, to perfection. We also have a qualitative dimension; the seventh day is a day of completion and perfection. Here again we see from God's resting on the seventh day not only a rhythm to life but also a quality of life characterized by completion and perfection.

What is the significance, in Genesis 2:3, of God blessing and hallowing the seventh day? Victor Hamilton noted, "Everything God made, as recorded in

Genesis, he called good. Only the Sabbath, however he sanctified, indicating perhaps that the climax of creation was not the creation of man, as is often stated, but the day of rest, the seventh day."[36] Actually, the purpose for which God blessed or hallowed the seventh day is not elaborated on in Genesis 2. Perhaps God blessed and hallowed this day simply because he rested and did not work on it. However, Roger Beckwith pointed out that it is difficult to supply these words with any meaning unless one interprets them to imply that God blessed and hallowed the day for the benefit of humankind whom he had just created.[37] Wolff saw a similarity between the blessing of both the fish of the sea and humans, with the blessing of the Sabbath.

> In Gen. 1:22, 28, God had previously blessed the fish of the sea and man. This blessing provided them with the power to be fruitful and to multiply. Now the day of rest is blessed. It, too, is provided with life-restoring powers, so that from it man's time might be made new and fruitful. In addition God also "hallowed" the Sabbath. That is, he separated it from the work-days. Like God's separation of light from darkness, his separating of rest-days from work-days is also an act of divine goodness.[38]

While Witherington argued that Genesis 2:1–3 does not establish a pattern of Sabbath observance, as it is retrospective not prospective,[39] other scholars believed that the intent of the seventh day is explained in the Sabbath commandment as written in Exodus 20:8–11, where Genesis 2:2–3 is alluded to and the words "blessed" and "made it holy" occur again: "Remember the Sabbath day by keeping it holy. . . . On it you shall not do any work. . . . For in six days the LORD made the heavens and the earth, the sea, and all that is in them, but he rested on the seventh day. Therefore the LORD blessed the Sabbath day and made it holy." Here we see that the seventh day was blessed and hallowed to be a day of rest. As Beckwith pointed out, "By a significant variation of language we are told that it was not the seventh day but the Sabbath day (Heb. *shabbat*, day of rest) which God blessed and sanctified at the creation."[40] G. Henry Waterman noted that the words of Jesus—"The Sabbath was made for people, not people for the Sabbath" (Mark 2:27)—point back before the Mosaic Law to the creation, and indicate that the Sabbath was created just after humanity came into being for its benefit and rest. Thus with Waterman I agree that the divine origin and establishment of one day's rest in seven occurred at the outset of human history when "God not only provided a divine example for keeping the seventh day as a day of rest, but also blessed and set apart the seventh day for the use and benefit of man."[41]

What have we learned from the creation account, specifically Genesis 2:2–3, for our study of leisure? First, the creation account establishes a seven-day rhythm to life—six days of work and one of rest. Second, rest, not only work, is basic to the nature of God and also to the nature of humans. As will be developed in more detail later, these two notions—the idea of rhythm to life and that of rest being integral to the nature of humans—are the two essential components in a holistic understanding of leisure.

Exodus 16

Apart from the creation account, no other mention is made of the Sabbath in Genesis. We are not told that the patriarchs observed the Sabbath. However, there is mention of periods of seven days in the account of Noah and the flood (Gen. 7:4, 10; 8:10, 12), and a week is mentioned in the story of Jacob and Rachel (Gen. 29:27). There is no mention of the word "Sabbath" in the Bible, nor is explicit reference made to Sabbath-keeping until Exodus 16, which outlines the regulations for the Israelites to gather and prepare manna while they are wandering in the wilderness.

Each day, while the Israelites were in the wilderness, God provided a fresh supply of manna; each day it had to be collected afresh, for the manna from the previous day would rot and smell. But on the sixth day God sent a double supply of manna. Obeying the instructions of the Lord, Moses commanded the people to gather and prepare double the amount of manna on the sixth day as on the other days (Exod. 16:5). After the leaders of the community informed Moses that the people had obeyed (16:22), Moses replied: "This is what the LORD commanded: 'Tomorrow is to be a day of sabbath rest, a holy sabbath to the LORD. So bake what you want to bake and boil what you want to boil. Save whatever is left and keep it until morning'" (16:23). What was saved for the seventh day "did not stink or get maggots in it" (16:24). Yet some of the people went out on the seventh day—just like modern people—to gather their manna, but we are told "they found none" (16:27). This comment, Wolff wrote, is "an almost humorous criticism of our restless, over-zealousness for work."[42] Work on the seventh day is ridiculed as foolish, for its results are nil; it fails to acknowledge that God supplies what is needed. Human life is not dependent on a human's unceasing work but on God's provision and care.

After some of these people had gone out to gather manna on the seventh day, the Lord said to Moses,

> "How long will you refuse to keep my commands and my instructions? Bear in mind that the LORD has given you the Sabbath; that is why on the sixth day he gives you bread for two days. Everyone is to stay where they are on the seventh day; no one is to go out." So the people rested on the seventh day. (vv. 28–30)

In these verses the Sabbath is described as a gift of God (v. 29) for the people's rest (v. 30). Work (i.e., to gather manna) was not necessary on the Sabbath, for a double supply had been provided on the previous day. In conclusion, then, Exodus 16 relativizes human work—one day in seven is to be set aside for rest. This is possible since it is God who provides what is needed to live. While Witherington explained that the Sabbath day was introduced in Exodus 16 as a way for Israel, after years of work and slavery in Egypt, to focus on the worship of God, we will see when we examine the motivations for observing the Sabbath commandment that they include God's rest on the seventh day in addition to the remembrance of deliverance from slavery.[43]

The Mosaic Law and the Sabbath Commandment

The Sabbath Commandment is found in all accounts of the Mosaic Law (Exod. 20:8–11; 23:12; 31:12–17; 34:21; 35:1–3; Lev. 19:3; 23:1–3; 26:2; Deut. 5:12–15). In an examination of this material two questions need to be considered. First, what reasons are given for observing the Sabbath? Second, how is the Sabbath to be observed?

Why Is the Sabbath to Be Observed?

What reasons are given for observing the Sabbath? Hamilton identified four motives given in the Mosaic Law for observing the Sabbath: (1) Exodus 20:8–11 "connects observance of the Sabbath with the fact that God himself rested on the seventh day after six days of work (Gen. 2:2–3)"; (2) Deuteronomy 5:15 "connects the Sabbath with deliverance from Egypt described in Exodus"; (3) Exodus 20:10; 23:12; and Deuteronomy 5:14–15 point to the Sabbath as a social or humanitarian ordinance that provides dependent laborers with a day of rest; and (4) Exodus 31:13–17 identifies the Sabbath as a sign of the covenant through which Israel "affirms her loyalty to Yahweh and guarantees his saving presence."[44] Let us examine, in some detail, each of these motivations for observing the Sabbath.

The Analogy of God Resting. In Exodus 20:8–11 we encounter the first reason provided for observing the Sabbath day: the analogy of God resting at the end of the creation account.

> Remember the Sabbath day by keeping it holy. Six days you shall labor and do all your work, but the seventh day is a sabbath to the LORD your God. On it you shall not do any work, neither you, nor your son or daughter, nor your male or female servant, nor your animals, nor any foreigner residing in your towns. For in six days the LORD made the heavens and the earth, the sea and all that is in them, but he rested on the seventh day. Therefore the LORD blessed the Sabbath day and made it holy.

The last clause of Exodus 20:11 specifically appeals to God's rhythm in creation and adopts the wording of blessing and hallowing from Genesis 2:2–3, now applying these words to the Sabbath instead of the seventh day. On the basis of his own rhythm of six days of activity and one of rest, God blesses and hallows the Sabbath day for Israel; the model is six days of work and a seventh day Sabbath (Exod. 20:9). What is the significance of this motivation for Sabbath observance? First, as we have already observed in our discussion of the creation account, the appeal to the creation account in the Sabbath commandment demonstrates that the rhythm of God's six days of activity and one of rest is to be the pattern for a rhythm of six days of work and one of rest in human life.

Second, the appeal to the creation account suggests that Sabbath observance is to be characterized by a certain attitude or posture before God. By recalling that God rested on the seventh day, the Israelite, in the act of Sabbath rest, "experienced his God as a God whose very nature was one of rest."[45] Furthermore, the Sabbath, as outlined here in Exodus 20:11, "is an invitation to rejoice in God's creation, and recognize God's sovereignty over time."[46] Heschel wrote: "To observe the seventh day does not mean merely to obey or to conform to the strictness of a divine command. To observe is to celebrate the creation of the world and to create the seventh day all over again, the majesty of holiness in time, 'a day of rest, a day of freedom,' a day which is like 'a lord and king of all other days.'"[47]

Since God has blessed and hallowed the Sabbath, it is fundamentally God's day, a day that belongs to God. According to W. Gunther Plaut, the Sabbath was not primarily for restorative purposes but time to be "viewed simply as God's time"; a time to consider God and his purposes.[48] Dumbrell wrote, "On the sabbath . . . Israel is to reflect upon the question of ultimate purposes for herself as a nation, and for the world over which she is set."[49] The appeal to the creation account in the command to observe the Sabbath seems to suggest that the Sabbath is a time for the Israelites to recognize that life is a gift from God and not just the result of human work. As such the Sabbath qualifies the Israelite's workaday world by putting their six days of work into proper perspective. Exodus 20:11 suggests that the day of rest forcefully reminds humans, once every seven days, that humans live in a world that contains not only all one needs but also many other things to enjoy. "So the Sabbath, which brings to an end the week, becomes for Israel an invitation to enter into, and rejoice in the blessings of creation."[50] Thus, wrote Heschel, the Sabbath is a day of the body as well as of the soul: "Comfort and pleasure are an integral part of the Sabbath observance."[51] It is a day of joy and celebration. David Ehrenfeld and Philip Bentley noted that "even Jews in the meanest circumstances will find a little wine, two loaves of Sabbath bread, attractive candlesticks, and a nice tablecloth to grace the Sabbath table. Thus the Sabbath becomes a celebration of our tenancy and stewardship on earth."[52] Thus Sabbath, explained Stevens, suggests not only a threefold harmony of God, humans, and creation but also that "*being* is more important than *doing*."[53] Or as Jürgen Moltmann put it, "Existence precedes activity. . . . The celebration of the sabbath leads to an intensified capacity for perceiving the loveliness of everything—food, clothing, the body, the soul—because existence itself is glorious."[54] Creating is important for both God and humans, Loren Wilkinson explained, but it is even more important to rest and delight in what is created.[55]

In summary, the first motivation given for observing the Sabbath, the appeal to creation theology in Exodus 20:11, suggests two dimensions to Sabbath observance. Quantitatively the Sabbath is to be a one-day break from the other six days of work that is patterned on God's six days of work and one of rest in the creation account; qualitatively the Sabbath is an invitation to experience God as a God whose very nature is one of rest and also to rejoice and celebrate in God's creation.

The Remembrance of Deliverance from Egypt. Although the Ten Commandments as recorded in Exodus 20 are almost the same as the account of them in Deuteronomy 5, the Sabbath commandment is a noticeable exception. A different motive for the observance of the Sabbath is found in the Deuteronomic account of the Decalogue where the Sabbath command is linked with God's deliverance of the Israelites from bondage in Egypt.

> Observe the Sabbath day by keeping it holy, as the LORD your God has commanded you. Six days you shall labor and do all your work, but the seventh day is a sabbath to the LORD your God. On it you shall not do any work, neither you, nor your son or daughter, nor your male or female servant, nor your ox, your donkey or any of your animals, nor any foreigner residing in your towns, so that your male servant and female servant may rest, as you do. Remember that you were slaves in Egypt and that the LORD your God brought you out of there with a mighty hand and an outstretched arm. Therefore the LORD your God has commanded you to observe the Sabbath day. (Deut. 5:12–15)

In this account the reasons for keeping the Sabbath day is the affirmation that Yahweh has liberated and delivered Israel from bondage in Egypt. Every seventh day Israel is to recall that her God is an emancipator able to put an end to all affliction. As such, "the Sabbath was a remembrance that Israel rested ultimately in God's graciousness."[56]

We have seen how the two accounts of the Ten Commandments base their injunctions to observe the Sabbath on different motivations. Appeals to both creation theology and salvation history (redemptive theology) are given as the reason for Sabbath-keeping. Is there any significance to the fact that there are two different motivations? Are the two reasons in conflict with each other?

Young argued that the reason given in Exodus for the observance of the Sabbath is not in conflict with the reason given in Deuteronomy 5:12–15.[57] In Deuteronomy the people are instructed to keep the Sabbath in a way similar to that which the Lord had previously commanded them in Exodus 20:8–11, and again it is stated that "the seventh day is a Sabbath to the LORD" (Deut. 5:14). However, another reason (because of God's redemptive acts) is simply added for the keeping of the command.

Dumbrell went further, seeing a parallel presentation of the Ten Commandments in Deuteronomy 5 to be complementary to Exodus 20.[58] In Exodus 20:8–11 the Sabbath prefigures the rest that the completion of creation had foreshadowed for humanity. However, it is the Exodus redemption that makes possible the new life in the land, and thereby the Edenic rest. Thus the reason given for observing the Sabbath in Deuteronomy is not simply additional, but it is necessary, for without the redemptive activity of God, the original notion of Sabbath rest is impossible. Yet the expectation of "rest" was not realized in Israel's experience, and finally Israel was exiled from the land. As we will see in more detail later, the Epistle to the Hebrews reminds us that although Israel did not enter this rest (Heb. 4:8–10), there still exists a Sabbath rest for believers, which is a fulfillment of creation's purpose.

In light of the fact that Israel did not enter the promised rest, it is interesting to note, with Johnston, that the later Deuteronomic account shifts "from a focus on God to a stronger emphasis on the need for relief from the oppressive reality of much work."[59] The Hebrew *shamor* ("observe the Sabbath day") has a definite ethical connotation as compared with the Hebrew word *zakor* ("remembering the Sabbath") that is found in Exodus 20:8. Furthermore, the Deuteronomic version of the fourth commandment includes the ethical justification "that your male and female servants may rest, as you do" (5:14). Here is the humanitarian emphasis. The necessity to abstain from human toil on the Sabbath for human benefit is emphasized in the phrase "may rest, as you do." Perhaps the humanitarian stress in Deuteronomy reflects that Israel will not experience the original Edenic Sabbath rest in a qualitative sense, therefore it is necessary to be strict about observing the Sabbath in a quantitative sense in order that all who work may rest. As such, the Sabbath is for human restoration. Johnston wrote: "Whether it be rest from unrest, refreshment from drudgery, or release from endless competition, the sabbath exists to serve humankind . . . the sabbath is meant as a time of rest from the world . . . [which] sanctifies and refreshes ongoing life."[60]

The Sabbath as a Humanitarian Ordinance. A third motivation for observing the Sabbath, a humanitarian one that we have already noted in Deuteronomy 5:14–15, is more clearly stated in the Book of the Covenant: "Six days do your work, but on the seventh day do not work, so that your ox and your donkey may rest, and so that the slave born in your household and the foreigner living among you may be refreshed" (Exod. 23:12). In this verse the only purpose given for the day of rest is so that the dependent laborers and domestic animals experience rest and recuperation. The word "refreshed," *weyinnaphesh*, which is used to describe the Sabbath benefit for the foreigner or the slave born into an Israelite household, is the exact same word that is used to describe God's rest on the seventh day in Exodus 31:17. When an Israelite master did not consider it wise to give his or her slave a particular task, the master would likely expect the slave's son or a foreign laborer to perform it. It is to these disadvantaged persons that this commandment is addressed. According to Exodus 23:12, then, the Sabbath was especially for the benefit of those who are severely burdened with work and are under the orders of others.

In light of this practice, it is only logical that the dependent laborers are identified in the longer formulations of the Sabbath commandment within the accounts of the Ten Commandments. In Exodus 20:10 we read, "On it [the Sabbath] you shall not do any work, neither you, nor your son or daughter, nor your male or female servant, nor your animals, nor any foreigner residing in your towns." To these words the parallel version in Deuteronomy 5:14 adds: "so that your male and female servants may rest, as you do." Here the commandment of a day of rest suggests an equality of all people before God.

The implication of this humanitarian motive for observance of the Sabbath is that all members of society should both work and rest. In our self-centered obsession with our own work, we all too readily ignore those who are burdened by the drudgery of the work they are required to perform. But the Sabbath provides an opportunity to close the gap that separates us. As Gerhard Hasel pointed out, the Sabbath reminds us of the "social emphasis on equality of all human beings (free persons and servants) under God."[61] Thus the biblical view does not lend support to the social structuring of society as in the Greece of Aristotle's day, when slaves made it possible for a few to have a life of leisure, nor does it support a leisure class who live a life of conspicuous consumption at the expense of a working class such as is described in Veblen's *Theory of the Leisure Class*. The humanitarian motivation for the Sabbath suggests that all are entitled to a break from work, and therefore leisure in at least a quantitative sense.

The Sabbath as a Sign of the Covenant. The fourth motivation for observance of the Sabbath is that it is a sign of the covenant: "The Israelites are to observe the Sabbath, celebrating it for the generations to come as a lasting covenant. It will be a sign between me and the Israelites forever, for in six days the LORD made the heavens and the earth, and on the seventh day he abstained from work and rested" (Exod. 31:16–17). In this passage the Sabbath is not only a sign of the covenant but also is called a covenant. Sabbath observance is also claimed to be a sign of Israel's allegiance to God in Exodus 31:13. In addition, the Sabbath commandment was an essential component of the covenant that God made with Israel at Sinai. This Sinaitic Covenant, consisting of the Decalogue uttered by the Lord himself from the mount (Deut. 4:13; 5:2–21; see also Neh. 9:14) in which the fourth commandment has a central place, established a relationship between God and Israel. Thus the Sabbath was to be observed not only within the context of a relationship with God, but it was also a sign of the relationship.

What implications does this covenant motivation for Sabbath observance have for our study of leisure? While some benefits may accrue from observance of one day's rest in seven, leisure like the Sabbath may find its true meaning and reach its fullest potential when one lives in relationship with God.

In summary, our review of the four motivations for Sabbath observance suggests a fourfold significance of the Sabbath for the study of leisure. Exodus 20:8–11, which connects observance of the Sabbath with the fact that God rested on the seventh day after six days of work (Gen. 2:2–3), suggests that there should be a rhythm of work and rest in human life. In addition, the appeal to creation theology is an invitation to experience the God of creation as a God whose very nature is one of rest and also to rejoice and celebrate in the gift of God's good creation. Thus leisure has a qualitative dimension to it that is characterized by rest and celebration. This qualitative dimension underlies a rhythm to life composed of work and rest. Second, we have seen how Deuteronomy 5:12–15 introduces an ethical and humanitarian emphasis to Sabbath observance. As such the Sabbath is provided for human rest, restoration, and re-creation. Third, Exodus 20:10; 23:12; and Deuteronomy 5:14–15 point to the Sabbath as a social or humanitarian ordinance that emphasizes the social equality of all persons under God. All, then, are entitled to a day of rest, or leisure in at least a quantitative sense. Fourth, Exodus 31:16 identifies the Sabbath as a sign of the covenant. It follows that the Sabbath, and likewise leisure, finds its deepest meaning and fullest potential within the context of a relationship with God.

How Is the Sabbath to Be Observed?

How, in the Old Testament, is the Sabbath to be observed? While Genesis presents the divine rest, the sabbatical legislation that gives regulations for the observance of the Sabbath is distributed throughout the remaining four books of the Pentateuch. The widespread distribution of this Sabbath legislation illustrates that the Sabbath commandment is central to Old Testament law (e.g., Exod. 31:13–16; 34:21; 35:2–3; Lev. 19:3, 30; 23:3, 38).

In the Mosaic covenant, the Sabbath rest is a matter of detailed regulations. All work is forbidden. In addition, what constituted work is delineated with great precision. Yet the stipulations for the observance of the Sabbath in the Mosaic legislation are fairly straightforward. The Sabbath is to be kept by all on every seventh day. The references to the family, servants and all other members of the Hebrew household, animals, and sojourners listed in Exodus 20:10 and Deuteronomy 5:14 guarantee that no one over whom the male Israelite had authority would have to work; therefore everyone would be able to rest from work.

It is not only laborious work that is prohibited, as is the case on many of the holy days; on the Sabbath "you are not to do *any* work" (Lev. 23:3; cf. with "do no *regular* work" of Lev. 23:7, 8, 21, 35, 36; Num. 28:18, 25, 26; 29:1, 12, 35). The gathering of food, the lighting of fires, and the collecting of firewood are all forbidden (Exod. 16:25–30; 35:1–3; Num. 15:32–36). No pressure could change the absolute nature of the command. The phrase in Exodus 34:21, "even during the plowing season and harvest you must rest," stresses that even at the busiest time of the year in an agricultural society the Sabbath was still to be kept. Especially in such busy times humans need a day of rest.

The sanction of the death penalty for profaning the Sabbath by doing any work on it (Exod. 31:14–15; 35:2) emphasizes the absolute nature of the Sabbath command. In Numbers 15:32–36 we read of a man who was found gathering wood on the Sabbath day. God, through a special revelation, ordered that the man be put to death since he had ignored the basic principle of the Sabbath. This incident illustrates the seriousness of keeping the Sabbath commandment and the importance of not working on the Sabbath. The day belongs to the Lord and therefore is to be observed in accordance with the Lord's instructions.

Due to these detailed regulations, the ungodly frequently resented the Mosaic Sabbath. But, properly observed, it was not an encumbrance but a "gift" (Exod. 16:29) and, as we will see in more detail later, a "delight" (Isa. 58:13–14). The Israelite who titled Psalm 92 "A song. For the sabbath day" must have appreciated the Sabbath as a gift and a delight.

In conclusion, how the Sabbath was to be observed is summarized in Exodus 34:21a: "For six days you shall work, but on the seventh day you shall cease work!" (NEB). The sabbatical legislation declared that life was best lived in a rhythm wherein all humankind both worked and then refrained from work. In this sense the Sabbath was a quantity of time in which no work was performed. Likewise, leisure, in a quantitative sense, is a period of time in which no work is performed.

But was the Sabbath only a quantity of time in which no work was performed? Differing opinions exist as to whether the Sabbath was a day of worship in addition to a day of rest. Certainly, the Sabbath was not a day of complete inactivity. The priests carried on their duties about the tabernacle. The ordinary daily sacrifices continue on the Sabbath (Num. 28:10), but the Sabbath had its own additional and special sacrifices of a burnt offering along with drink and grain offerings (Num. 28:9; Ezek. 46:4–8), together with the showbread—the Bread of the Presence—which was renewed every Sabbath day by being set on the table in the holy place (Lev. 24:8; 1 Chron. 9:32).

The Sabbath is enumerated among the sacred festivals, "the appointed festivals of the LORD" (Lev. 23:1–3). The Sabbath, like the festivals, was proclaimed to be a "sacred assembly" (23:3). The Sabbath and worship are linked together by the joint command given both in Leviticus 19:30 and 26:2: "Observe my Sabbaths and have reverence for my sanctuary." Based on this evidence, Waterman concluded that the Sabbath was a day of worship for Israel: "In the early history of the Israelites, the Sabbath was a day of welcome rest from labour and of solemn worship at the sanctuary of God."[62]

Wolff differs with Waterman and wrote that the Sabbath was primarily a day of rest and not of worship.[63] He argued that the regulations for the daily morning and evening sacrifices that give the Sabbath a cultic character by requiring that instead of one lamb, two (Num. 28:9–10) or even six (Ezek. 46:4–5) be offered on the Sabbath, together with grain and drink offerings, are very late and poorly attested. In addition, being attached to the sacrificial requirements for the other days of the week, he believed these requirements of sacrifices on the Sabbath practically confirm that the Sabbath day was not given a special cultic distinction, as if it were qualitatively different. Wolff quoted Albrecht Alt: "Originally the Sabbath was characterized merely by the prohibition of all work, and in Israel's early history has nothing to do with the specific cultic worship of Yahweh as such."[64] Rather, the Sabbath was characterized by a cessation of labor following six days of business.

Beckwith advocated a more helpful approach: "The disjunction between a day of rest and a day of worship ignores the fact that, to the Jew, rest was itself an expression of worship." The distinction between rest and worship is a false one: resting was worship, for on the Sabbath the Israelites "did not merely rest as they rested at night, involuntarily, to restore and refresh their powers of body and mind; on the Sabbath they rested deliberately, in obedience to God's command, in commemoration of his creative work, and in imitation of his own rest at the end of that work." Beckwith also argued that "the sabbath rest was of the nature of worship, . . . a way of symbolizing God's rest at creation, and . . . of symbolizing also Israel's rest when delivered from the servitude of Egypt, and her special relationship with the God who delivered her."[65] Similarly, Johnston wrote, "In the act of Sabbath rest, the Israelite experienced his God as a God whose very nature was one of rest."[66] Thus, as Lincoln pointed out, the emphasis on the physical rest through the cessation of work "hardly does justice to the significance of the Mosaic Sabbath in the O.T."[67] In conclusion, the Old Testament teaches that the Sabbath is to be observed not only by a cessation from work but also by a rest that is of the nature of worship.

The Prophets and the Sabbath

The prophets' utterances concerning the Sabbath are in accordance with the Pentateuchal legislation; they apply only what has already been revealed in the Pentateuch. They often spoke of the Sabbaths and the New Moon celebrations at the same time (2 Kings 4:23; Isa. 1:13; Ezek. 46:3; Amos 8:5; Hosea 2:11). Although the prophets spoke critically of the practices that occurred on these days, they were not condemning the Sabbath itself but a misuse of the Sabbath along with the other Pentateuchal institutions. It was necessary to admonish those who polluted the Sabbath and did evil on that day. Yet the prophets also pointed out the blessings that accrue from a correct observance of the Sabbath (Isa. 56:2–7).

For example, Isaiah decries the ritualistic Sabbath observance of his day (Isa. 1:12–13) and in a classic passage (below) outlines what will follow from a true observance of the Sabbath. The Sabbath is not a day on which humans can do what they please but rather one on which they are to pursue the will of God. Thus God, not humans, specify how the Sabbath is to be kept. Isaiah interprets true Sabbath-keeping as a forsaking of one's ways and pleasures to take delight in the Lord. Acknowledging that the day is holy and is the Lord's will bring the true enjoyment of his promises.

> "If you keep your feet from breaking the Sabbath and from doing as you
>   please on my holy day,
> if you call the Sabbath a delight and the LORD's holy day honorable,
> and if you honor it by not going your own way and not doing as you
>   please or speaking idle words,
> then you will find your joy in the LORD,
> and I will cause you to ride in triumph on the heights of the land
> and to feast on the inheritance of your father Jacob."
> For the mouth of the LORD has spoken. (Isa. 58:13–14)

Thus the admonitions to observe the Sabbath are based in a joy and delight of the Lord rather than a fear of punishment.

Amos, who passionately contends against the many abuses in the sacrificial cult (4:4–5; 5:21–27), brought down judgment on the grain dealers who could not wait for the Sabbath to be over so they could sell their wheat and deceive the people through "skimping on the measure, / boosting the price / and cheating with dishonest scales" (8:5). The misuse of the Sabbath is also condemned elsewhere by Amos and other prophets (Jer. 17:21–27; Ezek. 22:8; Amos 8:4) who interpreted the destruction of Jerusalem and subsequent exile of the Israelites to be partly the result of the desecration of the Sabbath (Jer. 17:27; Ezek. 20:23–24). Hosea prophesies that God will cause the termination of Israel's Sabbaths due to her unfaithfulness (Hosea 2:11); that this termination of Sabbath observance was not to be permanent is stressed by Isaiah and Ezekiel (Isa. 66:23; Ezek. 44:24).

During the period of exile, emphasis was again placed on Sabbath-keeping, and the Sabbath (in comparison with the other religious observances of the Jews) became more important as it was independent of the temple at Jerusalem, while the other observances were associated and partly dependent on the temple. After the return from exile, Sabbath observance was reestablished in Palestine, largely through Nehemiah's reforms. Back in Palestine, Nehemiah was horrified to observe extensive desecration of the Sabbath day. People were treading winepresses, harvesting and loading grain, and transporting wine, grapes, figs, and other kinds of food; people from Tyre were "bringing in fish and all kinds of merchandise and selling them in Jerusalem on the Sabbath to the people of Judah" (Neh. 13:16). Nehemiah rebuked the nobles of Judah: "What is this wicked thing you are doing—desecrating the Sabbath day? Didn't your ancestors do the same things, so that our God brought all this calamity on us and on this city? Now you are stirring up more wrath against Israel by desecrating the Sabbath" (13:17–18). From then on Nehemiah had the gates of Jerusalem closed each Sabbath. His serious efforts at reform greatly contributed to the Sabbath being set aside as a day of universal rest among the Palestinian Jews.

In conclusion, the prophets' words contradict humanity's natural inclination to make life secure or add to life's abundance by nonstop, uninterrupted work. Obviously many people thought that the Sabbath rest was a hindrance to their economic well-being. Yet, as W. Vischer noted, "Human life has a higher significance than being merely a struggle for existence."[68] Work is only to occupy six days of the week. Work on the seventh day is not only unnecessary but also prohibited. So there is a rhythm to life—six days of work and one of rest from work. But the Sabbath also has a qualitative dimension as seen in Isaiah 58, where it is described as a delight.

Jesus and the Sabbath

By the beginning of Jesus's ministry, the true meaning of the Sabbath had been hidden by the many restrictions governing its observance. Sabbath-keeping was primarily external and formal. Rigid observance of a day was put before the needs of the people. Thus Jesus entered a situation in which human tradition was confused with the commands of God.

Jesus's observance of the Sabbath was in harmony with the Old Testament teaching to observe the day "as holy to the Lord." For example, he made a habit of attending the synagogue on the Sabbath (Mark 1:21; 3:1; Luke 4:16; 13:10). Meanwhile, his teaching on the Sabbath was not in contradiction to the Old Testament teaching; rather, he upheld the authority and validity of the Old Testament law. But he did react against the Pharisees who stifled the Word of God with their restricting oral tradition. In contrast to the Pharisees, Jesus's emphasis was on the spontaneous fulfillment of God's will, which was the basis for the law, and not on the external performance of it (Matt. 5:17–48; 19:3–9). Therefore it is of no surprise that Jesus, on six different occasions, clashed with the Jewish leaders in regard to the Sabbath. Let us look briefly at each of these six occasions.

On one occasion Jesus defends his disciples against the Pharisees for picking grain on the Sabbath by referring to the occasion when David and his companions entered the house of God and ate the consecrated bread that was lawful only for priests to eat (Matt. 12:1–4; Mark 2:23–26; Luke 6:1–4). Jesus's response teaches that human need had priority over the legal stipulations of the Sabbath. On the same occasion, Jesus explains the true purpose of the Sabbath by stating the original reason for its institution: "The Sabbath was made for people, not people for the Sabbath" (Mark 2:27). With these words he suggests that the Sabbath was provided for human need and well-being rather than as a restricting legal requirement. On this same occasion Jesus declares his lordship over the Sabbath when he says: "The Son of Man is Lord of the Sabbath" (Luke 6:5; see also Matt. 12:8; Mark 2:28). Young wrote, "In so speaking, he was not depreciating the importance and significance of the Sabbath nor in any way contravening the Old Testament legislation. He was simply pointing out the true significance of the Sabbath with respect to man."[69]

In Capernaum Jesus, after expressing anger over the Pharisees at the synagogue who were more concerned with the precise observance of the Sabbath than for a man with a shriveled hand, proceeds, on the Sabbath, to heal the man (Mark 3:1–5). On another Sabbath, when the synagogue ruler becomes indignant because Jesus heals a woman who has been crippled by a spirit for eighteen years, Jesus supports his action by referring to the normal custom of untying one's domestic animals and leading them to water on the Sabbath (Luke 13:10–17). In a somewhat similar incident, Jesus, under the careful watch of the Pharisees, heals a man suffering from dropsy on the Sabbath. He maintains it is right to heal on the Sabbath by questioning his critics if they would not rescue an ox or an ass that had fallen into a well on the Sabbath (14:1–6).

John records two other times when Jesus's behavior on the Sabbath causes him to clash with the Jewish leaders. In John 5:1–8 we read of the invalid at the pool of Bethesda who is healed. On this occasion Jesus defends his authority to heal on the Sabbath on the basis that his Father does not discontinue his work on that day (5:17). In John 9:1–41 we read of the healing, on the Sabbath, of the man born blind. Here Jesus defends his action by denouncing the Pharisee's spiritual blindness (9:40–41).

On all these occasions, Jesus puts human need above formal external compliance with the Sabbath legislation. It was not wrong to pick and eat grain on the Sabbath. Nor was it unlawful to perform works of mercy or to heal on the Sabbath day (see also John 5:1–18; Luke 13:10–17; 14:1–6). Yet Jesus never does or says anything to indicate that he intends to abolish the Sabbath along with the relaxation and other benefits such a day of rest offers. Rather, in his conflict with the Pharisees (Matt. 12:1–14; Mark 2:23–28; Luke 6:1–11) Jesus warns the Jews of their total misunderstanding of the Old Testament teaching on the Sabbath wherein they attempt to make the observance stricter than God had intended. However, Jesus emphasizes keeping the spirit of the law, not just externally observing the law (Matt. 5:17–48). Jesus explains the true meaning of the Sabbath by teaching that it "was made for people, not people for the Sabbath" (Mark 2:27). Rather than not observing the Sabbath, as he was accused, or abolishing the Sabbath, as many Christians believe, Jesus *fulfilled* the Sabbath.[70] As we shall see later in our discussion of Matthew 11:28, he came to offer Sabbath rest in his own person.

What are the implications of Jesus's teaching on the Sabbath for our study of leisure? If connections can be drawn between the Sabbath and leisure, Jesus's teaching would seem to imply that leisure is more than quantitative; it also has a qualitative dimension to it. The Sabbath's one day of rest in seven is not just a day of inactivity. It is not just a time period. It is a time set aside for humans, a time for bringing healing and wholeness. It is the same with leisure. Leisure is not just a quantitative segment of life but also a quality of life closely related to wholeness and fullness.

The New Testament Church and the Sabbath

The first Christians as faithful Jews worshiped each day in the temple at Jerusalem (Acts 2:46; 5:42), went to the synagogue (Acts 9:20; 13:14; 14:1; 17:1–2, 10; 18:4), and respected the law (21:20). So it was very likely that the early Jewish Christians continued to keep the Sabbath.

In the Epistle to the Colossians (2:16–17), the Sabbath, along with religious festivals and the New Moon celebrations, is to be understood as "a shadow of the things that were to come; the reality, however, is found in Christ." Romans 14:5–6 reads, "Some consider one day more sacred than another; others consider every day alike. Everyone should be fully convinced in their own mind. Those who regard one day as special do so to the Lord." Commenting on these verses, Stevens explained that Paul makes it "absolutely clear" that Sabbath is not now optional in New Testament times, as he adds the phrase "for we do not live to ourselves alone" (Rom. 14:7). "Sabbath can now be one day or *every* day *or both*."[71] As we will discuss in more detail in the next chapter, the writer of the Hebrews describes the Sabbath solely as a type of "God's rest"—"a Sabbath-rest for the people of God" (Heb. 4:1–10). Instead of instructing Christians to observe the Sabbath, he exhorts them to "make every effort to enter that rest" (4:11). Banks summarized the teaching of the New Testament on the Sabbath for us: while Christians were no longer obliged to relax on a set day of the week (see Rom. 14:5; Col. 2:16–17) and believed that they had already begun to enter an eternal Sabbath (see Heb. 4:3), the principle of taking proper physical and spiritual rest remained important.[72] Stevens concluded: "Some form of Sabbath is not an optional extra for the New Testament Christian. It is fundamental to spiritual health, and even to emotional health."[73]

Summary on the Sabbath

In concluding our discussion of the biblical Sabbath, let us review the general principles that are applicable to our discussion of leisure. At least three principles may be derived: first, the Sabbath reminds us of the social equality of all humans under God; second, the Sabbath points to a rhythm in life; and third, the Sabbath has a qualitative aspect as well as a quantitative aspect. We will discuss each of these in turn.

First, all who work and labor, especially those burdened by work, are entitled to one day's rest in seven (Exod. 20:10; 23:12; Deut. 5:14–15). Thus a society in which a few members enjoy a life of leisure based on the endless work of the many is inconsistent with the teaching of Scripture. Humans have been given the task of ruling over creation, to work it, and to take care of it. Humans have also been instructed in the Sabbath commandment to labor six days and do all their work. But they are to rest on the seventh day. All who work are entitled to a day of rest. Therefore all are entitled to leisure at least in a quantitative or free time sense. From a biblical point of view, this social equality emphasis of the Sabbath legislation would seem to negate any attempt to define leisure in terms of a leisure class. Thus the biblical view does not lend support to the phenomenon of a leisure class as in the Greek society of Aristotle's day or to the nineteenth-century leisure class as described in Veblen's *Theory of the Leisure Class*.

Second, the Sabbath points to a rhythm in life—a rhythm of work and non-work (leisure in a quantitative sense). We have seen the importance of rhythm in the creation account (God's six days of activity and one of rest), in Exodus 16 (where the Israelites were not to collect manna on the seventh day), and in the fourth commandment (which instructs that all humans, regardless of social position, and their animals too, are to work six days and abstain from work on the Sabbath). We can also illustrate the idea of rhythm from God's command for the ground to be left fallow every seventh year so the land would rejuvenate itself (Exod. 23:10–11; Lev. 26:34–35), and from the Jubilee Year, the crowning point of all the festivals. I have documented how the Mosaic legislation and also the prophets stressed that no work was to be done on the Sabbath. So the Sabbath inculcated that Israel's life, in addition to work, also possessed time free from work. It taught Israel that work should occupy six-sevenths of life rather than all of it. So there is a rhythm to life—six days of work and one of nonwork. The implication for our study is that the Sabbath suggests some rhythm or cycle of work and leisure (in a quantitative sense) is necessary for well-being and wholeness.

After the instruction not to work on the Sabbath, the Deuteronomic account of the Sabbath commandment includes the phrase, "so that your male and female servant may rest, as you do," which emphasizes the necessity for all humans to abstain from work on the Sabbath for the purpose of human rest, restoration, and re-creation. The Sabbath commandment still remains instructive regarding God's concern for the physical rest of humans. If God commanded his people to rest one day in seven in the Old Testament and it was beneficial, such rest will be just as valuable today. In the New Testament the principle of taking proper physical and spiritual rest continued to be important. Jesus, in his earthly life, demonstrates a rhythm of work and rest and teaches his disciples to take rest: "Come with me by yourselves to a quiet place and get some rest" (Mark 6:31). The need for physical rest and recreation is worth emphasizing, especially when many Christians rationalize their addiction to work as serving God.

The rhythmic pattern to life that the Sabbath suggests should constantly serve as a model for us in shaping and scheduling the entire week—something that the Sabbath has been doing directly or indirectly throughout the history of

Judaism and Christianity. Lincoln concluded, "Societies that have adopted the arrangement of making Sunday a rest day for their members have benefitted from this in a variety of ways."[74] Yet some modern societies have altered the weekly cycle of rest and either have replaced it with different time intervals or have completely abolished a regular day of rest. Commenting on this situation, Roland Harrison wrote,

> Some persons appear to survive for a time without a regular "sabbath" interval, but it is doubtful that they are performing at anything approaching their maximum and they are certainly making themselves vulnerable to physical or mental breakdown. Thus the biblical concept of the Sabbath has not merely positive and recuperative values for the individual but also serves to guard against disease.[75]

Packer wrote,

> This prescribed rhythm of work and rest is part of the order of creation. Human beings are so made that they need this six-plus-one rhythm, and we suffer in one way or another if we do not get it. The leisure, or at least semi-leisure, of a weekly day of worship and rest is a divine ordinance that our work-oriented world ignores to the peril of its health.[76]

Not only does the Sabbath have health benefits, but, as Winter explained, it allows us to rest without feeling guilty.

> The biblical command to rest for one day of the week is an important God-given principle for our health and sanity. We neglect it at our peril. Some people feel very guilty if they are not doing something "worthwhile" with their time. They cannot rest with a clear conscience. The Christian understanding of the Sabbath is that it is given by God as a symbol of our being able to rest in his presence with easy consciences.[77]

As we will see in chapter 12, recent empirical research has documented some of these benefits of Sabbath observance. Thus, with Hasel, I agree that the great benefit of Sabbath rest is providing special time each week for physical, mental, spiritual, and emotional renewal that leads to health both for the individual and society.[78]

Although the Sabbath suggests a rhythm to life in which one day in seven is needed for human restoration and rest, the Sabbath is much more than this. Philo, the spokesperson for the Greek-speaking Jews of Alexandria, defended the Sabbath solely in terms of this narrow function of rest.

> On this day we are commanded to abstain from all work, not because the law inculcates slackness. . . . Its object is rather to give man relaxation from continuous and unending toil and by refreshing their bodies with a regularly calculated system of remissions to send them out to their old activities. For a breathing spell enables not merely ordinary people but also athletes to collect their strength with

a stronger force behind them to undertake promptly and patiently each of the tasks set before them.[79]

According to Heschel,[80] the Sabbath, as here represented by Philo, is not in the spirit of the Bible but in the spirit of Aristotle, who, as we saw in chapter 3, wrote, "We need rest because we are not able to go on working without a break, and therefore it is not an end."[81] However, to the biblical mind, the Sabbath, as a day of abstaining from work, is not entirely for the purpose of restoring one's lost strength and enhancing the efficiency of one's future work. Rather than simply an interlude between periods of work, it is the climax of living. Heschel went on to describe the Sabbath as "not a date but an atmosphere . . . a taste of eternity—the world to come."[82]

Thus the third major principle that we can derive from our study of the Sabbath is that leisure needs to be defined in more than a quantitative sense, for the Sabbath is more than a time period, more than one day in seven. The Sabbath suggests the attitude for human's basic posture in relation to God. I have argued from the creation account that rest is basic to the nature of humans. I have stated that the divine intention for humans is not work but the eternal rest that has been suggested by the rest of the seventh day. Thus the chief end of humans is not to labor but to enjoy God forever. We also saw that the rest of the seventh day could be interpreted in terms of completion and perfection. As such it is closely connected with the ancient rabbinic teaching that the seventh day brought *menuha*—tranquility, serenity, peace, and repose. The appeal to creation theology in the Exodus account of the Sabbath commandment suggests that the Sabbath is an invitation to the Israelite, in the act of Sabbath rest, to experience one's God as a God whose very nature is one of rest and to rejoice in and celebrate in God's gift of creation. The sabbatical legislation commanded a Sabbath rest that was of the nature of worship. The prophet Isaiah described the Sabbath as a delight. Jesus taught that the Sabbath was a time for bringing healing and wholeness. All this evidence conclusively suggests that the Sabbath, and likewise leisure, is more than a time of nonwork; it has a qualitative dimension.

I agree with Heschel, who wrote: "Observance of the seventh day is more than a technique of fulfilling a commandment. The Sabbath is the presence of God in the world, open to the soul of man. It is possible to respond in affection, to enter into fellowship with the consecrated day."[83] For the Christian believer fellowship with the presence of God in the world is fulfilled through Jesus Christ, through whom we enter God's own Sabbath rest (Heb. 4:9–10).

Next we will turn to the biblical concept of rest and trace its meaning through Scripture to its culmination in Hebrews 4 where it is joined together with the concept of Sabbath. But first, we conclude that the biblical Sabbath teaches us that leisure should not merely be an external cessation from work in the rhythm of human life but that it should also be an internal spiritual attitude; leisure reaches its fullest potential when our lives are lived in relationship with God.

6

the biblical concept of rest

Leisure is frequently equated with the biblical concept of rest. Several writers, including Dahl,[1] Houston,[2] Sherrow,[3] and Bertha Cato[4] draw parallels between leisure and Christ's offer of rest in Matthew 11:28–30. Thus it is fruitful for us to examine the biblical concept of rest and see what implications it has for our study of leisure.

Before proceeding, two introductory comments can be made. First, it is natural that we should move from an examination of the Sabbath to a discussion of the theology of rest, for although the developed Old Testament theology of rest utilizes different terminology than that used in Genesis 2:1–4, Dumbrell pointed out that the close link "between such 'rest' and the Sabbath which epitomized the concept was always maintained (cf. Exod. 20:11 where the two concepts of 'sabbath' and 'rest' are brought together)."[5] As we will see, the close link between rest and Sabbath culminates in the Sabbath rest of Hebrews 4:9.

Second, the belief is expressed throughout the Bible that God will give, or has given, rest to his people. Yet as Gerhard von Rad noted, "Among the many benefits of redemption offered to man by Holy Scripture, that of 'rest' has been almost overlooked in biblical theology."[6] Perhaps this overlooking of the biblical concept of rest partly explains, as I noted in the introduction, why Christians have a well-developed theology of work but not of leisure. In a paper titled "Re-creation and Recreation in the Eighties [the 1980s]," Gordon Preece explained how biblical theology has stressed salvation history as something distinct from earthly concerns. It has ignored large portions of biblical revelation, including the wisdom literature and the nature psalms. Salvation has been narrowed to mere deliverance, and the significant themes of blessing, land, and rest have been ignored. Preece commented: "This neglect was not decisive in the fields of Feudal society, but in the Bourgeoise society, the Industrial Revolution and the coming Leisure Age, it is disastrous."[7] Although the coming of a Leisure Age looks less likely than it did in the 1980s, Preece's point is still valid.

The Theological Uses of "Rest"

Let us now turn our attention to the biblical concept of rest, first by examining the Hebrew root for the word "rest" and its major theological uses, and then by tracing the development of the concept of rest through Scripture. According to Leonard J. Coppes, writing in the *Theological Wordbook of the Old Testament*, the Hebrew root of "rest" (*nuakh*) "signifies not only absence of movement but being settled in a particular place [whether concrete or abstract] with overtones of finality, or [when speaking abstractly] of victory, salvation etc."[8] At least four important theological uses are associated with this root: psychological-spiritual (personal) peace, soteriological (salvation rest), martial (rest from enemies), and a use related to death. If leisure includes a quantitative dimension related to a condition of our being, then the psychological-spiritual and soteriological (salvation) uses of rest must have some relevance for our understanding of leisure. Let us look at these two uses of rest in more detail. Since the martial use (rest from enemies) is developmentally linked to the soteriological use, we will also examine it.

The psychological-spiritual use of rest is seen in Job 3:26 when Job laments that he has no peace, no quietness, no rest, "but only turmoil." Proverbs 29:17 counsels the disciplining of one's children so that they will give one rest in a psychological sense, or (as the following phrase states it) "the delights you desire." Spiritual rest (the absence of distress) is depicted in Isaiah 14:3–7 (see also Prov. 29:9), and most vividly in Isaiah 28:12, which also has clear soteriological overtones. God is the one true source of spiritual rest (*manoakh*, Ps. 116:7). *Menukhah*, a state or place of *nuakh*, is a state of no strife, fighting, fear, or distrust that is the essence of the good life. As such it is a characteristic of true leisure.

The martial use of rest involves God's promise (Deut. 12:10) and the subsequent fulfillment (Josh. 21:44) to conquer Israel's enemies and give Israel rest, in terms of victory and security, in the Promised Land. Prolonged rest (2 Sam. 7:1) was conditional on Israel's obedience (Num. 32:15). While David, a man of war, was not permitted to build a place of rest for God, his son Solomon was. Solomon was designated a man of peace and rest because God gave him rest from all his enemies on every side during his reign as king (1 Chron. 22:9).

The soteriological use of rest develops in association with the theology of the Sabbath. While *shabbat* is used to describe God's rest (cessation from labor in Gen. 2:2–3), *nuakh* is used in Exodus 20:11. Thus humans are not only to refrain from their work (Exod. 31:12–17; Isa. 58:13–14) but are also to enter into a condition of victory/salvation rest (Josh. 1:13; cf. Deut. 25:19). This rest is only possible through the presence and provision of God (Exod. 33:14; see also Isa. 14:3–7). Through the Messiah, God will ultimately bring true rest to his people (Isa. 63:14; see also Heb. 3:7–4:13).

The Deuteronomic Notion of Rest: Rest in the Land

Since these theological uses of the word "rest" are not completely distinct but to some extent are developmentally linked, let us now trace the concept of rest through the Bible. We first meet the promise of rest in Deuteronomy.

> You have not yet reached the resting place and the inheritance the LORD your God is giving you. (Deut. 12:9)

> When the LORD your God gives you rest from all the enemies around you in the land he is giving you to possess as an inheritance, . . . (Deut. 25:19)

In Deuteronomy the concept of rest is grounded in and equivalent with possession of the land. Canaan as Israel's inheritance was to be a place of rest. Von Rad stressed that we must not spiritualize this concept of rest that was a direct gift from the hand of God: "[It] is not peace of mind, but the altogether tangible peace granted to a nation plagued by enemies and weary of wandering."[9]

The concept of rest to which Deuteronomy frequently refers is associated with the notion of a pleasant, secure, and blessed life in the land (15:4; 23:20; 28:8; 30:16). Dumbrell connected this pleasant life in the land with the creation account.

> Israel will enjoy the gifts of creation in the way in which they had been meant to be used. In this theology of rest we are clearly returning to the purposes of creation set forth in Genesis 1:1–2:4a and typified by the Eden narrative, namely that mankind was created to rejoice before the deity and to enjoy the blessing of creation in the divine presence. The notion of rest in both Genesis 2:2 and the book of Deuteronomy implies this.[10]

There is a sense in which the promise of rest was fulfilled in the Old Testament, in terms of rest in the land, and this fulfillment is first expressed in the book of Joshua.

> So the LORD gave Israel all the land he had sworn to give their ancestors, and they took possession of it and settled there. The LORD gave them rest on every side, just as he had sworn to their ancestors. Not one of their enemies withstood them; the LORD gave all their enemies into their hands. Not one of all the LORD's good promises to the house of Israel failed; every one was fulfilled. (21:43–45; see also 1:13–15; 22:4)

Later in 2 Samuel, we read that the Lord had given rest in the land and will continue to do so during David's reign as king: "The LORD had given him rest from all his enemies around him" (7:1). Then the word of the Lord came to Nathan instructing him to tell David that, among other things, the Lord Almighty "will also give you rest from all your enemies" (7:11b).

The fulfillment of the promise of rest may be identified, even more clearly, with the time of Solomon. In Solomon's blessing that followed his prayer of dedication for the temple he acknowledges the fulfillment of God's promise to give his people rest: "Praise be to the LORD, who has given rest to his people Israel just as he promised. Not one word has failed of all the good promises he gave through his servant Moses" (1 Kings 8:56). Thus it can be said that the divinely given rest was experienced by the nation of Israel during the times of Joshua, David, and Solomon. Yet, as we will see later in our discussion of Hebrews 3 and 4, there is a real sense in which the promise of rest was not fulfilled in the Old Testament.

The Chronicler's Notion of Rest: The LORD God Resting among His People

The Chronicler's notion of rest, as von Rad illustrated, swings away from the Deuteronomic conception of rest. "Rest from all your enemies" becomes a gift that God bestows periodically on pious kings. Solomon is a "man of peace and rest" (1 Chron. 22:9); God also grants rest during the reigns of King Asa (2 Chron. 15:15) and King Jehoshaphat (2 Chron. 20:30). In these passages von Rad detected a sense of anxiety in case the Deuteronomic notion of rest will not be preserved to its full extent. He also noted that Solomon is now considered a "man of peace" in an entirely new way, the fundamental characteristic of which is not that Israel obtains rest but that God comes to rest in the midst of the Israelite people.[11] Solomon ends his long prayer of dedication for the temple with the following exalted messianic invocation:

> Now arise, LORD God, and come to your resting place,
>   you and the ark of your might.
> May your priests, LORD God, be clothed with salvation,
>   . . . .
> LORD God, do not reject your anointed one.
>   Remember the great love promised to David your servant.
>   (2 Chron. 6:41–42)

Now added to the promise that Israel as a nation would receive rest is the anticipation that God will come to rest among his people. This anticipation, which von Rad described as a "stabilization of the nation's relationship to God,"[12] is a quotation from Psalm 132. The anticipation is that the LORD God will finally arise and come to his resting place among his people Israel.

At this point let me summarize the strands in the complex of ideas about rest in the Old Testament. One strand is seen in Deuteronomy, where the land is called Israel's resting place, for Israel was to obtain rest from all her enemies in the land she would inherit (12:9–10; 25:19; see also 3:20). A second strand of ideas concerning rest suggests that God has his resting place in the land and particularly in his sanctuary at Zion. This idea is especially evident in Psalm 132:7–8, 13–14 (see also 2 Chron. 6:41) and Isaiah 66:1. Elsewhere these two strands are joined so that the people's resting place is simultaneously God's resting place (Deut. 12:9–11). An excellent example of this synthesis of the two motifs is recorded in 1 Chronicles 23:25, when David says, "The LORD, the God of Israel, has granted rest to his people and has come to dwell in Jerusalem forever."

Rest in Psalm 95

Another development in the concept of rest is found in Psalm 95, where the resting place of the people is not only the resting place of God but also is God's rest itself.

> Today, if only you would hear his voice,
> "Do not harden your hearts as you did at Meribah,
>   as you did that day at Massah in the wilderness,
> where your ancestors tested me;
>   they tried me, though they had seen what I did.
> For forty years I was angry with that generation;
>   I said, 'They are a people whose hearts go astray,
>   and they have not known my ways.'
> So I declared on oath in my anger,
>   'They shall never enter my rest.'" (7b–11)

"Today" presents a new hope of salvation in contrast to the one forfeited by those who participated in the desert wanderings. This saying depends on the concept of rest articulated in Deuteronomy in that the nation is still the subject of the rest. However, the place of rest is now different. The Lord God says, "They shall never enter my rest." The resting place is God's rest. This refers to a gift of rest that Israel will reach only by a totally personal entering into her God. It is in this form that the Old Testament concept of rest is taken up by the writer to the Hebrews.

Rest in Hebrews 3 and 4

Let us now turn to the concept of rest in Hebrews 3 and 4. Here the word "rest" (*katapausis*), which is first introduced in the quotation from Psalm 95 in 3:11, is repeated in 3:18 and is found six more times in chapter 4, including two times where the first quotation is repeated. The cognate verb is found in 4:4, 8, 10 (twice by quotation of Gen. 2:2). The only other occurrence of *katapausis* in the New Testament is in Acts 7:49, where Isaiah 66:1 is quoted. *Anapausis* is the more prevalent term for "rest" in the New Testament and also in the Septuagint.

Donald Hagner pointed out that the writer to the Hebrews refers to three distinct but related types of rest:

1. literal rest in the land of Canaan (see Deut. 12:9);
2. God's own rest (Heb. 4:4);
3. the rest that is meant to be the portion of Christians (this indeed may be subdivided into the rest available at present and the future rest of eschatology proper).[13]

The first type of rest, the Deuteronomic rest in the land, is alluded to in the use of Psalm 95 quoted in Hebrews 3:7–11 and again in 4:3. And the affirmation that God rested after completing the work of creation (Gen. 2:2) is cited in 4:4. This is immediately followed by a repetition of the quotation from Psalm 95, "They shall never enter my rest" in verse 5. By connecting Psalm 95:11 and Genesis 2:2 in Hebrews 4:3–4 the rest in the land of Canaan may be regarded as a type of God's creation rest. Therefore the resting place remaining for the people of God may be viewed as a component of the divine rest that has existed since creation and is still available. As von Rad wrote, the joining of these two texts

> is an indication of the scope of the promised rest of the New Testament. This rest is an eschatological expectation, a fulfillment of the prophecies of redemption, an entering into that rest which there has always been from the beginning, with God. In the fulfillment of this hope the whole purpose of creation and the whole purpose of redemption are reunited. Such is the insight vouchsafed to the writer in the simple juxtaposition of these two texts![14]

God's rest is now viewed as the realization of his intention in the creation to bestow such a rest on humanity. After the fall, God's initial purposes for humanity's enjoyment of rest are made possible through his redemptive acts among his people. But the resting place in the Promised Land and in the temple at Jerusalem aim only toward the realization of God's purposes in creation. Now in Hebrews the final consummation is depicted as a heavenly rest, the antitype of the rest in the Promised Land alluded to in Psalm 95:11. There is no doubt that the final consummation rest is future as is suggested by the exhortation in Hebrews 4:11 to "make every effort to enter that rest," but it would be incorrect to accept the opinion of many commentators who believe "my rest" to be totally in the future. In response to this prevalent misunderstanding Lincoln argued from four angles that this rest is now a reality for Christian believers.[15]

First, one theme in Hebrews is that the heavenly realities, including rest, are available through Christ to those who believe.

Second, the present dimension of the rest is supported by the notion of faith spoken of in 4:3: "Now we who have *believed* enter that rest." As Charles Barrett indicated, in Hebrews faith "is not merely a waiting for the fulfillment of the promise; it means through the promise a present grasp upon invisible truth."[16] In Hebrews 11:1 we learn that through faith, that which is future, unseen, and heavenly is made sure and certain in the present. Therefore those who have believed may be described as having already entered into God's rest.

Third, as Hagner pointed out, the view that rest is now available is supported by the exhortation in 4:11 to "make every effort to enter that rest."[17] Furthermore, by inserting *eiserchomai* emphatically at the beginning of the sentence "we enter that rest," the writer affirms that God's rest has become a present reality.

Fourth, the present availability of rest is consistent with the use of "today" throughout the passage. The "today" in 4:7 "suggests not only that the rest remains to be entered, but that the invitation extends to, and finds its true meaning in, the present."[18] The author of Hebrews can apply the "today" of Psalm 95:7 (see also Heb. 3:7) to the present (Heb. 3:13, 15) because, as is explained in Hebrews 4:7–8, God, through David, had set a date in the future when his rest would be available: "Today, if you hear his voice." This "today" had now come since the readers of the epistle had heard God's voice spoken through Christ in these last days (1:1–2) and had received the promise of entering God's rest (4:3). Lincoln wrote, "On this new day the rest has become a reality for those who believe but remains a promise that some may fail to achieve through disobedience, so that all are exhorted to strive to enter it."[19]

The time frame of the rest in Hebrews is summed up by Barrett: "The 'rest', precisely because it is God's, is both present and future; [we] enter it, and must strive to enter it. This is paradoxical."[20] The tension we see between the indicative ("we who have believed enter that rest" in 4:3) and the imperative ("make every effort to enter that rest" in 4:11) merely reflects the tension between realized and future eschatology.

Christ is the one who has enabled the consummation of the promise of rest. Those who believe enter the heavenly rest because they participate in the heavenly calling (3:1) with Christ the great High Priest who has gone through the heavens (4:14). From 4:8 we learn that Joshua did not bring total rest to the people; his entry into the Promised Land and the concomitant rest in the land can be seen as a parallel to that of the high priest serving in the sanctuary that "is a copy and shadow of what is in heaven" (8:5). The final consummation of God's promise of rest did not occur until Christ opened the way for his people to enter God's heavenly rest.

If Joshua did not give the people rest (Heb. 4:8), how is the rest obtained by Israel under Joshua (Josh. 1:13, 15; 11:23; 21:44; 22:4; 23:1) to be explained?

Joshua's generation did dwell in the Promised Land and did attain the rest of deliverance from their enemies, along with a peaceful existence and pleasant life in the land. It would seem that the rest given in Joshua's day is a type of rest, a shallower dimension of the complete content of God's rest. In this typological relationship (between rest in the land of Canaan and the rest God intends for Christians), the blessings of the one foreshadow those of the other. But the physical aspects of rest cannot be separated from the spiritual aspects, nor can the promise of the physical land and the associated peaceful existence and pleasant life be separated from the spiritual kingdom of God. The former incarnates the embryo of the latter, and in a sense is brought to fulfillment in the latter. The promise of rest has not changed from the beginning (from the divine goal of rest in Gen. 2:2), but has advanced from the physical Canaan to the heavenly land portrayed in Hebrews 12:22–24 and the concomitant rest.

In Hebrews 4:9 the writer adds a new dimension to the concept of rest. When the writer says, "There remains, then, a Sabbath-rest for the people of God," he completes the same point he made in 4:6, "it still remains for some to enter that rest." This is the only occurrence of the term *sabbatismos* in the New Testament, and it seems to have been intentionally substituted for *katapausis*. This substitution is possible because *katapausis* has previously been associated with God's rest on the seventh day (4:4) and also had been used for the Sabbath rest in the Septuagint version of Exodus 35:2 and 2 Maccabees 15:1.

What is the Sabbath rest for the people of God? It involves entering God's rest and therein ceasing from one's own work (Heb. 4:10). This passage has been likened to the heavenly rest of Revelation 14:13: "'Blessed are the dead who die in the Lord from now on.' . . . 'They will rest from their labor, for their deeds will follow them.'" While the final consummation of this rest "will involve the removal of all curse on work and the enjoyment of that state of completion and harmony experienced by God after His creative work and intended by Him for humanity,"[21] this passage, as we have already seen, is "primarily concerned with the present rather than with the future, with the believer's rest here, and heaven only as its completing and culminating point."[22]

It should be noted that the Sabbath rest resembles God's resting from all his works at the end of creation (Heb. 4:10, see also 4:4). Donald Guthrie noted that the "reference back to creation . . . would seem to suggest that it is part of God's intention for [humans]." He continued,

> What believers can now enter is none other than the same kind of rest which the Creator enjoyed when he had completed his works, which means that the rest idea is of completion and not inactivity. . . . Indeed this whole passage suggests that after the act of creation, God began his rest, which presumably still continues. There is no suggestion that God withdrew from any further interest in the created order.[23]

So here rest is not to be thought of as simply inactivity and thereby imply that work is a misfortune. Guthrie wrote that "the reference back to creation places the idea on the widest possible basis."[24]

Jean Hering commented that this rest "must not invoke merely the notion of repose, but also those of peace, joy and concord."[25] Some, such as Calvin,[26] have associated Sabbath rest with the Sabbath day that is a day of rest and gladness. This could be true, especially if we consider the qualitative dimension and spiritual attitude of the Sabbath that was developed in the previous chapter. Lincoln wrote that this rest "will involve the realization of everything that God had intended by his own Sabbath rest."[27] Hagner believed that

> the author has in mind the ideal qualities of the Sabbath-rest, namely peace, well-being and security—that is, a frame of mind that by virtue of its confidence and trust in God possesses these qualities in contradiction to the surrounding circumstances. In short, the author may well have in mind that peace and sense of ultimate security "which is far beyond human understanding" (Phil. 4:7).[28]

In his book *The Rest of Life*, Witherington describes this rest as a "state of being," which obviously may have some insight for a "state of being" understanding of leisure: "The author of Hebrews calls us to enter that eschatological rest of God—not as a resting place or resting time, but as a state of being, living by faith, with the peace of Christ in our hearts, looking forward without anxiety about the future, because the future is as bright as God's promises and dawning Kingdom."[29] This rest is a quality of life that has generally eluded humans and cannot be attained except through fellowship with God, by way of a personal experience with Jesus Christ. As Jesus invited people to come to him to receive rest in Matthew 11:28–30, we will now turn our attention to this passage.

Rest in Matthew 11:28–30

According to Robert Hensel and Colin Brown, "The concept of rest finds its ultimate and deepest development" in Matthew 11:28–30.[30] As mentioned at the beginning of this chapter, the rest Jesus offers in this passage has frequently been equated with leisure by a number of Christian writers. Let us look at this passage in detail to see if it has anything to say concerning leisure. Jesus says, "Come to me, all you who are weary and burdened, and I will give you rest. Take my yoke upon you and learn from me, for I am gentle and humble in heart, and you will find rest for your souls. For my yoke is easy and my burden is light." According to Hans Dieter Betz, this passage presents an interesting hermeneutical phenomenon: "The meaning of the passage is unclarified. . . . [T]he passage is open to meaning, i.e., it is like a vessel which itself has no content, but which stands ready to be filled."[31] For our purposes, three questions need to be considered. To whom is the rest offered? How is the rest received? What is this rest?

To Whom Is the Rest Offered? Betz noted that the logion of the Easy Yoke and of Rest takes on a definite meaning from the hermeneutic context into which Matthew places it: "For the theological content in Matthew two things are decisive: the anti-Pharisaic tendency and the connection with vv. 25–27."[32] Thus most commentators, such as Willoughby Allen, believe "there is throughout this passage an underlying contrast between the Pharisaic conception of religion and the teaching of Jesus."[33] The Pharisaic interpretation of the law made it a heavy burden, while Christ's teaching was an easy yoke and a light burden. Thus William Hendriksen considered the invitation to rest to be "to all those who are oppressed by the heavy load of rules and regulations placed upon their shoulders by scribes and Pharisees."[34] Similarly, Randolph Tasker wrote that the invitation "is addressed in the first instance to those upon whom the Pharisees were laying heavy burdens by demanding meticulous obedience not only to the law itself but to their own intricate elaboration of it."[35]

While we may agree that in the original context this was the primary intention, Theodore Robinson argued that there is no need to limit the invitation to any particular kind of toil or weariness. Perhaps the invitation is making reference to the burdens of the law laid on the Jew by the scribe, "but on the whole we are bound to assume that the invitation is wider."[36] Calvin, who also argued for the universality of the invitation, believed that those "who limit the burden and labour to ceremonies of the law, take a very narrow view of Christ's meaning. . . . Christ stretches out his hand to all . . . without exception, who labour and are burdened." [37]

Some scholars make a distinction between those who are "weary" and those who are "burdened."[38] Those who are weary are considered to be those who are trying to work out their salvation, while those who are burdened are identified as those who have let others load them down with requirements for salvation. However, as Richard Lenski pointed out, these terms actually apply to everyone, for no one has true rest except those who come to Christ: "All the vain, fruitless striving after peace, contentment, happiness, rest and joy, . . . is this constant labouring."[39] Thus the invitation to come to Jesus for rest is addressed to everyone whose life is marked by a lack of peace and security, whether they are Jews under the law or gentiles far off from God.[40]

How Is the Rest Received? These verses, noted Eduard Schweizer, obviously imply that toil and labors do not lead to rest.[41] Rather, it is through coming to Jesus that one will find rest. David Hill wrote, "The rest is identical with the yoke of discipleship."[42] From their union with Jesus, his disciples will receive refreshment and renewal that will enable them to carry their load without finding it heavy and burdensome (cf. 2 Cor. 4:16).[43]

W. Robertson Nicoll pointed out that the literal translation is, "I will rest you," which means more than "give you rest."[44] Indeed, there is rest in Christ. The Christian finds rest for his or her soul through the assurance of the presence of the risen Lord, for Jesus, as Robinson wrote, "has a unique power and authority; he is, as it were, the sole repository of the whole resources of an infinite God, and so he is able to make an appeal and an offer to labouring and burdened humanity."[45]

What Is This Rest? The rest may be described as a present reality, discipleship not inactivity, peace in God, and as a rest for the whole person. First, the rest is present. The future tense—"you will find rest"—indicates not a future hope, or a rest in heaven, but a rest immediately available to all who follow Jesus.

Second, the rest is not that of inactivity or idleness; it includes a yoke of discipleship. And as Floyd Filson noted, there is no discipleship without a task.[46] Jesus does not promise freedom from toil or burden but a rest or relief that will make all burdens light. Tasker summarized: "Certainly Jesus does not promise His disciples a life of inactivity or repose, nor freedom from sorrow and struggle, but He does assure them that, if they keep close to Him, they will find relief from such crushing burdens as crippling anxiety, the sense of frustration and futility, and the misery of a sin-laden conscience."[47]

Third, the rest consists of the free pardon of all sin, rest flowing from peace with God: "Here true rest is found, not the invulnerability and calm of the Stoic, but peace, contentment and security in God, the Father God revealed by Jesus."[48] Lenski wrote, "The souls that animate our bodies shall find themselves free from every strain and burden, with no wrong, no fears and no distress."[49] This rest, according to Hendriksen, is not only freedom from uncertainty, fear, anxiety, and despair, but it also includes peace of mind and heart (Isa. 26:3; John 14:27; 16:33; Rom. 5:1) and assurance of salvation (2 Cor. 5:1; 2 Tim. 1:12; 4:7–8; 2 Pet. 1:10–11).[50]

Fourth, Henry Ellison pointed out that "rest for your souls" refers not merely to the inner person but to the whole person.[51] Hendriksen, who believed this fact is generally ignored, suggested that Jesus offers rest that is not only beneficial to the soul but also to the body. The rest—peace of heart and mind—that Jesus offers here is the very opposite of the aggravated mental stress that manifests itself in physical ailments, such as ulcers, colitis, high blood pressure, and heart attacks. The rest of Jesus, wrote Hendriksen, can "have a curative effect on the entire person, soul and body. He is a complete Saviour!"[52]

Summary on Rest

As we come to the end of this long and convoluted discussion of the biblical concept of rest, the question to be asked is what all this has to do with the concept of leisure? Well, if we accept the classical concept of leisure as a condition of life and a state of being, then for the Christian the biblical concept of rest is very descriptive of what leisure may be. While we cannot derive an operational definition of leisure from our discussion of rest, our discussion supplies a wide variety of clues that are descriptive of leisure: a pleasant, secure, and blessed life in the land (for as Preece noted, "We don't rest in a doctrine, we need a place to put our feet up, but a place in which God is personally present"[53]); a rest of completion, not inactivity, such as the Creator enjoyed when the works of creation were completed; a Sabbath rest of peace, joy, well-being, concord, and security; a relief and repose from labors and burdens; a peace and contentment of body, soul, and mind in God. It must be stressed that while these elements of rest available through fellowship with God will be consummated in the heavenly rest, they are at least partially a present reality. These elements of rest are one way of describing the quality of life we have in Jesus Christ, a quality of life that is synonymous with the qualitative dimension of leisure.

The qualitative dimension of leisure could be further explored and elaborated on by an examination of several other New Testament verses, which we will only briefly touch on, that describe the quality of life we have in Christ. We have seen how Hagner made connections between Sabbath rest and "the peace of God, which transcends all understanding" (Phil. 4:7). Similarly, Hendriksen made connections between the rest Christ offers and peace of mind and heart. Those who live in Christ have peace (John 16:33; see also Rom. 5:1), for Jesus said to his disciples: "Peace I leave with you; my peace I give you" (John 14:27). Certainly peace is a characteristic of life in Christ and also of true leisure.

The quote from the leisure education textbook in the introduction to this book links leisure with the full and abundant life that Jesus offers to us in John 10:10. In the process of defining leisure, Dahl commented on this verse as follows:

> When Jesus said, "I come that they may have life, and have it abundantly," he was promising much more than the satisfaction of physical and social needs. He came offering [men and women] a quality and style of life that went far beyond comfort and convenience. . . . [H]e called [men and women] away from the pursuit of these mundane interests and pointed them toward a fuller, more wonderful, more exciting, more beautiful experience of human life.[54]

In connection with John 10:10, leisure scholar Sherrow wrote, "Leisure is the opportunity for discovering Life (with a capital L!) in Jesus Christ."[55] Cato, another leisure scholar, in a paper titled "Leisure and Jesus' Rest: Making the Connection," wrote, "It is in leisure that one finds truth, peace and becomes the person Christ would have him/her to be."[56]

Very often a relationship is seen between leisure and freedom.[57] Jesus said that "the truth will set you free" (John 8:32). Dahl commented: "A Christian experiences leisure when [he or she] comes into full awareness of the freedom [he or she] has in Christ, the freedom from fear and guilt because of sin but, even more important, the freedom to be and become the new [person] after Christ's own . . . example."[58] Freedom, abundance, and peace, along with rest, are descriptive of the qualitative dimension of leisure, the quality of life one has in Christ. Doohan wrote that leisure "is a freedom for the rest, peace, joy and blessing that the Lord Jesus brings."[59]

Conclusion on Sabbath and Rest

My study of the biblical concepts of Sabbath and rest has revealed that leisure should encompass two dimensions—a quantitative and a qualitative, one related to our doing and the other to our being. First, the Sabbath teaches a rhythm to life—six days of work and one of nonwork. Second, the Sabbath inculcates a spiritual attitude for a human's basic posture in relation to God—one of rest, joy, freedom, and celebration in God and the gift of God's creation. This qualitative dimension to life, descriptive of leisure, can also be seen in the biblical concept of rest. Sabbath and rest are closely linked throughout the Bible, from the creation account (Gen. 2:2–3) to the idea of Sabbath rest in Hebrews 4:9. Rest in its ultimate and deepest sense is available through Jesus Christ (Matt. 11:28–29). This rest along with peace (John 16:33; 14:27; Phil. 4:7), abundant life (John 10:10), and freedom (John 8:32) are descriptive of the quality of life we have in Christ, and as such explicate the qualitative dimension of leisure.

In chapter 3 we saw how, in history, there has been a distinction between the *vita contemplativa* and the *vita activa*. The medieval monastic culture defined leisure primarily in terms of the qualitative dimension—that is, in relation to our being. In contrast, those in the Protestant tradition tended to view leisure in a quantitative sense, as non-work time to be used to restore and refresh one to go back to work. As such those in the Protestant tradition were following the rhythmic pattern of work and rest (which we have shown, in the previous chapter, to be a scriptural principle). The rhythmic pattern of the Protestant tradition emphasized "doing" (i.e., the active life). However, this chapter and the previous one have illustrated that an important scriptural emphasis is "being"— that is, recognizing the Sabbath as a spiritual attitude and embracing the rest and quality of life we have in Christ. In the next chapter we will examine biblical verses related to this spiritual attitude, but we will focus more on passages related to leisure as activity.

7

other biblical words and themes related to leisure

While the main focus of part 3, the biblical background of leisure, is focused on the biblical concepts of Sabbath and rest, there are other biblical words and themes that are instructive for our study of leisure, and in particular are relevant to an understanding of leisure as activity. In this chapter I will explore words in Scripture related to leisure and also examine the biblical themes of festivals, feasts, dance, hospitality, friendships, and leisure practices in Luke's Gospel.

Words in Scripture Related to Leisure

Are there words related to leisure in the Old and New Testaments that might help provide insight into a Christian understanding of leisure? As we saw in chapter 1, our English word "leisure" can be traced back to the Greek word *scholē*. Thus we might be more likely to find corresponding words in the Greek New Testament rather than the Hebrew Old Testament. However these words are few.

Mark 6:31

One example is the verb *eukaireō*, and its cognate noun *eukairia*, which may be translated "opportunity, seasonable time, spend time or leisure."[1] This Greek word is used in Mark 6:31, and in some English versions, such as the Revised

Standard Version, it is translated "leisure": "And he [Jesus] said to them, 'Come away by yourselves to a lonely place, and rest a while.' For many were coming and going, and they had no leisure even to eat." The disciples were so busy that they did not have an opportunity to eat, a regular and necessary human activity. In this verse Jesus sees the need for his disciples to take a break from their busy activity, so he instructed them to go with him to a quiet place where they could rest, which in Greek is the word *anapauō*.[2] In the context of Mark 6:31, *anapauo* means to abstain from work in order to be rejuvenated and restore strength. This Greek word is often translated "be refreshed" and can also denote keeping quiet, ceasing all movement, or a dimension of sleep, such as in Mark 14:41 when Jesus in Gethsemane asks his disciples, "Are you still sleeping and resting?" In the context of Mark 6:31 Jesus and his disciples needed to get away and be refreshed. Commenting on this passage, Ryken noted that Jesus, through both his instructions and example, drew a boundary around work, including the work of preaching the gospel and serving the needs of others, even those who were especially needy.[3]

In the context of this passage, we read that the disciples are gathered around Jesus telling him all their recent activities: preaching, healing, and casting out demons.[4] Jesus replies that the disciples are to leave for a quiet place by themselves to rest as they did not have leisure to eat. Eric Springsted suggested that Jesus is telling the disciples they need some leisure in their lives.[5] While the disciples needed rest and food, Springsted explained that the mention of eating has a deeper meaning in this passage, as is often the case when food is mentioned in the Gospels. The disciples needed "the very bread of life. They needed the sort of leisure that lets us hear the word of God that we live by."[6] In the call for the disciples to go to a deserted place, Jesus is recommending more than food for the stomach and rest for the body. This call reflects Jesus's regular practice of leaving the crowds behind to go "up on a mountainside to pray" (Mark 6:46). Springsted concluded,

> To look at things this way is to have a very different sense of what leisure is and what it is for. Leisure on this view is not rest for the bones, so that the bones can go back to work where real meaning is. Rather, leisure *is* the time of fulfillment, a time that is more fulfilling than any other for it is the time when most of all we actually encounter God, and pay most attention to the neighbor we are to love. It is fulfilling because we are being filled with the bread of life. It is not simply time off, but is more essentially time away from time, a sense of eternity itself, a taste of eternal life. It is a time, oddly enough, when more that is important happens to us than during any time of work and energy. It is a time when, being quiet, we are filled with the Word and its words.[7]

Greek words related to *anapauo* are the noun *katapausis*, which indicates a place of rest, and the corresponding cognate verb *katapauō*, which expresses "to take rest" or "give rest." This is the Greek word used in Hebrews 4:4, 8, 10, which we explored in the previous chapter, to refer to God's rest on the seventh day in Genesis 2:2. God rested on the seventh day after his work of creation.

"Have Leisure and Know That I Am God" (Ps. 46:10)

Another word of possible relevance to leisure is found in Psalm 46:10. Writings on leisure sometimes quote or paraphrase the Septuagint version of this verse: "Have leisure and know that I am God."[8] This verse is probably most well known in the leisure studies field because Pieper quoted it at the beginning of his *Leisure: The Basis of Culture*.[9] Does this verse provide biblical support for leisure or does it actually have nothing to do with leisure? If the verse is related to leisure, is it representative of the biblical teaching on leisure? An understanding of the historical and linguistic context of Psalm 46 is necessary to answer these questions.

Historical Context. While earlier scholarship thought that the historical context for Psalm 46 was the deliverance of Jerusalem from the Assyrians in 701 BCE during King Hezekiah's rule when the city was saved from imminent peril (2 Kings 18:13–19:36), more recent scholarship suggests that the psalm is not necessarily tied to this historical episode.[10] The psalm does not provide specific details suggesting this historical event, and even with poetic exaggeration, the psalm's language transcends any known historical event.[11] Thus the psalm may have originated in the Jerusalem cult (worship) and its ancient traditions. John Hebert Eaton suggested, "The 'events' are better understood as the universal issues of life and death, good and evil, as presented in Jerusalem's dramatic rituals."[12]

Literary Context. Psalm 46, with Psalms 47 and 48, appear to form a trilogy as they communicate the same theme, use similar language, and reflect a confidence in God's protection and kingship.[13] The theme of Psalm 46 is introduced in verse 1: "God is our refuge and strength, an ever-present help in trouble" and then is reinforced in the refrains of identical verses 7 and 11: "The Lord Almighty is with us; the God of Jacob is our fortress." These refrains and the use of the term "Selah" at the end of verses 3, 7, and 11 give the psalm its structure.[14] The psalm can be divided into three strophes or sections: 1–3; 4–7; 8–11. The theme in each of these strophes is to trust in God in the face of danger. In the first strophe the dangers are natural catastrophes. Using powerful imagery, the psalmist writes of an earthquake, mountains falling into the sea, tidal waves, and mountains trembling. Although the language is poetic and alludes to a deeper level, earthquakes were a common experience for the residents in this area.[15] Within this context, the people have no need to fear (v. 2) for God is a refuge, strength, and ever-present help. The second strophe (vv. 4–7) makes the same point, but now the focus is national and international catastrophes related to the political realm of nations and kingdoms. As in the previous strophe, God is seen as being present and a source of help (v. 5). The third strophe (vv. 8–11) is the climax where God is seen as a refuge for both natural and national powers. Unlike the previous strophes, this one uses direct speech. God is in control of the earth (v. 8) and as the peacemaker brings wars to an end (v. 9). Thus we come to verse 10, which describes how the reader is to respond to God's protection and presence: "Be still and know that I am God."

The psalms were originally written in Hebrew. The Septuagint (the ancient Greek version of the Old Testament of Hellenistic times that was completed in Egypt at the beginning of the second century BCE) used the Greek word *scholē* in this verse, so in English it reads, "Have leisure and know that I am God." Also of note is the Vulgate (Jerome's fourth-century Latin translation from the Hebrew) version of this verse: *vacate et videte quoniam ego sum Deus*—"be at leisure and see that I am God." Unlike the Hebrew and Greek, the Latin communicates the notion of the "vision of God" rather than "knowing God," which might be due to alliterative purposes—*vacate et videte*.[16] The English "be still" and the Greek *scholē* are translated from the Hebrew stem of the verb *raphah*, which means "to release, to let go, to be weak" and can be translated as "let yourselves become weak" or "cause yourselves to let go."[17] The noun form *repha'im* could be used in poetic contexts as a synonym for the dead. One commentator suggested the verb means "to abate, to relax, to sink," or in the causative mode it indicates "to abandon, to drop hands from, and to be still."[18] It is important to note that in Hebrew grammar the emphasis is on the second coordinate imperative ("know" rather than "be still"). Thus the goal of being still is to know God. Hence the people may be still or relax as they can be confident in God as protector, and they can know God as the Lord of nature and history rather than relying on themselves.[19]

Application to Leisure. To understand the "Have leisure and know that I am God" translation of Psalm 46:10, one has to understand the historical and literary context of this psalm. In a paper on hermeneutics within the leisure studies field, Sylvester wrote, "Ideas do not come freeze-dried in vacuum-sealed pouches, conveniently ready to heat and serve as operational constructs. Instead, ideas are deeply embedded in the flux and flow of history."[20] Thus we cannot remove Psalm 46:10 from its context and simply state that this verse is providing biblical support for many contemporary understandings of leisure (e.g., free-time, activity, "state-of-mind" psychological experience, holistic leisure). Once we understand the context we realize that this verse is not providing support for these contemporary understandings of leisure. Yet it is apparent that many statements Pieper made about leisure are generally consistent with the original understanding of this verse, especially as Pieper connected his understanding of leisure to divine worship.

> Leisure, it must be clearly understood, is a mental and spiritual attitude. . . . It is in the first place, an attitude of mind, a condition of the soul. . . . For leisure

is a receptive attitude of mind, a contemplative attitude, and it is not only the occasion but also the capacity for steeping oneself in the whole of creation.[21]

In particular, the following quotes from Pieper suggest an attitude similar to Parsons's[22] explanation that the Hebrew verb *raphah* in Psalm 46:10 means "to let go."

> Leisure implies . . . inward calm . . . letting things happen. . . . Leisure is not the attitude of mind of those who actively intervene, but of those who are open to everything; not of those who grab and grab hold, but of those who leave the reins loose and who are free and easy themselves—almost like a man falling asleep, for one can only fall asleep by "letting oneself go."[23]

Pieper's further statement that "a man at leisure is not unlike a man asleep"[24] may reflect the connection between the Hebrew verb *raphah* and the noun form *rephah'im* used in poetry as a synonym for the dead. As explained by Witherington, the term "sleep" in the Bible, which sometimes is loosely applied to the dead, is a metaphor for trusting God in the sense of "letting go and letting God."[25] Thus I tentatively conclude that Psalm 46:10 supports a Christianized classical view of leisure such as Pieper[26] and others (e.g., Doohan[27]) have articulated.

In regard to whether this verse is representative of biblical teaching on leisure, as we have already seen at the beginning of chapter 5, there have been many biblical themes and elements (such as God's rest, Sabbath rest, Old Testament festivals, the advice of Qoheleth in Ecclesiastes, and Jesus's lifestyle) that have been explored to support a biblical understanding of leisure.[28] These themes and elements, many of which reoccur in Scripture, probably provide stronger support for leisure than does Psalm 46:10. However Ryken, Wilhoit, and Longman noted that Psalm 46:10 reflects a latent leisure motif.[29] Furthermore, Psalm 46:10 is reflective of two of the major biblical themes related to leisure (Sabbath and rest) that we observed in the two previous chapters. Sabbath inculcates a spiritual attitude for a person's basic posture in relation to God—one of rest, joy, freedom, and celebration in God and the gift of his creation. This qualitative dimension to life, descriptive of leisure, can also be seen in the biblical concept of rest that includes a peace and contentment of body, soul, and mind in God. This spiritual attitude for a person's basic posture in relation to God is similar to that being suggested by Psalm 46:10. Actually, one commentator makes a direct link between Psalm 46:10 and the Sabbath.[30] The Exodus (20:11) version of the Sabbath commandment connects Sabbath observance with God's creation of the world (Gen. 1), while the Deuteronomy (5:15) version of the Sabbath commandment connects Sabbath remembrance with God bringing the nation of Israel out of bondage in Egypt (Exod. 15:1–18). According to Peter Craigie, the first focus of the Sabbath commandment corresponds to God's kingship over nature in the first strophe of Psalm 46 (vv. 1–3), while the second focus corresponds to God's kingship over history and nations in the second strophe of Psalm 46 (vv. 4–7).[31]

In conclusion, Psalm 46:10 provides support, not for contemporary concepts of leisure such as free time, activity, or psychological experience, but for understandings of leisure as a spiritual attitude such as Pieper held.[32] It is less likely that the verse can be interpreted in the contemporary context as Lee did: "Stop what you are doing, you busy little man, who thinks he has no leisure, and choose leisure!"[33] While there are larger themes and elements in Scripture that offer support for developing a philosophy of leisure in our present culture (and are probably better starting places for developing a philosophy of leisure), Psalm 46 is consistent with these other themes, especially the biblical themes of Sabbath and rest.

Biblical Themes Relevant to Leisure as Activity

Although words related to leisure are not prominent in the Bible, various modern-day writers have identified a number of biblical elements that may inform an understanding of leisure as activity. These include festivals, feasts, dance, hospitality, friendships, and leisure practices in Luke's gospel.

Festivals

Israel's festivals, as described in the Old Testament, are a significant image of leisure in the Bible.[34] For the Israelite of the Old Testament, a set of religious festivals and holy days, chiefly agricultural, provided an orientation and lifestyle of celebration, thanksgiving, and joy. As we have already seen, among Jewish holy days and festivals, the Sabbath was the most significant. The second most frequent holy days were the New Moon festivals held at the outset of each month. These festivals, related to lunar changes, were the foundation for the liturgical calendar.

Instructions for yearly festivals occur in each of the four books of the law (Exod. 23; Lev. 23; Num. 28–29; Deut. 16). In Deuteronomy 16, Moses describes the three major festivals in Israel's life to the people of Israel gathered before him on the plains of Moab: the Feast of the Passover and the Unleavened Bread to be held in the spring (vv. 1–8); the Feast of Weeks, Pentecost, or Firstfruits to be held in the summer (vv. 9–12); and the Feast of Booths, Ingathering, or Tabernacles to be held in the fall (vv. 13–15).

All three principal annual festivals, each a week long, were celebrated in conjunction with the harvesting of the fields. Although agrarian-based, these festivals were not pagan orgies. Rather, as Elmer Martens noted, "Love to God and love to neighbour came to expression in the festivals."[35] First, love to God was expressed in presenting gifts to Yahweh, gifts consisting of firstfruits of grain and fruit, in addition to animal offerings. During these festivals or holidays a pilgrimage was made by the people to Yahweh's sanctuary, where the people congregated together as a community and for seven days celebrated the Lord's goodness in furnishing food. Thus these festivals "to Yahweh" were religious occasions.

According to the directions in Deuteronomy, the festivals, while primarily festivals for Yahweh, were also to be for the people. Johnston noted that the description of Deuteronomy 16 patterns the festivals "on a sabbatical scheme, reinforcing the idea that they are to be a time of rest, not work."[36] In addition, the festivals had a social orientation, with feasting and celebration to take place for seven days. Yet, as already mentioned, they were not self-centered pagan orgies since, in addition to love of God, love of neighbor was also expressed in the festivals. Although in all three festivals the men presented themselves at the sanctuary, the festivals included all—sons and daughters, servants and Levites. The fatherless and widows are especially mentioned, and the sojourners were also to share in the celebrations (Deut. 16:11, 14). The festivals were not to be exclusivist but were to exhibit a humanitarian concern as the non-Israelite was to be involved. This humanitarian concern was motivated by remembering that the people of Israel had been slaves in Egypt (Deut. 16:12).

Finally, the mood of these festivals needs to be noted: "And rejoice before the LORD your God" (Deut. 16:11); "Be joyful at your festival" (Deut. 16:14); "rejoice before the LORD your God for seven days" (Lev. 23:40). In Deuteronomy 16:15 we read that if the people celebrate the Feast to the Lord their God, the people's joy would be complete. The instruction to rejoice implies the basic attitude for the Israelite. Martens pointed out that the festivals, as commanded by Yahweh, "were an expression of a joyful mood."[37]

The Jubilee Year, as the crowning point of all the festivals, completed the entire life cycle of sabbatical days, months, and years. Leviticus 25:9 instructs that a trumpet should announce the Jubilee Year throughout Israel on the Day of Atonement (the tenth day of the seventh month) after the passing of seven sabbatical years (forty-nine years). The Jubilee Year was a year of liberty; property was to return to its original owner (v. 10; see also v. 13) and those who, forced by poverty, had sold themselves as slaves were to become free (v. 10; see also vv. 39–41). Also, the Jubilee Year had the function of the ordinary sabbatical year; that is, there was not to be any sowing, reaping, or harvesting of vines. Everybody was to live off the fields, and no attempt was to be made to accumulate the fruits of the land (vv. 11–12). Thus the land was to lie fallow for two successive years. The Jubilee Year was a significant time of rest from the efforts of work.

It is interesting to read in the book of Nehemiah that after the Israelites congregated to listen to Ezra read from the law of Moses, Nehemiah, along with Ezra and the Levites, reproved the Israelites for not celebrating their God.

"This day is holy to the Lord your God. Do not mourn or weep." For all the people had been weeping as they listened to the words of the Law. Nehemiah said, "Go and enjoy choice food and sweet drinks, and send some to those who have nothing prepared. This day is holy to our Lord. Do not grieve, for the joy of the Lord is your strength." (Neh. 8:9–10)

Nehemiah's summons to festivity suggests that there was more to Israelite life than toil and drudgery. He encouraged the people to enjoy choice food and sweet drinks. Furthermore, to guarantee that everyone would partake in the celebration, he instructed that food and drink be sent to those who had not prepared any food. The festival was for all. On the next day, Ezra read from the Law concerning the Feast of Booths (vv. 13–14). Afterward the people "celebrated the festival for seven days" (v. 18), "and their joy was very great" (v. 17). In verse 17 we read that the Israelites had not celebrated the festival like this since the days of Joshua.

In conclusion, as Johnston noted, "Religious festivals were occasions for a break from life's larger concerns, a special time, or a 'parenthesis' within life, consecrated to the Lord in joy."[38] Thus an examination of Israel's festivals indicates that the Hebraic lifestyle was not totally dominated by work; there were also times of celebration and rejoicing. From the Hebraic festivals we can learn that all of our life should not be consumed by work. Ryken remarked that although Christians do not celebrate the Old Testament festivals, these festivals offer a model of how leisure activity can meet human needs for festivity and communal rituals.[39]

Feasts

Significant events in the life of an Israelite frequently involved a feast in the form of a meal that included celebration as well as physical nourishment.[40] For example, "Abraham held a great feast" (Gen. 21:8) when Sarah weaned Isaac. Likewise a feast was prepared to celebrate Jacob's marriage (Gen. 29). These feasts, associated with special moments in Israelite life, are "symbolic of God's gracious presence with" his people.[41]

Feasts were part of both Jesus's experience, such as his participation in the Cana wedding feast, and his teaching that used feasts symbolically as in the case of the parable of the prodigal son (Luke 15:11, 31; see also Matt. 9:14–17; 22:1–14; 25:1–13).[42] A recurring event in the Gospels is Jesus's participation in parties and dinners.[43] At the Cana wedding feast Jesus transformed water into wine (John 2). C. S. Lewis wrote, "The miracle at Cana in Galilee by sanctifying an innocent, sensuous pleasure could be taken to sanctify . . . a recreational use of culture—mere 'entertainment.'"[44] Jeffrey Crittenden explained how the account of Jesus feeding the five thousand (Luke 9:12–17) is an excellent example of Jesus welcoming large crowds to eat together in community.[45] Everyone had something to eat and everyone sat together rather than some being placed above others in places of honor. Thus all are invited to participate in leisure regardless of their ability or situation.

Likewise, Jesus uses examples of feasts in his teaching. For example, in the parable of the prodigal son (Luke 15; see also Matt. 9:14–17; 22:1–14; 25:1–13) Jesus describes the joyful feasting that occurs when the prodigal son returns home.[46] This parable, when considered within its context, is a response to criticism Jesus receives that he is not feasting with the right type of people (Luke 7:31–35). Since feasting is part of Israel's customs, he is not being criticized for the activity but for those with whom he is feasting. Jesus demonstrates balance in the life of celebration, avoiding the extremes of excessive indulgence and asceticism.[47] He teaches, explained Crittenden, that celebration involves enjoying life in God's creation without hoarding, addiction, or obsession: "In walking the fine line between asceticism and drunkenness and gluttony, Jesus was sending a clear message that God provided humanity with an abundance of good food and drink, but this providence was not to be abused."[48] Thus Jesus values celebration of life in a totally different way.

> Jesus reinterpreted celebration by distancing his understanding of it from the drunkenness and recreation of the Greeks and Romans as well as from the strictly legalistic practices of the Jewish Sabbath. Instead, Jesus moved toward an understanding of Holy leisure in celebration as a celebration of trust in God's grace and care for each one of us. . . . In thanksgiving and freedom one experiences Holy leisure in God, in relationships and in the simple pleasures found everyday, e.g., such as eating together.[49]

Even the Last Supper, which is a model for the Lord's Supper, was a time where the disciples sat together for a meal. Kenneth Ross explained that the Lord's Supper, as the supreme symbol of the gospel and human response to it, is not something to be achieved or work to be accomplished but a time for Christians to sit together for a meal.[50] While it memorializes Christ's suffering for our salvation, there is also a dimension of celebration and joy.

Witherington pointed out that there are several passages in the Gospels that describe that the coming kingdom will involve a celebratory feast that includes eating and drinking (Matt. 8:11–12; 22:1–14; 25:1–13).[51] Jesus anticipated that eating and drinking will typify the future kingdom after his return (although there may not be marriage) because eating and drinking with others is one of the most important ways in which intimate relationships are developed, and koinonia and communion facilitated. Eating was not intended to be a private indulgence but a social activity.[52]

When considering feasting in the Bible, Witherington cautioned us that this is not a justification for overeating and overdrinking in today's society where "many of us . . . in our leisure, have become couch potatoes for Jesus."[53] He explained that feasting in the Bible was not an everyday occurrence but took place on special occasions such as festivals or weddings.[54] He pointed out that gluttony, which refers to overeating and overdrinking, is currently the pleasure of choice for many people, including Christians, although it was once known as one of the seven deadly sins and can keep a person from entering the eschatological kingdom.[55] While keeping this caution in mind, I agree with Packer that "all through the Bible the feast table is the place and the emblem of refreshing, celebratory fellowship—a very proper leisure activity, and certainly one to encourage."[56]

Dance

The Old Testament mentions dance on numerous occasions.[57] The psalmist instructs the Israelites to praise the Lord "with dancing" (Ps. 149:3; see also Ps. 150:4). Psalm 68 (see also Ps. 118:27) describes a processional dance of timbrel players and singers up to Zion. Judges 21 records the dance of Shiloh's daughters, which most likely occurred during a fall harvest festival. The famous passage from Ecclesiastes 3 that begins with "There is a time for everything" (v. 1) notes that there is "a time to dance" (v. 4). Jeremiah laments that "our dancing has turned to mourning" (Lam. 5:15; see also Ps. 30:11; Jer. 31:13) when Jerusalem is destroyed. However he anticipates a future time after exile when the Israelites will "go out to dance with the joyful" (Jer. 31:4) as they again celebrate their festivals.

Dance was a feature of Israelite celebrations.[58] After David defeated the Philistines, as "the men were returning home . . . the women came out of all the towns of Israel to meet King Saul with singing and dancing, with joyful songs and with timbrels and lyres. As they danced, they sang" (1 Sam. 18:6–7; see also Judg. 11:34; Exod. 15:20–21). When David brought the ark of the covenant to Zion, "David was dancing before the LORD with all his might" (2 Sam. 6:14). While in some of these passages singing and dancing went together, as Witherington pointed out, the Bible also includes much to say about the activity of music (see Job 21:11–12 and the psalter, which was Israel's songbook).[59] Thus I agree with Ross that dancing "features strongly in the Old Testament as a means of expressing celebration and worship."[60] As Ross pointed out, while Western Christianity has downplayed dance, African Christianity has resonated with dance as a way of expressing worship and celebration.

Hospitality

For Israelites, providing hospitality for, and taking care of, a sojourner or stranger was a holy and needed reciprocal responsibility as public places to stay were few and the danger of robbery was great.[61] Very high priority was given to hospitality in the ancient Near East, including Israel, even hospitality to enemies.[62] The neglect of hospitality was viewed as a serious sin worthy of severe punishment. For example, Ezekiel 16:49 informs us that the central sin of Sodom was not sexual sin but the lack of hospitality. Another example is in the book of Judges where the Benjaminites of Gibeah are attacked by the Israelites (Judg. 20) for inhospitality toward a travelling Levite (Judg. 19:15).[63] A guest, even if an enemy, was to receive protection and respect for up to three days. This was a basic ordinance of Israelite life (Gen. 24:22–32; Exod. 2:20; Deut. 23:4; Judg. 13:15; 1 Sam. 25; 2 Sam. 12:1–6; 1 Kings 17:8–16; Neh. 5:17–19; Job 22:7; 31:32). An example of these three days of hospitality is seen earlier in Judges 19 where the traveling Levite is taken in: "He remained with him three days, eating and drinking, and sleeping there" (Judg. 19:4). Actually the host pleaded with the visitor to stay five days, and during this time he made the heart of the guest merry. Since his goal was that the guest be happy, the host put aside other concerns in order to drink and eat with the guest.

Yet another example of the importance of hospitality can be seen in Genesis 18 and 19 when Abraham arranged a feast for the divine messengers although he did not know they were heavenly guests.[64] According to Ryken this classic story of hospitality is also a leisure occasion as it is set apart from daily life, involves the rest of the visitors, a lavish meal, and conversation between host and visitors.[65] Likewise the next day Lot took the visitors to his home so that they could bathe their feet, eat, and be safe from attack. Johnston concluded: "The ethical force of the obligation to be hospitable was formidable in ancient Israel. But being gracious to one's guests had another side as well. Not only were the guest and his party to be *cared* for, they were to be *entertained*. Hospitality was not only a *duty*; it was meant to be a delight."[66]

Friendships

Friendships were important to Jesus.[67] Jesus distinguished between his hospitable way of life and John the Baptist's ascetic lifestyle in Luke 7. Jesus personified the joy of the kingdom while John focused on repentance. Jesus appreciated the presence of others while John was more of a recluse. Indeed Jesus was criticized for his companionship with others who were seen as questionable: "Here is a glutton and a drunkard, a friend of tax collectors and sinners!" (Luke 7:34). Furthermore, according to Johnston Jesus was a friend of the woman who anointed his feet (Luke 7:38), as is suggested by his comments later in the passage that he is aware of her sins.[68]

Jesus's companionship with the unwelcomed and the unwanted is also suggested in Matthew 21:31–32, where Jesus associated with "tax collectors and the prostitutes." Not only did he associate with these people but he also claimed that these types of people will enter into God's kingdom. Jesus demonstrated a similar companionship with Zacchaeus (Luke 19:1–10) and with the woman caught in adultery (John 8:2–11). These types of relationships led I. Howard

Marshall to write that Jesus "brought to sinners the offer of divine forgiveness and friendship."[69]

Later in his life, there was a second anointing of Jesus by a woman in Bethany (Matt. 26:6–13; Mark 14:3–9; John 12:1–8). John mentioned that the woman is Jesus's close friend Mary, and that Mary's brother and sister, Lazarus and Martha, were also present, which led Johnston to conclude that the occasion was a "warm, friendly dinner party."[70] Johnston suggested that friendship is also highlighted in the account of Jesus's visit to Bethany to share a meal with Mary and Martha in their home (Luke 10). In this passage Martha's preparation of a meal is contrasted with Mary who sat at Jesus's feet and listened to him. Although many commentators on this passage stress the importance of listening to Jesus, Johnston emphasized that Jesus was highlighting the importance of friendly conversation: "Hospitality should involve more than a sumptuous banquet. It should also include friendly attention. It should be an occasion for enjoyment . . . and not merely a duty."[71]

Leisure Practices in Luke's Gospel

In a study titled "Does the Gospel of Luke Suggest a Christian-Judaic Form of Leisure in the Graeco-Roman World?" Karen Fox argued that the Gospel of Luke presents Jesus as challenging and modifying the leisure practices of the Graeco-Roman world as this Gospel focuses on activities and settings normally associated with leisure activity: socializing, traveling, sharing and eating food, partaking in outdoor meals, and visiting wilderness.[72] Recognizing that the word *scholē* does not appear in Luke's Gospel, she suggested, however, that the Gospel is haunted by this concept through the use of parables and examples. Graeco-Roman leisure practices included eating, social relationships, and hospitality, so it made sense that Luke situated his text within such a context. Fox drew on Byrne's view of Luke's metaphor of hospitality as extending beyond meals, visitors, and guests, to making a stranger feel "at home," so that the hospitality is a metaphor for ethical Christian behaviors and values. Byrne wrote,

> Luke sees the whole life and ministry of Jesus as a "*visitation*" on God's part to Israel and the world [note Luke 19:44]. . . . The One who comes as visitor and guest in fact becomes host and offers a hospitality in which human beings and, potentially, the entire world, can become truly human, be at home, can know salvation in the depths of their hearts.[73]

Fox claimed that a significant portion of Luke's Gospel (4:16–22, 31–35; 6:1–10; 13:10–17; 14:1–6) criticizes an emphasis on piety and law associated with leisure actions that lacks compassion and benefaction. The portions of narrative and parables that focus on food and eating practices encourage the values of generosity, sharing, and hospitality.

A number of parables (Luke 5:27–32; 7:36–50; 15:1–24; 19:1–10) criticize the values and practices of the upper-class banquet tradition that involved formal dining practices and are far removed from the Jewish peasants' communal meals. Dining practices of the upper class included dining areas decorated with fancy art and architecture, service by attendants and slaves, hierarchical seating arrangements, and dining couches on which to recline. These banquets reinforced the ruling class's legitimacy. Luke challenges the banquet's hierarchical features by sitting Jesus at tables with prostitutes, tax collectors, and other sinners, which would be unusual for a literate person like Jesus who was able to converse with Pharisees and other members of the upper classes. The least recognized within society are shown by Luke as accepting Jesus and providing him with hospitality. In Luke 16:19–31 and 20:45–47, Luke's focus on leisure practices teaches that if leisure exacts a cost on others, it is wrong.[74] Fox concluded, "These parables posited a Christian-Judaic leisure that challenged the normative and hierarchical structure of the Graeco-Roman banquet and promoted a 'table fellowship' that invited all to participate and share without regard to worth or status."[75] Eating together and sharing food is a significant theme in Luke's Gospel. "Jesus was known as someone who hugely enjoyed a good dinner with friends."[76] Fox explained that "Jesus seemed to understand that taste, smell, touch, and the daily attentions of one person to another comprised much of what was 'good' in human life."[77] In summary, Jesus's life and teaching are connected with various food practices that are interrelated with leisure, such as Luke's accounts of a few loaves and fishes being multiplied, Jesus eating with prostitutes and sinners, the Last Supper itself, many parables related to the growing of food, and Jesus's criticisms of eating practices.[78]

Conclusion

I began part 3 with a quotation from Richardson stating that people in biblical times spent their days working. In this chapter we have seen that there is much biblical evidence that life in biblical times was more than just work. The biblical themes of festivals, feasts, dance, hospitality, friendships, and leisure practices in Luke's Gospel are all descriptive of the concept of leisure as activity as practiced in biblical times. In chapters 5 and 6, my exploration of the biblical concepts of Sabbath and rest provided much biblical support for the classical understanding of leisure as a state of being or a spiritual attitude that permeates all of life. The biblical themes in this chapter support an activity view of leisure, thus suggesting that in Scripture we see support for both the classical and the activity views of leisure. In chapter 10 I will return to how we can integrate these two concepts of leisure into a Christian understanding of leisure, but first we need to investigate the idea of work in chapters 8 and 9.

part 4

leisure
and work

/\
8

work today and
in the past

A Christian philosophy of leisure cannot be developed without looking at the other dimensions of life, in particular work; therefore chapters 8 and 9 will focus on work. The structure of these chapters will reflect the methodology used for this book as a whole—that is, that the theological task consists of a dialogue between biblical, traditional, and contemporary sources. I will begin by looking at work in the contemporary context, then review the concept of work throughout Western history. In the next chapter (chapter 9) I examine the biblical view of work and later in chapter 11 I discuss how we should see the relationship between work and leisure in contemporary society.

Work in the Contemporary Context

Work for Americans is often not considered as enjoyable as it was in the past. In response to the question "Which do you enjoy more, the hours when you are on the job, or the hours when you are not on the job?" 44 percent of workers in 1955 enjoyed the job hours more, while only 16 percent enjoyed job hours more in 1999.[1] Also, approximately three times the number of full-time employed women in the late 1990s stated they worked for financial reasons, compared to those who stated they worked for personal satisfaction.[2] Another study found that life satisfaction decreased with increased weekly hours of work.[3]

The paradox is that we require work in order to earn an income, yet many people dislike their work. In 1972 Dahl wrote that most people "tend to worship their work, to work at their play, and to play at their worship."[4] While this statement may have been true when Dahl wrote it, now instead of worshiping work, people often worship the income that work (defined in terms of a job) provides. People tend to choose jobs that provide the greatest income for the effort expended. We desire the financial benefits of work so that we can purchase "all the 'goodies' for a 'happy life,'" but we hate the work itself."[5] The view that work is for God's glory, or is even a service to humanity, is largely ignored in the contemporary view of jobs and work. However, the financial benefits alone are no longer sufficient to make people satisfied with work.[6]

Calvin Redekop suggested that people's dislike for work is the result of work becoming divorced from its productive role in the community, a development that has accompanied the industrialization and bureaucratization of Western society.[7] It is this divorcing of work for income (i.e., a job) from the broader context of the community that has led to people being alienated from their work, and that has produced the unusual paradox of the necessity of work despite the disparagement of work.

In contrast to contemporary Western society, *Gemeinschaft* (strong communities) characterized earlier societies. Work performed for different reasons—for the physical, social, or spiritual benefit of the community—was not differentiated. For example, the work of a homemaker (done for the social maintenance of a family) or the work of a priest (done for the spiritual benefit of the individual or community) was not delineated. There was no specification of jobs, only work in general. Indeed, there was no clear separation between work and leisure either.[8]

While in the past work was closely associated—spatially and otherwise—with family and community life, work for contemporary North Americans has become extremely differentiated, specialized, and removed from the family and community context. The "non-remunerative, spontaneous, casual, relaxed, and indefinite" dimensions of work have been replaced by an abstract entity, called the job, that has become a means to an end—income, power, prestige, and so on. Work has become synonymous with the job: "The job defines the type of work that is to be done, where, when, with whom, and how it is to be done."[9]

Furthermore, in contemporary society the job has come to define the person. A person's basic status, security, prestige, and esteem are usually determined by one's job and the prestige associated with it. A person's job "is as good a clue as any to the course of his life, and to his social being and identity."[10] "What do you do?" is the question invariably asked when a person is introduced in a new situation. Hence North Americans tend to believe that what a person does defines who he or she is. A job therefore carries far too much significance, for there are other dimensions of human worth. Since work is now defined as a job, when one is not on the job, one has leisure time. This distinction has become so generally accepted that satisfaction in life tends to be separated from work and associated primarily with leisure time. Free time pursuits have emerged as enjoyable and are categorized as leisure because one is not obligated to work during non-job hours.[11]

Therefore many people in Western society find themselves in the strange paradox of being required to work to live, to enjoy the good life, and to bring self-identity, but being unable to find satisfaction in work. Many believe that work is essential for human fulfillment but detest their work. The tension between participating in an activity essential to human life, yet that is often disliked, is a concern of today's society. Fortunately, the steps to humanize work in recent years are a step in the right direction. For Christians, the problems associated with work in today's society can be informed by the biblical understanding of work and in understanding how to reintegrate it into today's family, community, and societal situation. Thus we will look at biblical teaching on work in the next chapter. First, let us turn to a historical review of the concept of work.

Work throughout History

The Ancient World

The educated people in Greek and Roman societies regarded work with some contempt, a contempt that extended to the workers themselves. Cicero, who lived just prior to the Common Era, wrote: "The toil of a hired worker, who is paid only for his toil and not for artistic skill is unworthy of a free man and is sordid in character."[12] In ancient Greece only those free from the necessity to work were regarded as true citizens. While work was despised, leisure was idealized. As we have seen previously, the word "work" in both Greek and Latin was designated as the absence of leisure (unleisure).

An exception to the prevalent Greek view was Stoic philosophy, which conferred work with intrinsic value and taught that work did not prevent one from living the virtuous life. Yet this only meant such work was not an obstacle to the higher life; philosophical activity was still considered the best way of life. The soul was considered more important than the body. In contrast, the apostle Paul regarded all kinds of work—spiritual and physical—as potentially equal in service to God.

Early Christianity

Christians in the early centuries viewed work as a necessary part of life.[13] While the early Christians recognized the necessity of work as taught by the Bible, they did not overemphasize it or idolize it. De Grazia wrote,

Early Christianity kept well in mind what Jesus Christ had said about the birds of the air: "They sow not, neither do they reap nor gather into barns; yet your heavenly Father feedeth them. Are you not much better than they?" (Matthew, vi:26). Christians were not to waste their time thinking, planning and working for the morrow. . . . For the patristic age the end was salvation, the other life. The first thing was to save one's soul, to bring it closer to God. Work, in a sense, was something one did in his free time.[14]

The Middle Ages

During the Middle Ages, under the leadership of monks, forests were cleared, large areas were reclaimed from the sea, and commercial cities and trading centers started to prosper. Through the influence of monks, the church became the first institution to emphasize the value of physical work—especially agricultural labor but also craftsmanship.

In the sixth century work was designated as a spiritual discipline by St. Benedict. The Benedictine adage "To labor is to pray" stressed the divine approval that was given to work. Monastery bells rang to call the monks to pray and also to summon them to manual labor. A Benedictine rule reads, "Idleness is the enemy of the soul. And therefore, at fixed times, the brothers ought to be occupied in manual labor, and, again at fixed times, in sacred reading." Don Fabun pointed out that the contemporary definition of work was fostered here in the sixth century: "For the first time not work as such, but work for a stipulated time, became integral to Western thought. In later years we were to confuse the two, so that 'putting in time' became more important than the work."[15] Thomas Aquinas viewed work as part of both the law of nature and the divine order. Work was a right and a necessity for survival; consequently, society should supply opportunities for all to work. In addition, work made it possible for a person to give alms and, hence, obtain merit.

Of greater significance for our study, Aquinas categorized people into classes and occupations, and ranked work according to the value of what was produced. In the Thomistic view, a person's life was divided into two realms: the spiritual and the economic or secular. This medieval Catholic doctrine that dichotomized human life into sacred and secular categories developed partly from the contempt that the early Christians had for the things of this world and from their desire to see the coming of the kingdom of God.

This dichotomization of life into sacred and secular categories encouraged the development of a notion of vocation in which the Christian's primary task was to offer spiritual works of prayer and meditation unto God while at the same time denying the desires of the flesh. Those who adopted this vocation entered special religious orders and usually withdrew to monasteries where they could focus on spiritual disciplines with a minimum of worldly distraction. The special vocation of monks along with the spiritual works of monastic life were viewed as better than all secular forms of work. Secular work had spiritual value when its results were given to the church or to charity.

In summary, the medieval church differentiated between three kinds of work.

1. The spiritual work performed by the clergy, especially prayer, fasting, and the giving of alms.
2. The work of peasants and craftsmen (less exalted, yet highly honored).
3. The work of merchants and financiers (though necessary, generally considered sinful and work that Christians should not engage in).[16]

A major problem of the medieval view of work was this unnatural division of work derived from an incomplete biblical understanding of human activity in the world. So-called religious work and physical labor were regarded to be pleasing to God, while the remainder of human activity was considered to be an inevitable evil.

While some aspects of the medieval work ethic, such as the secular-sacred dichotomy, were unbiblical, there were also positive dimensions of the medieval way of life that are helpful for our understanding of work and leisure today. In the Middle Ages work was not only characterized by a leisurely pace but it also provided a deep sense of satisfaction. The leisurely manner in which work was carried out was unlike the feverish pace of today's society. For example, in the final years of the Middle Ages there were at least 150 statutory holidays, mainly days commemorating saints. France, which preserved the medieval way of life longer than most European countries, retained a great number of statutory holidays until the French Revolution in 1789. Due to the many compulsory holidays, the first inhabitants of Canada, in what was then called New France, complained to Louis XIV's finance minister, Colbert, that they were unable to complete the work of settling the new land, since after holidays only ninety working days remained in the year.[17]

In addition to the medieval world of work being characterized by a leisurely pace of life, what was produced through work was of good quality and had a spiritual significance. In the medieval world the goal in life was to reach the kingdom of heaven; this life was but a stepping-stone to the life hereafter. Work focused on creating goods that had significance beyond earthly life, something more than a mere utensil to be used, worn out, and discarded. An object was produced, used, and cared for as having a value that pointed to God. This is probably best seen in cathedrals and public buildings constructed during this period and later during the Reformation period.

The Reformation

The Reformers' rediscovery of the Bible had a profound impact on the direction of Western society. Luther, Calvin, and the other Reformers made a spiritual break with the dualistic structure of life in the Middle Ages and affirmed that all types of work were of equal value and were pleasing to God. The notion of vocation (God's calling to his service) was enlarged to encompass the "callings of the common life," in contrast to the narrower and special calling of the monk in the medieval world. As Weber wrote, "The whole world became a monastery and every man a monk."[18]

Luther condemned the system of spiritual works in the medieval church as being not only corrupt but also unfaithful to Scripture. Although his main point was that no type of work contributes to salvation, Luther contended that the spiritual works of the medieval church were no better than ordinary work in the eyes of God. Along with the other Reformers, Luther repudiated the medieval position that the monastic disciplines were the only expression of divine calling and therefore in a distinct category from secular work. Luther expanded the notion of vocation to all worthwhile occupations and employments in life. Luther considered all honest work as honorable; while he considered the life of the peasant to be the most admirable, the work of the craftsman was also honorable because craftsmen served the community through their calling.[19] Luther believed that God in his sovereignty had placed every person in a station in society to do the work of that station.

Although Luther's theology was crucial in undermining the medieval church's system of spiritual works, it was actually Calvin's theology that had more influence on the origins of the modern work ethic. Of the Reformers, Calvin may have been the most forceful in his exhortations to work. For Calvin, the chief goal of humans was not limited to personal salvation but encompassed the glorification of God through all activities, including diligent work and not just spiritual activities. He emphasized useful activity; as Dahl pointed out, "Calvin taught that men are called, neither to spiritual exercise nor to quiet acceptance of grace, but to actively glorify God in their work."[20] Calvinists took the task of being stewards of God's creation very seriously, which meant that they were very involved in economic activities. The belief that it is a human's responsibility and honor to work led to tremendous economic development in the regions influenced by the Reformation.

There were definitely weaknesses in the Reformers' views on work, but in general their teaching was substantially that of the New Testament: all work is of equal value; all work is to be service to God and done as unto God; and this world with its responsibilities is the realm of a person's work. Marshall concisely summarized, although somewhat simplistically, the evolution of the view of work through the medieval monastic and Reformation period: "It is hard to escape the impression that the followers of Augustine and Aquinas were to serve in the world only when necessary, that Luther's followers were ushered out to serve in the world, and that Calvin's followers were let loose to transform the world."[21]

The Confusion of Vocation, Work, and Job

Earlier in this chapter I mentioned how in today's society work has often become synonymous with a job. Marshall documented how this present problem arose from the Reformers' understanding of vocation, work, and job. One of the important verses in the Reformers' understanding of work was 1 Corinthians 7:20, "Abide in the calling in which you were called" (as translated in Marshall[22]). Almost all the Reformers interpreted the word "calling" (*klēsis*) in this verse as the work and station in life that a Christian was already in. Such an explication was a misinterpretation of Paul unless he was giving the word "calling" a meaning that was not found elsewhere in his or other Greek writings. It is most probable, argued Marshall, that Paul insisted that one's type of work should be relatively unimportant (vv. 21–24); what was most important was that people remain in their callings as Christians.[23]

When the Reformers based their understanding of work on this interpretation of 1 Corinthians 7:20, they deviated from the biblical understanding of work. A calling tended to be narrowed to the work associated with a specific position in society. Thus a calling might entail being a baker, a farmer, a homemaker, a merchant, or a preacher. Service in the world was focused on a specific kind of work for each person. The consequence of this interpretation of calling was that Christians were instructed to serve God in the world; however, the world and its callings were never questioned. Christians were to be bakers, farmers, merchants, and homemakers but never to consider whether working as such was really a beneficial and just service. While Christians were exhorted to be honest and hard working, the actual content of their work was never questioned.

During the next century, with the increase in jobs (i.e., paid work), the notion of calling was reduced even further. Calling came to signify a type of job. One result of this change was that unpaid work was degraded. Real work was paid work; activities such as helping the needy, comforting the bereaved, visiting the sick, or assisting the poor were all right but were not considered to be real work.

This confusion of vocation, work, and job had implications for leisure. Work came to be defined as time devoted to a job. As such, life was fragmentized, and a dichotomy between work and leisure was created. While the tendency to reduce work to a job was not developed by the Reformers themselves, it later arose from their narrow understanding of calling and came to overshadow the biblical understanding of work and vocation.

The Deification of Work

Another distortion of the biblical understanding of work within Protestantism was the deification of work. English and American Puritans, along with German and Dutch Pietists, although in the tradition of the Reformation, developed a work ethic that drastically departed from the Reformers' ideas. For the Puritans, work was a divine mandate, while leisure was looked on as idleness. Success was sometimes viewed as a sign of God's favor, and the way to success was hard work and thrift. The Puritans, according to Vanderkloet, considered shalom as the reward for diligence and not a free gift from God that must pervade one's whole life.[24] But as Bob Goudzwaard pointed out, "Shalom is never attained in this way, for shalom is not the result of our work and our activities. Acceptance with God is the basis for our life and work!" The Puritan's interpretation of the Sabbath commandment often stressed "six days you shall labor" more than "remember the Sabbath (rest) day." Again the comments of Goudzwaard are helpful: "The Torah first says, 'Remember the Sabbath day to keep it holy,' and then adds, 'Six days you shall labour and do all your work.' Shalom thus precedes work and gives it its framework."[25]

Following in the Puritan tradition, there was a strong tendency to overvalue work in eighteenth- and nineteenth-century Protestantism. For example, John Wesley considered hard work and frugality to be of benefit to the soul, while later Charles Spurgeon instructed that work was a means of defense against the temptations of the devil.[26] The result has been an overemphasis of work within Protestantism. However, as we have seen from the biblical material presented in chapters 5 and 6, rest, in addition to work, is basic to the created nature of humans. Protestantism has generally overemphasized work at the expense of rest.

The Secularization of the Protestant Work Ethic

Let us summarize so far. The medieval theologians glorified spiritual work, relegated physical labor to secondary importance, and discouraged all economic activities. Calvin and Luther returned work to its intended place in creation as a God-given task and stressed that all work is to be of service to God and done as unto God. However, over time a number of changes in economic, political, and social thought and action converged in the Renaissance, the Enlightenment, and the subsequent Industrial Revolution, to overshadow the religious dimensions of the Protestant work ethic and thereby modify it into a more secularized view of work. Successive generations were decreasingly interested in the theological foundation of the work ethic and increasingly interested in its practical utility.

The secularization of the Protestant work ethic was influenced by the deistic rationalism of the Enlightenment, which placed humans at the center of life. God was no longer viewed as the living God who desired people to serve him and one another. Rather God was considered as a distant being who, following the creation of the world, had left the world to humans. Thus the world was compared to a clock that God had wound up and then left to operate on its own. In this world humans were guided by reason and not God's revelation.

Since humans were guided by reason and not God's revelation, humans were seen to be autonomous and at the center of life; God and his kingdom were demoted to a place of secondary importance. Work came to be motivated by a humanistic work ethic founded on the Renaissance faith that autonomous humans can conquer the world by means of one's own intellect and effort. Christian belief in the sinfulness of humans and the necessity of God's grace for salvation was replaced by a humanistic belief in the eventual perfectability of humans and human society through devotion to work. For example, the Puritan virtues of hard work and frugality were useful to Benjamin Franklin, but he severed them from the Christian faith that had embodied them. Hard work and frugality became important in and of themselves, and they were viewed to bring rewards in this world. It was thought that humans were self-sufficient; through intellectual effort, moral striving, and hard work a person could obtain all that he or she wanted. The world was a good and fruitful place; humans had only to take initiative and make the most of it. Work became a means to elevate and glorify humans, instead of a way to glorify God.

The social evolutionary theories of Herbert Spencer provided additional support to the belief that humans prosper by their own efforts. Through a free and unhindered quest for wealth, the strong would succeed while the weak and lazy would fall by the wayside. The secular work ethic gained further support from the view that "the progress of a society or a culture is something like the natural progress of a man; as he grows older and works harder, he accumulates more wisdom and more material things. . . . [Therefore] the idea of social progress and the sanctity of work as a means to achieve it grew into a now virtually unexamined ethic."[27] The religion of deistic rationalism provided the context necessary for the development of free enterprise and the idea of laissez-faire (the lack of government regulation and interference in the economy), which subsequently greatly influenced the purpose and conducting of work. While the medieval theologians and the Reformers believed that Christians should refrain from seeking their own end, Adam Smith raised the principle of self-interest to the dominant motivation in society. It was no longer necessary to consciously serve God and one another. Instead of people attempting to do good, goodwill emerges as the by-product of self-interest. According to Smith, the supposed "invisible hand" of the market will guarantee that everyone receives his or her due. Thus the government should not interfere in the market. God was nearly pushed out of the realm of work to be replaced by the god of profit and gain. Vanderkloet wrote that this humanist work ethic "was based on the so-called iron laws of nature; not on God's law of love."[28]

Although the Protestant work ethic had become secularized, Ryken pointed out that many confuse the secular work ethic with the Protestant work ethic. He points out six misconceptions of the Protestant ethic that are actually characteristics of the secular work ethic.

1. Work should absorb nearly all one's time.
2. Self-interest is the motivation for work.
3. Getting rich is the goal of life.
4. People can be successful through their own efforts.
5. Wealth is a sign of God's favor and evidence of one's salvation.
6. The Protestant work ethic approved of all types of business competition.[29]

Ryken concluded, "What goes by the name of 'the Protestant ethic' today is nearly the opposite of what the original Protestants actually advocated and practiced. Only when the religious conscience and theological framework had been removed did the original Protestant ethic acquire the traits that are mistakenly attributed to it."[30]

Unlike the medieval theologians and Reformers who condemned the ambition to become wealthy in this world and disciplined those who pursued material well-being out of economic self-interest, Renaissance thinkers and leaders approved of the desire to obtain wealth. Therefore wealth became the motivating force behind industrial development, and the means to that end became work. Renaissance entrepreneurs put into practice the idea (developed by John Locke, Smith, David Ricardo, and others) that the labor value is the real value of every commodity. Hence the worker was only valued in terms of his or her capacity to perform work. During the early part of the Industrial Revolution, this notion of the worker as a commodity was adopted by industrialists who were to drastically change the nature of work and leisure. The subsequent industrialization resulted in terribly inhuman working conditions. After the tremendous technological development of the second half of the eighteenth century, industrialization accelerated, and the miserable working conditions that followed were beyond description and were virtually unparalleled in Western history. Workdays of fourteen and sixteen hours were commonplace. Young children were taken to the factories as early as four in the morning. Fabun pointed out that the work of the Industrial Age was not like the kind of work that had been conducted in previous eras: "It was specially oriented in space (in the factory or foundry) and structured in time (the necessity for the worker to be in a certain place, at certain times, performing certain prescribed activities)."[31]

During the first half of the nineteenth century, the work ethic of unceasing labor began to take on the nature of a religion. In 1851, on the occasion of the opening of the Great Exhibition in the Crystal Palace in London, a showpiece of what work and industry had accomplished, *The Economist* printed the following editorial:

> We may briefly notice its [the Exhibition's] moral significance. The Queen of the mightiest empire of the globe—the empire in which industry is the most successfully cultivated, and in which its triumphs have been greatest—was fittingly occupied in consecrating the temple erected to its honour. . . . [T]he former disdain . . . for humble industry, and the present honour it bestows, telling of a future when the hand or the skill of the labourer shall be held in still higher honour . . . are convincing proofs of the moral improvements already made; and they give us irresistible assurances that a yet higher destiny awaits our successors even on earth.[32]

This glorification of work that accompanied industrialization led to an increasing separation of work and leisure. The economically productive functions became the most significant aspects of life, while leisure was relegated to the status of free time.

As the primarily agrarian society shifted toward an industrialized, urban society, the work ethic further developed into a "gospel of wealth," popularized by Andrew Carnegie, in which it was believed that wealth could greatly extend humanity's influence for good. In summarizing the belief system that is the basis of the gospel of wealth ethic, Albert T. Rasmussen identified the following principles that he gathered from *The American Business Creed*:

1. central emphasis on the individual;
2. self-reliance;
3. productivity: volume of material production as the chief measure of well-being;
4. activism as the most honored way of life;
5. progress as chief goal and hope;
6. optimism as the only valid personal and historical attitude;
7. competition as the key regulator of the economic system;
8. consumer sovereignty as ruler of production; and
9. self-interest or the profit motive as the decisive incentive in human effort.[33]

If these convictions are characteristic of the modern work ethic, Rasmussen was correct in concluding that "the demise and reversal of the Reformed view was virtually complete."[34] Thus the Protestant work ethic of the seventeenth and eighteenth centuries became the secular work ethic of the nineteenth and twentieth centuries. Perhaps the secular work ethic could be called the gospel of hard work, since, as Harvey Cox wrote, "disciplined work had become the secular substitute for religious devotion."[35]

The religious devotion with which work was to be pursued is reflected in a 1939 syndicated newspaper article by a columnist from the Midwest United States: "Work is divine. God is revealed as the great worker and it is through work that men become like God. It is through work that man finds his life and his life is measured by work. . . . To run away from work is to run away from life. To repudiate work is to commit suicide."[36] Some thirty years later, U.S. President Richard Nixon's view of work was not that much different: "The 'work ethic' holds that labor is good in itself; that a man or a woman becomes a better person by virtue of the act of working. America's competitive spirit, the 'work ethic' of this people, is alive and well on Labor Day, 1971."[37] This modern belief in work was summarized by Wayne Oates as follows: "(a) a religious virtue, (b) a form of patriotism, (c) the way to win friends and influence people, and (d) the way to be healthy, wealthy, and wise."[38]

That work is a virtue is not unique to Western society. Marxists have also exalted work, although in doing so they have deviated to some extent from Karl Marx's teachings. Although Marx believed that a person becomes fully human only through work, he envisioned a world in which the worker would not only be able to work at various tasks but also could devote much of his time to leisure. However, Marx's colleague, Friedrich Engels, who grew up in a pietist home (as did many of his followers), increasingly exalted work as an end in itself. Consequently, in Marxist countries, religious significance was given to the worker and his work. Aleksandr Solzhenitsyn wrote in his *Gulag Archipelago* that the administrators of the Gulag's labor camps viewed hard work as a purifying and cleansing experience.[39]

The Decline of the Work Ethic

Today there is an increasing awareness that work is no longer considered as the moral and religious center of life. In 1972 Dahl wrote that instead of work, the present ethic of today "is that life revolves around leisure activities and leisure goods, that money is to be spent before it is ever earned, and that pleasure is to be pursued."[40] Although this shift away from a work orientation has manifested itself only in recent decades, it is the result of several major societal forces—including the increasing value placed on wealth and prosperity, the philosophy of utilitarianism, and technological advancements—over the past century or more.

As I have already noted, the desire to become wealthy was one of the significant factors that contributed to the industrial development of the nineteenth century. During the past two centuries in Western societies, increasing value has been placed on wealth and property. Hence the primary motivations in our culture are no longer service to God and neighbor, but self-fulfillment and the accumulation of material possessions. This philosophy of life has been influenced by utilitarianism.

With utilitarianism, pain and pleasure became the new determinants of good and evil. Both manufacturers and consumers adopted the utilitarian approach and began to regard the ownership of material possessions as pleasure (hence good) and the carrying out of work as pain (hence evil). With utilitarianism, work was no longer deified and exalted but became a necessary pain. Obviously these ideas are in opposition to what the Bible teaches when it often warns against idolatry of material possessions and upholds work as part of God's purpose for humans in creation.

Another factor that has led to the demise of the work ethic was the increasing use of technology. Technology has made it possible to produce more goods in a shorter period of time. Ironically, it is not the work ethic's failure but its success that has led to its demise. Motivated by their high view of work in the past, North Americans have produced such an abundance of material possessions and technological conveniences that now they cannot resist the temptation to enjoy it! Actually, the continued growth of the North American economy is dependent on residents' increasing ability to consume all the goods and conveniences they have toiled so hard to produce. In the past the economy required as many members of society as possible to be involved in the production process. In its early stages, the North American economy did not need people who spent and consumed. Rather, it needed frugal, hard workers and consumers who could invest. For many years expansion of the economy came through the transformation of raw materials into finished products. Today, "its expansion is dependent upon speeding the flow of goods from the assembly line to the trash heap."[41] Furthermore, since the concept of deferred rewards is no longer economically functional, our credit-based economy demands that we consume the commodities and services we produce as quickly as possible. In recent decades the health of the economy has depended on aggregate demand being sufficient to purchase goods; therefore since the 1940s politicians and business people have been persuading people to consume.

At present, secularized North Americans are experiencing a transition between the two ethics as the new consumption-ethic has created a new set of values that are destructive of the work ethic. Our society now appears to be experiencing tension between the traditional values associated with the work ethic, which taught that work was a virtue that contributed to moral character, and the rising trend to pursue leisure (really pleasure and consumption) through experiencing, gratifying, playing, getting as much discretionary time as possible, living it up, acting on impulse, doing what feels good now, and so on.

Meanwhile, it is likely that the average citizen lives out the paradox documented in the first part of this chapter. He or she is less than satisfied with work, yet at the same time knows that work should be a central part of meaningful human experience. In addition, work is seen as a necessity in order to purchase the consumer goods for a "comfortable life," which is mistakenly believed to be the life of leisure. The average person experiences a tension between the work ethic and the consumption ethic, or what some people would call a leisure ethic. Let us turn to examine how this tension may be resolved from a biblical perspective.

9

the biblical view of work

In this chapter I first look at what the Old Testament teaches concerning work, then move on to the New Testament instructions about work, before seeking guidance from the book of Ecclesiastes concerning the relationship between work and leisure.

The Old Testament View of Work

I will first summarize Old Testament teaching, then look more specifically at work as portrayed in Genesis 1–3, and finally elaborate on three biblical reasons to work. Much of the information in this section is gleaned from Richardson's *The Biblical Doctrine of Work*, which is a concise summary of his interpretation of the biblical position on work.[1]

According to Richardson, the biblical concept of work "includes everything from the activity of God in creation to the toil of the meanest slave. The same word is used in the Old Testament to cover work, effort, labour, toil, service and even worship."[2] When the biblical writers employed the word "work" in reference to humans they usually were thinking of "ordinary, everyday, more-or-less monotonous toil." Rarely did they refer to the type of work that today is called creative. Thus the most frequent usage of the word "work" in the Bible is in the sense of men's and women's "ordinary, everyday, routine labour, by which [they earn their] daily bread."[3] It may be described as ongoing work, such as cooking and cleaning, planting and harvesting, without which people would not have food, clothing, and other necessities for a healthy life, and without which society would be unable to function. Work in this sense of everyday routine is regarded as a normal, appropriate, and inevitable part of human life, and as such it is a regular part of the created order of the world just as the sun rises or lions hunt: "Then people go out to their work, to their labor until evening" (Ps. 104:23). The wisdom literature contains many warnings against idleness and exhortations to work with diligence (e.g., Prov. 6:6), while some of the prophets' most severe condemnations are directed toward the idle rich (e.g., Amos 6:3–6).

In contrast to the Greeks, who considered that working for one's livelihood was below the honor of a gentleman, the biblical writers never regarded work as humiliating. The Hebrews viewed daily work as an accepted component of the divine ordering of creation from which no one was exempt. Generally in the Old Testament there was no stigma associated with working as a servant ('ebed). It was not even degrading for a king to do physical work. Saul's plowing with his oxen did not detract from his royal dignity (1 Sam. 11:5). Likewise David, a shepherd, became the ideal king.

The instruction of the Old Testament concerning work may be summarized by saying that work is an indispensable and God-ordained function of human existence. In the biblical writings work is assumed to be part of a divinely ordered structure of the world and of human nature. So widespread and accepted is this assumption in biblical thought that it is not stated in a specific commandment, such as, "Thou shalt not be idle." This is even more significant since, as we saw previously, there is a command to abstain from work on the Sabbath—a commandment that contains the subsidiary clause, "Six days you shall labor and do all your work" (Exod. 20:9). However, this clause seems to be more a statement of a fact than a command. That the Sabbath commandment is an order to rest from work suggests that humans, by their very nature, are workers. A human is so created, wrote Richardson, "that not only can he not satisfy his material needs without working, but also he cannot satisfy his spiritual needs or fulfill his function as a human being."[4] This biblical insight is reflected in the lives of some unemployed people today.

The Teaching of Genesis 1–3

The teaching of the Old Testament on work, which I have just summarized, reflects Genesis 1–3 where we see that work was a part of God's original purpose for humans at the time of creation. The creation account of Genesis 1–2 in which the ordinance of work has a central place, along with the account of humanity's fall in Genesis 3, gives us much insight into a biblical understanding of work.

In Genesis 1 and 2 God is portrayed as a worker. Day by day his creative work unfolds. Then when he creates man and woman he makes them workers too. In verse 26 and again in verses 27 and 28 of chapter 1, the relationship between humans created in the image of God (v. 27) and the human task to rule over creation is emphasized: "Be fruitful and increase in number; fill the earth and subdue it. Rule over the fish in the sea and the birds in the sky and over every living creature that moves on the ground" (v. 28). Thus God created humans to be his stewards to care for the earth on his behalf.

In Genesis 2 we read that humans are put into a well-watered garden—planted by God—of "trees that were pleasing to the eye and good for food" (v. 9). Humans are placed in this garden for the purpose of cultivating it: "The LORD God took the man and put him in the Garden of Eden to work it and take care of it" (v. 15). Later in this account (v. 19) humans are called on to name each living creature.

In summary, what have we learned about work from the creation account? First, work—in the sense of subduing the earth and of ruling over nature (1:28), of tilling and caring (2:15), of ordering and organizing (2:19)—is essential to God's purposes for human life. Second, work is also an activity that reflects the divine image.

The account of humanity's fall immediately after the account of creation implies, according to Graham Dow, that both these accounts should illumine our understanding of the world: "That is, we are to view human society through the interpretive keys of both creation and fall, held firmly together." As we have seen, the first two chapters of Genesis reveal that humans have the privilege, honor, and task to develop, through work, the world under God (Gen. 1:28). However, the story of the fall tells us that work now turns into a sweat and struggle to stay alive (Gen. 3:19). So the accounts of the creation and of the fall, wrote Dow, "offers us opposite extremes and the whole range of human work lies somewhere on the range between them, interpreted in the light of both."[5]

Although it is sometimes claimed that the Bible instructs that work is inflicted by God on humanity as a punishment for sin, the Genesis account does not depict work as a consequence of sin but rather as part of the very purpose of God in creation of both the world and humans that occurred before the fall. Therefore work in itself should not be described as a "curse" or as a punishment for sin. Nevertheless, the account of the fall in Genesis 3 informs us that human work is placed under a curse.

> Cursed is the ground because of you;
>> through painful toil you will eat food from it
>> all the days of your life.
> It will produce thorns and thistles for you,
>> and you will eat the plants of the field.
> By the sweat of your brow
>> you will eat your food
> until you return to the ground,
>> since from it you were taken;
> for dust you are
>> and to dust you will return. (vv. 17–19)

In this passage we see that the curse displays itself especially in the realm of work; empirical verification of this biblical insight is common to our own experience. That the ground produces thorns and thistles reflects the cosmic disordering of creation, which is the consequence of humanity's rebellion against God. This cosmic disordering of creation greatly influences the conditions of human work. I agree with Marshall "that in Genesis the curse was not the imposition of labour as such but only that labour would become harsh and painful; it is clear that work was considered one of the blessings before the fall."[6]

It is from these Genesis accounts of creation and the fall that we must develop a biblical understanding of work. From these accounts, Richardson articulated six points about work that I will briefly summarize and where possible relate to our discussion of leisure.[7]

First, work is a necessary element of human life; humans are created to be workers. Therefore to not have the opportunity to work is to be "something less than a human being, created in the image of God, who is himself represented as a worker (cf. Gen. 2:3)."[8] In the chapter on Sabbath we saw how rest is an integral part of human nature. Hence we can conclude that both rest and work are basic to human's created nature.

Second, to perform the work that humans have been instructed by God to do—to rule the earth and to care for it—is to fulfill the purpose of God in creation. Thus work is in itself a privilege and not a curse. When work is seen as a privilege and not a curse, the tendency to hate work and to overvalue leisure, which often leads to a dichotomizing of the two, will be minimized.

Third, although work is a privilege given to humans by God, work has been thwarted by human sin: the whole domain of human work, which should have been the realm of humanity's happy cooperation with God for creation's benefit, has become a sphere of self-seeking, competition, and mismanagement. The good intention of God in creation is partly hindered. Thus we need to keep work in its proper perspective; we should not overvalue work (and in so doing devalue leisure), nor should we believe that work alone will solve all the world's problems.

Fourth, since humans try to ignore or hide from the reality of sin, they dream of a Utopia brought about via technological advances through which the drudgery of work, although not totally removed, will be greatly reduced. This dream is expressed in talk, less prevalent now as a few decades ago, of a future leisure society. However, it must be emphasized that ideas, such as that work in itself is bad or dehumanizing, or that science and technology will lead us into a workless paradise, are not consistent with the biblical idea of humans as workers.

Fifth, following from point four, human ignorance does not nullify the creational ordinance of work. This does not mean that we are not to try via technological or other advancements to alleviate the drudgery of work; rather, it is our Christian responsibility to reduce in whatever way possible "the 'curse of

Adam' to eradicate the 'thorns and thistles' and to wipe off the 'sweat' from the face of man."[9] Yet God's command, "Six days you shall labor and do all your work," still remains. Although this command should not be taken too literally, it certainly does imply that it is a human responsibility to put in an honest week's work. We cannot escape our responsibility to work by living a life of only leisure time or leisure activity. As we have already seen in a previous chapter, life is to consist of a rhythm of rest and work.

Sixth, the creational ordinance of work must be seen within the totality of biblical teaching, which is given for the well-being and blessing of humans. Although work at times seems oppressive and hateful, it is actually one element of God's goodness to humans. The task of work that is given to humans is for their own good, however unattractive working may appear. Thus "the good life" includes not only leisure but also work. Mark Geldard wrote,

> God calls man to be a worker—to dominion and service. This mandate embodies a picture of the good life. Thus whilst forms of activity which do not come under the theological categories of dominion and care may yet be important in terms of rest, relaxation and pure fun, they cannot ever be regarded as a substitute for work.[10]

Three Biblical Reasons to Work

To further demonstrate how, according to the Bible, work is a blessing and why humans are to work and not have only leisure, let us elaborate on three biblical reasons why we are to work: (1) work is a means to meet human needs; (2) work is a means of human fulfillment; and (3) work is for the stewardship of God's creation.[11]

Work Is a Means to Meet Human Needs. Work is closely connected with the satisfaction of basic subsistence needs. Within the Genesis account it is evident that an integral part of human work in creation is to be that harmonious interaction with the created world through which one's basic needs are met. In Genesis 1:29, God says, "I give you every seed-bearing plant on the face of the whole earth and every tree that has fruit with seed in it. They will be yours for food." John Stott speculated that by working and caring for the garden of Eden, Adam fed and possibly clothed his family.[12] After the fall, however, food did not come so easily: "By the sweat of your brow you will eat your food" (Gen. 3:19). So before and after the fall, work was necessary for the meeting of basic subsistence needs.

Besides providing for subsistence needs, the Bible also stresses work as productive service to others. The Old Testament covenant codes teach that work is not just to be for the benefit of a person and the person's immediate family but also for the whole community (Lev. 23:22; Deut. 24:19–22). The poor, the foreigner, the fatherless, and the widow were also to share in the produce of the land. Work must be a service designed for the benefit of society since, as Stott wrote, "though we depend on God for life, we depend on each other for the necessities of life, not only of physical life (food, clothing, shelter, warmth and health) but of social life too (everything that goes to make up civilized society)."[13]

Work Is a Means of Human Fulfillment. Work is intended to be a means of human fulfillment. Since work-related satisfaction was part of God's intention for humans in creation, the human spirit suffers without work. Dow claimed it is impossible not to conclude that human work reflects the Creator's creativity, for God is clearly depicted in Genesis as the archetypal worker who worked six days and rested one during creation. As we saw previously, there is an obvious analogy between God's rhythm in the creation account and the Sabbath commandment wherein Israel was to work six days and rest one. Thus the human function of work, like that of rest, "is to be understood as grounded in the being and activity of God."[14]

Furthermore, the two parts of Genesis 1:26 go together: "Let us make human beings in our image" and "so that they may rule over" all the creatures. Likewise, the instruction to subdue the earth in verse 28 is introduced by the affirmation in verse 27 that God created humans in his own image. It is due to our being created in God's image that we are to rule over the earth. Thus human capacity for creative work, claimed Stott, is an integral part of one's godlike humanness, and without work one is not completely human.[15] Since we are made in the image of God and since God was obviously satisfied with all he had created when he described creation as being "very good" (Gen. 1:31), we may then infer with Dow "that man's activity to develop the world under God is intended to be creative and satisfying."[16]

We can perhaps articulate this notion of creativity in work from a slightly different angle. According to Geldard the creative aspect of work is rooted in the very structure of the created world.[17] At one level the work of creation is completed (Gen. 2:1–2), yet at another, it is not. God has left immense scope for humans to use their creativity and resourcefulness in caring for creation. The world was created with such great diversity (see Gen. 2:10–27) that humanity's work of subduing, ruling, tilling, caring, and naming has overflowed with numerous creative possibilities from the beginning. As Derek Kidner wrote, humans were "blessed with an immense creative task from the first."[18] The very fact of creation's incredible diversity—together with the great variety of human need—requires that human work must involve creativity and therefore requires a large input of physical, mental, emotional, and social energy.

In conclusion, work should leave us with a deep sense of satisfaction and self-fulfillment. If instead of being active we are idle, or instead of being creative we are destructive, we are not fully human and thereby not self-fulfilled. It is therefore very tragic that many people in our society, due to the conditions of their work, do not have the opportunity for this satisfaction and fulfillment. As a result, Vanderkloet noted, these people "are virtually forced to seek happiness in their leisure and the possession of goods."[19] It is regrettable that the opportunity for creative satisfaction in work has been so eliminated that paid employment for many people has been reduced to the means for earning an income so that their non-work time (leisure in a quantitative sense) may be enjoyed. From the biblical perspective, this is tragic for "there is nothing better for a person than to enjoy their work" (Eccles. 3:22; see also 2:24).

Work Is for the Stewardship of God's Creation. Work involves our stewardly care of all the potentialities and resources of creation. We have already seen from Genesis 1:26, 28 and 2:15, 19 that God calls us to be co-creators and co-stewards with him. God has intentionally humbled himself to enlist the cooperation of humans in tending creation. He created the world but assigned to humans the work of subduing it. He planted a garden but commissioned a gardener to till and keep it. Stott wrote, "Creation and cultivation, nature and culture, raw materials and craftsmanship belong together."[20]

This work of tending creation has been described in numerous ways: creative management under God; stewardship; collaboration or partnership with God; and humanization.[21] The idea of divine-human cooperation applies to all honorable work. God has so created life in this world as to rely on our work. Therefore "whatever our work, we need to see it as being—either directly or indirectly—cooperation with God" to fulfill the intentions of creation.[22]

As cooperation with God in fulfilling the intentions of creation, work is a form of worship and a way to glorify God. St. Bernard of Clairvaux said, "He who labors as he prays lifts his heart to God with his hands." Jesus said, "Let your light shine before others, that they may see your good deeds and glorify your Father in heaven" (Matt. 5:16). Since the worship of God is expressed in the work a person does to fulfill his or her role as steward, human worship will be complete only if a person cares for God's creation in a way in which God is honored and the welfare of the person's neighbor is truly served.

Human stewardship of creation is not only a task and a form of worship but also a means of blessing and satisfaction, for it enhances the enjoyment of leisure and rest, as Vanderkloet elaborated.

> In history we see that God blesses man when he performs his task in obedience to the divine norms of stewardship. The faithful servant, who will be busy when the Master comes, shall be rewarded in the present as well as in the hereafter. Despite the curse of sin, many may enjoy the fruits of his labours and may rejoice in the product of his hands, because his handiwork mirrors God's handiwork. Man is not doomed to slavish labour all the days of his life. The satisfaction derived from his daily work and the joyful reflection on his accomplishments presuppose the enjoyment of leisure and rest.[23]

In summary, the Old Testment illustrates that work is a regular part of everyday life. The creation account tells us that work is essential to God's purposes for human life. Work, like rest, is basic to the created nature of humans. Furthermore, the biblical account informs us that work is a necessity to meet

The New Testament View of Work

In the New Testament the word "work" is often used but rarely in the sense of human's daily toil for survival. The New Testament does not say much concerning human's working life since the New Testament writers were more concerned with the central truth of the gospel. The primary New Testament usage of the word "work," according to Richardson, is the special task of Christians, which is "the furtherance of the Gospel and the service of the purpose of God."[24]

Although not much is said about working life in the New Testament, it is assumed throughout that daily work is not a hindrance in Christian living but is a necessary element of it. The people of the New Testament were immersed in the life and difficulties of the working world. Most of the apostles were from a humble working background and occasionally returned to their work after becoming disciples. Jesus was a carpenter for the majority of his adult life.

As far as we know the apostle Paul did not develop any systematic teaching on work. However, his epistles include a consistent argument against idleness, and he wrote several exhortations on work (see 2 Thess. 3:6–10). He does not distinguish between physical and spiritual work. For example, he uses the same words to describe both the physical work by which he made a living and the spiritual work of his apostolic service (see Rom. 16:12; 1 Cor. 4:12; 15:10; 16:16; Gal. 4:11; Eph. 4:28; Phil. 2:16; Col. 1:29; 1 Thess. 5:12). Frequently it is difficult to determine to which he is referring. For him all work begins in faith. Work for him is not confined to liberal pursuits; it is physical labor that he most frequently refers to. When he describes the life of the "new self, created to be like God in true righteousness and holiness," he exhorts believers to "work, doing something useful with their own hands" (Eph. 4:24, 28; see also verses 17–32). Paul did physical work so as not to burden the church. In spite of his good education, he did manual work to support others, and he advocated the same practice for other Christians (Acts 20:35; 2 Cor. 11:9; 12:13; 1 Thess. 4:11; 2 Thess. 3:8).

The House-Tables

The so-called house-tables found in the Epistles (Eph. 6:5–9; Col. 3:22–4:1; 1 Tim. 6:1–2; Titus 2:9–10; and 1 Pet. 2:18–25) contain the only specific teaching that we find in the New Testament on the subject of daily work. Called "house-tables" by Luther, these household codes in Paul are teachings to various members of the household according to their role and status (husbands/wives, parents/children, masters/slaves).[25] According to Richardson, these passages expound the attitude and responsibilities of Christian slaves (*douloi*, i.e., workers) who carried out the daily labor of the household, farm, and workshop in the biblical world; although not directly comparable to workers today, they were the laboring classes of their day.[26] Paul's advice to slaves does not mean he uncritically accepted slavery, but illustrates that he did not look down on the work of slaves, but viewed it as service to God just like his own work.[27]

The house-tables go beyond Stoic teachings about faithfulness in work and are based on the truth that it is to Christ that the Christian primarily performs his or her work and not to those who are "earthly masters." Thus the motivation for work, according to the New Testament, is not natural law, as the Stoic would suggest, or even the keeping of an Old Testament ordinance, but obedience to Christ, the Christian's heavenly master: "Slaves, obey your earthly masters with respect and fear, and with sincerity of heart, just as you would obey Christ. Obey them not only to win their favor when their eye is on you, but as slaves of Christ, doing the will of God from your heart. Serve wholeheartedly, as if you were serving the Lord, not people" (Eph. 6:5–7). The house-tables demonstrate that a new attitude toward work has been initiated through faith in Jesus Christ and that by following Christ's example, a Christian's work is foremost something offered to the Lord and not to humans. Here we do not simply have a rule or code of work that is to be legalistically followed but instead an attitude, a spirit. The house-tables suggest that the fulfillment of the creational ordinance of work is possible due to the transformed heart of the redeemed person. When a person repents and puts his or her faith in Christ, all areas of life, including work, have the potential of being sanctified. As Peter Nijkamp wrote, "Clearly, the fall into sin exerted a destructive influence, but through Christ Jesus the original human task has been restored, so that labour renders a service to the coming kingdom of God."[28]

Christians do not work out of obedience to law or duty as a Stoic; nor do they work simply under the pressure of necessity or fear, or out of the desire for reward or profit (as an "economic human"), but their motive is one of thanksgiving to their divine master—"doing the will of God from your heart" (Eph. 6:6; cf. Col. 3:23). The faithfulness of Christians in their work is an expression of their grateful appreciation to God for what he has done for them in Christ. What had previously been done as a duty, or for self-expression and fulfillment, is now carried out "as if you were serving the Lord," and becomes an activity of free service, as well as a source of profound satisfaction. The Christian knows that when his or her work is performed "as if you were serving the Lord, not people," then his or her indescribable reward is "from the Lord." In working "as if you were serving the Lord," the Christian finds true liberty: "freedom from the enslavement to 'duty', from ambitions of worldly reward and fears of earthly penalties from the frustrations of limiting circumstances and from the anxiety about his status, reputation or 'security.'"[29]

In conclusion, work as seen from the perspective of the New Testament is the expression of an attitude, a spirit of thanksgiving to Christ, one's divine master. As such, our work, our doing, flows from our being, from our life in Christ. If we remember from previous chapters that leisure can be a condition of our being, then the artificial dichotomy between being and doing, between work and leisure, prevalent in our society is broken down. We may be able to experience leisure as we work. Work, our doing, may flow from our attitude of leisure.

An Aside on 2 Thessalonians 3:7–12

As leisure textbooks sometimes quote 2 Thessalonians 3:10 to illustrate and explain a biblical view of work, it is helpful to take an in-depth look at this passage. For example, Henderson and colleagues directly quoted part of this verse, "If any would not work, neither shall he eat," to support their statement that "diligent work is praised as a virtue in several Biblical passages."[30] While Henderson and colleagues made reference to one other verse (1 Thess. 4:11), the partial quotation of 2 Thessalonians 3:10 is the only direct quotation they made from the biblical record to support their statement. In a discussion of Christianity and work, Goodale and Godbey did not reference or directly quote 2 Thessalonians 3:10 but they alluded to it in a paraphrase: "And Paul, in his missionary work, was quite clear; if you want to eat, then you must work," and then incorrectly attributed to Paul the phrase from Genesis, "From the sweat of thy brow."[31] In a discussion of the Judeo-Christian view of leisure, Sylvester[32] also quoted this verse, and included the two subsequent verses as well: "If any would not work, neither should he eat. For we hear that there are some who walk among you disorderly, working not at all, but are busybodies. Now them that are such we command and exhort by our Lord Jesus Christ, that with quietness they work, and eat their own bread (3:10–13)." Neither Henderson and colleagues, Goodale and Godbey, nor Sylvester explained the context of this passage. While Sylvester referenced and quoted other biblical passages, the majority of these referred to God's work (Gen. 2:2; 1 Cor. 3:10; Pss. 7:28; 22:24) or what we would commonly refer to today as spiritual activities (1 Cor. 3:9; Matt. 4:19).

Historical Context. To understand this passage we need to be aware of its historical and literary context. In regard to historical context, during his second missionary journey, the apostle Paul visits Thessalonica for several weeks (as recounted in Acts 17:1–10) probably in the early summer of 50 CE.[33] However, opposition forces him to leave the city before he is able to deliver all the instructions that he thought are necessary for a newly formed Christian community (1 Thess. 3:10). The newly formed church in Thessalonica has experienced active persecution. Paul sends his companion Timothy back to Thessalonica. When Timothy returns to Paul he reports that the Thessalonian Christians are standing firm in spite of persecution. However, there are several topics on which they want further teaching, in particular, teaching about the return of Christ. Paul is pleased with Timothy's good report and writes to encourage these Thessalonian Christians and to respond to their practical problems. His letter, what we know as the first Epistle to the Thessalonians, is thought to have been written toward the end of 50 CE. The letter is primarily a missionary's letter to new Christians that includes teaching on eschatology (final times) and the parousia (the personal presence, coming of Christ) in order to clarify some confusion on this topic (1 Thess. 2:19; 3:13; 4:13–5:4, 23; cf. 2 Thess. 2:1–12).[34] The second Epistle to the Thessalonians to a large extent deals with a similar situation as that of the first Epistle. The persecution of the Thessalonian Christians seems to have been less at this time, but excitement and confusion about the return of Christ still existed.[35] Thus a primary reason for writing 2 Thessalonians was to clarify a misconception about the parousia: "Its main aim is to tell them certain things which will calm their hysteria and make them wait, not in excited idleness, but in patient and diligent attendance to the day's work."[36]

Literary Context. In terms of literary context, Paul's instruction about work in 2 Thessalonians 3:10 must be seen in conjunction with his teaching in his first Epistle to the Thessalonians. In 1 Thessalonians 4:11, Paul writes, "Make it your ambition to lead a quiet life: You should mind your own business and work with your hands, just as we told you, so that your daily life may win the respect of outsiders and so that you will not be dependent on anybody." Commentators see these instructions as a response to the unhealthy situation where there was an overemphasis and hysteria about the second coming of Christ. Some Christians in Thessalonica had a fanatical expectancy about Christ's return and neglected their work and daily responsibilities, which made them a burden on others and gave the church a bad name.[37] In 2 Thessalonians 3:6–14, Paul addresses a situation similar to the one he addressed in 1 Thessalonians, where some Christians think that Christ's return is so imminent that they give up their work and their normal everyday activities to wait about in excited and restless idleness.[38] However, only some were involved; the problem was not widespread.[39] The verb Paul uses to describe the idleness of these people is *ataktōs*, which means "to play truant." Within this context he refers to both his own example of working while with them and his previous teaching. He continues with a play on words in the Greek, *mēden ergazomenous alla periergazomenous*, which is captured in the TNIV as "They are not busy; they are busybodies" (v. 11). In other words, they have not only neglected their own activities but they have also interfered in the activities of others.

Application. The saying "Anyone who is unwilling to work shall not eat" occurs in a very specific context where the original readers had a confused understanding of eschatology and expected the immediate return of Christ. Therefore direct applications to other contexts require caution. It should be noted that this frequently quoted and misunderstood saying was not a callous expression toward those who were unable to support themselves. The verse states, "Anyone who is unwilling to work shall not eat," and not, "Anyone who does not work shall not eat." Stott noted that "it was addressed to the voluntary, not involuntary, unemployed; it condemns laziness not redundancy."[40] Denys Whitely stated, "The passage deals with refusal to work, not with inability to do so. In the 1930s it was necessary to stress this fact because millions were unemployed against their will."[41] John Vernon McGee provided an example of a modern situation that might be similar to the original context of this verse when he described a situation where two students at a theological seminary sat in their dormitory and did not show up for meals or engage in the daily activities, as they thought they would receive some sort of special revelation if they waited patiently.[42] Paul Marshall interpreted this verse as follows: "He [Paul] was asserting that a life of leisure or one solely devoted to religious contemplation was a deficient life—that all members of the church should be involved in useful activity."[43]

The saying "Anyone who is unwilling to work shall not eat," from 2 Thessalonians 3:10, has no doubt been quoted out of context by Christians (e.g., Falwell[44]) and leisure scholars. If it is not put into its historical and literary context, the saying definitely suggests a strong work orientation and even sounds overly harsh and callous to contemporary readers. It is important to understand this verse within its original context and within the total biblical teaching on work, which is conditioned by other biblical elements suggestive of leisure.

Paul's statement in 2 Thessalonians 3:7–12 is also a confirmation that until the second coming of Christ the creational ordinance of work is to continue. The New Testament provides no evidence to those who ceased taking their work seriously but expected a consummation in the present, a consummation that will actually occur only when Christ returns. Today there are some who believe progress in history will culminate in a utopian leisure society in which work will no longer be necessary. From a biblical perspective these people are victims of an incorrect eschatology or futurology just as much as were those in the Thessalonian church.

The Balance of Work and Leisure in Ecclesiastes

The book of Ecclesiastes addresses both those who espouse a compulsive work ethic and those who live a hedonistic leisure ethic, but it also points a way to a true alternative—the enjoyment of the life, including work, that God has given us. Let us look at what Qoheleth, the writer of Ecclesiastes, has to say about each of these three ways of life.

The Work Ethic

Johnston, in his essay "'Confessions of a Workaholic': A Reappraisal of Qoheleth," believed that Qoheleth juxtaposes two alternatives for one's controlling attitude toward life: the meaninglessness of human work over against an acknowledgment that life is to be lived in joy or, to put it simply, work versus joy. Instead of concentrating on the joy inherent in life itself, Qoheleth focuses on the misuse of work that results from a work-oriented lifestyle. Hence Johnston understood Qoheleth to be primarily concerned with the limits of human work, which include

> that man's common lot, his destiny, is death (cf. 9:2, 3; 2:15; 3:1; 5:12–16; 6:6; 7:2; 8:8; 12:1–7) . . . the realization that man lives out his life amidst an indiscernible moral order (cf. 7:15; 8:14); that wisdom is transitory at best and life uncertain (cf. 4:13–16; 9:13–16); and that wisdom is fragile and easily defeated in the presence of riches and folly (cf. 9:16–10:1).[45]

Thus Qoheleth questions human effort to master life through work. According to Qoheleth, the attempt to master life is mistaken not only because the realities of life frequently frustrate the attempt (the good person is not always the most successful) but also because it is an insult to God's independence. Since God is sovereign and beyond our understanding, we cannot presume to comprehend his ways (Eccles. 3:11; 6:10; 7:13–14, 23–24; 8:17).[46]

Gordis pointed out that throughout Ecclesiastes, and especially in 4:4–16, Qoheleth emphasizes the folly of hard work.[47] Let us look at a few selected texts that can offer advice on work before examining 4:4–16 in some detail.

Ecclesiastes 2:17–26. In this passage Qoheleth suggests that work has no ultimate value since humans frequently must, without any say in the matter, leave the result of their work to someone else (vv. 18–23). Instead a person is "to eat and drink and find satisfaction in their toil" (2:24a). But Qoheleth immediately informs his readers that this satisfaction comes "from the hand of God" (2:24b). God's grace, not a person's work, is the source of human satisfaction.

Ecclesiastes 5:9–16. Here Qoheleth describes the futility of working to achieve life's meaning through the possession of transitory riches.

> They take nothing from their toil
>   that they can carry in their hands.
>   This too is a grievous evil:
> As everyone comes, so they depart,
>   and what do they gain,
>   since they toil for the wind? (5:15b–16)

Ecclesiastes 6:7–9. Here Qoheleth begins with a negative conclusion that may be paraphrased: "There is no advantage, no self-profit, either in toil or in wisdom."[48] He then continues with the positive affirmation in 6:9, "Better what the eye sees / than the roving of the appetite." This is qualified by the concluding phrase, "This too is meaningless, / a chasing after the wind."

Ecclesiastes 4:4–16. In these verses, Qoheleth again discusses the futility of work but in more detail. Throughout history the value of diligence and hard work has often been stressed. In this passage Qoheleth refutes three arguments often put forward in support of hard work: the need to achieve (v. 4); the desire for wealth (v. 8); and the desire to gain fame (vv. 13–16).

The Need to Achieve. Verses 4–6 consist of a sample of attitudes toward work that remind us of the familiar contemporary extremes. Verse 4 reads: "And I saw that all toil and all achievement spring from one person's envy of another. This too is meaningless, a chasing after the wind." Here Qoheleth suggests all work and all skill in work are motivated by rivalry or greed. The creative skill that people glory in is really a disguise for their desire to outdo or not be out-done by others. Thus human rivalry or greed is the chief motivation in work. The precise idea, suggested Eaton, is not that work leads to rivalry but that it arises from rivalry. Effort put forth in work, along with the skills demonstrated, frequently hides the struggles for wealth, authority, power, or prestige. Beneath the surface is a restless desire to surpass others. Yet, Eaton wrote, if work "origi-nates in ambition (4:4), if its progress is liable to be inherited by folly (2:19, 21) if its results may be nil (1:3; 5:15), any hope of gain can come only from God (3:13; 5:18f.)."[49]

The second portrait of attitudes toward work (4:5) illustrates the opposite extreme—escaping from the working life. From the conclusion of verse 4 ("This [all labor and all achievement] too is meaningless, a chasing after the wind"), it might seem warranted to simply forget about work altogether since it is so caught up with rivalry. Commenting on this verse, Walter C. Kaiser Jr. asked, "Why should anyone want to work so hard in a dog-eat-dog world, only to be envied as the reward for his success?"[50] Nevertheless, Qoheleth admonishes that the problems of the working life, such as competitiveness, should not be an excuse to drop out. And to make his point he inserts the proverb "Fools fold their hands / and ruin themselves" (v. 5). Eaton pointed out that the phrase "to fold the hands" means to be idle (see Prov. 6:10).[51] This portrait, then, is the contrary of 4:4.

We move from the person caught up in the rat race who works frantically to achieve status and power, to the drop-out who scorns endless activity. He is called a "fool," for his avoidance of work is as much an error as those who are frantically busy. He is the image of total complacency and unknowing self-destruction, for this observation of him identifies a greater danger than a deple-tion of his monetary savings. He figuratively "eats his own flesh" after consuming the food he has stored up. His condition is described as self-cannibalism since he consumes his own flesh. Kidner wrote that the fool's idleness eats away not only at one's possessions but also who one is, therefore eroding one's self-control, one's grasp of reality, one's capacity for care, and, in the end, one's self-respect.[52]

To both these extreme attitudes concerning work Qoheleth offers a true al-ternative. Instead of frantic competitiveness in work and slothfulness in activity, Qoheleth recommends moderation.

> Better one handful with tranquillity
>   than two handfuls with toil
>   and chasing after the wind. (v. 6)

The "one handful with tranquillity" is the middle way between the hectic working of verse 4 and the escapism of verse 5. The writer proclaims that one handful attained with tranquillity is better than two handfuls earned through much work. Kidner explained that the expression "one handful with tranquillity" conveys the twofold idea of modest demands and inner peace: an attitude toward work that is radically different from the worker's struggle for preeminence and the fool's selfish idleness and ease.[53] Eaton wrote, "The way of wisdom will attempt much (one handful) but not too much (two hands full), and so will find life within its grasp (one handful) not an impossible strain (striving for wind)." Such a life is "a gift" (5:19; see also 9:7–10) "from the hand of God" (2:24). This middle way is also seen in the proverbs "Better a little with the fear of the LORD / than great wealth with turmoil" (Prov. 15:16; see also v. 17), and "Better a little with righteousness / than much gain with injustice" (Prov. 16:8), as well as in the Pauline injunction "godliness with contentment is great gain" (1 Tim. 6:6). Eaton pointed out that this way is embodied by Christ "who withdrew from 'twohands full' of trouble (Matt. 12:14f.), but was noted for his 'handful of quietness' (Matt. 12:19f.)."[54] In conclusion, this middle way needs to be heard in the contemporary situation that is well described by these verses (Eccles. 4:4–6): a frantic achievement orientation in work at one extreme, and a disastrous opting out for the life of ease at the other extreme.

The Desire for Wealth. Verses 7 and 8 depict the person who works to increase one's wealth.

> There was a man all alone;
>   he had neither son nor brother.
> There was no end to his toil,
>   yet his eyes were not content with his wealth.
> "For whom am I toiling," he asked,
>   "and why am I depriving myself of enjoyment?"
> This too is meaningless—
>   a miserable business!

Here the self-centered compulsive worker is dehumanized for he has surrendered to the endless process of gratifying a mere craving for more wealth. However, life is intended to be lived in community (vv. 9–12), hence all egocentric work is meaningless. Kidner noted that the image in these verses of lonely, aimless busyness (along with that of jealous competitiveness in verse 4) counters any arguments we might wish to advance for the virtue of excessive and hard work.[55]

The Desire to Gain Fame. In verses 13–16 Qoheleth argues that the pursuit of fame is an empty justification for exertion and hard work. Fame is the worst delusion of all, for people are soon forgotten by those who follow after.

In this passage (vv. 4–16), Qoheleth illustrates that the reasons normally presented for hard work—the desire to achieve (v. 4), to increase one's wealth (vv. 7–8), and to gain fame (vv. 13–16)—are all invalid. The conclusion is unavoidable: hard work is foolish and only moderation is sensible.

The Leisure-as-Pleasure Ethic

Qoheleth also addresses those at the other extreme from the workaholic, those who hold a consumptive or hedonistic ethic, a pleasure-seeking understanding of leisure. Although Qoheleth calls us to enjoy the good gifts of God's creation, pleasure-seeking is not the ultimate goal of humans. A life of unreserved pleasure-seeking is "meaningless, a chasing after the wind" (2:11). Qoheleth comes to this conclusion at the end of a section (2:1–11) in which he describes how he has experimented "with pleasure to find out what was good" (2:1). At one time during his life he pursued and endeavored to experience all the possible pleasures life offered. Although there is debate over whether Solomon wrote Ecclesiastes, Qoheleth seems to link himself with King Solomon. William LaSor, David Hubbard, and Fredric Bush suggested that "Solomon himself could serve as a model of the life Qoheleth was striving to evaluate."[56] It should be noted that the Solomonic era was one in Old Testament history when, due to the wealth available, it was possible to try a variety of pleasures and indulgences. Furthermore, Solomon as king was in a better position than most people to take advantage of every opportunity for pleasure. The writer's experiment is very relevant to our day, for we too have the affluence and means to try a variety of pleasures and indulgences.

In these verses Qoheleth argues that pleasure-seeking cannot satisfy his spiritual thirst. The passage is organized as follows: his resolve (v. 1a); his conclusions (vv. 1b–2); a detailed description of his endeavors (vv. 3–8); the great extent of splendor and self-indulgence he achieved (vv. 9–10); and his conclusions (v. 11). Characteristically the conclusion precedes his observation: "I said to myself, 'Come now, I will test you with pleasure to find out what is good.' But that also proved to be meaningless" (v. 1).

Pleasure-seeking shares in the meaninglessness of all earthly phenomena. In verse 2, two items are identified, laughter (*sekhoq*) and pleasure (*simkhah*). The first is superficial merrymaking as in the fun of a game (Prov. 10:23) or a party (Eccles. 10:19). Though the distinction is not always clear, *simkhah* is thoughtful pleasure.[57] In this context it describes the amusements and delights of life that bring momentary happiness. One paraphrase, suggested Louis Goldberg, could be, "he amused himself with a lot of fun."[58] Both types of pleasure-seeking are given appropriate verdicts. The first, laughter, explained Eaton, is sheer madness or foolishness rather than taking life realistically; "The merry-maker drowns the hard facts in a sea of frivolity."[59] As for the more serious pleasure (*simkhah*), Qoheleth simply asks, "What does pleasure accomplish?" The obvious implication of this rhetorical question, concluded Eaton, is that "all pleasure, highbrow and lowbrow alike, fail to meet the needs of the man whose horizon remains 'under the sun.'"[60]

In verse 3 Qoheleth provides the specifics of his pleasure-seeking. His pursuit of pleasure was deliberate and serious ("my mind still guiding me with wisdom"), persistent ("I wanted to see"), and limited to a definite area ("under the heavens").

In verse 4 the general statement "I undertook great projects" is followed by the details.

> I built houses for myself and planted vineyards. I made gardens and parks and planted all kinds of fruit trees in them. I made reservoirs to water groves of flourishing trees. I bought male and female slaves and had other slaves who were born in my house. I also owned more herds and flocks than anyone in Jerusalem before me. I amassed silver and gold for myself, and the treasure of kings and provinces. I acquired male and female singers, and a harem as well—the delights of a man's heart. I became greater by far than anyone in Jerusalem before me. In all this my wisdom stayed with me.
>
> >I denied myself nothing my eyes desired;
> >   I refused my heart no pleasure.
> >My heart took delight in all my labor,
> >   and this was the reward for all my toil. (vv. 4–10)

The picture increasingly progresses to the splendor achieved by Solomon. His underlying motivation is revealed by some variant of the refrain "for myself," repeated six times in verses 4–8.

In verse 10 the words "eyes" and "heart" express the external and internal dimensions of his pleasures. Everything that might be outwardly entertaining or inwardly satisfying was experienced. Indeed, in verse 10 we read that his "heart took delight." Nevertheless, the verse concludes on a more somber tone. The activity gives satisfaction, but after the accomplishment the pleasure begins to fade.

In verse 11 he comes to what Eaton suggested may be described as "the morning after the night before."[61] A verdict is now passed on pleasure.

> >Yet when I surveyed all that my hands had done
> >   and what I had toiled to achieve,
> >everything was meaningless, a chasing after the wind;
> >   nothing was gained under the sun. (v. 11)

All of Qoheleth's key words come together in this verse: "toil," "meaninglessness," "chasing after the wind," "nothing was gained," and "under the sun."

The combination of these words conveys bitter disillusionment. It is not the morality of human pleasure-seeking that is under consideration, but rather, as Eaton put it, "secular man is being shown the failure of his life-style, on its own premises."[62] Thus if leisure is understood as pleasure-seeking and becomes one's all-consuming end, it is ultimately not fulfilling, and hence cannot be considered as true leisure. Qoheleth's conclusion is as appropriate in our day as it was at the time it was written.

The alternative lifestyle to hedonistic pleasure-seeking is presented at the end of Ecclesiastes 2. Qoheleth tells us life is to be enjoyed: "People can do nothing better than to eat and drink and find satisfaction in their toil" (2:24a). Eaton noted that "to eat and drink is expressive of companionship, joy and satisfaction . . . the symbol of a contented and happy life."[63] Thus in Ecclesiastes 2, Qoheleth holds before his readers two ways of life: the vicious pursuit of temporary pleasures versus an enjoyable life accepted from the hand of God. Let us now turn to look at the alternative lifestyle of joy.

The Enjoyment of Life

The alternative lifestyle to pleasure-seeking is presented at the end of chapter 2 (vv. 24–26) and is elaborated on in several other passages throughout Ecclesiastes. Although Qoheleth rejects hedonistic pleasure-seeking, he does, as we have just seen, advocate that life is to be enjoyed: "People can do nothing better than to eat and drink and find satisfaction in their toil" (v. 24a). Commenting on this verse, Winter wrote, "After seeking pleasure in every possible way, the writer of Ecclesiastes concludes that the simple, ordinary, everyday routines of eating, drinking, and work—seen in the bigger framework of living in relation to God—bring the deepest enjoyment and satisfaction."[64] Roger Whybray pointed out that this is the first of seven passages "arranged in such a way as to state their theme with steadily increasing emphasis" that "recommends the whole-hearted pursuit of enjoyment."[65]

The first passage, 2:24a, is a plain statement, but the next three passages that recommend a life of joy begin with phrases that positively affirm this way of life.

I know that there is nothing better for people than to be happy and do good while they live. (3:12)

So I saw that there is nothing better for a person than to enjoy their work. (3:22a)

This is what I have observed to be good: that it is appropriate for a person to eat, to drink, and to find satisfaction in their toilsome labor. (5:18a)

And the fifth is expressed in even more forceful words.

So I commend the enjoyment of life, because there is nothing better for a person under the sun than to eat and drink and be glad. (8:15a)

The sixth passage begins with a statement in the imperative mood. Qoheleth now positively urges his reader to follow his advice.

Go, eat your food with gladness, and drink your wine with a joyful heart. . . . Always be clothed in white, and always anoint your head with oil. Enjoy life with your wife, whom you love. (9:7a, 8–9a)

In the seventh and last passage the advice is again given in the imperative and is personally addressed to the young.

You who are young, be happy while you are young,
    and let your heart give you joy in the days of your youth.
Follow the ways of your heart
    . . . banish anxiety . . .
Remember your Creator. (11:9a, 10a; 12:1a)

These seven texts punctuate Ecclesiastes, creating a kind of leitmotif or theme. The main point is that God has given humans the opportunity to enjoy life. Whybray summarized Qoheleth's teaching as follows:

1. What good things God has given us are intended for our enjoyment, and in the giving of them he has shown his approval of our actions. To enjoy them is actually to do his will.
2. We must accept our ignorance of God's purposes . . . we must take life as we find it and enjoy what we can because
    a. we cannot change the fate which God has chosen for us;
    b. we cannot know what God has in store for us;
    c. life is short and death is inevitable.
3. The recognition that toil is part of what God has allotted to us in this life, and that reliance on our own efforts is vain, enables us to find enjoyment even in our toil.[66]

Whybray, who in giving weight to the joyous side of Ecclesiastes, is one of the more recent scholars who has recognized the theme in this book that life is meant for our enjoyment. Johnston wrote, "Qoheleth's stance toward life has been clouded by commentators unable to break out of their alien (to Qoheleth) work-dominated mind-sets."[67] In the past, most biblical scholars have subordinated the recurring theme in Ecclesiastes—that humans are to enjoy life (2:24–26; 3:12–13, 22; 5:17–19; 7:14; 8:15; 9:7–9; 11:9–12:1)—to some variant of the vanity motif as the principal focus of the book. The view that the vanity motif pervades Ecclesiastes was so prevalent that in 1960 Frederick

Moriarty wrote, "That Qoheleth is sceptical goes without saying."[68] In recent decades this view has been changing. For example, Eaton wrote: "The fear of God which he (Qoheleth) recommends (3:14; 5:7; 8:12; 12:13) is not only the beginning of wisdom; it is the beginning of joy, of contentment and of an energetic and purposeful life."[69] Likewise Gordis, in his book *Koheleth—The Man and His World*, recognized that "*simkhah*, the enjoyment of life" is the "basic theme of the book": "For Koheleth, joy is God's categorical imperative for man, not in an anemic or spiritualized sense, but rather as a full-blooded and tangible experience, expressing itself in the play of the body and the activity of mind, the contemplation of nature and the pleasures of love."[70] A similar viewpoint was articulated by Norbert Lohfink, who believed Qoheleth wrote from a perspective dominated by a recognition of life's joys: we should accept "the gift of happiness in the present moment from the hand of God."[71]

For Johnston, as we have already seen, Qoheleth is primarily concerned with the limits of human work and thus "argues for the importance of enjoying life from God as a gift while we can. 'Enjoyment,' not 'work,' is to be our controlling metaphor of life." Johnston elaborated,

> Having noted (1) a range of limits imposed on man's experience, and (2) the resultant folly of man's attempt to master life, Qoheleth (3) reasserts the sage advice that man's lot (*kheleq*) is to enjoy (*ra'ah* or *samakh*) the life that God gives (*natan*) him. Man's active participation and engagement in the world is not to be manipulative or assertive, but rather a "seeing" (*ra'ah*: 2:24; 3:13; 5:17; cf. 9:9), or a rejoicing (*samakh*: 5:18; cf. 3:22; 3:13; 5:17; cf. 9:9) in the good in all his labor, and affirming as "good" (*tob*) of his eating and drinking (2:24–26; 5:17; 8:15; 9:7), a rejoicing in all one's present activities (3:22), and an affirmation that life was meant to be lived joyfully in community (9:9; 4:9–12). Qoheleth preaches that there must be an acceptance of life as given by God with both its joys and sorrows (7:14), and he argues for an active participation and engagement with life, despite its uncertainties (11:1–6).[72]

Johnston proceeded to illustrate a link between Qoheleth's counsel to enjoy life and a theology of creation based on the Genesis accounts. For example (and this is possibly the most important connection), Ecclesiastes and Genesis substantially agree concerning the focal point of the creation motif—"that life is to be celebrated as a 'good' creation of God."[73] On seven occasions in the first chapter of Genesis, God observes creation and describes it as "good" (*tob*). Likewise, Qoheleth observes life and concludes, "People can do nothing better [lit., *tob*, 'good'] than to eat and drink and find satisfaction [*tob*] in their toil. This too, I see, is from the hand of God" (2:24). After considering this and other agreements between Genesis and Ecclesiastes, Johnston concluded that "it is not in the least surprising that Qoheleth seeks to affirm life as something to be celebrated and enjoyed as good, as something to be beheld reverently and interacted with joyously."[74]

Eaton also saw a connection between Genesis and Ecclesiastes. Qoheleth is suggesting that the created realm is basically good and intended for our enjoyment (Eccles. 2:24; 3:12, 22; 8:15; see also Gen. 2:9). Likewise human work is to be enjoyed. Thus Qoheleth reflects the orthodox Israelite view of the earthly realm: God brings

> forth food from the earth:
> wine that gladdens human hearts,
>   oil to make their faces shine,
>   and bread that sustains their hearts. (Ps. 104:14–15)

Qoheleth's perspective reflects what Walter Eichrodt described as the Old Testament exaltation of "earthly possessions, many children, long life, friendship and love. . . . When human life is thus surrounded and upheld by God's blessed will, man's basic mood in relation to his task and his destiny is one of joy."[75]

The joy that Qoheleth advocates is similar to the rejoicing in creation that we saw was suggested by the appeal to creation theology in the account of the Sabbath commandment in Exodus 20. This enjoyment of the gift of God's good creation is not worldliness, and thus is to be differentiated from the consumption-ethic of the rich fool who says to himself, "You have plenty of grain laid up for many years. Take life easy; eat, drink and be merry" (Luke 12:19), or the exclusively earthly horizon of the unbeliever, "Let us eat and drink, / for tomorrow we die" (1 Cor. 15:32). Self-centered pleasure-seeking leads to despair. The life of enjoyment is the gift of God, "for without him, who can eat or find enjoyment?" (Eccles. 2:25). Qoheleth advises not hedonism but joy and contentment. A New Testament parallel is 1 Timothy 4:4, "For everything God created is good, and nothing is to be rejected if it is received with thanksgiving."

In our discussion of Ecclesiastes as it relates to the balance of work and leisure today, we have digressed somewhat from the topic of this chapter—that is, work. However, the advice of Qoheleth has shown itself to be very applicable to contemporary life where there appears to be a tension between a work ethic and a leisure ethic. Qoheleth helps to restore some balance. He shows the vanity of exalting work, as has been the case in the secularized work ethic (dare we say also in the Protestant work ethic). Part of Qoheleth's intention in writing is to assist his readers to rediscover a God-centered joy. Thus Qoheleth dispels our false and illusory hopes of what can be accomplished through our work. To those obsessed with work, he affirms the value of enjoying life in and of itself. Our leisure need not be merely rest and refreshment to serve our work. Rather, we are to enjoy life.

At the same time Qoheleth illustrates the vanity of pleasure-seeking that all too often characterizes what some people call a "leisure ethic." Instead, Qoheleth advocates an enjoyment of life in creation, which is a gift of God. It should be noted that work is one of these gifts of creation to be enjoyed (2:24; 3:22; 5:17). Our life entails more than leisure; it also includes work, and we are to find joy in it. Thus work is not to be exalted, but yet it is not to be rejected for it is one of the joys of creation. This is the way out of the paradox described at the beginning of this chapter—we are not always satisfied with work, yet we know that work must not disappear.

Conclusion

Let us summarize what we have learned from this part of the book on work, and especially its relationship to leisure. First, we saw how there is a paradox concerning work in contemporary society: we want to work yet we are not always satisfied with work. This is partly because work has become synonymous with our job, and while the job is seen as a necessity to earn an income to provide for the good life, the job is sometimes disliked because it is no longer a source of satisfaction. Yet we know that work should be at the center of meaningful human experience. For some, one's job is satisfying because it is a means of self-expression and self-fulfillment. But the idea that work is for the glory of God or is even to provide a service or contribution to society is largely ignored in the contemporary view of jobs and work. We need to recover a biblical understanding of work.

Turning to the biblical account we learned that work—in the sense of subduing the earth and of ruling over nature (Gen. 1:28), of tilling and caring (Gen. 2:15), of ordering and organizing (Gen. 2:19)—is essential to God's purposes for human life and is also an activity in which the divine image is displayed. Furthermore, work provides for the needs of the individual and society, is a means of human fulfillment, and is a means of fulfilling the task to be stewards of creation. The biblical account teaches us that work is something that makes us fully human, for it is part of our created nature to be a worker. Therefore we cannot reject work in favor of a life of leisure. The New Testament teaches that through Jesus Christ the original creational mandate for humans has been restored, so that work offers a service to the coming kingdom of God. Furthermore, the New Testament shows the attitude in which work is to be done: an attitude or spirit of thanksgiving to Christ, one's divine master. As such, work is not to be done out of a sense of duty or for economic self-interest, but it is to flow from our being, from our life in Christ. Thus there is no need to dichotomize work and leisure, for both flow from our life in Christ.

We can learn much from tracing the concept of work through history. We need to avoid the mistake of the Middle Ages where a dichotomy was created between spiritual and secular work. The Bible teaches that all types of work are of equal value. Yet from the medieval period we can learn a more leisurely pace of life and that our work and the fruit of it should be done in view of eternity.

We need to overcome the confusion of vocation, work, and job that developed from the Reformers' confusion of calling. Thus work needs to be returned to its widest perspective and no longer be seen as a synonym for the job. When this is done there will be less of a dichotomy between work and leisure. We also have to restore the work ethic to its proper context—that is, remove it from its secular context and place it within the divine context as the Reformers saw it: all work is to be service to God and done as unto God.

When we say that work needs to be returned to the context of the divine we do not mean that it is to be exalted as it was previously in both the Protestant and secular work ethics. Rather, work needs to be viewed as it is in the creation account where it is one part of God's purpose for humans. The biblical teaching is that though humans are workers, this is not the whole truth about human nature and destiny; humans were created to glorify God and enjoy God forever. Both work and rest are basic to the created nature of humans.

From the book of Ecclesiastes we learn that we are to enjoy life as a gift from the hand of God. This life includes our work. We cannot escape from work, and therefore we cannot accept any leisure ethic that has no room for work, yet we cannot exalt work. There is a middle way between the traditional work ethic and an all-consuming leisure ethic.

part 5

christian
perspectives
on leisure

a critique of the concepts of leisure

In this chapter, I will develop a Christian perspective on the conceptualization of leisure, arising from a synthesis of biblical, historical, and contemporary sources presented in previous chapters. I will critique the seven concepts of leisure outlined in chapter 1 from a Christian perspective and argue that the biblical idea of a rhythm in life supports the view of leisure as non-work time or activity that refreshes and restores, which has been the dominant view of leisure within Protestantism. Meanwhile the concept of rest, reflective of the quality of life offered in Jesus Christ, provides support for what has historically been called the classical state-of-being view of leisure that originated in Greek society but was adapted by Augustine, Aquinas, and medieval monastics and that is more common within Roman Catholic spirituality. I will also argue that the classical and "Protestant" views of leisure are not mutually exclusive but together provide a comprehensive, holistic view of leisure. In the next chapter this holistic view of leisure will be related to patterns of work in contemporary society, and the ethics of leisure will be briefly discussed.

The Free-Time Concept of Leisure

The discretionary or free-time approach to conceptualizing leisure simply reduces leisure to a quantity of time. To conceive of leisure as free time is both limiting and confusing. While leisure is associated with freedom, freedom cannot be broken up into blocks of time. Dahl noted, "Free time is an alien and spurious notion to any Christian who reflects theologically upon the details and dynamics of his life."[1] All of a Christian's time is free since life is a free gift, given by God and intended to be freely accepted by the people of God. Therefore we cannot earn free time, for all of our time is freely given apart from any work on our part. At the same time none of our time is free, for it all comes under the Lordship of Christ, whether we are working or engaged in recreation. Free time implies that when a person is not working or otherwise obligated, one may do whatever one desires. But a Christian is not free to do anything one desires during non-work hours, for all of one's time is to be offered to God. In his discussion of Christian freedom, Luther characterized the Christian as always living simultaneously in total freedom and total responsibility.[2] A person cannot break up his or her life into distinct periods, some of which are regarded as free and others that are not. Therefore, for the Christian the notion of free time is not very helpful.

At least three problems arise from the attempt to define leisure as free time. First, the equation of leisure with free time is at the same time too broad and too narrow. It is too broad if it refers to all the time except for that time in which we are engaged in paid employment. Much of the time we spend away from our jobs is still devoted to work-related activities, such as household maintenance. Yet the notion of free time is too narrow if it implies that leisure is only the residual time left over after one has fulfilled all the obligations that contemporary life demands of a person. If this concept is brought to its logical conclusion, there would be almost no leisure, for if one completed all the expected role responsibilities of every area of one's life, the residual time would be minimal. As we saw in chapter 2, many people today are so busy that they simply discover they have no such thing as free time. Although some people may devote less time to paid employment than did people in the past, many are busy with other duties. Since these people frequently have an incomplete and misleading understanding of what leisure is, often equating it with free time, they conclude that they do not have any leisure.

Likely the only people in today's society who have plenty of free time are those in hospitals or prisons, and those involuntarily unemployed or retired. However, except for some of those retired it would be wrong to describe the situation of the people in these groups as free, and it definitely cannot be termed leisure.

The second problem of defining leisure entirely in terms of time is that it does not give any normative guidance for leisure. While the notion of free time is helpful in presenting sociological data on the uses of time, such as was done in chapter 2, it implies nothing about the moral direction of leisure. The concept of free time runs counter to responsible involvement in our interdependent society. Free time assumes that people's work is their only real responsibility and implies that when people are not working, they can spend their time doing anything they desire to do. However, this is neither realistic nor desirable in our increasingly complex and interdependent society.[3] Sociologist Bennett Berger maintained that sociology "has taught us that no time is free of normative constraints."[4] While freedom and nonobligation are associated with leisure, discretionary time cannot be removed from the context of responsibility to God for our use of time. All time and activities are to be brought under God's sovereignty.

Third, to conceptualize leisure entirely in terms of time misses so much of the qualitative dimension of leisure described in Scripture: the spiritual attitude of rest, joy, freedom, and the rejoicing in God and the gift of his creation inculcated by the Sabbath, along with the quality of life characterized by rest, peace, abundant life, and freedom available to us in Jesus Christ as we saw in chapters 5 and 6. Not everything one does in one's discretionary time can be claimed to be leisure. Nevertheless, discretionary time or quantitative leisure may be used to develop and nurture the qualitative dimension of leisure as Nelvin Vos explained.

> Free time is only potentially a time of experiencing leisure. Rather than emphasizing time itself, we should focus on the person. Leisure depends not only on available time, but also on the person's freedom to experience all time qualitatively rather than quantitatively. Leisure is not a matter so much of time, free or otherwise, but rather is a quality of living, a way of looking at life.[5]

The time remaining after work and other obligations can be called discretionary time but not leisure. Discretionary time may be used in a variety of ways: it may remain as empty idleness, be filled with unproductive activities or the consumption of material goods, or used to cultivate and nurture the qualitative dimension of leisure. Therefore free time is only potential leisure.

In summary, free time is an element of leisure, but leisure should not be limited to segments of time. Yet freedom from work and other obligations is definitely an essential dimension of leisure. In chapter 5 we saw that, at one level, the creation of the Sabbath suggests that we need periods of time each week that are free from both work and all other work-related activities. Exodus 34:21a reads, "Six days you shall labor, but on the seventh day you shall rest." In addition, both the Mosaic legislation and the prophets stressed that no work is to be done on the Sabbath. The Sabbath taught that Israel's life, in addition to work, also possessed the element of free time. At this level the Sabbath was a quantity of time in which no work was performed. Likewise, leisure, in a quantitative sense, is a period of time in which no work is performed.

Yet we also saw that the Sabbath was more than a quantity of time in which no work was to be performed. The Old Testament taught that the Sabbath was to be observed not only by a cessation from work but also by a rest that was of the nature of worship. So while there is the necessity to have periods of time free from work and work-related activities in our lives, this is not the totality of leisure.

Leisure as a Symbol of Social Class

In *The Theory of the Leisure Class*, Veblen illustrated how the wealthy ruling classes, throughout history, have been identified by their possession and use of leisure.[6] Veblen was critical of the idle rich who exploited and lived on the toil of others while totally engaging themselves in a life of conspicuous consumption. From his analysis arose the conceptualization of a leisure class.

While the notion of a leisure class may be useful in a descriptive analysis of the sociological structure of a society, it cannot be normative in any Christian understanding of leisure. As we saw in chapter 5, the implication of the humanitarian motive for the observance of the Sabbath in Exodus 23:12 (see also Deut. 5:14), which teaches that the domestic slave and alien are also to rest on the Sabbath, is that all members of society are entitled to a break from work, and therefore entitled to leisure in at least a quantitative sense. The biblical view does not lend support to the social structuring of society such as in the Greece of Aristotle's day when slaves made it possible for a few to have a life of leisure, nor does it support a leisure class who live a life of conspicuous consumption at the expense of the working class, as Veblen described.[7] As Gordis pointed out, the Sabbath was not only the cornerstone and capstone of Jewish life but also provided a more democratic form of leisure than in Greek society.[8] Aristotle's leisure was based on the ancient Greek institution of slavery, while the Jewish Torah declared that everyone, including male and female servants, had an inalienable right to Sabbath rest. Crittenden commented that Jesus offers a radically different view from the elitist Greek view of leisure primarily as something for the educated.[9] In his dialogue with the Pharisees in Luke 17:20–21, Jesus's statement that "the kingdom of God is in your midst" suggests that the kingdom to which everyone is invited is rooted in everyday experience and is not an elitist search for truth.

Neville explained that Christians need to criticize any society that distributes the benefits of work so as to create a minority "leisure class."[10] In contrast to the wastefulness and vanity of a leisure class, the Christian model is that of stewardship. Packer wrote that money "is to be stewarded for the service of God and one's neighbor. Frugality, rather than conspicuous consumption, must mark the Christian, and if that means that he or she cannot keep up with the world's wealthiest Joneses, well, so be it."[11] More recently Witherington has argued that we need more Christians who are socially motivated and spiritually formed: "We need Christians who consciously think through their lives and de-enculturate themselves from many of the values of the dominant Western culture, including consumerism and conspicuous consumption, not to mention the disease of the health and wealth gospel."[12]

With the diffusion of culture, the spread of wealth, the greater influence of the mass media, greater mobility, and a reduction of working hours, there has been a democratization of the leisure class in modern society. Leisure, as associated with the concept of a leisure class, has become accessible to all. "Unfortunately," observed Doohan, "for many, the increase in non-working hours has led to a fruitless mimicking of a previous leisured class,"[13] or what is often called a "keeping up with the Jones."

As we saw in our discussion of leisure and consumption in chapter 2, a wide variety of entertainments, sports, weekend excursions, prepackaged holidays, and vacations are available to most North Americans for consumption. These pursuits often necessitate consumer goods—recreational vehicles, cottages, specialty clothes, DVD players, and so on. For many, leisure does not go beyond this consumption of non-work-related possessions and entertainments. This pursuit of leisure through the consumption of material goods prevalent in our society confuses the real meaning and true satisfaction of leisure with the purchasing of consumer goods. People who fill their free time with consumption activities do not understand or truly experience leisure.

The pursuit of leisure through the consumption of material goods in today's society is not that different from the acquisition of material possessions described in Ecclesiastes. The writer amassed houses, vineyards, gardens, parks, fruit trees, reservoirs, slaves, herds, flocks, silver, gold, treasures, singers, and a harem. Yet the writer concludes in 2:11,

> when I surveyed all that my hands had done
> and what I had toiled to achieve,
> everything was meaningless, a chasing after the wind;
> nothing was gained under the sun.

It is the same today, as nothing is gained by an accumulation of consumption goods. Leisure, if defined in terms of conspicuous consumption, does not lead to any ultimate satisfaction or meaning in life.

Leisure as a State of Mind

There has been very little Christian reflection on the social psychological concept of leisure as a state of mind or even connections made between Christianity and this understanding of leisure that dominated leisure studies in the 1980s and 1990s and is still prevalent today. Given its prevalence, I will devote considerable attention to critiquing it. One of the few connections between Christianity and this psychological state-of-mind view was made by Isabella Csikszentmihalyi in an investigation of why the Jesuit order of the Roman Catholic Church was so successful during the 1500s and 1600s. She provided a psychological explanation: the Jesuit rules offered an optimal set of conditions through which the young Jesuits could live the totality of their life as one religious flow experience; that is, the Jesuits were able to match personal skills with the opportunities provided by the order to produce enjoyment.[14] Csikszentmihalyi argued that the Jesuit practices and rules, because they were consistent with "biologically programmed goals," offered "a unified structure of consciousness whereby psychic energy could be invested in an ordered way."[15] While there may be some merits to Csikszentmihalyi's thesis, it seems to reduce the explanation to external conditions that existed rather than take into account deeper spiritual realities more in tune with the state-of-being understanding of leisure than the psychological state-of-mind understanding of leisure. She recognized that the founder of the Jesuits, Ignatius of Loyola, was deeply influenced by Thomas à Kempis's *Imitation of Christ* that emphasized not outward practices but a deeper inner life of the spirit and the need to personally imitate the life of Christ.

Marcia Carter has used the flow state (intensely absorbing experiences where the challenge of an activity matches the skill level of the individual so that the person loses track of both time and awareness of self) to explore how leisure and spiritual well-being can be integrated.[16] She explained that a Christian acts to move toward an optimal quality of life through spiritual and leisure behaviors that are proactive, positive, personal, and purposeful. Thus she concluded that both spirituality and leisure are dynamic and incorporate actions of total involvement that are comparable to the flow state. As characteristics of flow experiences are found in both spirituality and leisure, Christians can generate experiences that lead to both holistic well-being and spiritual freedom.[17]

The social-psychological approach to studying recreation engagements and leisure activities is a helpful approach to understand as well as maximize the benefits of these activities. However, a number of concerns and cautions are needed when considering leisure as a subjective experience or a state of mind. These concerns include too much emphasis on optimal experience, too much attention to individual behavior rather than social processes, little to say about the ethics of leisure, an overemphasis on the experience of happiness as an end itself, and little recognition of the importance of the eternal and of suffering.

Douglas Kleiber wrote that the state-of-mind or psychological view of leisure has focused too much on optimal experience as an ideal outcome, characterized by commitment, competence, and concentrated effort, and on a high intensity activity as a source of self-realization and satisfaction.[18] The concepts of relaxation, receptivity, and "just being" advocated by Pieper have been subordinated and neglected in the state-of-mind view of leisure, as have peacefulness, contemplation, appreciation, contentment, and serenity. In contrast to the optimal experience view, Kleiber stated that leisure is essentially a condition of relaxation, faithful openness to the present, and ease of thinking and moving. As illustrated by the work of Feldman Barrett and Russell (see fig. 10.1), positive affect can take place both when a person is activated and deactivated (e.g., contentment, calm, serenity, relaxation), and thus positive emotions can arise from relaxation as much as from action. However, leisure studies scholars tend to ignore these deactivated experiences.[19] Kleiber believed that understanding leisure as true relaxation, rather than optimal experience, is desirable. He advocated a view of leisure very similar to that of Pieper but noted: "For Pieper, faith in God is needed for true leisure. Perhaps that is so. But I would argue that disengagement and emotional security would be enough to give leisure meaning and value in our time."[20] However, for the Christian, as we have noted in our discussion of Sabbath as a sign of the covenant, leisure reaches its highest fulfillment within the context of a relationship with the divine. Also, as we have seen, the Septuagint version of Psalm 46:10 connects being still and having leisure, at least from a state-of-being perspective, with knowing God.

Figure 10.1
A Schematic Structure of Affect

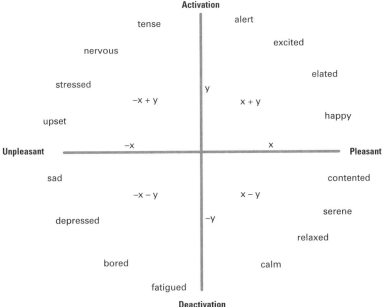

The letters x and y represent schematic components: x = pleasantness; y = activation.

Source: Lisa Feldman Barrett and James A. Russell, "The Structure of Current Affect: Controversies and Emerging Consensus," *Current Directions in Psychology* 8, no. 1 (1999), 11.

The social psychological paradigm for studying leisure as a subjective experience or a state of mind has been criticized, especially by feminists, for focusing too much on the individual person with not enough recognition of situational and social factors.[21] For example, Shaw critiqued the focus on matters related to individual behavior, experience, perception, and meaning that do not explore issues of macrosociology, social control, structural power relations, and cultural issues.[22] This state-of-mind concept tends to promote the belief that leisure is innocent with regard to significant and related social processes.[23] In a related critique, Crittenden questioned whether subjective states such as flow are applicable to everyone, at any time, and in all life circumstances, or whether there are racial, class, gender, and cultural limitations on who can experience these subjective states.[24] Furthermore, Crittenden critiqued the privatized nature of subjective states, such as flow, that are "anchored in an individual's experience that is private, unique and rooted in one's personal experience. There is nothing outside of one's individual experience. There is no common good or cause. Further, there are no obligations or responsibilities outside of the experience."[25] Rather, Crittenden argued for a Christianized understanding of the classical state-of-being view that he calls "Holy leisure."

> In Holy leisure one is free to participate in something much greater than an individual experience. Holy leisure is the experience of participating in the communion of saints or in identifying with others who have experienced Holy leisure both in the past and present. Consequently, there is a requirement or an obligation of the participant in Holy leisure to dedicate one's life and abilities to the spiritual disciplines and to serve one's fellow human beings. Therefore Holy leisure in a Christian understanding, is an experience that compels one to "pick up their cross and follow him (Jesus the Christ)."[26]

Rather than focusing on personally pleasing activities, Jesus, as Crittenden explained, directs people back to their physical and cultural environment where they are to focus on community, compassion, and service to others.

The state-of-mind view of leisure has also been criticized as being concerned with private psychological experiences characterized by satisfaction, contentment, and well-being, with little to say about the ethics and morality of these experiences. Sylvester claimed that psychologists of leisure, such as Neulinger, have confused the state-of-mind view of leisure with the classical state-of-being view.[27] However, Aristotle's classical understanding of leisure was not concerned with psychological happiness, feelings, or a state of mind. Rather, leisure was good action related to virtue and excellence. For Aristotle, leisure had moral substance; it was important to use leisure rightly. Thus the classical understanding of leisure involves moral judgment. In contrast the state-of-mind view suggests leisure is any activity that produces a feeling of freedom, even if the activity is unethical. For example, participation in criminal activity may provide an optimal psychological experience but not be ethical. Sylvester wrote,

> Any choice, including the illusion of choice, qualifies as subjective leisure as long as it produces feelings of freedom. Rooted in subjective feelings, "no activity is inherently not a leisure activity" (Neulinger, 1974, p. 35). Consequently, making "snuff" films, the depraved and horrific practice of kidnapping children for pornographic purposes and then torturously murdering them, subjectively counts as leisure alongside family strolls in the park. Yet according to the classical view only virtuous activity is inherently leisure.[28]

A similar argument focused on the ethical content of behavior was put forward by Chris Rojek, who wrote that without a consideration of context, flow and peak experiences are actually rather simplistic concepts. He claimed that serial killing, murder, masochism, sadism, theft, violent beatings, and mugging can all create the intense experiences described by peak and flow experiences.[29] Actually Mihaly Csikszentmihalyi, who developed the flow concept, agrees that "flow can be experienced in activities that are destructive rather than constructive, that lead to entropy instead of to harmony."[30] He gives the examples of Emperor Nero enjoying lions attacking innocent Christians and gladiators killing one another, physicists involved in the Manhattan Project being exhilarated in building the nuclear bomb, and thousands of people flocking to Las Vegas to gamble.

The above critiques of the state-of-mind view of leisure are not specific to Christianity. In his book *Still Bored in a Culture of Entertainment: Rediscovering Passion and Wonder*, Winter, a psychiatrist, offered some background that is helpful in critiquing the state-of-mind understanding of leisure from a Christian perspective.[31] Winter built on the work of Spacks, who documented the interrelationships between the decline of Christianity, a sense of entitlement to happiness, and a focus on inner or subjective experience.[32] Winter explained how in post-Enlightenment Europe and North America during the eighteenth and nineteenth centuries, there was a move away from the quest for God, where happiness was a by-product of a relationship with God rather than an end in and of itself, and a move toward a search for self-fulfillment and happiness for their own sake.[33] The death-of-God movement within philosophy advocated the view that human society, instead of religion, could provide everything humans needed, and as a result, a sense of entitlement to happiness developed. The U.S. Declaration of Independence reflected and enshrined the idea that citizens had a right to "life, liberty, and the pursuit of happiness."

Antireligious and humanistic ideas began to influence every academic discipline but were especially strong in the fields of psychology and sociology—two of the foundational disciplines for the study of leisure—which taught that happiness and truth could be discovered through subjective psychological experience, which is the central concept of the state-of-mind understanding of leisure. Winter, quoting Carl Rogers, wrote,

> *Experience is, for me, the highest authority.* . . . It is to experience that I must return again and again, to discover a closer approximation to truth as it is in the process of becoming in me. Neither the Bible nor the prophets—neither Freud nor research—neither the revelations of God or man—can take precedence over my own direct experience.[34]

For Rogers and others with similar views, the meaning of life and happiness are based on one's own subjective experience rather than an external referent, so self-fulfillment can be pursued without connection to any greater authority.

Winter concluded that a problem exists if self-fulfillment is the primary guiding principle in a person's life, as one's perception of what gives happiness and meets one's needs becomes the principal motivator of one's behavior.

> When my feelings rule me, I am intolerant of pain and boredom; I demand that my needs for pleasure and distraction be met as quickly as possible. Today, when there is no greater principle to guide us, we tend to allow our desires and passions (which are so easily shaped by the culture) to rule us. "Obey your thirst" and "unleash your lust" say the advertisements.[35]

Without an external reference point to give meaning and value, humans are left to find identity and meaning in "one intense experience after another—these give us a sense of being alive and important."[36] Winter, quoting Andrew Fellows, wrote,

> We run from one [mirror] to the next in this flimsy system, like ghosts trapped in an existential vacuum. How can a ghost feel alive and real? The answer is intense experience. In a world where the reality of things no longer gives life to the self, intense experience is all we have left. Moreover, because there is no truth outside of myself, there is no other ideal by which to measure these experiences. There is only intensity; some things feel better than others.[37]

With the loss of a Christian worldview, there is a consequent problem of living without any significant integration point for life. In his book *Flow: The Psychology of Optimal Experience*, Mihaly Csikszentmihalyi explained that purpose in life and a sense of meaning in life is needed to avoid boredom. Recognizing that this meaning and purpose can be found in religious belief he wrote, "Such implicit faith used to be widespread in our culture . . . but it is not easy to find now."[38] It is relatively easy to engage in leisure activities that will bring about a harmonious experience of flow for a short period of time, but it is much more difficult to create the conditions where there is a matching of skills with the challenges of the environment to bring about enjoyment throughout the totality of life. In other words, there is a difference between the state-of-mind subjective experience brought about by external factors and a deeper state of being associated with the classical spiritual understanding of leisure. Ultimate meaning is not found in experiences of the five senses: "Without a sense of ultimate meaning or purpose, without a story (or metanarrative) that makes sense of our individual story, without a connection to the deeper reality of how we are made,"[39] experiences of flow, and similar optimal leisure experiences, are not ultimately fulfilling. As Augustine put it: "You [God] have formed us for yourself; and our hearts are restless until they find rest in you."[40] Or in the words of Blaise Pascal,

> There was once in man a true happiness, of which all that now remains is the empty print and trace . . . This he tries in vain to fill with everything around him,

seeking in things that are not there the help he cannot find in those that are, though none can help, since this infinite abyss can be filled only with an infinite and immutable object; in other words, by God himself.[41]

Winter suggested that God has created us such that we need to live in a specific way to be most fulfilled. The specific way involves directing our desires and longings toward God and God's values. Since God has built a moral and aesthetic compass into human hearts, fulfillment will come as we allow this compass to direct us into what is good and beautiful while discerning what is bad and ugly. Pursuit of happiness is generally elusive if pursued directly but is usually the by-product of the pursuit of other things, such as goodness and beauty. Pope John Paul II was also critical of enjoyment as an end in itself: "It is not wrong to want to live better; what is wrong is a style of life which is presumed to be better when it is directed towards 'having' rather than 'being' and which wants to have more, not in order to be more but in order to spend life in enjoyment as an end in itself."[42]

Likewise Packer, in an essay on the theology of enjoyment, claimed that to seek subjective states of happiness, comfort, and pleasure is a way to guarantee that one will not experience them.[43] Rather, they are by-products of focusing on something else; for example, loving God leads to the subjective experience of peace in one's heart. Quoting the *Evangelical Dictionary of Theology*, Packer pointed out a distinction between joy and pleasure.

> Joy. A delight in life that runs deeper than pain or pleasure . . . not limited by nor tied solely to external circumstances[,] . . . a gift of God[,] . . . a quality of life and not simply a fleeting emotion. . . . The fullness of joy comes when there is a deep sense of the presence of God in one's life. . . . Jesus made it clear that joy is inseparably connected to love and to obedience (John 15:9–14). . . . There can also be joy in suffering or weakness when suffering is seen as having a redemptive purpose and weakness as bringing one to total dependency upon God (Matt. 5:12; 2 Cor. 12:9).[44]

Joy is active in that one *rejoices*, while pleasure (conscious enjoyment) is passive in the sense that one is pleased by an external circumstance.

Packer noted that Christian discipleship is not based on one's quest for pleasure through individual self-fulfillment, self-realization, self-discovery, and self-expression as life's supreme goals, but involves Jesus's call to follow him and take up one's cross in self-denial (Matt. 16:24; Mark 8:34; Luke 9:23).[45] Discipleship includes many forms of pain: distress, hurt, restriction, personal disappointment, and mental as well as physical discomfort (2 Cor. 4:7–11). These experiences of unpleasantness and pain are used by God to facilitate the fruit of the Spirit: "love, joy, peace, forbearance, kindness, goodness, faithfulness, gentleness, and self-control" (Gal. 5:22–23a). Thus pleasure, as a gift from God, needs to be kept in its proper place. Creation is God's good gift and therefore pleasures are gratefully accepted as gifts from God, but happiness is a by-product of our love for, obedience to, and hope in God. Life needs to be lived in light of heaven as "God will bring every deed into judgement," rewarding in heaven those Christians who have made their goal good rather than evil, and obedience rather than pleasure-seeking (see Eccles. 12:14).[46] Or as Tony Campolo put it in his book *The Kingdom of God Is a Party*, "It is the future breaking into the midst of our present sufferings that enables us to conquer our sorrows (Rom. 8:37). Christians cry: but on the other side of their sadness they know there is a party."[47] While the state-of-mind view of leisure focuses on immediate experience (e.g., flow, peak experience), from a Christian perspective this focus needs to be seen within the context of eternity—there is more to life than immediate experience.

Another concern with the state of mind's emphasis on optimal experience concerns the place of suffering in the Christian life.[48] For Christians, the evil and the pain associated with suffering, along with death, is part of the reality of life. Jesus says his followers must "take up their cross and follow me" (Matt. 16:24). As a Christian loses him- or herself in discipleship and the imitation of Christ, life is not necessarily a pursuit of optimal experiences but may involve the experience of suffering, which nevertheless leads to spiritual growth and development. At the very heart of Christianity is Christ's suffering on the cross followed by the joy of Easter. Christianity recognizes the reality of sin, illusion, and death, and also provides a way to transcend and transform them. This spiritual path may be incredibly difficult and not one of optimal experience. For people experiencing tragedy, sickness, loss, and death, actualizing oneself in optimal experiences may not be helpful. Paul Vitz wrote that suffering "is at the center of the meaning and hope of the religious life. By starting with an unsentimental realism about existence, religion is able to provide an honest and ultimately optimistic understanding of the human condition. Christianity starts with suffering and ends with joy."[49] An inordinate emphasis on leisure as subjective, optimal experience can become a substitute religion that denies meaning in suffering and death. From my own personal life experience that has included the loss of jobs that I have enjoyed, the deaths of my parents, my experience of cancer, and various disappointments, I have found the state-of-being spiritual understanding of leisure, which permeates all of life, rather than the state-of-mind subjective experience view of leisure, which is based on immediate experience, to be a solid foundation that helps me to stay close to God through the ups and downs of life. Nevertheless, the social-psychological approach is very helpful for leisure researchers and recreation practitioners to use in understanding and facilitating leisure experiences.

Feminist Leisure

There has been little, if any, Christian reflections on feminist leisure perspectives. Of the more recent Christian writers on leisure, Ryken discussed the feminist work ethic but not feminist leisure.[50] In his book *Free Time: Towards a Theology of Leisure*, Neville correctly observed that the unique situation of women has not been adequately documented in leisure literature.[51] He wrote critically of a 1989 book on the philosophy of leisure for which all nine contributors were male and that did not include any specific discussion of the uniqueness of women's leisure. He asked if there is any Christian judgment on this and described the yearning of many women for this situation to change. More than a dozen books on Christianity and leisure are identified in the introduction to this book, but only one was written by a woman.

Neville also noted that in past generations, churches and chapels offered respectable spaces for women to visit during their free time, since clubs and pubs were almost entirely male places. Women's activities in these churches and chapels included both worship and social activities resulting in a close association between worship and leisure. Feminist leisure scholars have made similar observations in recognizing the importance of church activities for women's social activities and women's social reform initiatives.[52] Church-related activities can provide a leisure container for leisure interactions and meanings.

Given the prevalence of feminist perspectives on leisure and the lack of Christian reflections on it, it is important that we consider these perspectives thoroughly. Feminist leisure scholars' emphasis on the equality of women and men is consistent with a Christian understanding of male and female equality. For hundreds of years, numerous biblical arguments have been made to support the equality of women and men.[53] John Stackhouse has summarized some of these arguments: both male and female are created in God's image and given the creation mandate (Gen. 1:27–28); marriage in Genesis 2:18–24 is an image of coequality and partnership; Jesus befriended and taught women in a way that crossed the gender lines of his culture and affirmed women (Mark 15:40–41; Luke 8:1–3; 10:38–42; John 4; 11:1–44; 12:1–8); the Holy Spirit is poured out on both men and women at Pentecost (Acts 2:16–18); Paul teaches that in Christ barriers between men and women are done away with (Gal. 3:28); spiritual gifts and church functions are not specified for men only (Rom. 12:6–8; 1 Cor. 12:8–10, 27–30; Eph. 4:11); and Paul commends various women who performed roles, such as deacon, coworker and apostle (Rom. 16:1–12).[54] Furthermore, Nicola Hoggard-Creegan explained that restrictions on women's equality are not congruent with many other gospel themes, such as the poor inheriting the earth, the payment of the worker arriving at the eleventh hour, and the first becoming the last, as the dishonored and weak in human terms are the ones honored in God's kingdom.[55]

As Chris Marshall noted, the briefest and best statement of Christian egalitarianism is probably Paul's incredible assertion in Galatians 3:28, "There is neither Jew nor Gentile, neither slave nor free, nor is there male and female, for you are all one in Christ Jesus."[56] Marshall described how the egalitarianism Paul is referring to is not simply spiritual equality, as this equality needs to be worked out in the way Christians relate to one another in everyday life. The spiritual notion of equality is extended to social practices including leisure practices. The preceding chapter of Galatians records Paul's accusation of Peter's hypocrisy for not participating in the social practice of sharing food at a common table with gentile believers in the Antioch church (Gal. 2:11–21). The gospel requires a social equality of Jews and gentiles, and the same is true between females and males. Marshall pointed out that this equality does not mean that everyone begins with the same position and has the same potential, as individuals are not equal in strengths, gifts, and talents. Therefore everyone does not have equal life opportunities. Rather, Marshall claimed that the equality of salvation and worth in Christ described in Galatians 2–3 requires that social practices be transformed, not in the sense that everyone has the exact same opportunity to do the exact same things in life but that everyone has the same opportunity to achieve his or her own created potential in all spheres of life without arbitrary restrictions being imposed by sex, class, or race in accordance with his or her individual abilities, talents, and gifts. This principle would then apply to leisure practices and the sphere of leisure.

After documenting that leisure time and leisure opportunities are usually much more restricted for women than for men, Neville wrote, "The freedom given in Christ, in whom there is neither male nor female, will enfranchise . . . [women] to explore ways of leisure which express that proper self-love within the Christian community which must not be lost in loving a family. That too, will be an exploration of God-given reality."[57] Such an approach leads to leisure entitlement for women rather than a life of responsibility that does not allow for leisure time and activities. Noting the great variability within humans, Neville suggested that there is the possibility for different patterns of free time fulfillment for women.

Women's equality has waxed and waned, although, as Hoggard-Creegan pointed out, good arguments have repeatedly been made in biblical studies, hermeneutics, and theology for the equality of women throughout the modern history of the Christian church.[58] Hoggard-Creegan explained this waxing and waning in terms of the natural human tendency to be aggressive and patriarchal as a result of the fall.

> I will make your pains in childbearing very severe;
>   with painful labor you will give birth to children.
> Your desire will be for your husband,
>   and he will rule over you. (Gen. 3:16)

One of the costs of unloving human dominion over the earth is unbalanced gender relationships that impact the lives of women. Thus, as Hoggard-Creegan explained, generation after generation of men and women replace God's intentions for humans with their own fallen intentions: "However we interpret the details of fall and original sin, we can at least affirm that sin and brokenness are deeply embedded in human life in a way that is obscure to us, and the gospel calls us to resist evil."[59] She concluded that feminist theology that recognizes the equality of women and men is stilled needed. Likewise, although gains have been made in women's leisure, gaps still remain,[60] and biblical notions of equality still need to be applied to the realm of leisure.

As we have seen in our discussion of feminist leisure in chapter 1, the feminist leisure perspective is concerned with removing oppression and working for equality, not only for women but also for other oppressed groups. There is plenty of biblical support for both goals. The feminist goals of working for equality and removing oppression is consistent with a biblical understanding of justice. As Stackhouse correctly stated, a Christian feminist perspective "echoes the fundamental biblical call to work for shalom, for the full flourishing of every woman and every man, every slave and every master, every child and every parent, as God gives us opportunity to do so."[61]

Applying this biblical equality to leisure, Crittenden noted in his discussion of the gospel eating stories that Jesus freely invites all people to participate in leisure because everyone is of value regardless of their social, religious, cultural, political, economic, or gender position.[62] Groups and individuals excluded from society were invited by Jesus into full participation in their community.[63] For example, Crittenden explained how the account of Jesus feeding the five thousand (Luke 9:12–17) is an excellent example of Jesus welcoming large crowds to eat together in community. Everyone had something to eat, and at this banquet everyone sat and ate together rather than being placed above others in places of honor.[64] Thus everyone is invited to participate in leisure, regardless of one's ability or situation. All people, regardless of their status, income, or gender are invited by Jesus to celebrate life with him.[65] As we have already seen in our discussion of Matthew 11:28–30 in chapter 6, Jesus's invitation, "Come to me, all you who are weary and burdened, and I will give you rest," is the gift of what Crittenden calls "Holy leisure" to everyone, whether they are male or female, Jew or gentile, slave or free.

A positive correction of the feminist leisure perspective is its emphasis on listening to women's voices, as most traditional concepts of leisure were articulated by men in positions of power. While listening to women's voices is very important, as Christians we also need to hear God's voice and word. Elaine Storkey has explained that three of the main branches of feminism—liberal, Marxist, and radical—all trace their roots to the Enlightenment and its "idea of human *autonomy*, personhood-without-God."[66] The implication for feminism was that it was "under the authority of neither man or God: woman on her own."[67] Furthermore, the humanism of the Enlightenment "was faith in a basically *good* humanity."[68]

In contrast to the three main branches of feminism that arose out of the Enlightenment, Christian feminism has its roots in nineteenth-century temperance movements, and in the United States it developed alongside abolitionist movements.[69] Unlike Enlightenment thought, the biblical account teaches that humans are sinful, that sin accounts for the oppressive situations humans find themselves in, and that it is through forgiveness that there is the possibility of freedom. Storkey explained that biblically inspired feminism is not based on the autonomy of the Enlightenment but on an understanding of people-under-God that accepts the reality of sin and necessity of salvation in all areas of life, including leisure. Patriarchy is a symptom of a deeper problem, the problem of sin in the human heart that perverts and distorts human relationships and social structures. Christian feminism recognizes the need for repentance, change, and reconciliation. Thus Christian feminism is not just about the liberation of women but of men as well. Christian liberation is not freedom to do whatever one wants but being free from sin before God. A Christian feminist perspective on leisure, then, is developed "in the context of our creatureliness rather than our independence and autonomy" and needs "to go hand in hand with respect for each other and for the rest of creation."[70] Storkey claimed that a Christian feminist perspective needs to be developed in every sphere of life. In regard to leisure arts she stated: "We live in God's world and it is ours to experience, enjoy and experiment with. Literature, song, painting and dance can be indeed used as our celebration of humanness and womanhood."[71]

The feminist critiques of both the time and activity views of leisure, outlined in chapter 1, are consistent with Christian critiques of these concepts. We have already identified Christian problems with the free time definition of leisure earlier in this chapter. In regard to the activity view, which we will examine shortly, the activity in and of itself is not as important as the activity acting as a leisure container for enjoyment and meaningful experience. The concept of an activity or time being a leisure container fits with the notion of leisure intensification, which will be explained at the end of the next chapter. Feminists' description of the holistic nature of some women's lives is also consistent with the Christian view of holistic leisure that will be articulated later in this chapter.

Furthermore, the feminist emphasis on enjoyment and meaningful experience is consistent with a Christian understanding of leisure. The Bible teaches the goodness of pleasure as stated clearly in Ecclesiastes 8:15: "I commend the enjoyment of life."[72] Of course, as we have seen from the previous chapter, from a Christian perspective this enjoyment is within the context of the pleasures of creation understood and accepted as gifts from God.

The feminist emphasis on affiliative leisure is an emphasis that Christians can enthusiastically support because social relationships, rather than an emphasis on leisure consumption, are an essential part of Christian lifestyle and church functioning.[73] According to Dietrich Bonhoeffer, within the realm of Christian freedom, friendship is both the most rare and valuable gift, for it is difficult to find in a world dominated by work, family, and governmental responsibilities.[74] Ryken, noting that Scripture depicts humans as relational people designed to live with one another, suggested that such a view of people makes the social dimension of leisure a significant Christian concern and a key component of Christian living.[75] In leisure time, when one is free from the responsibilities of work and the daily cares of life, people can enjoy one another for their own sake. The New Testament Epistles' teaching on the unity of believers can be expressed and fostered through the sharing of leisure activities, whether it be participating in activities together or visiting in others' homes.[76] Furthermore, Ryken claimed that friendships need the nurturing energy of leisure.[77] Likewise, Neville explained that leisure, similar to the heavenly life, frequently unites its participants in fellowship.[78] He described the type of society visualized by the prophets and that the New Testament writers assume as characterized by face-to-face contact rather than the passive consumer standardization of much of today's leisure activity.[79] He went on to explain that relationships, with God and with other people, including the sharing of leisure discoveries and interests with other people, enrich leisure.[80]

Leisure as Non-work Activity

The activity concept views leisure as non-work behavior or activity in which people engage during their free time. This activity quite often has a utilitarian purpose such as relaxation, entertainment, and personal development, and is frequently although not always seen as being subservient to work either as a reward for past work or as an activity that refreshes one to go back to work.

This activity concept of leisure is closely associated with the idea of a rhythm to life. However, the opportunity to engage in leisure activities has traditionally been organized around work, the dominant and primary element in the rhythm. Thus the opportunity to engage in leisure activities is not only scheduled around work but is also subservient to work and often serves work.

This concept of leisure has been the predominant one among Protestants, especially the Puritans. In chapter 4 we saw that the Puritan ethic was the foundation of an active life. Work tended to be the dominant activity in life. Yet the Puritans recognized the need for recreation in their life, although it tended to be utilitarian: "anything that gave refreshment to the body or spirit."[81] "Seasonable merriment" was used to describe recreation that was appropriate and that contributed to the main goal in life—devotion to a sovereign God through work. Since work tended to be the dominant reality in life, the other dimensions in life were not seen as separate. Rather, "Puritanism was rooted in a view of life as a unified whole under the sovereignty of God."[82] In this unified whole, there were periods of work and periods of seasonable merriment. In some respects, this rhythm to life in Puritanism reflects the biblical rhythm to life: periods of work interspersed with periods of nonwork on the Sabbath and during annual agricultural festivals.

Yet there are serious problems with the activity concept of leisure. Dahl pointed out that most people in today's society approach leisure with residual traces of the Puritan and rationalist tradition.[83] Not only is work made the center of their life, but it is also the reference point for all other aspects of life. This tradition emphasizes that all time must be used to *do* something. We must be constantly active, on the go, busy. We are culturally conditioned that to be busy is a sign of righteousness or virtue. A Western person is characterized as a doer, in perpetual motion, and always asking "What shall I do?" so that doing the right thing is more important than "being the right person." Spence wrote, "'Do, Do, Do,' is our motto. 'Rush, Rush, Rush'—we revolve in a 'Rat Race.' Holy is the man who keeps busy." If leisure is restricted to activity as is suggested by this concept, then "how deadly exhaustive and surely meaningless it would soon become."[84] Banks has enumerated the effects of this constant activity: the threat to physical and psychological health, the decline in social life including the weakening of interpersonal relationships, the decline in political life, the erosion of thought and leisure, and the undermining of religious sensitivity and the subversion of spiritual life.[85]

A second problem of this notion of leisure is that when leisure is subservient to work, it has no intrinsic value. If work is the center of life then leisure cannot be truly appreciated—any form of nonactivity is considered idleness and suspect unless it can be justified in terms of work. There is no time for the enjoyment of the created world, or much appreciation for contemplation unless its purpose is to purify the mind for more dedicated and disciplined work. Recreational activities reflect a work-orientation in that they usually are "designed to develop physical and mental skills that would be useful in work."[86] However, as the British 1924 Conference on Christian Politics, Economics and Citizenship Commission on Leisure pointed out, "Leisure is a part of God's positive purpose for men and women in the development of personality; not only a means of keeping fit for the daily toil."[87]

A third problem is that often when leisure is reduced to activity, the pursuit of leisure becomes a continual quest for entertainment and amusement, for something to fill one's time. While entertainment may be beneficial, enjoyable, and refreshing, to narrow leisure to the pursuit of entertainment ignores a great deal of the qualitative dimension of leisure as suggested by the biblical material of Sabbath and rest that was reviewed in chapters 5 and 6. The idea that leisure is primarily activity used to fill or kill time contributes to disillusionment and despair, for it neglects the "being" dimension of our lives. Bernard Hahn wrote, "When our leisure involves nothing but seeking entertainment, we soon forget who we are and why we are here."[88] The appeal to creation theology in the Exodus account of the Sabbath commandment suggests that the Sabbath is a time set aside for humans to reflect on God and his purpose, a time to recognize that life is a gift from God and not just the result of human work. Therefore to fill up our time with constant activity, amusement, and entertainment is to deny God. Leisure is not merely constructive activity, entertainment, or distraction.

Casual Leisure

Before leaving our discussion of the activity view of leisure we need to examine two more recent manifestations of this concept as developed by Stebbins: casual leisure and serious leisure. When we consider Stebbins's differentiation of casual and serious leisure, it is interesting to note that much earlier than his writings, the 1924 British Conference on Christian Politics, Economics and Citizenship distinguished short-term relaxation from a more extended imaginative and creative leisure.[89]

Casual leisure has similarities to what previously was called the anti-utilitarian concept of leisure.[90] The anti-utilitarian concept of leisure is characterized by "doing your own thing," creative self-development and self-expression, self-actualization, and the enjoyment of the natural existences and pleasures of life. One positive feature of this concept of leisure is that it bestows intrinsic value on leisure instead of making it subservient to work. It rejects the idea that every activity has to be utilitarian or work-oriented. It emphasizes our "being" over our "doing" in its belief that each person is free and unique and that a person's worth is not determined by his or her role in the economic system of production and consumption. Thus it reacts against the activity orientation of the traditional work ethic.

From a Christian perspective, a positive aspect of the "doing your own thing" ethic is, as Dahl wrote, "its clear affirmation of personal dignity and freedom in the face of all the depersonalizing forces of contemporary culture—including aspects of bureaucracy, technology, and mass-media."[91] Another positive aspect of this concept of leisure is its emphasis on the enjoyment of the natural existences and pleasures of life. The book of Ecclesiastes teaches that we are to enjoy all the gifts of God's good creation (2:24–26; 3:12–13, 22; 5:17–19; 7:14; 8:15; 9:7–9; 11:9–12:1). However, Christians have often ignored the gifts of this life in their overemphasis on the other worldly dimensions of salvation.

Nevertheless, there are at least three problems with the anti-utilitarian concept of leisure as it is generally conceived and practiced. First, in practice, due to humanity's sinful nature, the enjoyment of the natural existences and pleasures of life often turns into hedonistic pleasure-seeking, a gratification of fleshly desires. Stebbins actually recognizes the problematic nature of casual leisure: "The road to the Hell of bad health may be paved with a diet too rich in casual leisure,"[92] and as we saw in chapter 1 he advocates an "optimal leisure life-style" that complements one or more types of serious leisure with sensible amounts of project-based leisure and casual leisure.[93] As we have seen in chapter 9, Ecclesiastes teaches that pleasure seeking, both simple and sophisticated, shares in the meaninglessness of all earthly phenomena experienced within the earthly horizon unless there is recognition of the divine. Qoheleth concludes: "I said to myself, 'Come now, I will test you with pleasure to find out what is good.' But that also proved to be meaningless" (Eccles. 2:1). As Eaton pointed out, it is not the morality of pleasure-seeking that is under consideration here; rather, the secular person is shown the failure of a hedonistic and narcissistic lifestyle on its own premises.[94] Instead, Ecclesiastes teaches that life is to be enjoyed as a gift from God.

The second problem is the morality, or lack thereof, associated with anti-utilitarian leisure. In today's society many of the values and morals of the Christian faith have been rejected in favor of much more pragmatic and relativistic ones. Bregha described the result of this trend as follows:

> More and more people are occupying their leisure with a bewildering variety of acts and deeds that leave their trace on their neighbours and communities. The leisure of one becomes sometimes offensive to another one—morally as well as otherwise. To preach the sanctity of self-fulfillment in an increasingly interdependent society does not solve anything, to hide behind the jargon of "enabling everyone to reach his/her full potential" leads us nowhere. . . . After all, my self-actualization could be your de-actualization, my self-fulfillment achieved at the cost of your emptiness. To view leisure as morally neutral or even as "good per se" denotes a naivete that should have died out with Rousseau.[95]

Therefore not only is "doing your own thing" not ultimately satisfying, but there is the possibility that it will harm one's fellow citizens. Furthermore, comparing our society to that of Rome during its decline, Peter Kreeft explained, "If there is any certain symptom of social senility it is in indifference, shown in slogans like 'anything goes,' 'do your own thing,' 'different strokes for different folks,' or 'live and let live.'"[96]

Third, the hedonistic approach to self-discovery and self-development that is characteristic of this concept of leisure is usually carried out from a humanistic orientation that is not open to the divine. As we saw in chapter 1, a humanistic approach to life is not enough to guarantee the fruits of leisure. Rather, Doohan explained that "the integral human development that results must naturally include the religious" dimension, or an openness to the divine.[97] Or as Billy put it, "When separated from divine worship, leisure loses its power."[98]

It is true that in the last few decades there has been an increasing openness to spirituality. There is some good in this for there is a tendency in our society to be so busy in activity and doing that one is not in touch with the spiritual dimension of life as I documented in chapter 2. However, there are also some concerns.[99] First, much of this pursuit of spirituality is a kind of interiority. In this view, which often omits the concept of the divine, spirituality is basically a human dimension. Second, contemporary discussions of leisure and spirituality often focus on the inner self with little discussion of relationships with others or of community. The quest for spirituality is undertaken on an individual basis to gain private benefit. There is a desire to develop the inner self, to become self-actualized. However, biblical spirituality balances an inner spiritual focus with involvement in the world. Third, there is a need to go beyond spiritual experience to spiritual well-being. Immense significance is presently given to "experience" within discussions of leisure and spirituality. However, the focus of Scripture is not so much on spiritual experience but on a lifestyle that leads to spiritual transformation (Rom. 12:1–2; 2 Cor. 3:18; Eph. 4:22–24). It is not sufficient to get in touch with the deep inner self, for the inner self is itself the root of the problem. Only a radical change in one's innermost being, a change that only Jesus Christ can bring about, brings hope of a radical transformation of life.[100]

True self-development occurs when a person is brought into relationship with Christ and is able to fully become the person he or she was created and intended to be. Dahl wrote,

> Leisure means freedom, but not . . . the kind of sweaty freedom that comes from the defiance of social mores, nor the teary freedom that accompanies abandoned commitments and broken relationships. Leisure is rather that sense of freedom which is realized when a person experiences more fully his uniqueness and worth as an individual and his acceptance and relationship as part of the world around him. A person finds leisure when he discovers who he is, what he can do with his life, and what an abundance of happy circumstances and relationships in which his life is cast. A Christian experiences leisure when he comes into full awareness of the freedom he has in Christ, . . . the freedom to be and become the new man after Christ's own splendid example.[101]

True leisure, in the sense of the possibility to fulfill one's potential and uniqueness, is ultimately possible when one comes to Christ.

Neville connected this idea of freedom in Christ to freedom from the consequences of sin. He suggested that the notion of leisure as the realm of freedom in human life is challenged by the primary theological concern of freedom from sin. Sin, in one of its many forms, suggested Neville, denies humans their freedom. As stated in Galatians 5:1, "It is for freedom that Christ has set us free." Neville concluded by stating, "The only freedom worth talking about is the gift of God through Jesus Christ, and it certainly is not available only to the leisured."[102] This freedom, explained Packer, has four dimensions: from the necessity to work for salvation, from the restrictions of the Old Testament Law, for the enjoyment and use of everything that is created; and in the sense of contentment and fulfillment in serving God "whose service is perfect freedom."[103]

Serious Leisure

In chapter 1 we learned that serious leisure includes three types: amateurs, hobbyists, and volunteers. Thus some forms of serious leisure, such as volunteer work, may be consistent with Christian vocation. The Christian understanding of work is not restricted to paid employment but also includes those unpaid activities that serve others and care for God's creation. Although he does not use the terms "serious leisure" or "project-based leisure," Stott provided a long list of these types of leisure activities that he describes as a form of work.

> For creative leisure, though unpaid, is a form of work. The possibilities are numerous: "do-it-yourself" repairs, redecorations and improvements at home; servicing the car, motorbike or bicycle; self-education through evening classes, correspondence courses or Open University; cultivating the garden or allotment, growing your own vegetables, keeping pigs or chickens; working with wood or metal; dressmaking, knitting and embroidery; making music; painting, pottery and sculpting; reading and writing; and where possible doing these things together, spending more time with family and friends. Then there is the whole sphere of community service, either through the local church or a voluntary organization or on one's own initiative; visiting the sick, the elderly or prison inmates; redecorating an old person's home; working with mentally or physically handicapped people; baby-sitting; collecting other people's children from school; teaching [mentally challenged] children, or ethnic families for whom English is a second language, to read and write; helping in the local hospital, school, club or church.[104]

These types of activities are commendable as long as it is kept in mind that an excessive amount of some forms of serious leisure may reflect work orientation, work addiction, or lead to a life of work. As a result, the second part of Dahl's phrase, "We worship our work, we work at our play, and we play at our worship," becomes characteristic of one's life. Even Stebbins recognized too much volunteering may result in burnout.[105]

Not only may serious leisure have negative consequences if it becomes a form of overwork, but there is also the possibility that it becomes a central life interest to such a degree that it can detract one from one's worship and God's work. The appeal to creation theology in the Exodus account of the Sabbath commandment that was noted in chapter 5 suggests that life is more than constant activity: it is a gift of God and time needs to be set aside to reflect on God and his purposes. Thus to fill up our time with constant activity, hobbies, and volunteer work is to deny God. Serious leisure reflects a common idea that leisure should be creative and full of activities.[106] Yet "it is not necessarily the case that man is most fully human when he is achiever rather than receiver, active rather than passive, subject rather than object."[107]

Rojek is critical of Stebbins's serious leisure concept as it does not include a moral dimension in the six distinctive qualities that describe it, and thus it could be used to describe serial killers, gang rapists, pedophile rings, or drug subcultures.[108] He suggested that the serious leisure concept assumes that the concept applies to activities that improve society and enrich individuals and thus "the amorality of everyday life is a nonissue." To be fair to Stebbins, he has recently suggested that serious leisure needs to be connected to morality. An optimal leisure lifestyle, involving both serious and casual leisure, "has to be connected with ethical education, which is to train people how to realize the part of humanity they are responsible for. All activities chosen have to be in relation with their potential of added value to humankind."[109] In fact, empirical research has found that some forms of serious leisure, such as climbing[110] and dancing,[111] have been conducive to spiritual enrichment and meaning for some Christians.

Ramsay made a clear distinction between serious leisure and his notion of reflective leisure, what has traditionally been called contemplative leisure, when he noted that most examples of serious leisure are not particularly reflective.[112] Furthermore, Stebbins does not necessarily see religious contemplation as always being leisure.[113]

The Classical View of Leisure

The classical view of leisure emerged in ancient Greece. *Scholē* ("leisure") was a state of being that implied freedom or the absence of the necessity of being occupied.

A crucial question for Christians to ask is: If we accept the classical conception of leisure, are we accepting Greek categories of thinking instead of biblical ones? In his book, *The Christian at Play*, Johnston, although acknowledging that the theological task involves the consideration of traditional sources, quickly dismissed both the classical Greek model of play (leisure) and the Protestant model after only a brief one-page discussion of each, in favor of the "Hebraic" model.[114] Similarly, Ryken, in his book *Redeeming the Time*, devoted only two pages to the description of the Greek ideal of leisure that he believes "remains a standard for excellence in leisure."[115]

But we cannot dismiss the classical view of leisure so quickly, for at least three reasons. First, as Pieper pointed out, "the Christian and Western conception of the contemplative life is closely linked to the Aristotelian notion of leisure."[116] Second, the very concept of leisure originated in Greek society. If we want to do justice to the semantic background of leisure, we cannot simply ignore the classical concept. While we may disagree with its content, we can take it and fill it with Christian content, like the apostle John did when he used the Greek word *logos* (John 1), or Paul did when he referred to the statue of the unknown God in Athens (Acts 17). Indeed, this is what those of the medieval monastic period did as we saw in chapter 3. Third, as we also saw in chapter 3, Owens illustrated how Aristotle's conception of leisure "does not offer us any detailed blueprint. It requires us to do our own thinking."[117] The contemplative and intellectual life envisaged by Aristotle was left open for application and development down through the centuries. It has and can be embodied in different ways by different people, such as Augustine's "contemplative life" (*otium*) that was a reflection and meditation on God and God's truth; the *vita contemplativa* of Aquinas that was centered in the beatific vision of God and oriented to the eternal;[118] and the monastic life of leisure that anticipated eternal rest, as expressed in terms such as *otium* (leisure), *quies* (quiet), *vacatio* (freedom), and *sabbatum* (rest).[119] Unfortunately, as we saw in chapter 3, many contemporary leisure scholars turn to Aristotle for guidance in their thinking about leisure, but they completely ignore the biblical record and how the classical concept of leisure has been adapted by Christians throughout the centuries. As Christians we need to fill the classical concept of leisure with biblical content.

At this point it is helpful to discuss *Leisure: The Basis of Culture*, the work of Pieper, a Catholic philosopher who not only sought to revive the classical concept of leisure in the last century but also centered it in divine worship. Owens commented that Aristotle's concept is open to being developed in this direction.[120] Pieper considered leisure to be the primary basis of any culture in the past, present, or future. Culture depends on leisure for its very existence, and leisure in turn is only possible if it has a strong and vital link with divine worship.

> The soul of leisure, it can be said, lies in "celebration." Celebration is the point at which the three elements of leisure come to a focus: relaxation, effortlessness, and the superiority of "active leisure" to all functions.
>
> But if celebration is the core of leisure, then leisure can only be made possible and justifiable on the same basis as the celebration of a festival. *That basis is divine worship.*[121]

Leisure implies celebration, and celebration is rooted in divine worship; worship is therefore considered to be the well-spring of leisure. I concur with Pieper. Our leisure must be God-centered and God-directed in order to guarantee the fruits of leisure. In chapter 5 I inferred from the notion of the Sabbath as a sign of the covenant between God and humans (Exod. 31:16–17) that leisure finds its deepest meaning and fullest potential within the context of a relationship with God.

Separated from divine worship, leisure, according to Pieper, becomes idleness and laziness: "Idleness, . . . so far from being synonymous with leisure, is more nearly the inner prerequisite which renders leisure impossible: it might be described as the utter absence of leisure, or the very opposite of leisure. . . . Idleness and the incapacity for leisure correspond with one another. Leisure is the contrary of the both."[122] Pieper went on to define leisure: "Leisure, it must be clearly understood, is a mental and spiritual attitude—it is not simply the result of external factors, it is not the inevitable result of spare time, a holiday, a week-end or a vacation. It is, in the first place, an attitude of mind, a condition of the soul."[123]

Although Pieper did not explicitly provide a biblical background to his concept of leisure (other than quoting the Septuagint version of Psalm 46:10 at the beginning of his book), the mental and spiritual attitude of which he wrote is not all that different from the qualitative dimension of leisure that I developed in chapters 5 and 6 from the biblical account—the spiritual attitude of rest, joy, freedom, and the rejoicing in God instilled by the Sabbath, along with the quality of life characterized by rest, peace, abundant life, and freedom available to us in Jesus Christ.

Pieper continued, "Leisure is a form of silence, of that silence which is the prerequisite of the apprehension of reality. . . . For leisure is a receptive attitude of mind, a contemplative attitude, and it is not only the occasion but also the capacity for steeping oneself in the world of creation."[124] This steeping of oneself in the world of creation is similar to the idea expressed by the appeal to creation theology as a motivation for Sabbath observance in Exodus 20. Pieper made a connection between the creation account and leisure: "We may read in the first chapter of Genesis that God 'ended his work which he had made' and 'behold, it was very good.' In leisure, man too celebrates the end of his work by allowing his inner eye to dwell for a while upon the reality of the Creation. He looks and he affirms: it is good."[125] The Sabbath encourages an attitude of rejoicing and celebrating the gifts of God's good creation. Similarly, Qoheleth, in Ecclesiastes, teaches the enjoyment of creation, God's gift to humanity. Likewise leisure is that rejoicing and celebrating in, as well as enjoyment of, creation.

Thus leisure is characterized by a receptive and contemplative approach to life along with a celebrating and enjoying of creation that receives its vitality from divine worship, from a relationship with the God who has made himself known to us in Jesus Christ. Leisure in this spiritual sense not only provides inner direction, purpose, and meaning in life but is also the basis of culture.

The major problem with the classical view of leisure is the tendency to emphasize human *being* at the expense of human *doing*. In this view of leisure, as Johnston noted, "Contemplation, not activity becomes our goal; the monastery not the workbench, the place."[126] In Greek society, leisure (*scholē*) was idealized and work (*ascholē*) was disdained. In medieval monastic culture the monastic life of spiritual works was usually set above the active life. Neville pointed out that Aquinas was too reliant on Aristotle, and therefore contemplation is overemphasized while creativity is brushed aside: "It is a limitation in Aristotle's understanding of divinity that his gods did nothing but contemplate. The image of God revealed in the Christian scriptures is of one who creates and loves."[127] Pieper also seemed to idealize leisure above work: "Leisure . . . [is] utterly contrary to the ideal of 'worker' in each of its three aspects . . . as activity, as toil, as a social function."[128] The creational ordinance of work is minimized. In chapters 5 and 9 we saw that both rest and work are basic to the created nature of humanity. Even those whose writing is not articulated directly from a biblical perspective, such as leisure scholar Goodale, believe that humans are intended to be workers: "We live in a world of work and we have no reason to think we should not. We are workers and have no reason to think we should not be, not because Calvin walks in the land but because the world's work (dare we say God's work?) remains to be done. Surely there is no end to the worthwhile work that must be done."[129]

The Holistic Concept of Leisure

Traditionally Christians have held classical, activity, or time definitions of leisure. In general, Roman Catholics such as Pieper,[130] Doohan,[131] and others have articulated the classical view of leisure, while Protestants have advocated an activity (e.g., Ryken[132]) or time (e.g., Neville,[133] Sherrow[134]) view of leisure. More recently some Christians have advocated a more holistic understanding of leisure. For example, Dahl wrote,

> Work and leisure are not distinct; they lie on a continuum. . . . Leisure is being able to combine work, worship, and recreation in a free and loving, holistic way which integrates these three elements as much as possible. Although a person goes to different places to perform different functions, leisure lies in integrating these three aspects in order to experience wholeness in one's life, family, and community.[135]

Joblin advocated a holistic model of leisure that encompasses work, play, and worship in a way that is linked to spirituality and that does not reduce leisure to time or activities.[136] While Doohan primarily holds a classical understanding of leisure, he proposed a "holistic approach to life" that integrates leisure and work while recognizing the contribution of work to individuals, communities, and societies. In this approach "leisure is a necessary dimension of wellness and holistic living."[137]

The traditional concepts of leisure may be placed into one of two categories. The quantitative category includes the free time, social class function, and activity definitions of leisure. The second category, a qualitative one, includes both the classical state-of-being and the contemporary state-of-mind views of leisure. The former category includes behavioral and temporal definitions while the latter category includes attitudinal and existential definitions. The holistic concept of leisure encompasses both categories of definitions.[138]

A holistic approach unites the two previously opposed traditions of leisure, leisure as an end or as a means, as being or as doing, as a qualitative concept or as a quantitative concept. In the classical tradition, leisure is defined as a spiritual and mental attitude, as a style of life and a state of being that was first expressed by Aristotle and other Greek aristocrats, adapted in the medieval monastic practice of *otium*, and more recently advocated by Pieper. The strength of the classical view of leisure is its emphasis on humans' being, on the qualitative dimension of leisure. However, as we have seen, this view often minimizes the creational ordinance of work.

In contrast to the classical interpretation, the second tradition of post-Hellenic Christianity including the Protestant ethic emphasizes work and views "leisure as therapy, rest, relaxation, social control, recreation for subsequent productive effort—and generally, therefore, as instrumental in character."[139] In this Protestant ethic of serving God through much work and the forgoing of pleasures, leisure is viewed as a re-creative and restorative activity that is of secondary significance to the development and spreading of culture. This Protestant view of leisure, influenced by Calvinist theology, contributed to the separation of work and leisure since work was valued as the most important aspect of life while leisure, defined in terms of free time, was relegated to secondary importance.

The strengths of the Protestant view are its recognition of the creational ordinance of work along with the recognition of a rhythm to life—the alternation of periods of work and nonwork or quantitative leisure—that reflects the biblical pattern to life. However, the free time and activity concepts of leisure that the Protestant view incorporate are essentially quantitative approaches to the conceptualization of leisure, and as such leisure has no intrinsic value. The activity concept maintains that perpetual doing is much more important than our being, the qualitative dimension to leisure. But doing is not the primary element in any satisfactory conceptualization of leisure: "Leisure does not have to be a 'doing' . . . it can be just a 'being'—being quiet, being aware, being open to the world about us."[140] The time element is definitely necessary but not sufficient to develop a complete explanation of leisure. The "freedom from" (i.e., time free from work and other obligations as is suggested by the humanitarian motivation of the Sabbath) along with the "freedom for" (i.e., free for activity) are necessary, but these freedoms in and of themselves cannot be equated with leisure. Leisure consists of more than simply quantitative components.[141]

The holistic tendency unites these two historical traditions (which were reviewed in chapters 3 and 4)—leisure as an end and leisure as a means of relaxation and refreshment, the emphasis on being and on doing, the qualitative dimension and the quantitative dimension. In this blend the weaknesses of each tradition are counterbalanced by the strengths of the other tradition. Reflecting on Pieper's classical understanding of leisure, Ramsay recently wrote that "it is important to combine Pieper's spiritual and human insight into our transcendent needs with an account of the other, more familiar aspects of leisure—play, fun, rest, recovery, relaxation, recreation."[142]

The holistic concept of leisure is advocated here not primarily because it offers the opportunity to combine the two historical traditions, although this is a good reason, but because the holistic concept of leisure is able to encompass the variety and richness of the biblical material relevant to leisure. The examination of biblical materials in chapters 5–7 revealed that leisure encompasses quantitative and qualitative dimensions; one related to our doing and the other related to our being. First, the Sabbath teaches a rhythm to life—six days of work and one of nonwork (quantitative leisure), while a variety of biblical elements (e.g., festivals, feasts, dance, hospitality, and friendships) suggest the importance of leisure activities. Second, the qualitative dimension is seen in the spiritual attitude of rest, joy, freedom, and celebration in both God and his creation that is inculcated by the Sabbath and that culminates in the rest, peace, abundant life, and freedom available in Jesus Christ. The holistic concept of leisure is advocated here because it has the capacity to encompass both these quantitative and qualitative dimensions of leisure as inferred from Scripture.

11

leisure, work, and ethics

The previous chapter articulated a Christian holistic understanding of leisure that integrates the classical Roman Catholic understanding of leisure as a spiritual attitude and the Protestant view of leisure as activity. In this chapter I will consider the relationship of work and leisure through the lens of a holistic understanding of leisure. Since the classical view of leisure, which is incorporated into the holistic concept, is linked to virtue, ethics, and the life of proper conduct, the second part of this chapter will discuss leisure ethics as informed by the Golden Rule.

The Relationship of Work and Leisure

A Christian philosophy of leisure cannot be arrived at without considering the other dimensions of life. Both work and rest are basic to the created nature of humanity. Furthermore work flows from our being, from our life in Christ.

How do we relate our biblical understanding of work to the contemporary perceptions of the relationship of work and leisure? Kunio Odaka, in a study of Japanese industrial workers in the 1960s, classified workers according to five types of living related to work and leisure. These five perceptions of the relationship between work and leisure are defined as follows:

1. *Work-oriented-unilateral*: Work is a [person's duty]. I wish to devote myself wholly to my work without any thought of leisure.

2. *Leisure-oriented-unilateral*: Work is no more than a means for living. The enjoyment of leisure is what makes human life worth living.
3. *Identity*: There is no distinction between work and leisure. I therefore have no need of being liberated from work in order that I may enjoy leisure.
4. *Split*: Work is work and leisure is leisure. Modern [people get their] work done smartly, and enjoy their leisure moderately.
5. *Integrated*: Work makes leisure pleasurable, and leisure gives new energy to work. I wish to work with all my might, and to enjoy leisure.[1]

In his book *The Christian at Play*, Johnston adapted Odaka's classification for the purpose of articulating a Christian approach to work and play. He advocated that Christians accept an "integrated" relationship of work and play.[2] Using these same five lifestyles as a framework, I will discuss the relationship of work and leisure. Based on the understandings of leisure and work that I have developed from the biblical and historical sources, I will argue that the "identity" approach is the most appropriate response in most circumstances. Let us critique each of the five possible relationships individually. While there may be some value in Ryken's claim[3] that we should not try to find the Christian model for the relationship between work and leisure as Johnston and I do, how we conceptualize leisure is going to influence how we view the work and leisure relationship.

Work-Oriented-Unilateral Approach

In the "work-oriented-unilateral" lifestyle, work is the supreme value in life while leisure is subservient. This work-oriented-unilateral approach to life is characteristic of the Protestant and secular work ethics. In the religious and secular worldviews that have dominated Western society since the Reformation, humans have been regarded as *homo faber*, humans as workers, and one's main function has been to work at one's particular place in society. The saying "One does not work to live; one lives to work," is a good description of this approach to life. The problem with the emphasis on humans as *homo faber* is that the value of leisure is minimized. Margaret Mead observed, "Within traditional American culture . . . there runs a persistent belief that all leisure must be earned by work and good works. And second, while it is enjoyed it must be seen in a context of future work and good works."[4] When work becomes a person's only focus, it blinds him or her to the other dimensions of a person's created nature. Scripture suggests that work and rest are basic to the nature of humans. Although humans are workers, that is not the whole truth about humanity's nature and destiny; humanity was created to glorify and enjoy God forever.

Furthermore, for Christians work is never the central determinant of our worth. Berton wrote: "Work seems to be the one thoroughly acceptable way that a man can demonstrate his worth to himself and his peers."[5] Yet Houston wrote,

"The glorification of work and its rewards both distort the human psyche as well as obscure the true meaning of work. For the essence of 'man lies not in what he does, but in who he is.'"[6] Therefore we cannot accept the work-oriented-unilateral approach to the work-leisure relationship for it exalts humans as *homo faber* to the detriment of the other dimensions of human's created nature.

Leisure-Oriented-Unilateral Approach

In the "leisure-oriented-unilateral" approach to the relationship between work and leisure, the experiencing of leisure is the primary value in life. This approach can be seen in classical Greek culture where leisure was idealized and work despised, in some expressions of the medieval monastic culture where the contemplative life was emphasized at the expense of the active life, and in some expressions of the more recent casual or anti-utilitarian concept of leisure wherein hedonistic and narcissistic pursuits are valued above participation in society. In both the classical and monastic cultures, the notion of *homo faber*, humans as workers, was minimized in favor of the contemplative life. In the casual or anti-utilitarian view of leisure, *homo faber* is rejected in favor of *homo ludens*, humans as players. In all three cases, a human's "being" is emphasized above a human's "doing." The creational intention of humans as workers is minimized. But to emphasize leisure at the expense of work is contrary to our nature, as Jacques Ellul, among others, noted,

> To assert that the individual expresses his personality and cultivates himself in the course of his leisure is to accept the suppression of half of the human personality. History compels the judgement that it is in work that human beings develop and affirm their personality. When the human being is no longer responsible for his work and no longer figures in it, he feels spiritually outraged. . . . The annihilation of work and its compensation with leisure resolves the conflicts by referring them to a subhuman plane. . . . To gamble that leisure will enable man to live is . . . to cut him off completely from part of life.[7]

The biblical account teaches us that work is something that makes us fully human, therefore the leisure-oriented-unilateral approach to life, with its narrowing of work to a means for living, is not acceptable to the Christian.

Split Approach

The "split" approach to life views work and leisure as two separate categories. In this approach the human is both a worker, *homo faber*, and a player, *homo ludens*, but there is a clear distinction between the two roles in life. In chapter 8 we observed that in earlier societies, which reflected *Gemeinschaft* (strong communities), there was no clear distinction between work and leisure; rather, this distinction came about historically through a variety of influences that included:

(1) the fixed times in monastic culture for manual labor and for spiritual activities; (2) the confusion of vocation, work, and job that arose from the Reformers' understanding of the Christian's calling (1 Cor. 7:20) that ultimately tended to be narrowed to the work associated with a specific position in society—this contributed to work being defined as time devoted to a job;[8] and (3) the glorification of work that accompanied industrialism, through which work came to be the most significant aspect of life while leisure was relegated to free time. The divorcing of work and leisure is characteristic of the average worker today, who (as we observed at the beginning of chapter 8) often despairs of finding satisfaction in or through his or her job but believes work is a necessity in life in order to earn an income to provide for the good life.

Johnston noted that "a biblical notion of Christian vocation will have nothing to do with such compartmentalization and secularization."[9] Rather than separating work and leisure, we are to "do all to the glory of God." In my critique of the free time concept of leisure I suggested that all of life is freely given by God, and therefore we cannot divide life into distinct segments of work and leisure. Furthermore, Ecclesiastes teaches that all of life, including work, is to be enjoyed. It is not suggested that work is to be compartmentalized from the other elements of life that are to be enjoyed. Therefore I conclude that the "split" approach to life is not appropriate for the Christian.

Integrated Approach

In the "integrated" approach to life, "work makes leisure pleasurable and leisure gives new energy to work. I wish to work with all my might, and to enjoy leisure."[10] Johnston stated that this is the style of life God intended for us: "Christians are created and called to consecrate both their work and their play." However, Johnston proceeded, "play is God's appointment, his gift to humankind which is meant to relativize and refresh our endeavours, putting them in their God-intended perspective."[11] Although throughout his book Johnston writes about play as nonpurposeful activity with intrinsic value in itself, he now portrays play as a means "to relativize and refresh one's endeavours." In this view, humans are still both *homo faber* (humans as workers) and *homo ludens* (humans as players), however the worker serves the player and the player serves the worker. If one holds the activity view of leisure, then this approach to work and leisure might be appropriate; however, if leisure is also a spiritual attitude that permeates and undergirds all of life, then this approach fails to do complete justice to leisure.

Identity Approach

The "identity" approach to life, in which work and leisure are merged, is more consistent with the holistic concept of leisure that I advocate. The holistic perspective suggests that one's life is not fragmented into a number of spheres, such as work, leisure, family, and religion, but all aspects of life are considered as part of the whole. In the holistic view of life, work and leisure are inextricably related and fused. This does not mean that work and leisure, especially when leisure is considered as a spiritual attitude and a condition of being, can be equated with each other, but rather that they can be experienced at the same time, unlike the work-oriented-unilateral, leisure-oriented-unilateral, split, and integrated approaches to life that all make a clear temporal distinction between work and leisure.

The holistic, or Odaka's "identity," approach to life in which there is a fusion of work and leisure is a more helpful approach than the traditional approaches that place work and leisure in an antithesis. From a Christian perspective, the ultimate meaning in life is found neither in work nor leisure. As Arthur Holmes wrote, "In the final analysis a human being is neither *homo faber* nor *homo ludens*. A person at the heart of his being is *homo religeous*, his life to be lived in responsible relationship to God, and it is worship that is his most distinctive activity, not work and not play."[12] And as Pieper has shown, worship is the wellspring of leisure. Leisure originates in a right relationship with God. Thus leisure is primarily seen in a qualitative sense, as a spiritual attitude and as a condition of being. Oswald Chambers spoke of "the leisureliness that ought to characterize the children of God."[13] Vos suggested that "perhaps the adverb 'leisurely' conveys more accurately than the noun [leisure] that way of living, the style of life, which is the goal of the Christian."[14]

When leisure is considered as a spiritual attitude and a condition of being, then work and leisure may occur simultaneously. Our leisure, as a condition of our being, is reflective of the quality of life we have in Christ, and from this life in Christ flows our work, our activity, our doing. "Leisure is both the source and climax of genuine work," wrote Banks.[15] Work is an expression, in the form of service to God and humanity, of thanksgiving and gratitude to Christ, one's divine master. Thus Houston could write,

> True leisure then is the expression that we give to the Lordship of Jesus Christ
> . . . the constant recognition that our identity does not lie in our work roles, that
> our identity is only in Jesus Christ, and that the stronger our identity grows in
> Christ, the less neurotic our activities will become and the freer we shall be from
> the enslavement of work. . . . Our vocation will then look less and less like a job
> to do, and more and more a source of rejoicing in gratitude of what we are privi-
> leged to do to the glory of God.[16]

But how, in our daily lives, do we resolve the tension between being and doing, rest and work? Scripture teaches that both rest and work are basic to the created nature of humanity. To resolve such a tension William Still advocated simultaneous rest and work.

Therefore we must learn to act properly, with a due balance of rest and work, which we may say is to work *from* a position and attitude of rest. . . . [A]s Christians we ought to live with a restful ease, even in busyness and in energetic activity, which not only ought to enable us to get through our work, but to do so more efficiently and therefore also more enjoyably.[17]

So our work is to flow from a quality of life, a spiritual attitude characterized by rest in God. According to Still we are to have a "due balance of rest and work." This brings us to the second dimension of leisure, the quantitative dimension and the idea of rhythm to life. So far we have been emphasizing the qualitative dimension—leisure as a condition of our being.

In part 3 on the biblical background to leisure, I concluded that while most of the biblical material related to leisure supports a qualitative definition of leisure, the Bible also supports a quantitative dimension to leisure. The Sabbath teaches a rhythm to life—six days of work and one of nonwork. The implication is that the Sabbath suggests that some rhythm or cycle of work and leisure (in a quantitative sense) is necessary for well-being and wholeness. Thus in addition to leisure as a spiritual attitude that undergirds all of life, "periods are necessary when leisure is lived more intensely."[18] Doohan wrote,

We have a leisurely approach to life which must be nourished by times of intensified leisure. The latter will include, among other things, play, friendship, sharing, an absence of oppression in favor of a happy and cheerful affirmation of oneself, a feeling of at-homeness in the world, and a capacity to steep oneself in the beauty of the universe. It will demand a form of silence and inward calm leading to a receptive attitude of mind above all; it will be a varied celebration of life—men's and women's looking upon creation and seeing that it is good.[19]

Intensified leisure can also include those leisure activities reflective of biblical themes that we identified in chapter 7: festivals, feasts, dance, hospitality, and friendships.

In conclusion, then, a Christian holistic conceptualization of leisure has two dimensions: a qualitative and a quantitative. The qualitative dimension is the spiritual attitude and condition of being that reflects the quality of life available in Jesus Christ. This qualitative dimension of leisure is not limited to a certain time period, thus it may be experienced simultaneously with work; work may be conceived of as an expression of this attitude. The quantitative dimension of leisure consists of certain times and activities—ranging from silent contemplation to an active celebration and rejoicing in the gifts of creation—in which an intensification of leisure is experienced. Thus all of our life should be characterized by a spiritual attitude of leisure, but at the same time our life should exhibit a rhythm of periods of work and periods of intensified leisure.

Leisure Ethics

The classical understanding of leisure plays an important role in the holistic view of leisure that has just been articulated. As we saw in a number of places earlier, the classical understanding of leisure is linked to virtue, ethics, and the life of proper conduct. Therefore we need to consider the ethics of leisure. While many biblical passages may be used to develop a Christian perspective on the ethics of leisure, I will limit my discussion to the implications of the Golden Rule for leisure activity.

Jesus instructs his followers to "love your neighbor as yourself" (Matt. 22:39b), and in Luke 6:31 he commands them to "do to others as you would have them do to you." What are the implications of this Golden Rule for leisure? First, the Golden Rule presupposes self-love, that one will treat oneself well, for this is the model for behavior to others. Thus one's leisure behaviors will be for one's good. Neville suggested that leisure is the place of self-love where we learn to love ourselves and where we foster and appreciate our own uniqueness.[20] Neville explained that in Jesus's summary of the Law, loving God fulfills the religious, loving our neighbor fulfills the ethical, and loving ourself fulfills the aesthetic.[21] In a discussion of which recreation activities are acceptable, Goodale and Godbey suggested that acts harmful to oneself are not acceptable.[22] The Golden Rule, especially in its positive formulation as stated by Jesus, suggests a more positive and proactive approach. Individuals are encouraged to participate in those activities that are good for them, those activities that are best. It is through a healthy self-love that humans care for their physical, social, emotional, mental, and spiritual needs. Although leisure activities may be chosen primarily for their enjoyment, activities can be selected that enhance total health. Leisure activities can provide opportunities for improving bodily health, nurturing social relationships, promoting positive self-concept, expanding cognitive abilities, and increasing spiritual awareness.[23]

Secondly, the Golden Rule suggests that not only should one not participate in activities that would harm another person—again a criterion that Goodale and Godbey use to determine unacceptable activities—but one also should seek out what is best for the other person.[24] Jesus's "love your neighbor as yourself" suggests more than just ensuring one's activity is not harmful to another, more than just "tolerating" another's behavior as suggested by today's relativism, but suggests an active involvement in seeking the best for the other person. Neville explained, "In leisure, the love of neighbour is the simple, restful acceptance of the other person as God's creation and the object of his love."[25] He suggested that love of neighbor includes fostering and appreciating the uniqueness of another person, which is directly applicable to participation in many leisure activities.[26] Thus any leisure that tends to dehumanize people, whether it be through making them sex objects, shattering their self-respect, stifling their growth, or any leisure that is unloving, unjust, unfair, or needlessly violent is challenged by the Golden Rule.

Ron Johnson and Don McLean pointed out that as recreation programming has become more pluralistic, recreation provision has been guided more by excluding errant behavior than by emulating an ideal.[27] While this is consistent with the Golden Rule in the sense that recreation provision is excluding those activities that might harm one's neighbor and thus be in contradiction to "doing to others as you would have them do to you," Jesus's positive formulation of the Golden Rule suggests going a step further and selecting activities that are not only enjoyable but also enhance holistic health.

Much leisure activity in our society (e.g., games and sports) is dominated by a competitive attitude. Sometimes this competitive attitude turns into a cutthroat desire to win at all costs and to humiliate opponents. In its extreme form such an attitude leads to sports violence characterized more by retaliation than by "doing to others as you would have them do to you." The rule that is prevalent in much competitive sport is: "You did it to me, therefore I'll do it to you." Humiliation also takes a form of verbal intimidation. At sporting events we hear phrases such as, "We're going to get them the next time," or "Kill the ump." Coaches frequently use the motivation of revenge to prepare their players for the big game. All such behaviors, along with play to prove oneself better than others or to be "one up on" fellow players, is not consistent with "doing to others as you would have them do to you." Furthermore, as Neville put it, "The cult of competitiveness gives leisure the character of training for further conflict which is alien to the inner meaning of leisure itself."[28] However, friendly competition that challenges participants and brings out their best efforts, efforts that show one is ultimately performing for oneself, may be consistent with the spirit of the Golden Rule. For example, competitive athletes, such as swimmers or runners, may spur one another on to personal best times that they would not otherwise achieve outside competition. However, cooperative games that focus on playing and winning together may lend themselves more to an implementation of the Golden Rule than many competitive sports in our society.[29]

It has been suggested that the Golden Rule promotes love, compassion, and self-sacrificing concern for others.[30] This interpretation has implications for justice issues. How might my leisure activity be affecting the marginalized in our society or those in developing countries? Am I establishing or preserving dominance over others through my leisure? Am I participating in activities or consuming recreational goods that directly or indirectly support oppressive regimes or that exploit peoples in developing nations? Does my recreational behavior create barriers that prevent other people from maximizing their leisure; for example, do I misuse recreation environments, whether natural or human-made, in ways that will detract from another person's experience?

Furthermore, Neville instructed that we need to keep in mind the prophets' condemnation of those who exploit the needy and the poor (e.g., Amos 4:1) when we consider how the provision of leisure in today's society may exploit vulnerable groups, such as children and the poor. Noting that "the Bible includes prophetic denunciation of class exploitation," he explained that a "responsible attitude to the increasing leisure opportunities must include awareness of the context of exploitation in which they are frequently set."[31]

It has also been suggested that the Golden Rule promotes kindness and forgiveness.[32] Despite how good our intentions might be, there will still be times when one person's recreation has a negative impact or harmful effect on another person. Kindness and forgiveness, as suggested by the Golden Rule, instead of revenge and bitterness, are helpful virtues in resolving conflicts that arise in these situations.

part 6

a leisurely
spirituality

12

leisure and spiritual well-being

Given the holistic concept of leisure arrived at in the previous chapters, in which leisure is seen to comprise both a spiritual attitude to life and time periods or activities of intensified leisure that can strengthen one's spiritual attitude to life, it is logical that we examine the relationship between leisure and spiritual well-being. Even if one does not hold the holistic understanding of leisure, other conceptualizations of leisure are also associated with spirituality. As we saw in chapter 3, the classical definition of leisure has had spiritual overtones for centuries. When leisure is defined as free time, the free time can be used for spiritual growth. When leisure is defined as activity, spiritual activities may be included. Peak experience, optimal experience, and flow, which are associated with the state-of-mind view of leisure, have been used to describe spiritual experiences.

In chapter 2 we saw that the lack of a spiritual dimension to leisure is one of the leisure issues in our society. And, in the introduction, I summarized a number of the arguments made by Doohan for leisure being a spiritual need.[1] One of the strengths of Doohan's book (*Leisure: A Spiritual Need*) is the connection he made between leisure and spiritual growth. Table 12.1 summarizes a number of practical suggestions Doohan identified for enhancing spiritual growth and development during leisure time. A question we might consider is whether there is research evidence to support Doohan's claims that leisure is a spiritual need and an essential ingredient in spiritual development.

At about the same time that Doohan published his book (1990), leisure studies scholars Barbara McDonald and Richard Schreyer wrote about the spiritual benefits of leisure participation and leisure settings, which established the foundation for the social scientific study of the relationship between leisure and spirituality.[2] Some twenty years later a body of empirical literature has begun to be established on this topic. Some of these studies have gone beyond determining if leisure has spiritual benefits to investigate the leisure factors that produce spiritual benefits. As Chris Schmidt asked, "What is it about these experiences that contribute to spiritual benefits within leisure?"[3] Examples of spiritual benefits include spiritual experiences, spiritual well-being, and leisure-spiritual coping (to be discussed in the next chapter).[4] Spiritual well-being may be defined as

> a high level of faith, hope, and commitment in relation to a well-defined worldview or belief system that provides a sense of meaning and purpose to existence in general, and that offers an ethical path to personal fulfillment which includes connectedness with self, others, and a higher power or larger reality.[5]

A Christian understanding of spiritual well-being would be similar to the above definition but involve a well-defined Christian worldview or belief system, and include connectedness with self, others, and God.

Table 12.1

Leisure Time Practices to Enhance Spiritual Growth and Development

Contemplative Exercises: listening (Matt. 13:17); seeing (Luke 10:23); sitting still and doing nothing (Ps. 46:10); relaxation (Ps. 131:2); development of the senses of taste, smell, touch (Ps. 34:8); free association (Ps. 139:1); free expression (Ps. 51:15); worship by affirmation (Matt. 5:48); worship by detachment (Matt. 5:45); breathing exercises (Gen. 2:7)

Attitudes to Develop during Leisure: rest, read, relax, recreate, rethink, rejoice, refocus, renew, rejuvenate

Attitudes to Eliminate during Leisure: compulsiveness, complaining, sharing of the negative, the desire to have the complete leisure experience while neglecting attitudinal refocusing; feeling guilty about saying no to extra work

Strategies for Leisure: Choose the company of people who appreciate quality of life; slow down the pace of daily living; add exercise; develop a new self-concept not dependent on career (readjust values away from social pressures to conform); do something to counter the specific pressures of your normal life (a change)

Source: Leonard Doohan, *Leisure: A Spiritual Need* (Notre Dame, IN: Ave Maria, 1990), 87–93.

At least eight processes that link leisure and spirituality have been identified through empirical research.[6] Processes that may enhance spiritual well-being are a balance of work and leisure in life; time and space for spiritual activities; attitudes of gratefulness, openness, and celebration; leisure settings with personal or historical meaning; spending time in nature and engaging with it; getting away to a different environment; times of solitude and personal reflection; and connecting with others. We will discuss each of these processes in this chapter.

While empirical research on leisure and spirituality is recent, nonempirical knowledge and wisdom on spirituality has existed for centuries. Within the Christian tradition, the classics of spirituality outline and describe spiritual disciplines or practices that aid in spiritual growth.[7] A review of classic writings on Christian spirituality, often in the form of anthologies[8] or summaries,[9] is helpful in determining if the identified leisure processes are similar to traditional Christian spiritual practices and disciplines. Thus this chapter will investigate whether the leisure processes that have been empirically documented as contributing to spirituality are similar to the spiritual practices and disciplines that have been advocated for centuries as paths to spiritual growth in the Christian tradition.

While the processes that we will discuss may enhance spirituality, it is important to keep in mind that some leisure-spiritual processes may repress spirituality. Both quantitative and qualitative studies have documented how leisure can detract from, as well as enhance, spiritual well-being (see fig. 12.1). Thus it should not be presumed that leisure activities and programs are always spiritually beneficial for participants.

Figure 12.1
Model of Leisure and Spiritual Well-Being

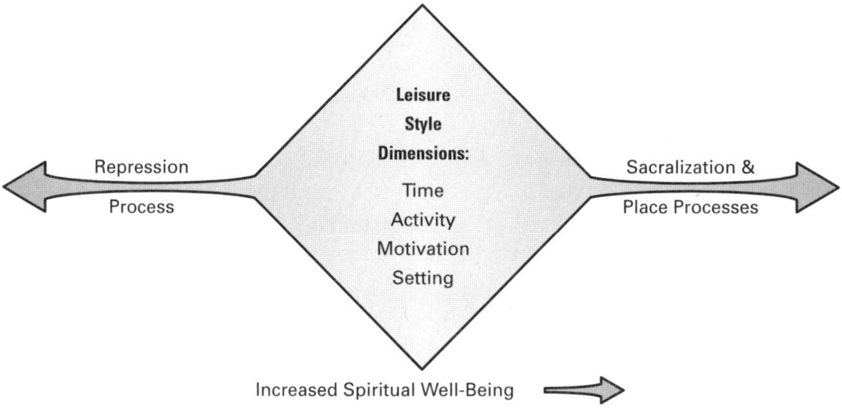

Source: Paul Heintzman, "Leisure and Spiritual Well-Being: A Social Scientific Exploration" (PhD diss., University of Waterloo, 1997), 245.

Balance in Life

Empirically a balance of work and leisure in life, in contrast to busyness, has been found to be conducive to spirituality. For example, in a qualitative study I conducted on leisure and spiritual well-being, balance in life, in contrast to busyness, was discovered to be conducive to spiritual well-being. [10] Balance involved daily, weekly, monthly, and yearly dimensions, while the exact nature of balance was different for each participant. Participants' reflections on balance included these comments:

> You need balance. . . . I believe God can be in leisure and in work, so I think you need balance in your life. . . . If one gets off [balance] then everything, just falls apart. (Andrea)

> I tend to get involved in projects that I don't see the end of because I have lots of time. . . . I let things take over my life . . . so then, it gives me problems a lot of the time. . . . It's a question of balance; I often get out of balance because I do have a lot of time and so I . . . tend to get immersed in things. (Diane)

> Balance is really important throughout the day . . . in both inward nurturing and also the connection with other people, and service is [an] important part of that too, so it's that interaction and the balance. (Fiona)

In Maria Anderegg and colleagues' study of mental health professionals, participants noted that balance tended to be actualized when boundaries were less rigid, when ordinary life was celebrated, and simple tasks, such as doing laundry, were viewed as spiritual. [11] Making time for and engaging in leisure helped people to take care of all the tasks and responsibilities in their life and the things they valued. Therefore leisure provided the opportunity to develop a balanced life. The notion of balance overlapped with the search for an integrated life (physical, psychological, emotional, spiritual), and it was "through the common image of being on a journey and the search for integration, that leisure seemed to be closest to spirituality." [12] Participants who integrated leisure into their life, as compared to compartmentalizing it, were more open to spiritual experiences.

This theme of balance has similarities with the early Christian notion of *otium sanctum*, or "holy leisure," which Richard Foster described as "a sense of balance in life, an ability to be at peace through the activities of the day, an ability to rest and take time to enjoy beauty, an ability to pace ourselves." [13] This ability to have a sense of balance in life and to be at peace during daily activities, which grew out of menial service in a monastic kitchen, is seen in the life of Brother Lawrence as described in the spiritual classic *Practicing the Presence of God*. For example, after a section on his work in the kitchen and shoe shop it is stated "that he was more united to God in his ordinary activities than when he devoted himself to religious activities." [14] Furthermore, as we saw in chapter 3, medieval monastics advocated a balance wherein *otium* (leisure) was viewed halfway between the two dangers of *otiositas* (idleness) and *negotium* (business). [15]

Leisure as Time and Space

Empirical research has documented that leisure creates time and space for activities with a spiritual dimension. Participants in my qualitative study on leisure and spiritual well-being noted that leisure provided the time for spiritual development and the space necessary to create an environment for spiritual well-being.[16] The following examples from participants explain how leisure creates time and space for spiritual well-being:

> It [leisure] is more restful, you can be more focused, you can be more fully present, it allows for creativity and it is less doing or task-oriented. (Andrea)

> I think in some ways it's [spiritual development] easier with leisure activities because there's a sense of space, which is important to me, . . . and [if] I've chosen to take that time and create that space, chances are I will be more open to the spiritual dimensions within myself and those who are with me and in a wider context. (Fiona)

> More and more my life has become more leisurely, I have become more spiritual for sure because . . . I have needed to create more space for leisure in my life in order to allow myself to get in touch with an environment that helps me to have spiritual growth. (Hilary)

In another qualitative study by Chris Schmidt and Donna Little, it was discovered that leisure gave participants the time and space to learn more about themselves and to increase their spiritual awareness.[17] Time meant not only time for activity but also time away from expectations and responsibilities. Space meant creating space for self in a specific location or activity. This time and space allowed participants to experience spirituality, know God, or to be aware of a power greater than the self.

In their study of mental health professionals, Anderegg and colleagues discovered that leisure provided the opportunity for spiritual experience.

> Leisure provides one with the opportunity to reflect and become more in touch with self and focus on self-care. For many participants, leisure became a space in which reflection took place. It allowed participants to connect with their needs, count their blessings and feel thankful for what they have achieved in their lives.[18]

Interestingly it was observed that the mental health professionals who had integrated leisure into their lives, in comparison to those who were trying hard to set aside a special time for leisure, were more receptive to spiritual experiences that appeared during the course of everyday life. In a study that involved photo elicitation interviews, where the participants received disposable cameras with the instruction to take photos of places that were special to them, followed by interviews that explored the ways that spirituality and religion does or does not operate in each place, Roman Williams discovered that some people create space for God in their leisure settings, such as in their homes, bedrooms, gardens, or at the beach.[19]

These findings are consistent with classical and contemporary Christian writings on spirituality that suggest leisure is necessary for spiritual development. For example, Doohan stated, "A leisured approach to life is a basic element in the first stages of spiritual growth,"[20] while Teaff wrote that it has long been recognized that "Christian spirituality thrives best in a leisure atmosphere where time and space are allotted for 'being' as well as 'doing.'"[21] Henri Nouwen explained "we need to set aside a time and space to give him [God] our undivided attention."[22]

Attitude of Openness

An attitude of receptivity, gratitude, and celebration during leisure has been empirically shown to enhance spirituality. In my qualitative study of leisure and spiritual well-being, I discovered that while leisure created time and space to cultivate spiritual well-being, time did not necessarily guarantee spiritual well-being. A key factor was the attitude that participants brought to their activities: an attitude characterized by terms such as "keeping awareness open," "seeing with new eyes," "gratitude," "gratefulness," "focus," a "different way of seeing things," "intentionality," "discernment," and "being awake to seeing."[23] Fiona spoke of a "frame of mind" an "attitude" that involved "being awake to seeing," and that determined whether or not leisure activities were helpful to her spiritual well-being.

> There's some mornings when I walk the dog and there is this wonderful sense of being awake, surrounded by the air . . . and there's a sense of being open to that. But I could also go out and it could be another beautiful day and I'm preoccupied with thinking about the project I'm supposed to be doing, maybe I'm worried about a relationship . . . and I can just be spinning around in my head and not even see anything as I walk along. . . . I think I believe that they all [leisure activities] are [spiritual] but I don't always recognize it and that's part of how I would approach it, because . . . if part of what we are is spirit . . . they are but it is *whether or not we are awake to seeing* that. . . . So if I'm doing the compulsive sort of . . . spinning my wheels kind of thing as I'm walking the dog, . . . that can be a block to spiritual well-being but, it doesn't mean it's not spiritual.

Another participant, George, mentioned a "kind of discernment," "an intentionality or focus," a "different way of seeing things" that involved gratefulness and gratitude as being necessary for leisure to be associated with spiritual well-being.

When I stop and think about it or bring them [leisure activities and experiences] to, I suppose bring them to prayer, then in some ways they all become part of my spiritual life and can contribute to that spiritual well-being. . . . But they can also just be activities in the day. I think it is just a *different way of seeing things* . . . so I think all those activities can contribute in some way to my spiritual life and my spiritual well-being if I let them or if I consciously bring them into it . . . through prayer, through reflection, . . . the whole thing of just being able to go through the day with *gratitude*.

Similarly, Anderegg and colleagues' study of mental health professionals discovered that there was a "space" or state of mind associated with the participants' leisure in which a person experienced fewer demands, and less worry, stress, and pressure. Participants reported that when they were in this "space" they felt more open, more receptive, and aware of new possibilities for renewal and relaxation. Anderegg and colleagues also noted a sense of gratitude and a celebration of life and creation; when leisure became a celebration of life in all its forms, there was a connection with spirituality. Closely related was a sense the participants had of "being in the moment," which gave the participants a fresh perspective on the world: "It gave them new eyes, which rested firmly on the fullness of the present moment, changing even the most ordinary of experiences into something extraordinary, miraculous and spiritual."[24]

The attitude of celebration is advocated in the Christian spiritual tradition. As suggested by the title of his book *Celebration of Discipline*, Foster wrote: "Celebration is central to all the Spiritual Disciplines. Without a joyful spirit of festivity the Disciplines become dull. . . . Every Discipline should be characterized by carefree gaiety and a sense of thanksgiving."[25] Thanksgiving and gratitude are at the heart of the Christian life, as Thomas Merton explained.

To be grateful is to recognize the love of God in everything He has given us—and He has given us everything. Every breath we draw is a gift of His love, every moment of existence is a grace, for it brings with it immense graces from Him. Gratitude . . . is constantly awakening to new wonder and to praise of the goodness of God. . . . Gratefulness . . . is the heart of the Christian life.[26]

Doohan explained that Christian spiritual development is dependent on a "sense of appreciation, wonder, awe, and mystery."[27] An attitude of openness was taught by Teresa of Avila, a sixteenth-century Spanish mystic, who emphasized that people do not develop spiritually by effort and hard work but by passively accepting the gifts of God. She wrote about the need for passivity, relaxation, listening, quiet, and reflection in her seven stages of the spiritual life.[28] As Neville put it, leisure "through receptivity will open communication both with God who is personal and with humanity which receives its personality from him."[29]

Leisure Settings of Personal or Human History

Empirical studies have documented how leisure settings of personal or human history enhance spirituality. Participants in my study on leisure and spiritual well-being noted that settings that had a sense of personal history (places associated with childhood or earlier periods of life) or human history (old buildings, ancient cultures) tended to be conducive to spiritual well-being.[30] For example, Fiona, when asked if she associated any geographical settings or any particular settings of her leisure activities with spiritual growth, referred to the geographical area where she grew up.

> Muskoka, it's where I grew up and it's very much a sense of that landscape having formed who I am and also formed my spirituality. It influences the images that I have of God, it influences images of all kinds of things, it is just very much a part of me, so Canadian Shield, water, trees growing out of rocks along the water edge. I mean that's where I feel most at home. I don't live there anymore. I do have the capacity . . . in different settings of seeing the wonder there, but it comes most easily when I'm home.

Not only places of personal history, but settings of human history were associated with spiritual well-being. Andrea described her experience of walking into an old church.

> I ended up being by myself [in the church], I went into the sanctuary and the windows were open. . . . [I]t's just the stained glass and the trees outside and the leaves, I mean, you look at those stones going all the way up the church and like, you know, very high ceilings and you're thinking "oh" and how long it's been there, the people have been worshiping there and it just gives you that sense of, of timelessness that, that there's been other generations.

Andrea contrasted this timelessness with much of the transitory nature of urban architecture: "It is just I think part of the problem too, you know, in the city is that as soon as something gets decrepit or not that well done, they tear it down and put something else up."

In a qualitative study of women's wilderness experience, Fox found that associations with history and ancient items were conducive to spiritual experience.[31] Somewhat related, Schmidt and Little identified ritual and tradition as a trigger that sparked the spiritual dimension of leisure experiences.[32] For example, lifestyle habits, such as the ritual of a morning walk or the annual attendance at a specific festival, triggered a spiritual response and outcome.

There is less direct support of this process in the classics of Christian spirituality compared to the other processes; however, within some Christian traditions there is an emphasis on visits or pilgrimages to sacred sites.[33] For example, within the Celtic spiritual tradition there is a sense that some places are "thin";

spiritual realities could be sensed more directly and acutely in these places. In an introduction to the Celtic Northumbria Community, Foster described four encounters that he had in four places special to this community: Cuthbert's Cave; Lindisfarne (also called Holy Island) with the statue of St. Aiden, the priory ruins, and the "prayer hole"; the small chapel at Old Bewick; and the prayer chapel in the ancient grottolike cellar of Northumbria Community's Mother House and retreat center called Nether Springs.[34] The "prayer hole" in particular reminded Foster of the words of Jeremiah 6:16: "Stand at the crossroads, and look, and ask for the ancient paths, where the good way lies; and walk in it, and find rest for your souls." In a book on the history of Christian spirituality, Bradley Holt recommended going on a pilgrimage to a place that is personally meaningful, such as a place where God was heard at an earlier time, a grave of a loved one, or the locale of a well-known spiritual writer.[35] In terms of regular practices of going to certain places, we read that Jesus "on the Sabbath day . . . went into the synagogue, as was his custom" (Luke 4:16; see also Mark 1:21; 3:1; Luke 4:16; 13:10).

Being in Nature

Extensive empirical research suggests that opportunities in leisure to experience nature and develop a relationship with it is conducive to spirituality.[36] Numerous quantitative studies suggest that spiritual benefits are one of many benefits sought by a majority of wilderness visitors. Furthermore, research studies suggest that more natural settings, nature-oriented activities, and being alone in these settings are more likely to be associated with spirituality.[37] Researchers have discovered various reasons why wilderness recreation produces spiritual benefits: it "provides a place to find inner peace and tranquility, solitude, beauty and spiritual rekindling";[38] its biophysical characteristics and opportunity for direct contact with nature are spiritually inspiring;[39] wilderness nature is seen as powerful, therapeutic, and spiritual;[40] and wilderness is conducive to spiritual well-being as it generates intrigue, reflection, awe and wonder, and creates a sense of vulnerability.[41]

In addition to studies on wilderness experience, studies on leisure in all settings have also identified the important role of nature in spiritual benefits. In Anderegg and colleagues' study of mental health professionals, it was discovered that nature settings and activities were by far the most evident connection between leisure and spirituality.[42] Their study demonstrated that nature instilled a sense of amazement, wonder, and awe that led to spiritual meditation and reflection. Livengood's study of New Paradigm Christians found that recreation in natural settings provided participants with the opportunity to connect with God and also to experience and enjoy God's creation.[43] Other studies have discovered that nature settings are conducive to spiritual well-being for a variety of reasons: nature elicits a sense of wonder and awe, as in the Anderegg and colleagues study;[44] nature helps some participants connect with God,[45] as in the Livengood study; nature is life giving;[46] and nature provides a sense of peacefulness, calm, and stillness.[47] One of the participants in my qualitative study on leisure and spiritual well-being provided the following explanation:

> Being out in nature is, I think, just about the best way to experience God. I've always liked the outdoors, I like eating outside; I like doing anything outside and I think often talk to God and pray in nature and you know, God talks to you. I think it is a really good . . . place to pray . . . talking and praying seem to go with nature. . . . So that's why I like gardening too. I think I'm having conversations with God in the garden and because I think we're part of nature. We're part of the universe and we belong out there. I think we are green on the inside, it's peaceful, it's quiet, it's nourishing, and all those things that you connect them more with the spiritual being.[48]

This nature factor is similar to the ancient tradition of meditating on creation, "that first form of contemplation which the old mystics sometimes called 'discovery of God in His creatures.'"[49] Several biblical verses allude to this discovery of God in creation (e.g., Job 12:7–9; 37:14; Ps. 19:1; Matt. 6:28–29; Rom. 1:20). For example, Psalm 19:1 reads, "The heavens declare the glory of God; / the skies proclaim the works of his hands." Numerous Christian writers through the centuries have described how the created world aids in spiritual growth.[50] For example, St. Athanasius (297–373) wrote,

> For creation, as if written in characters and by means of its order and harmony, delares in a loud voice its own Master and Creator. . . . For this reason, God, by his own Word, gave creation such order as is found therein, so that while He is by nature invisible, men might yet be able to know Him through His works.[51]

St. Bonaventure (1217–1274) stated, "Throughout the entire creation, the wisdom of God shines forth . . . as in a mirror containing the beauty of all forms and lights as in a book in which all things are written according to the deep secrets of God. . . . Truly, whoever reads this book will find life and will draw salvation from the Lord."[52] Calvin (1509–1564) explained, "It is the wisdom of men to search out God's works, and to set their minds wholly upon them. And God has also ordained the world to be like a theatre upon which to behold his goodness."[53]

Being Away

Being in a different environment may be as important as the natural environment itself. Opportunities to be in a different environment during leisure have been empirically documented to be conducive to spirituality. Being away is one of four features of restorative environments theory, which explains why some settings are more conducive to restoration than others.[54] This feature of the theory suggests that a conceptually or physically different setting from one's everyday environment is conducive to restorative experiences. L. Allison Stringer and Leo McAvoy, in a study of wilderness experience, observed that the greater opportunities and enhancement of spiritual experiences in the wilderness setting were usually ascribed to the lack of constraints and responsibilities in the wilderness compared to the participants' everyday life.[55] Since all the participants lived in or near large urban areas, these constraints were associated with urban living, while wilderness presented a different living environment. Stringer and McAvoy speculated that a different environment, without the usual time and energy constraints, was the operative factor for some participants, and it did not matter if it was wilderness. Some of the participants in my qualitative study on leisure and spiritual well-being identified being away to natural areas as conducive to their spiritual well-being.[56] Diane noted that on canoe trips she was able to leave the everyday world behind and focus on basics.

> [My husband] and I get really connected, our spirits are connected on [canoe] trips . . . leaving everything behind, and getting down to basics and I think that's very meditative too because when we meditate we're just there with God, it's very simple and we don't need anything else really. And so when you go on a canoe trip or a camping trip, you just take a few things. And you . . . don't really need a lot of stuff especially for our spirits, for our spiritual growth or enhancement.

Fiona noted that getting away and canoeing, or going to a place like Algonquin Park (a large provincial park in Ontario, Canada), enabled one to get away from the everyday demands and expectations and to focus on one's spiritual well-being. When asked, "What sorts of things would you do if you wanted to rejuvenate or renew your spirituality?" she replied, "The best thing would be, to go off by myself . . . take a canoe and just being by the water." When probed about what it is about the solitude and nature that she finds rejuvenating, Fiona replied,

> For me it's about listening to God in that space . . . it's clear of any distractions, that would be part of it, and sometimes all the demands of everyday life are just really, they can be joyful, and they can be very distracting as well and losing that sense of focus, that sense of centered. . . . I think that when I, for example, when we go to Algonquin I'm certainly aware of the possibility of feeling more centred, of feeling more connected with God.

"Being away" has been identified as facilitating spiritual benefits in studies of youth residential campers who found that the camp setting provided a nonurban experience away from their everyday lives that were dominated by technology, pollution, and busy cities;[57] men on wilderness canoe trips for whom wilderness provided an opportunity to get away from the everyday routine to focus on the spiritual;[58] vacationers to Montana who explained how the naturalness and wide open spaces of the landscape helped them get away and become spiritually grounded, recentered, and refocused;[59] and individuals who visited monasteries as a leisure activity.[60]

In the life of Jesus we see this practice of being away: before he began his ministry he spent forty days in the wilderness (Matt. 4:1–11); before he chose his disciples he spent the night in the desert (Luke 6:12); when he heard of John the Baptist's death he withdrew in a boat to a place apart (Matt. 14:13); after the feeding of the five thousand he went up into the hills (Matt. 14:23); after a long night of work he got up early and went to a lonely place (Mark 1:35); when the disciples had returned from a mission, he instructed them to come away to a lonely place (Mark 6:31); following the healing of a leper he withdrew to the wilderness (Luke 5:16); with three disciples he went up a mountain for the transfiguration (Matt. 17:1–9); and before his death he went to the garden of Gethsemane (Matt. 26:36–46).[61]

This notion of being away to another place is advocated in the Christian practice of retreats. For example, St. Ignatius of Loyola realized that Christians need retreats to "come aside and rest awhile," as Jesus taught his disciples to do.[62] In encouraging retreats, Foster recommended, "The best place is anywhere as long as it is away from home. To leave the house not only sets you free from the telephone and domestic responsibilities but it also sets your mind into a learning mode."[63]

Solitude

Times for solitude and personal reflection within leisure activities and programs have been empirically documented as important to spirituality. Fox found that solitude in wilderness was important for women due to factors such as peace, tranquility, inner journey, and time for self thoughts.[64] Time alone in nature also enhanced time to listen, watch, explore, and reflect on nature. Likewise, Laura Fredrickson and Dorothy Anderson discovered that during periods of solitude, wilderness participants contemplated life's deepest questions that they did not have time to reflect on in their everyday life. This solitude left them renewed and rejuvenated.[65] Stringer and McAvoy observed that the major factor that inhibited spiritual experiences in the wilderness was a lack of time alone or not enough time off.[66] In a study of hiking alone, the solitude inherent in solo hiking was found to allow some participants to relax, experience peace and calm, and thereby become spiritually revitalized.[67] This factor of solitude was also discovered in a large-scale, quantitative study of campers at Ontario Provincial Parks.[68]

Solitude has been found to be an important factor in producing spiritual benefits in other leisure settings as well. My study with Mary Sweatman of youth residential camp experience discovered that time alone had a positive spiritual impact on the youth. Time alone included both experiences on their own time (unstructured) as well as solitary activities planned by their leaders (structured).[69] Furthermore, participants in my study on leisure and well-being noted that settings of silence, solitude, and quiet were conducive to spiritual well-being.[70] For example, when asked what is it about quiet leisure settings that is helpful to her spiritual well-being, Andrea responded,

> The quiet . . . makes me more sensitive to the things around me. . . . Quietness . . . puts you more in touch, an awareness of those things, puts you more in touch with yourself, it puts you more in touch with being able [to] . . . entertain God in the sense that you would think about things that he's said through scripture or you'd think about an experience perhaps in prayer, or you'd think, about . . . Jesus, so it just gives you that peace, that tranquility. . . . More time to think about, to use your mind, to think about him, rather than, "I gotta do."

George described how solitude occurred for him in the form of regularly scheduled retreats.

> As the word ["retreat"] implies going back to things. And in my tradition, we have this kind of almost commitment . . . on a yearly basis to take eight days to just kind of withdraw from our responsibilities, commitments and the world and the work and just go to a quiet place like that and spend time in prayers and spend time in solitude and preferably with somebody you know with a spiritual director or counselor who could help keep one focused.

I can identify with both Andrea's and George's explanations. For five years I held a very busy position as executive director of a camp and conference center. I lived at the center, so it was very difficult to get away from work responsibilities. On a couple of occasions I went on a two- or three-day solo hiking or cross-country skiing trip where I had time alone with God in creation to pray, read Scripture, and journal, and thereby be spiritually rejuvenated. During this period in my life, I also went on a weeklong solitary retreat and then later, while I was working on my PhD, participated in weekend silent retreats once a year. These retreats provided me with time to focus on spiritual matters and forget about the demands of my work or studies.

The desert fathers were known for their practice of solitude, as is suggested by the following saying: "A certain brother went to Abbot Moses in Scete, and asked him for a good word. And the elder said to him, 'Go, sit in your cell, and your cell will teach you everything.'"[71] The Christian monastic tradition also emphasizes solitude.[72] Thomas à Kempis (c. 1379–1471) explained that "the person who wants to arrive at interiority and spirituality has to leave the crowd behind. . . . In quiet and silence the faithful soul makes progress."[73] More recently, John Main stated, "Now to tread the spiritual path we must learn to be silent. What is required of us is a journey into profound silence."[74] Similarly, Henri Nouwen wrote, "Without solitude it is virtually impossible to live a spiritual life," and continued, ". . . solitude allows us gradually to come in touch with this hopeful presence of God in our lives, and allows us also to taste even now the beginnings of the joy and peace which belong to the new heaven and the new earth."[75]

Connections with Others

Activities that help people to explore and develop their connections with one another in leisure have also been found to be helpful to spirituality. In their study of wilderness experience, Stringer and McAvoy observed that the sharing between group members and the range of experiences, opinions, and ideas that each wilderness participant brought to the group was an important factor that contributed to spiritual experience.[76] Fox discovered that women experienced a sense of spirituality through being part of a women-only wilderness experience and that working as a team with other women enhanced their spiritual experience.[77] Similarly, Fredrickson and Anderson found that aspects related to being part of an all-women's group ("group trust and emotional support," "sharing common life changes," "noncompetitive atmosphere") contributed to the meaningful dimensions of the wilderness trip.[78] My study of a three-day men's informal and unstructured canoe trip, composed of seven men from an urban church, discovered that the theme that characterized the impact of the canoe trip on spiritual well-being was spiritual friendship.[79] Bruce elaborated on the spiritual impact of the trip: "A sense of getting to know each other better I think. Not only as people, but as Christians, as brothers . . . having contributed to their spiritual life and getting a sense of their heart and mind." Spiritual friendships that developed through the trip were facilitated by informal conversations and discussions. The most frequently mentioned context of these conversations was the evening campfires. Dan explained why the campfire conversations were so important to his spiritual well-being:

> It's not very often in life that I find . . . opportunities to discuss one's beliefs or explore other people or listen to other people expressing their thoughts. . . . [T]here's a non-threatening environment . . . [while] some environments are not that way. . . . The dynamic seems to be right for that kind of expression. And also I suppose there's no hurry, there's lots of time, we're not on schedule, and that really helps too.

Participants observed that being part of a men-only group provided a different dynamic than if it had been a mixed group. Andrew elaborated,

> We talk about things . . . that we wouldn't talk about if there were women present . . . or maybe we wouldn't talk about it in exactly the same fashion. And so that

creates a different experience. I think that can help build your spirituality in a way. . . . I suppose that we're able to address certain issues that we would probably be reluctant to address in a male/female environment and therefore we're able to do certain things with a male-only group.

Connections with others is also an important characteristic of leisure experiences in nonwilderness settings that contribute to spirituality. While the participants in my study of leisure and spiritual well-being viewed silence, quiet, and solitude as important to their spiritual well-being, this theme was not to be confused with isolation.[80] Rather, solitude was balanced with community and connecting with other people. Similarly for the youth in an outdoor residential camp setting, formal and informal social experiences with camp staff and other camp participants went together with solitude to contribute to spirituality.[81] One of the outcomes of leisure experiences that Schmidt and Little observed was that of connection—connection with God, with self, and with others.[82] Similarly Little and Schmidt found that the experience of leisure travel had spiritual meaning and impact for participants, including greater connection with self, God, and with something beyond the self.[83]

Christian spirituality encourages both fellowship (*koinōnia*) and spiritual friendship, which may be defined as "companionship and mutual encouragement along the path of discipleship."[84] Proverbs 27:17 reads, "As iron sharpens iron, / so one person sharpens another." Basil of Caesarea (c. 330–379) wrote that "God the Creator arranged things so that we need each other,"[85] while Richard Rolle (c. 1300–1349) stated, "It is of God that we should be sustained . . . by the advice and assistance of friends."[86] In his classic *On Spiritual Friendship*, Aelred of Rievaulx (1109–1167) explained that a spiritual friend is

> someone to whom you dare to speak on terms of equality as to another self, one to whom you need have no fear to confess your failings; one to whom you can unblushingly make known what progress you have made in the spiritual life; one to whom you can entrust all the secrets of your heart and before whom you can place all your plans.[87]

Combination of Factors

Sometimes it is a combination of experiences that are associated with spirituality. For example, in their study of wilderness hikers and canoeists, Stringer and McAvoy identified two main factors that were influential in contributing to spiritual experiences during wilderness trips: (1) other people on the trip, and (2) being in a wilderness environment.[88] Fredrickson and Anderson arrived at a similar conclusion concerning the women hikers and canoeists in their study: "It is a unique combination of social interactions and landscape characteristics that render a place as spiritually inspirational."[89]

Another example is the combination of being with a group and having solitude in wilderness. For example, in my study of a men's wilderness canoe trip, I found that the variety of social settings in a wilderness trip, such as being with one or two other people and being in a group, along with times to be alone, including opportunity for an overnight solo, was viewed as important to spiritual well-being:[90]

> The others are open to talk or discussion but . . . if people want to find their own space, people are free to do that as well. . . . [S]o there's lots of time for self but there's also lots of time to participate . . . in a group with fellow men if you wish. (Arthur)

> I think that I found some spiritual jewels, some spiritual treasures in all the social settings, being alone definitely, being around the fire with the entire group definitely, and just in one-on-one conversations with people. (Bob)

> I at least, went back and forth between group and solitude throughout the day, throughout the series of days. It was a nice alteration. . . . To the extent that friendship and camaraderie is an element of spiritual well-being, there was quite a bit of opportunity for that. Sometimes with everybody together and sometimes one on one. Two or three people. (Ernie)

While it may seem contradictory that both group experiences and times of solitude are associated with spirituality, it seems that both types of experiences on the same wilderness trip may be critical factors in spiritual experience.[91] The balance of both types of experiences was also found to be important in youth camp experiences.[92]

This paradox also appears in the Christian spiritual tradition. In a description of the lives and spiritual sayings of desert Christians (from the third through fifth centuries), Edward Sellner wrote that

> two seemingly contradictory characteristics consistently appear: . . . despite their love of solitude, or perhaps precisely because of that love, friendship had a special meaning for them. . . . [T]hese desert guides, revered for their friendship, hospitality and compassion, also valued silence and solitude, even when they lived within monasteries.[93]

Similarly Celtic Christians valued solitude in the midst of familial and communal responsibilities, and sought out isolated places or "soul-space" to develop silence and greater intimacy with God.[94] In his book *Life Together*, Bonhoeffer titled one chapter "The Day Together" and the following chapter "The Day Alone," as he saw both community and solitude essential for spiritual growth.

Let him who cannot be alone beware of community. . . . Let him who is not in community beware of being alone. . . . Each by itself has profound pitfalls and perils. One who wants fellowship without solitude plunges into the void of words and feelings, and one who seeks solitude without fellowship perishes in the abyss of vanity, self-infatuation, and despair.[95]

Conclusion

The author of the Old Testament book of Ecclesiastes wrote, "There is nothing new under the sun" (1:9). In this chapter we have seen that the leisure processes or factors that have been shown by research studies to be conducive to spirituality are not necessarily new; these practices have been advocated within Christian spirituality for centuries. However, these studies confirm the practices, with a different type of knowledge—empirical knowledge, the experiential knowledge and wisdom that has been passed down through the centuries in the Christian spiritual tradition. Most of these processes have to do with some dimension of leisure as activity, or intensified leisure (settings of personal and human history, being in nature, being away, solitude, connections with others); however, one of them is concerned with time (time and space), one with leisure as an attitude (openness), and one with a holistic approach to life (a balance in life). Thus they illustrate how the different dimensions of holistic leisure may be influential in spiritual growth and development.

13

leisure-spiritual coping

In his book *Leisure: A Spiritual Need*, Doohan explained that leisure is necessary to cope with the constant change, tension, and stress of contemporary life; to counterbalance the pressures of contemporary life; and to bring balance in life.[1] This chapter builds on the leisure-spiritual processes presented in the previous chapter and presents a model of leisure-spiritual coping that synthesizes theory and research findings on leisure, stress, and spiritual coping (see fig. 13.1).[2] "Spiritual coping" refers to the ways that people receive help from spiritual resources (e.g., God, spiritual practices, faith community) during times of life stress, whereas "leisure-spiritual coping" is spiritual coping that takes place within the context of one's leisure. The model takes into account five dimensions of leisure-spiritual coping: spiritual appraisals; personal factors (e.g., religious orientation); leisure-spiritual coping behaviors (e.g., sacralization and grounding, contemplative leisure, leisure as time and space, being away); leisure-spiritual coping resources (e.g., connections with nature, others, and God); and leisure-spiritual meaning-making (e.g., life purpose, transformation, growth).

Spiritual Appraisals

At the first stage of the appraisal process, attributing spiritual cause (e.g., God, the devil, fate) is a common way to understand stressful circumstances, such as an injury or an illness.[3] For example, attributing cause to God may help people maintain a sense of justice in the world[4] that enables them to sustain a sense of personal control in the midst of an unmanageable circumstance.[5]

An example of primary appraisal is desecration—that is, a spiritual evalua-tion of harm/loss: to what extent has an event negatively affected a dimension

Figure 13.1

Leisure-Spiritual Coping Model

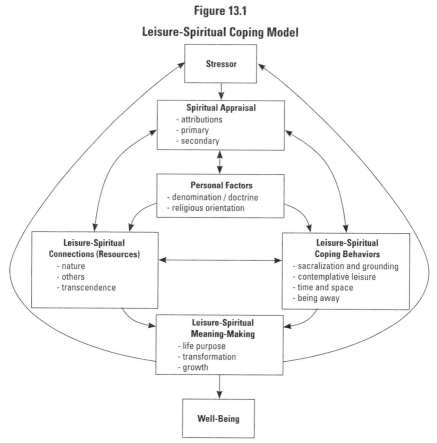

Source: Paul Heintzman, "Leisure-Spiritual Coping: A Model for Therapeutic Recreation and Leisure Services," *Therapeutic Recreation Journal* 42, no. 1 (2008), 59. Adapted from Terry Lynn Gall et al., "Understanding the Nature and Role of Spirituality in Relation to Coping and Health: A Conceptual Framework," Canadian Psychology/ *Psychologie canadienne* 46, no. 2 (2005), 89.

of a person's life that is considered to be sacred or related to God?[6] Secondary appraisal refers to a person's assessment of the accessibility and possible helpfulness of particular spiritual coping strategies that could be utilized in reaction to stress.[7] These appraisals have implications for the choice of particular coping behaviors.[8]

Personal Factors

Religious Denomination and Doctrine

For religious people, including Christians, personal beliefs are integrated with beliefs of their religious group to create a source of social support and social norms that influence their behavior. Thus religious beliefs can affect how a person will cope with stress. Research has documented that religiously oriented lifestyles tend to be healthier.[9] In studies on the stress-coping of marginalized groups (e.g., individuals with disabilities, older people suffering from diabetes), Yoshitika Iwasaki and colleagues noted that the spirituality of participants was rooted in different religious groups or traditions, including Christianity.[10]

Religious Orientation

A distinction may be made between extrinsic and intrinsic religious orientation.[11] An extrinsic orientation is characterized by being religious to gain personal benefits, including comfort and safety; religious practices are not the result of faith but the result of guilt, anxiety, or external pressure. An intrinsic orientation is characterized by a selfless motivation to pursue purpose and meaning in life for its own sake and an internalized understanding of transcendence based on "faith, hope, and love for others, God, and self."[12] An extrinsic religious orientation, which is thought to be less effective than an intrinsic orientation when coping with stress,[13] has been found to be associated with a sense of inadequacy when coping with a stressful situation and is less likely to be associated with the feeling that the stressful experience will be an opportunity for growth.[14] In contrast, during times of crisis, particularly times when a situation is beyond a person's control, people with high intrinsic religiosity tend to rely on their religious resources. An intrinsic religious orientation is also associated with the perception of a stressful event as an opportunity for personal growth, reliance on problem-solving coping during stress, and a sense of meaning during severe stress.[15]

Leisure-Spiritual Coping Behaviors

Spiritual coping behavior is a common response to stress and has a significant relationship to a great diversity of adjustment factors.[16] These behaviors may be classified as organized religious behaviors, private spiritual or religious practices, and nontraditional spiritual practices. Organized religious behaviors involve participation in activities such as attendance at religious services and volunteer activity offered by formal religious organizations.[17] Private spiritual or religious practices are personal and private behaviors, such as studying sacred texts, praying, watching religious television, and singing.[18] Nontraditional spiritual practices are those that differ from traditional religious expressions.[19] Of particular relevance to leisure-spiritual coping behavior are the nontraditional spiritual coping practices that may include leisure activities with a spiritual dimension.

A study on the relevance of spirituality for people with mental illness by Chyrell Bellamy and colleagues found that all three categories of spiritual coping behavior were identified: public spiritual activities (i.e., formal religious activities, such as attending worship services and Bible study groups); private spiritual activities (e.g., praying, reading the Bible and other spiritual books, meditating); and other activities including both recreational activities (e.g., playing and watching sports, fishing, reading, participating in social activities) and mutual support activities (e.g., attending Alcoholic Anonymous meetings, helping others, providing community service).[20] Bellamy and colleagues noted that while the activities in this last category are not normally viewed as religious or spiritual, they may include significant religious and spiritual elements, such as social support and fellowship. Similarly, in their research on marginalized groups, Iwasaki and colleagues found that all three classifications of spiritual coping behavior have been useful in coping with stress. Spiritual coping behavior ranged from praying, reading the Bible, or being connected with a church, to meditating during a long bath that offered the occasion to "think things through."[21]

Of particular relevance to this study is the third category of nontraditional spiritual coping practices, which may include leisure activities with a spiritual dimension. An important question to ask as we consider leisure as a nontraditional spiritual coping practice is how leisure functions as a spiritual coping practice. We will consider this question under the headings of sacralization and grounding; contemplative leisure; leisure as time and space; and being away.

Sacralization and Grounding

Sacralization refers to a process where a person is sensitized to the spiritual. Leisure activities such as meditation and relaxation may assist in sacralization. Preliminary research that I conducted with Roger Mannell suggests that the spiritual function of sacralization may serve as a coping strategy to ameliorate the negative influence of time pressure on spiritual well-being.[22] "Sacrilization" as a spiritual function of leisure refers to the use of leisure for nurturing the spiritual dimension of life, and use of leisure to provide the time and space to develop spirituality. In our quantitative study that used structural equation modeling we found that the effects of time pressure on spiritual well-being were mediated by the spiritual functions of leisure. Time pressure's adverse impact was indirect through its adverse influence on the amount of leisure time the respondents had available. As we might expect, the more time pressure experienced by the respondents, the less leisure time they reported. This relationship was quite strong. Those respondents with less leisure time were less likely to experience the spiritual functions of leisure, and in turn were more likely to experience lower levels of spiritual well-being. This finding is consistent with suggestions in classical and contemporary writings on spirituality that time and balance in life are needed to develop spirituality,[23] and with research findings on time pressure and mental health that demonstrate that excessive levels of time pressure are negatively related to mental health.[24]

The link between leisure time and the spiritual functions of leisure was much stronger when time pressure was introduced into the model. This finding is not too surprising. When experiencing time pressure and a consequent decrease in leisure time, time becomes a much more important resource or factor in the ability to use leisure for its spiritual functions. Interestingly, the experience of higher levels of time pressure appeared to trigger the greater use of leisure for its spiritual functions. In other words, time pressure in daily life can make it difficult to stay in touch with the spiritual aspects of life. These pressures may not allow people to increase their level of leisure participation or time, and may reduce leisure time, but they may also trigger increased efforts to maintain spiritual well-being through the leisure time and activities that they have available. Furthermore, people who may have lost sight of the spiritual dimension of their life due to the pressures and hassles of everyday life may use their leisure as an opportunity to become sensitized or resensitized to the spiritual. This process of sacralization can ultimately lead to the pursuit of spiritual development. In stressful situations, leisure activities may also "ground" a person and divert his or her attention away from the stress and thus perform a function similar to palliative coping.[25]

Contemplative Leisure

As we have seen in earlier chapters, leisure has been considered not only as an activity but also as an attitude. For example, Pieper's conceptualization of leisure as "a mental and spiritual attitude . . . a condition of the soul . . . a receptive attitude of mind, a contemplative attitude"[26] reflects a contemplative leisure that can be traced back to Augustine and Aquinas. Contemplative leisure has been viewed as one of the steps of the spiritual journey that empowers an individual through transcendent life-giving powers to cope with the stresses of the everyday world.[27] As contemplation and celebration of life, leisure is a restorative remedy to burnout. In support of this view, empirical research has shown that a leisure attitude of "being open" and "being aware" has contributed to spiritual well-being,[28] while for older women with HIV/AIDS, spiritual transcendence has been facilitated by the quiet of contemplative leisure.[29] Some middle-aged and older people suffering from arthritis reported that spiritual contemplation and prayer was an effective means of coping with stress.[30]

Leisure as Time and Space

Some studies suggest that participants deliberately create a leisure space or an oasis where they can renew themselves; these leisure spaces could be a spiritual leisure space.[31] This idea of a leisure space is consistent with findings reviewed in the previous chapter, that leisure may be viewed as time and space for spiritual well-being.[32] Specifically related to coping, Soti Grafanaki and colleagues' study on the experience and role of leisure in the life of counselors and psychologists discovered that leisure provided opportunity for spiritual experience, thereby helping participants achieve balance and integration in everyday life and cope with the demands of their work.[33]

Leisure as time and space has been historically associated with religious holidays and the practice of Sabbath. The importance of holidays and the Sabbath for coping with stress has been noted in both therapeutic and psychology literature. Holidays or "holy days" that remember national, religious, or personal events are special and significant times that provide a time-out from daily routines, present distractions from mental or physical problems, and let people express their inner selves.[34] These holidays may provide a buffer to daily stresses and help individuals fill their spiritual needs. As meaningful spiritual activities, holiday celebrations have four therapeutic implications. First, as a religious celebration, holidays enhance religious and spiritual expression by facilitating transcendence, which helps individuals cope with the uncertainty and conflict they face. Second, as cultural activities, holidays help people feel socially integrated into their community and society. Third, holidays can help people organize their time by facilitating time orientation through the notions of "before" and "after." Fourth, as leisure, they provide meaning, enjoyment, entertainment, and satisfaction.

Related to holidays is the growing interest in North America to rediscover models of Sabbath-keeping as a counterbalance to the stresses and fragmentation of life. According to Margaret Diddams, Lisa Klein Surdyk, and Denise Daniels, Sabbath-keeping may take different forms: (1) life segmentation, where individuals deliberately segment their lives in order to create relief from stress; (2) prescribed meaning, where individuals give positive and spiritual meaning to life segmentation; and (3) integrated Sabbath, where Sabbath-keeping is observed as an integrated belief structure of reflection, rest, and relationship development on a daily basis.[35]

Empirical studies are beginning to appear on the benefits of Sabbath-keeping. Based on the assumption that the Sabbath's cyclical rhythm of activity and rest helps to fulfill the human need for spiritual renewal, Joyce Earickson concluded from a qualitative study that Sabbath-keeping promoted spiritual well-being and psychological health.[36] In a study of Sabbath-keeping by Protestant ministers, Traci Lee discovered that ceasing from work was correlated positively with autonomy, whereas rest was correlated positively with relatedness, competence, and autonomy.[37] Both ceasing and resting were correlated negatively with emotional exhaustion. Structural Equation Modeling (SEM) found that rest was the critical dimension of Sabbath-keeping. Matilda Burian Anhalt investigated the relationship between stress and the Jewish Sabbath among Sabbath-observant and nonobservant groups.[38] The Sabbath-keeping group had significantly lower Saturday (Sabbath) stress as compared to their weekday stress and also significantly decreased Saturday stress compared to the Saturday stress level of the nonobservant group. Research has also been conducted on the influence of Sabbath-keeping on human relationships and functioning. Jane Boyd found individuals who were intrinsically motivated to observe the Sabbath experienced greater marital intimacy than did individuals who were extrinsically motivated.[39] Bianca Stern discovered that meaningful Sabbath ritual activities rooted in retained long-term memories play a facilitative role in enabling meaningful engagements and sustaining personhood for those with mild to moderate dementia.[40] Thus these empirical studies document the benefits of Sabbath-keeping and how leisure time provides time and space for spiritual coping.

Being Away

Building on the notion of leisure as time and space, leisure provides the opportunity to get away from the everyday world, consistent with the "being away" feature of Stephen Kaplan's restorative environments theory that was explained in the previous chapter.[41] For example, studies by Pierre Ouellette and colleagues document how a monastery may function as a spiritually restorative environment for individuals who visit them as a leisure activity.[42] Stringer and McAvoy found that for wilderness adventure participants, some of whom had disabilities, enhanced spirituality and spiritual experience were due to being in a different setting, free from usual constraints on energy and time.[43] Thus leisure provided the opportunity to be away, which contributed to spiritual growth and development that ultimately could help in dealing with stress. Likewise, in Fredrickson and Anderson's study of women's wilderness experience, all the women had experienced a major life change (deterioration of personal health, major career change, death of a loved one), so the trip provided the opportunity to leave the stresses of everyday life to have an experience of spiritual rejuvenation in the wilderness environment.[44]

Leisure-Spiritual Coping Resources

Leisure-spiritual coping resources, along with spiritual appraisals and leisure-spiritual coping behaviors, act as mediating factors in the stress-coping process. These leisure-spiritual coping resources take the form of connections with nature, others, and God.

Connections with Nature

As we saw in the first part of this chapter Christian spirituality is frequently associated with a connection with creation. One of the most frequently mentioned combinations of spiritual experience with leisure is the wilderness or nature experience.[45] In the previously mentioned studies on wilderness experience, it was found that wilderness is conducive to spiritual development and that direct contact with the biophysical characteristics of nature in undisturbed wilderness played an important role in spiritual inspiration and led to a more contemplative and self-reflective trip experience.[46] Gardening as a leisure activity has been found to be a spiritual enabler providing meaningfulness and stress reduction under extreme circumstances, such as cancer,[47] and sustaining spiritual development and renewal in older people.[48] Margaret Schneider and Roger Mannell's study of parents with children who had cancer discovered that one aspect of the parents' spiritual coping mechanism was contact with nature.[49] Examples included enjoying the sunshine and trees while reading on the porch, visiting a remote cottage, enjoying the environment while driving the car, and appreciating the beauty of trees.

Connections with Others

Social support and care from others during leisure activities may also contribute to leisure-spiritual coping. In Fredrickson and Anderson's study of wilderness experience, where the women participants all recently encountered a major life change, a significant theme that contributed to spiritual meaning was group trust and emotional safety.[50] Continuous verbal encouragement and ongoing emotional support from other group members, which led to personal bonding and emotional safety, were mentioned as significant contributions to the more spiritually inspirational aspects of the trip. These findings are consistent with a Christian perspective on therapeutic recreation that encourages relationships with others through a love of one's neighbor, compassion, and self-sacrifice; the resultant social relationships provide a sense of connectedness and play a significant role in restoring wholeness.[51]

Connections with God

Research suggests that a relationship with God has a significant role in coping with stress, particularly if God is viewed to be available, protective, comforting, loving, and nurturing.[52] In a study on the potential of leisure to engage the human soul, Schmidt and Little observed that in leisure the participants "transcended the everyday assault of their lives."

> In their time and space the co-researchers [participants] did not just recharge the body; they recharged the soul. Wholly engaged, not just one element of the self was involved. Rather their leisure allowed them to experience the spiritual . . . to know God . . . and to intensely be aware of a power beyond the individual. In the achieved moment of leisure, the [participants] experienced a transcendent realization that there is more to life than the ordinary.[53]

Carol Gosselink and Susan Myllykangas's study of older women living with HIV/AIDS found that leisure provided spiritual transcendence—which for some women meant connection with God—that strengthened over time as their disease progressed.[54]

Leisure-Spiritual Meaning-Making

Research has documented that spirituality and religion perform a significant role in discovering meaning in a stressful situation.[55] Leisure can provide the context for this spiritual meaning-making to take place. In their studies on marginal groups, Iwasaki and colleagues have examined the role of leisure as a contributor to coping with stress.[56] They found that using active leisure to cope with stress included both spiritual activities and spiritual meanings. That is, spiritual activities (e.g., spiritual reading) were pursued in leisure to cope with stress, and active leisure provided the opportunity to obtain spiritual meaning. For example, in a study of Aboriginals with diabetes, many participants mentioned the role of culturally appropriate leisure in bringing about spiritual rejuvenation that had cultural meanings: "Regardless of the type of activities described from escaping the city, going to reserves, and going to camping or the lake, to walking, reading and sewing, one key stress-coping mechanism of leisure relevant to participants seemed to involve the facilitation of spiritual or psychological renewal in a culturally meaningful way."[57]

Another illustration of meaning-making through leisure-spiritual coping is provided by a study of the leisure experiences of older women who were living with HIV/AIDS.[58] The women in the study were disenfranchised and encountered economic, social, and structural constraints. Following HIV/AIDS diagnosis, the meaning of leisure was transformed for all the women in the study. As their disease progressed the women experienced spiritual transcendence and developed a spiritual view of leisure, which became a metaphor for meaning in life. For some, church took on new meaning in terms of prayer, connecting with self and God, and a place of acceptance of their disease. For others spirituality meant a stronger spiritual connection with self, nature, and others. At the same time, leisure advanced the women's well-being through therapeutic benefits, such as resilience in transcending systemic barriers they faced as a result of being female, over age fifty, and infected with HIV/AIDS. As the disease progressed, the women's transcendence matured and their resolve to overcome obstacles increased. The newfound spirituality of all the women "continued to grow and provide meaning such that they viewed nature, animals, friends, family and advocacy as leisure vehicles through which they could express their spirituality."[59]

Summary and Case Study

The empirical research that I have reviewed suggests that leisure may be a fruitful context for spiritual coping to help alleviate, overcome, and transcend many of the stresses and challenges that people face. The leisure-spiritual coping model is an attempt to capture and organize the complexity of factors involved in leisure-spiritual coping. Although the model is to some extent hierarchical in that some components affect one another in a linear sequence, it is recursive. For example, leisure-spiritual coping can lead to leisure-spiritual meaning-making, and the effects of meaning-making may feed back to the spiritual appraisal component and thus indirectly to leisure-spiritual coping as a person tries to adapt to a stressful situation. The following case study, based on my personal experience, illustrates the components of the leisure-spiritual coping model (the components of the model are italicized in this case study).

In 1994 I was diagnosed with cancer, which was followed by surgery to remove a cancerous tumor and subsequently chemotherapy to eradicate the cancer that had spread elsewhere. At the time of diagnosis I was experiencing multiple forms of stress. As executive director of an understaffed and under-funded Christian camp and conference center, I was overworked and had no regular or consistent time off work. I had been experiencing overwork and burnout for a number of years. For the previous few years I had also been taking care of the affairs of my uncle, who had Alzheimer's disease and lived 160 kilometers away. My uncle died five months prior to my cancer diagnosis, and I was now executor of my uncle's estate. I also had some responsibilities for my father, who was in his late eighties and lived alone in the family home 100 kilometers away. I had also been primary caregiver to my mother, who had died six years earlier of cancer.

In regard to the *attribution* stage of *spiritual appraisal*, I was initially quite shocked and perplexed to receive a diagnosis of cancer as I had been very healthy all my life. *Primary spiritual appraisal* involved the realization that death might be a reality in the near future. In terms of *secondary spiritual appraisal*, I realized changes in my lifestyle were necessary and that spiritual resources were essential to bring about these changes. In terms of *personal factors*, my beliefs (*religious denomination and doctrine*) were rooted in Christian spiritual faith, which provided the contextual framework for understanding and responding to this stress. I had been brought up in a Christian home and during my teenage years this faith became personalized into a faith of my own (*intrinsic religious orientation*).

From the time of diagnosis until the completion of chemotherapy, I drastically cut my hours of work to a normal workweek. This allowed more time than usual for spiritual practices of a traditional nature, but also *leisure-spiritual coping behaviors*. Although lacking the usual amount of energy, I jogged two miles each day during chemotherapy, which acted as a *grounding* activity, diverting my attention from my cancer to something positive. Reduced work time led to opportunities to focus on spirituality through *sacralization* and *contemplation*. For example, I participated in a weekend retreat on life changes at a spiritual retreat center just prior to my surgery, which also offered the opportunity to *be away* to another setting. In terms of *leisure as time and space*, although I strongly believed in the concept of *Sabbath* and had practiced what Diddams and colleagues call an integrated form of Sabbath-keeping for most of my life, I had been unable to do so for the previous four years due to the nature of my work. During the period of cancer I returned to Sabbath-keeping by abstaining from work on Sundays. Also during this time I experienced *being away* from my usual work setting of the remote camp and conference center to my father's home in an urban area. While this change of environment related mainly to my work and living situation, it also affected the context for leisure activities and provided for leisure opportunities that were not available in the remote setting.

In regard to *leisure-spiritual connections*, although opportunities for *connection with nature* were less accessible in the urban environment, when possible I continued to participate in nature-based recreation, which usually provided opportunities for meditation, prayer, and reflection that strengthened my *connection with God* and thereby played a significant role in coping with this situation. *Connections with others*, which were now easier to pursue due to the urban setting, were also enhanced during this time. Spiritual friendships that were a source of inspiration and comfort were renewed and strengthened. Some of the opportunities for connections with others were within the leisure context. A particular highlight was a weekly Saturday morning hockey game with others from the church I attended prior to moving to the camp and conference center.

All the components of the leisure-spiritual model had an influence on *meaning-making,* which led to a reappraisal of beliefs and attitudes, and my ability to cope. I sometimes refer to this period in my life as a holiday, as my stress level was drastically reduced from previous levels. During this time I reevaluated the priorities in my life—developing connections with God and with others took on greater value, while I questioned whether I should continue in my job. I decided to resign from the position I held with no definite next step. Meaning-making also fed back to *spiritual appraisal*: while others suggested possible reasons for the cancer, I accepted it as a mystery, and to some extent a gift, for which only God knew the reason.

epilogue

a   c o n c i s e   a n d   i l l u s t r a t e d   t h e o l o g y
o f   l e i s u r e

In this epilogue I will present a concise theology of leisure that includes the principles of Sabbath-keeping, rest, and a balanced rhythm of work and leisure presented earlier in the book and that is illustrated by quotes and examples from one of my role models. At least once every winter during my teenage and university years, I visited the home of Bill and Joyce Mason. Bill was a legendary Canadian filmmaker, canoeist, and artist. A typical visit to the Mason home in Quebec's Gatineau Hills would involve a church or university group playing broomball or hockey on the Masons' backyard rink, then possibly going trail skiing, followed by eating a hot meal and watching one of the fruits of Bill's work—an already-popular or yet-to-be-completed film. Although I studied recreation at university, there was much I learned from Bill about a Christian understanding of leisure. Bill's life personified a Christian understanding of work and leisure.

Sabbath-Keeping

As Christians we need to ask ourselves: How do we understand and practice leisure? How do we forge a lifestyle of leisure and work that is consistent with Scripture and respectful of other people and God's creation? What place should leisure have in Christian discipleship?

Several biblical principles can help us to understand leisure. Let us start with the biblical concept of Sabbath. The Sabbath reminds us that there is more to life than work. In the creation account, the Sabbath points to a rhythm of work and nonwork (Gen. 1–2). The same Sabbath rhythm is suggested in the account of God's provision of manna in the desert (Exod. 16), in the Mosaic law (Exod. 34:21; Lev. 23:1–3; Num. 28:18), and in the words of the prophets (Amos 8:5;

Isa. 58:13–14). The Sabbath principle suggests that the rhythm of work and non-work, or leisure, is necessary for our well-being. Jesus demonstrated this rhythm in his life on earth. During his ministry he regularly took time alone in the hills or solitary places to rest and pray (Mark 1:35; 6:31–32, 45). Rhythms were evident in Bill Mason's life. In his feature film *Waterwalker* he tells about enjoying the company of his whitewater buddies but also needing to get away and be alone.[1]

In the Exodus account of the Sabbath commandment (20:8–11) we encounter the first reason God gives for observing the Sabbath: we should rest from our work just as God did after calling creation into being. The Sabbath was given not primarily for restorative purposes but was a time to recognize that life is a gift from God and we are to respond with our worship and thanksgiving. Exodus 20:11 suggests that observing a day of rest forcefully reminds us that we live in a world that contains all we need as well as many other things to enjoy. So the Sabbath is an invitation to experience the blessings of God's good gift of creation and delight in them. Leisure, like the Sabbath, is more than a time period or an activity; it is an attitude.

Such delight in God's creation is evident in *Waterwalker*. Gazing at the wilderness around him, Mason says in the film, "I look around me at the colors, the textures, the designs. It is like being in an art gallery. God is the artist. And he has given us the ability to enjoy all this, and to wonder, and in our own small way, to express ourselves in our own creativity, and that's why I like being here."[2]

Deuteronomy's version of the Sabbath commandment provides another reason why we are to stop working: "so that your male and female servants may rest, as you do" (5:14). The Sabbath, therefore, is for human rest, restoration, and re-creation. It is a "day of sacred assembly" (Lev. 23:3)—a day set aside to worship the One who created and sustains us. Jesus also taught that the Sabbath was a time for bringing healing and wholeness (Matt. 12:1–14; Mark 2:23–27; 3:1–5; Luke 6:1–4; 13:10–17; 14:1–6; John 9:1–41).

A third motivation for observing the Sabbath, a humanitarian one that we have already noted in Deuteronomy 5:14–15, is more clearly stated in the Book of the Covenant: "Six days do your work, but on the seventh day do not work, so that your ox and your donkey may rest and the slave born in your household, and the foreigner among you as well, may be refreshed" (Exod. 23:12). In this verse the only purpose given for the day of rest is that the dependent laborers and domestic animals experience rest and recuperation. The Sabbath was especially for the benefit of those who are severely burdened with work and are under the orders of others. Our leisure activity needs to be respectful of other people as well as of God's creatures and creation. Mason wrote about the importance of "compassion for our fellow humans and for all other living things. They were all created as a part of the whole and have a right to exist."[3] Our leisure activities should reflect concern for other people and creatures, and we should be careful not to intentionally or unintentionally exploit them during our leisure activity.

A fourth motivation for observance of the Sabbath is that it is a sign of the covenant: "The Israelites are to observe the Sabbath, celebrating it for the generations to come as a lasting covenant. It will be a sign between me and the Israelites forever" (Exod. 31:16, 17a). Thus the Sabbath was to be observed not only within the context of a relationship with God, but also as a sign of the relationship. Applied to leisure, while some benefits may accrue from observance of one day's rest in seven, leisure like the Sabbath may find its true meaning and reach its fullest potential when one lives in relationship with God. Even when close to death, Bill Mason recognized that life was best when lived in relationship with God: "My optimism is rooted in my faith that God has not forsaken us. My relationship with God is in his son Jesus Christ, and with a relationship like that there's really not a lot that can go wrong."[4]

Taken together, the Exodus and Deuteronomy accounts of the Sabbath suggest that our recreation should be for both enjoying God and God's creation, and for personal renewal.

Rest

Like the principle of Sabbath, the biblical concept of rest also reminds us that there is more to life than work. Biblical rest includes a range of physical and spiritual dimensions: a pleasant, secure, and blessed life in the land (Deut. 12:9–10); an entering into God's rest (Ps. 91:1); a rest of completion such as God enjoyed after creation (Gen. 2:2); a Sabbath rest of peace, joy, and well-being (Heb. 4:9–11); and a relief from labors and burdens, as well as a peace and contentment of body, soul, and mind in Jesus (Matt. 11:28–30).

While we may not fully experience all these physical and spiritual dimensions of rest until God's kingdom has fully come, we can begin to experience them now. These elements of rest are part of the good life on God's good earth, and they provide insights into how we understand leisure. The Deuteronomic notion of rest in the land is of particular importance for our understanding of leisure as activity, or what can be called intensified leisure. As theologian Preece noted, "We don't rest in a doctrine, we need a place to put our feet up, but a place in which God is personally present."[5] God's creation provides the context for our rest and leisure. God's creation contains many good gifts for us to enjoy. As we saw in chapter 7, the biblical themes of festivals, feasts, dance, hospitality, and friendships are all examples of leisure activities that provide an opportunity to enjoy God's good creation. And as explained in chapter 11, these leisure activities may be seen as an intensification of leisure that nourishes our spiritual attitude of leisure and a leisurely approach to life. In addition to a physical dimension, the biblical concept of rest also has a spiritual dimension, which suggests to us that leisure is more than recreation, more than leisure as activity. It also involves an attitude or a condition of our being. Leisure, in the classical sense, refers to an attitude or a state of being characterized by peace, contentment, joy, and celebration. Bill Mason's play and life in general, was characterized by joy and celebration. In *Path of the Paddle* he wrote about the joy of his canoe trips: "The joy of these trips that I experienced as a young man is now only equaled by having my family who share my enthusiasm accompany me."[6] He also wrote about the joy of being in the wilderness: "Out there it is possible to rediscover the joy to be derived from just looking, listening, and thinking."[7] His film *Song of the Paddle* is an excellent illustration of the joy of a canoe trip with his family.[8] His joy is confirmed by Ken Buck, who informs us that Mason's cartoons usually "expressed joy and happiness . . . and being alive,"[9] and by Chris Chapman, who in the foreword to *Canoescapes* reports receiving cartoons from Mason showing "himself jumping up and down with joyous abandon. This was Bill. When he was excited, he was ecstatic."[10] Chapman also described Mason's "profusion of joy over our natural heritage."[11] Mason himself reflected on joy as follows:

> Life. Is it merely a sentimental delusion, a "pathetic fallacy," to think that one sees in the animal a capacity for joy which man himself is tending to lose? We have invented exercise, recreation, pleasure, amusement, and the rest. To "have fun" is a desire often expressed by those who live in this age of anxiety and most of us have at times actually "had fun." But recreation, pleasure, amusement, fun and all the rest are poor substitutes for joy; and joy, I am convinced, has its roots in something from which civilization tends to cut us off.[12]

There was a connection between Mason's joy and his relationship with God. He referred to "the joy I got out of being out there [wilderness] because of my belief that the same God who lived in me created that."[13]

Work and Leisure Balance

The book of Ecclesiastes critiques those who distort God's intended rhythm of work and leisure by pursuing either a compulsive work ethic or a hedonistic leisure ethic based on consuming goods. The book points to an alternative for true disciples: enjoying the good life on the good earth God has given us. Throughout Ecclesiastes (2:17–26; 5:9–16; 6:7–9; esp. 4:4–16) the author emphasizes the folly of compulsive work and refutes three arguments often put forward in its support: the need to achieve (4:4); the desire for wealth (4:8); and the desire to gain fame (4:13–16). The conclusion is unavoidable—overwork is foolish, and moderation is sensible. Bill Mason was a worker. In his lifetime he produced twenty-two films, authored three books, and created numerous paintings, among other things. He wrote about finding much satisfaction in work: "The compulsion to create is something that I was born with. I am happiest when I am painting, photographing or writing. Or put it another way, I'm unhappy when I am not creating." However, his life was more than work, as he completed this sentence with the phrase "unless I am doing something active, like running whitewater, or skiing, or playing hockey."[14] His life also included quieter and more contemplative activities, such as "just looking, listening, and thinking"[15] and contemplating creation.

Although Mason produced much creative work, he did not let work prevent him from engaging in leisure activity. Recounting an experience of telemark skiing near Roger's Pass, he wrote,

> Telemark skiing presents a problem. I enjoy the thrill and challenge of cross-country and telemarking skiing so much that it cuts into my painting time. I should have been sitting on the saddle sketching and painting among the peaks. Instead I spent a riotous day of telemarking with my friends. I often envy Turner's single-mindedness of purpose. However, I'm sure I have had a lot more fun than he did![16]

In Ecclesiastes, the writer addresses those who hold a hedonistic, consumptive recreation ethic. A life of unreserved pleasure-seeking and acquisition of possessions is "meaningless, a chasing after the wind" (2:1–11). Evidently, leisure activity that is focused on pleasure-seeking, on consumption and acquisition, or that becomes one's all-consuming end is ultimately not fulfilling. Bill Mason was quite aware of the danger of a leisure ethic becoming all-consuming and idolatrous.

> When I get together with people I talk about the canoe so much because I feel sorry for them if they're not sharing in the beautiful experience of paddling a canoe on a calm, misty morning. And I've got to tell people about that. This is why sometimes I feel that—I feel, my gosh, if I could have this same enthusiasm for spreading or sharing with people the love of Christ. . . . I've got to struggle with it so that it [the canoe] doesn't really become the centre of my life because I almost talk more about the canoe than I do about the person of Christ. It's almost the cart before the horse.[17]

The recommended lifestyle, in contrast to a compulsive work ethic and a hedonistic leisure ethic, comes at the end of Ecclesiastes 2. Here we learn that life is to be enjoyed: "People can do nothing better than to eat and drink and find satisfaction in their toil" (v. 24). Commentators suggest that this phrase stands for a contented and happy life characterized by joy, companionship, and satisfaction. The writer of Ecclesiastes further elaborates on the theme of enjoying the life God has given us (2:24–26; 3:12–13, 22; 5:18–19; 9:7–9; 11:9–12:1). God has given humans the opportunity and the encouragement to enjoy the good life on God's good earth. As we have seen above, Bill Mason's life was characterized by a deep sense of joy. Even when near death, he appreciated what life had to offer: "We live and cherish each day at a time, as always.

I want to spend as much time as I can painting, writing, smelling the flowers and watching the clouds."[18]

This advice in Ecclesiastes to enjoy life reflects the Genesis account, in which God repeatedly pronounces the creation "good." It also reflects the rejoicing in creation suggested by the Exodus account of the Sabbath commandment, and the orthodox Israelite view of the earthly realm, in which God brings "forth food from earth: wine that gladdens the human hearts, oil to make their faces shine, and bread that sustains their hearts" (Ps. 104:14b–15).

Since most of us work indoors, only during our leisure activity or recreation do we have time to develop our awareness and knowledge of the created world. As the word "recreation" itself suggests, we can be *re-created* in the environment of *creation*, and during recreation we can care for and preserve creation.[19] Bill Mason cared deeply for creation and was wildly enthusiastic about creation-based recreation.

Being good stewards of God's good creation implies that we should choose forms of leisure activity that help us to conserve rather than consume or exploit that creation. We have already seen how the Sabbath suggests that leisure activity is for enjoyment of creation and personal renewal, but it also suggests that our leisure activity should reflect care of creation. For example, both the Exodus and Deuteronomy versions of the Sabbath commandment (Exod. 20:10; Deut. 5:12–14) state that the Israelites' animals were not to work on the Sabbath, thus the Sabbath was also for the benefit of the animals: "Six days do your work, but on the seventh day do not work, so that your ox and your donkey may rest" (Exod. 23:12). Mason was concerned about these creatures. In *Path of the Paddle*, he stated, "I believe that we have a moral obligation to preserve and care for the habitat of animals and plant life because, like us, they were created by God and have a right to exist too."[20] In his book *Song of the Paddle* (which has the same title as one of his films), he added, "Not just for your sake or mine or that of our children, but for the sake of all the myriad forms of life that live there we have a responsibility to ensure that they continue to exist."[21]

Often our leisure activities can be detrimental to creation, especially when they are technology-based and involve rebuilding creation to amuse ourselves with consumer goods. Bill Mason wrote, "We have become so totally committed to changing our environment that we have become oblivious to the fact that the world around us is a creation itself—God's creation."[22] Our leisure activities need to respect, not exploit, God's creatures and the creation. That means we need to raise questions about activities that use scarce energy resources and emit noxious fumes, such as auto-racing, jet-skiing, or traveling to distant resorts; or that abuse animals, such as bullfighting or hunting for "sport" rather than for food or other purposes.[23] We need to question any activity that needlessly upsets ecosystems or defaces natural beauty.

Instead we should choose forms of leisure activity that allow us to see, hear, and experience the majesty of God's creation. In his book *Path of the Paddle*,

Bill Mason wrote about his visit to Banff National Park. By choosing to hike up Mount Rundle rather than take the gondola up Sulphur Mountain, he was able to experience that majesty firsthand. "I made it almost to the peak before the clouds lowered and it began to snow. . . . As I sat there in silence, I was very glad there was no easy way up Mt. Rundle."[24] In the same book, Mason contrasted motorboat travel with canoe travel. He observed, "A journey by canoe along ancient waterways is a good way to rediscover our lost relationship with the natural world and the Creator who put it all together so long ago."[25] Such leisure activities are consistent with the ancient tradition of meditating on creation—a form of contemplation that the mystics called the "discovery of God in his creatures" (see Pss. 8; 19) and that helps to develop the qualitative spiritual dimension of leisure that permeates all of life.

In his film *Waterwalker* Mason continued the tradition of contemplating creation when he quoted Job 12:7–9:

> But ask the animals, and they will teach you,
>   or the birds of the air, and they will tell you;
> or speak to the earth, and it will teach you,
>   or let the fish of the sea inform you.
> Which of all these does not know
>   that the hand of the LORD has done this?

Elsewhere he wrote that in wilderness "it is possible to rediscover the joy to be derived from just looking, listening, and thinking."[26] He reflected on God speaking to him through creation in the catalog for his 1980 art show, *Wilderness Impressions: A Dialogue with the Arts*: "It has taken me almost a lifetime to learn to look and to listen to what God has to say through His creation."[27] In summary, these biblical passages and Bill Mason's example teach us that leisure is part of God's lifestyle for us: for rest; for renewal; and for learning about, appreciating, and enjoying God and God's gift of creation.

notes

Introduction

1. Witold Rybczynski, *Waiting for the Weekend* (New York: Viking, 1991), 224.

2. Kathleen Norris, *Acedia and Me: A Marriage, Monks, and A Writer's Life* (New York: Penguin, 2008), 194.

3. Jean Mundy and Linda Odum, *Leisure Education: Theory and Practice* (Toronto: John Wiley and Sons, 1979), 178–79.

4. Indur M. Goklany, "Economic Growth and Human Well-Being," in *Sustainable Development*, ed. Julian Morris (London: Profile Books, 2002), 31, cited in Tim Robinson, *Work, Leisure and the Environment: The Vicious Cycle of Overwork and Over Consumption* (Northampton, MA: Edward Elgar, 2006), 25.

5. Michael Cox and Richard Alm, cited in Robinson, *Work, Leisure and the Environment*, 22.

6. Jesse H. Ausubel and Arnulf Grübler, "Working Less and Living Longer: Long-Term Trends in Working Time and Time Budgets," *Technological Forecasting and Social Change* 50, no. 3 (1995): 195.

7. Antoine Zalatan, "Work Utility and Disposable Time: The Canadian Evidence," *Leisure Studies* 3, no. 1 (1984): 89, 90, 94, tables 1 and 2.

8. Sebastian de Grazia, *Of Time, Work and Leisure* (New York: The Twentieth Century Fund, 1964), 89–90.

9. Geoffrey Godbey, *Leisure and Leisure Services in the 21st Century: Toward Mid Century* (State College, PA: Venture, 2006), 179.

10. J. I. Packer, "Leisure and Life-Style: Leisure, Pleasure, and Treasure," in *God and Culture: Essays in Honour of Carl F. H. Henry*, ed. Donald A. Carson and John D. Woodbridge (Grand Rapids: Eerdmans, 1993), 357.

11. Godbey, *Leisure and Leisure Services*, 179.

12. Chris Rojek, Susan M. Shaw, and Anthony James Veal, introduction to *A Handbook of Leisure Studies*, ed. Chris Rojek, Susan Shaw, and Anthony James Veal (New York: Palgrave Macmillan, 2006), 1.

13. Ibid., 1–2.

14. Ibid., 19.

15. Margo Hilbrecht, "Leisure and the Changing Workplace," in *Leisure for Canadians*, ed. Ron McCarville and Kelly MacKay (State College, PA: Venture, 2007), 89–90.

16. Margo Hilbrecht, "Leisure and the Changing Workplace," in *Leisure for Canadians*, 2nd ed, ed. Ron McCarville and Kelly MacKay (State College, PA: Venture, 2013), 104.

17. Godbey, *Leisure and Leisure Services*, 180.

18. Packer, "Leisure and Life-Style," 357.

19. J. I. Packer, "Hot Tub Religion: Toward a Theology of Enjoyment," in *God's Plans for You* (Wheaton: Crossway, 2001), 70.

20. Margaret Hothem, "The Integration of Christian Faith and Leisure: A Qualitative Study" (EdD diss., Boston University, 1983). See also Margaret Trunfio, "A Theological Perspective on the Ethics of Leisure," in *Leisure and Ethics: Reflections on the Philosophy of Leisure*, ed. Gerald Fain (Reston, VA: American Association for Leisure and Recreation, 1991), 151.

21. Packer, "Leisure and Life-Style," 356.

22. Paul Stevens, *Seven Days of Faith* (Colorado Springs: NavPress, 2001), 205.

23. Tim Hansel, *When I Relax I Feel Guilty* (Elgin, IL: David C. Cook, 1979).

24. Gordon Dahl, *Work, Play and Worship in a Leisure-Oriented Society* (Minneapolis: Augsburg, 1972), 114.

25. Leland Ryken, *Redeeming the Time: A Christian Approach to Work and Leisure* (Grand Rapids: Baker Books, 1995), 239.

26. Karl Johnson, "From Sabbath to Weekend: Recreation, Sabbatarianism, and the Emergence of the Weekend" (PhD diss., Cornell University, 2011), 220.

27. Packer, "Leisure and Life-Style," 363.

28. Beverly L. Driver, Perry J. Brown, and George L. Peterson, "Research on Leisure Benefits: An Introduction to This Volume" in *Benefits of Leisure*, ed. Beverly L. Driver, Perry J. Brown, and George L. Peterson (State College, PA: Venture, 1991), 4.

29. Roger C. Mannell and Daniel J. Stynes, "A Retrospective: The Benefits of Leisure," in *Benefits of Leisure*, ed. Beverly L. Driver, Perry J. Brown, and George L. Peterson (State College, PA: Venture, 1991), 461.

30. Parks and Recreation Federation of Ontario, *The Benefits of Parks and Recreation: A Catalogue* (North York, ON: Parks and Recreation Federation of Ontario, 1992).

31. Mannell and Stynes, "A Retrospective," 472.

32. Edgar L. Jackson, ed., *Leisure and the Quality of Life: Impacts on Social, Economic and Cultural Development: Hangzhou Consensus* (Hangzhou, China: Zheijiang University Press, 2006).

33. James F. Murphy, "A Rediscovery of the Spiritual Side of Leisure," *California Parks and Recreation* (December 1972/January 1973): 22–23.

34. Stanley Parker, *The Sociology of Leisure* (New York: International Publications Service, 1976), 107.

35. Geoffrey Godbey, "Implications of Recreation and Leisure Research for Professionals," in *Understanding Leisure and Recreation: Mapping the Past, Charting the Future*, ed. Edgar L. Jackson and Thomas L. Burton (State College, PA: Venture, 1989), 622.

36. Thomas L. Goodale, "Legitimizing Leisure Anew" (paper presented at the 25th anniversary of the Leisure Studies Department, University of Ottawa, May 14, 1994), 2.

37. Robert Lee, *Religion and Leisure in America: A Study in Four Dimensions* (New York: Abingdon, 1964).

38. Gwen W. Wright, "Spirituality and Creative Leisure," *Pastoral Psychology* 32, no. 3 (1984): 192–203.

39. Leonard Doohan, *Leisure: A Spiritual Need* (Notre Dame, IN: Ave Maria, 1990), 26.

40. Ibid., 20.

41. Ibid., 32.

42. Ibid.

43. Ibid., 33.

44. Ibid., 35.

45. Ibid., 55.

46. Ibid., 56.

47. Ibid., 56–57.

48. Ibid., 57.

49. Ibid., 60.

50. Ibid., 64.

51. Jennifer Livengood, "The Role of Leisure in the Spirituality of New Paradigm Christians," *Leisure/Loisir* 33, no. 2 (2009): 419–45.

52. Paul Heintzman, "Men's Wilderness Experience and Spirituality: Further Explorations," in *Proceedings of the 2007 Northeastern Recreation Research Symposium*, comp. Cherie LeBlanc and Christine Vogt (Gen. Tech. Rep. NRS-P-23) (Newton Square, PA: U.S. Department of Agriculture, Forest Service, Northern Research Station, 2008), 55–59.

53. Vera Berkers, "Religion, Spirituality and Leisure: A Relational Approach. The Experience of Religion and Spirituality of Dutch New Christians and New Spirituals during Leisure Activities" (Master's thesis, Utrecht University, 2001), v.

54. Lee, *Religion and Leisure in America*, 22.

55. Hothem, "Integration of Christian Faith and Leisure." See also Trunfio, "Theological Perspective on the Ethics of Leisure," 152–53.

56. Ben Witherington III, *The Rest of Life: Rest, Play, Eating, Studying, Sex from a Kingdom Perspective* (Grand Rapids: Eerdmans, 2012), 153.

57. Edward Fitzgerald, "A Time for Play? I: The New Leisure," *Clergy Review* 59, no. 4 (1974): 283.

58. Doohan, *Leisure: A Spiritual Need*, 13.

59. John Schulz and Chris Auld, "A Social Psychological Investigation of the Relationship between Christianity and Contemporary Meanings of Leisure: An Australian Perspective," *Leisure/Loisir* 33, no. 1 (2009): 121–46.

60. James Houston, "The Theology of Work," in *Looking at Lifestyles Professional Priorities—A Christian Perspective*, Proceedings from the Conference for Physicians and Dentists, Banff, May 2–8, 1981 (Vancouver: Christian Medical and Dental Society of Canada, 1981), 45–46.

61. Dahl, *Work, Play and Worship*, 60.

62. Ibid.

63. Josef Pieper, *Leisure: The Basis of Culture* (New York: Random House, 1963), 40, 56.

64. Lee, *Religion and Leisure in America*, 199–263.

65. Rudolf F. Norden, *The Christian Encounters the New Leisure* (Saint Louis: Concordia, 1965), 68–69, 96–98.

66. Dahl, *Work, Play and Worship*, 71.

67. David A. Spence, *Towards a Theology of Leisure with Special Reference to Creativity* (Ottawa: Canadian Parks/Recreation Association, 1973), iv, v.

68. Harold D. Lehman, *In Praise of Leisure* (Kitchener, ON: Herald, 1974), 133–44.

69. Robert K. Johnston, *The Christian at Play* (Grand Rapids: Eerdmans, 1983), 137.

70. John Oswalt, *The Leisure Crisis: A Biblical Perspective on Guilt-Free Leisure* (Wheaton: Victor, 1987).

71. Jeanne E. Sherrow, *It's About Time: A Look at Leisure, Lifestyle, and Christianity* (Grand Rapids: Zondervan, 1984).

72. Leland Ryken, *Work and Leisure in Christian Perspective* (Portland, OR: Multnomah, 1987).

73. Doohan, *Leisure: A Spiritual Need*.

74. Packer, "Leisure and Life-Style."

75. Douglas Joblin, "Leisure and Spirituality: An Engaged and Responsible Pursuit of Freedom in Work, Play, and Worship," *Leisure/Loisir* 33, no. 1 (2009): 95–120.

76. Ryken, *Redeeming the Time*.

77. Paul Heintzman, Glen E. Van Andel, and Tom L. Visker, eds., *Christianity and Leisure: Issues in a Pluralistic Society*, rev. ed. (Sioux Center, IA: Dordt College Press, 2006).

78. Graham Neville, *Free Time: Towards a Theology of Leisure* (Birmingham, UK: University of Birmingham Press, 2004).

79. Witherington, *Rest of Life*.

80. Doohan, *Leisure: A Spiritual Need*.

81. Johnston, *Christian at Play*, 5.

82. Gregory Baum, "Peter L. Berger's Unfinished Symphony," *Commonweal*, May 9, 1980, 266, quoted in Johnston, *The Christian at Play*, 86.

Chapter 1: Concepts of Leisure

1. Gordon Dahl, *Work, Play and Worship in a Leisure-Oriented Society* (Minneapolis: Augsburg, 1972), 114.

2. Graham Neville, *Free Time: Towards a Theology of Leisure* (Birmingham, UK: University of Birmingham Press, 2004), 133.

3. Francis Bregha, "Philosophy of Leisure: Unanswered Questions," *Recreation Research Review* 8, no. 1 (July 1980): 16–17.

4. Ibid., 18.

5. Ibid.

6. Ibid., 15.

7. Francis J. Bregha. "Leisure and Freedom Re-examined," in *Recreation and Leisure: Issues in an Era of Change*, ed. Thomas L. Goodale and Peter A. Witt (State College, PA: Venture, 1980), 36.

8. Ibid., 37.

9. Leonard Doohan, "The Spiritual Value of Leisure," *Spirituality Today* 31, no. 2 (1981): 157–67.

10. Bregha, "Philosophy of Leisure," 15.

11. Ibid.

12. Robert K. Johnston, *The Christian at Play* (Grand Rapids: Eerdmans, 1983), 5.

13. Charles Sylvester, "Interpretation and Leisure Science: A Hermeneutical Example of Past and Present Oracles," *Journal of Leisure Research* 32, no. 1 (1990): 292.

14. Richard Kraus, *Recreation and Leisure in Modern Society*, 3rd ed. (Glenview, IL: Scott Foresman, 1984), 41–47.

15. James F. Murphy, *Concepts of Leisure: Philosophical Implications* (Englewood Cliffs, NJ: Prentice Hall, 1974), 3–5.

16. Paul Heintzman, "Defining Leisure," in *Leisure for Canadians*, 2nd ed., ed. Ron McCarville and Kelly MacKay (State College, PA: Venture, 2013), 3–14.

17. Murphy, *Concepts of Leisure*, 3; cf. 72, 75.

18. Kraus, *Recreation and Leisure*, 42.

19. David E. Gray, "This Alien Thing Called Leisure" (paper presented at Oregon State University, July 8, 1971), quoted in Murphy, *Concepts of Leisure*, 42.

20. Charles Sylvester, "The Western Idea of Work and Leisure: Traditions, Transformations, and the Future," in *Leisure Studies: Prospects for the Twenty-First Century*, ed. Edgar L. Jackson and Thomas L. Burton (State College, PA: Venture, 1999), 21–23.

21. Josef Pieper, *Leisure: The Basis of Culture* (New York: Random House, 1963), 40–41.

22. Sebastian de Grazia, *Of Time, Work and Leisure* (New York: The Twentieth Century Fund, 1964).

23. Murphy, *Concepts of Leisure*, 3.

24. de Grazia, *Of Time, Work and Leisure*, 8.

25. L. Joseph Hebert Jr., "Be Still and See: Leisure, Labor, and Human Dignity in Josef Pieper and Blessed John Paul II," *Logos: A Journal of Catholic Thought and Culture* 16, no. 2 (Spring 2013): 144.

26. Leonard Doohan, *Leisure: A Spiritual Need* (Notre Dame, IN: Ave Maria, 1990).

27. Dennis J. Billy, "The Call to Holy Rest," *New Blackfriars* 82, no. 962 (April 2001): 182–87.

28. Thomas DuBay, *The Evidential Power of Beauty: Science and Theology Meet* (San Francisco: Ignatius, 1999), 340.

29. James J. O'Rourke, "Work, Leisure and Contemplation," *American Benedictine Review* 28, no. 4 (1977): 351–72.

30. Joseph Teaff, "Contemplative Leisure within Christian Spirituality," in *Christianity and Leisure: Issues in a Pluralistic Society*, rev. ed., ed. Paul Heintzman, Glen E. Van Andel, and Thomas L. Visker (Sioux Center, IA: Dordt College Press, 2006), 113–14.

31. Douglas V. Steere, "Contemplation and Leisure," *Humanitas* 8, no. 3 (1972): 287–306.

32. Sylvester, "Interpretation and Leisure Science."

33. John Hemingway, "Lesiure [*sic*] and Civility: Reflections on a Greek Ideal," *Leisure Sciences* 10, no. 3 (1988): 179–91.

34. Anand Kashyap, "Leisure: An Indian Classical Perspective," *World Leisure and Recreation* 33, no. 2 (1991): 6–8.

35. Murphy, *Concepts of Leisure*, 4.

36. International Study Group on Leisure and Social Sciences, quoted in Isobel Cosgrove and Richard Jackson, *The Geography of Recreation and Leisure* (London: Hutchinson University Library, 1972), 13.

37. Kenneth Roberts, *Leisure* (London: Longman, 1970), 13.

38. Robert A. Stebbins, "Serious Leisure: A Conceptual Statement," *The Pacific Sociological Review* 25, no. 2 (1982): 268.

39. de Grazia, *Of Time, Work and Leisure*, 22.

40. Joffre Dumazedier, *Toward a Society of Leisure*, trans. Stewart E. McClure (New York: Free Press, 1967), 16–17.

41. Ibid., 14–16.

42. Joffre Dumazedier, *Sociology of Leisure,* trans. Marea A. McKenzie (New York: Elsevier, 1974), 75.

43. Packer, "Leisure and Life-Style: Leisure, Pleasure, and Treasure," in *God and Culture: Essays in Honour of Carl F. H. Henry*, ed. Donald A. Carson and John D. Woodbridge (Grand Rapids: Eerdmans, 1993), 363.

44. Robert A. Stebbins, "Serious Leisure," in *Leisure Studies: Prospects for the Twenty-First Century*, ed. Edgar L. Jackson and Thomas L. Burton (State College, PA: Venture, 1999), 69.

45. Ibid., 70–71.

46. Robert A. Stebbins, "Serious Leisure," in *A Handbook of Leisure Studies,* ed. Chris Rojek, Susan M. Shaw, and Anthony James Veal (New York: Palgrave Macmillan, 2006), 455.

47. Karen Gallant, Susan Arai, and Bryan Smale, "Celebrating, Challenging, and Re-Envisioning Serious Leisure," *Leisure/Loisir* 37, no. 2 (2013): 104.

48. Robert A. Stebbins, "Casual Leisure: A Conceptual Statement," *Leisure Studies* 16, no. 1 (1997): 18.

49. Murphy, *Concepts of Leisure*, 145–50.

50. Gray, "This Alien Thing Called Leisure," quoted in Murphy, *Concepts of Leisure*, 42.

51. Charles Reich, *The Greening of America* (New York: Random House, 1970), cited in Murphy, *Concepts of Leisure*, 145.

52. Walter Kerr, *The Decline of Pleasure* (New York: Simon & Schuster, 1962), cited in Murphy, *Concepts of Leisure*, 146.

53. Robert A. Stebbins, "Project-based Leisure: Theoretical Neglect of a Common Use of Free Time," *Leisure Studies* 24, no. 1 (2005): 2.

54. Robert A. Stebbins, *The Idea of Leisure: First Principles* (New Brunswick, NJ: Transaction, 2012), 40.

55. Susan M. Shaw, "Conceptualizing Resistance: Women's Leisure as Political Practice," *Journal of Leisure Research* 33, no. 2 (2001): 186–201.

56. Heather Mair, "Civil Leisure? Exploring the Relationship between Leisure, Activism and Social Change," *Leisure/Loisir* 27, nos. 3–4 (2002–3): 213–37.

57. William H. Martin and Sandra Mason, "Leisure in an Islamic Context," *World Leisure* 46, no. 1 (2004): 4–13.

58. Hilmi Ibrahim, "Leisure and Islam," in *Leisure and Ethics: Reflections on the Philosophy of Leisure*, ed. Gerald S. Fain (Reston, VA: American Association for the Study of Leisure and Recreation, 1991), 206.

59. de Grazia, *Of Time, Work and Leisure*, 246.

60. John R. Kelly, *Leisure*, 2nd ed. (Englewood Cliffs, NJ: Prentice-Hall, 1990), 27.

61. Murphy, *Concepts of Leisure*, 3; cf. 72, 75.

62. Henry Pratt Fairchild, ed., *Dictionary of Sociology* (Totowa, NJ: Littlefield, Adams & Co., 1976), 175.

63. Gray, "This Alien Thing Called Leisure," quoted in Murphy, *Concepts of Leisure*, 42.

64. Abraham Joshua Heschel, *The Sabbath* (New York: Harper & Row, 1966), 21.

65. Robert Gordis, "The Sabbath—Cornerstone and Capstone of Jewish Life," *Judaism* 31 (1982): 6–11.

66. Robert D. Crabtree, "Leisure in Ancient Israel" (PhD diss., Texas A&M University, 1982). See also Dain A. Trafton, "In Praise of Three Traditional Ideas of Leisure," in *Transitions to Leisure: Conceptual and Human Issues*, ed. Billy G. Gunter, Jay Stanley, and Robert St. Clair (Lanham, MD: University Press of America, 1985), 23–31.

67. Murphy, *Concepts of Leisure*, 92.

68. Thorstein Veblen, *The Theory of the Leisure Class* (New York: The New American Library, 1899/1953), 46.

69. Ibid., 63–64.

70. Kraus, *Recreation and Leisure*, 43.

71. Maryam Siddiqi, "Ridiculously, Deliciously Conspicuous Consumption," *Financial Post*, December 20, 2003, IN1.

72. Murphy, *Concepts of Leisure*, 100.

73. Rudi Colloredo-Mansfeld, *The Native Leisure Class: Consumption and Cultural Creativity in the Andes* (Chicago: University of Chicago Press, 1999).

74. Beverly L. Driver and S. Ross Tocher, "Toward a Behavioral Interpretation of Recreational Engagements, with Implications for Planning," in *Elements of Outdoor Recreation Planning*, ed. Beverly L. Driver (Ann Arbor: University of Michigan Press, 1970), 10.

75. Douglas A. Kleiber, Gordon J. Walker, and Roger C. Mannell, *A Social Psychology of Leisure*, 2nd ed. (State College, PA: Venture, 2011), 103–4.

76. Abraham H. Maslow, *Toward a Psychology of Being*, 2nd ed. (Toronto: Van Nos Reinhold, 1968), 73.

77. John Neulinger, *The Psychology of Leisure* (Springfield, IL: Charles C. Thomas, 1981), 18.

78. Mihaly Csikszentmihalyi, *Beyond Boredom and Anxiety: The Experience of Play in Work and Games* (San Francisco: Jossey Bass, 1975).

79. Jianyu Wang and L. Allison Stringer, "The Impact of Taoism on Chinese Leisure," *World Leisure* 42, no. 3 (2000): 33–41.

80. Gordon J. Walker and Jinyeng Deng, "Comparing Leisure as Subjective Experience with the Chinese Experience of Rùmí," *Leisure/Loisir* 28, nos. 3–4 (2003–4): 245–76.

81. Johan Huizinga, *Homo Ludens: A Study of the Play-Element in Culture* (Boston: Beacon, 1955), 13.

82. Karla A. Henderson et al., *Both Gaps and Gains: Feminist Perspectives on Women's Leisure* (State College, PA: Venture, 1996), 99–120. See also Valerie J. Freysinger et al., *Leisure, Women and Gender* (State College, PA: Venture, 2013).

83. Karla A. Henderson et al., *A Leisure of One's Own: A Feminist Perspective on Women's Leisure* (State College, PA: Venture, 1989), 46.

84. Ibid., 10.

85. Henderson et al., *Both Gaps and Gains*, 195–206.

86. Henderson et al., *A Leisure of One's Own*, 11.

87. Henderson et al., *Both Gaps and Gains*, 107–16.

88. Chiang-Tzu Lucetta Tsai, "Research Note: The Influence of Confucianism on Women's Leisure in Taiwan," *Leisure Studies* 25, no. 4 (2006): 469–76; Chiang-Tzu Lucetta Tsai, "Women's Leisure, Leisurely Women? Feminist Perspectives on the Leisure Practice in Taiwan," *Asian Journal of Exercise and Sports Science* 5, no. 1 (2008): 39–47; and Chiang-Tzu Lucetta Tsai, "A Reflection on Cultural Conflicts in Women's Leisure," *Leisure Sciences* 32, no. 4 (2010): 386–90.

89. Murphy, *Concepts of Leisure*, 223.

90. Max Kaplan, "Implications for Gerontology from a General Theory of Leisure" (paper presented at the Third International Course, "Leisure and the Third Age," Dubrovnik, Yugoslavia, May 15–19, 1972), cited in Murphy, *Concepts of Leisure*, 223.

91. Anthony W. Bacon, "Leisure and Research: A Critical Review of the Main Concepts Employed in Contemporary Research," *Society and Leisure* 4, no. 2 (1972): 83.

92. Kaplan, "Implications for Gerontology," quoted in Murphy, *Concepts of Leisure*, 223.

93. Max Kaplan, "Leisure and Design" (paper presented at the American Iron and Steel Institute, Chicago, March 23, 1972), quoted in Murphy, *Concepts of Leisure*, 225.

94. Max Kaplan, "New Concepts of Leisure Today," in James F. Murphy, *Concepts of Leisure: Philosophical Implications*, ed. James F. Murphy (Englewood Cliffs, NJ: Prentice Hall, 1974), 232.

95. Murphy, *Concepts of Leisure*, 213–28.

96. Alvin Toffler, *Future Shock* (New York: Bantam, 1971).

97. Thomas Goodale and Geoffrey C. Godbey, *The Evolution of Leisure: Historical and Philosophical Perspectives* (State College, PA: Venture, 1988), 195–97.

98. Joy Beatty and William R. Torbert, "YIN AND YANG: The Relationship of Leisure and Work," in *Routledge Handbook of Leisure Studies*, ed. Tony Blackshaw (New York: Routledge, 2013): 468–79.

99. Crabtree, "Leisure in Ancient Israel."

100. Jean Leclercq, "Otium Monasticum as a Context for Artistic Creativity," in *Monasticism and the Arts*, ed. Timothy G. Verdun (Syracuse: Syracuse University Press, 1984), 69.

101. Henderson et al., *Both Gaps and Gains*, 97.

102. Donald G. Reid and Sue Welke, "Leisure and Traditional Culture in First Nations Communities," *Journal of Leisurability* 25, no. 1 (1998): 26–36.

103. Daniel McDonald and Leo McAvoy, "Native Americans and Leisure: State of the Research and Future Directions," *Journal of Leisure Research* 29, no. 2 (1997): 145–66.

Chapter 2: Contemporary Leisure Trends and Issues

1. Margo Hilbrecht, "Leisure and the Changing Workplace," in *Leisure for Canadians*, ed. Ron McCarville and Kelly MacKay (State College, PA: Venture, 2007), 89.

2. Juliet Schor, *The Overworked American: The Unexpected Decline of Leisure* (New York: Basic Books, 1991).

3. John P. Robinson and Geoffrey Godbey, *Time for Life: The Surprising Ways Americans Use Their Time* (University Park: Pennsylvania State University Press, 1997).

4. Hilbrecht, "Leisure and the Changing Workplace," 89.

5. Juliet Schor, "The (Even More) Overworked American," in *Take Back Your Time: Fighting Overwork and Time Poverty in America*, ed. John de Graaf (San Francisco: Berrett-Koehler, 2003), 6.

6. Ibid., 10.

7. Juliette Schor, "Overturning the Modernist Predictions: Recent Trends in Work and Leisure in the OECD," in *A Handbook of Leisure Studies*, ed. Chris Rojek, Susan M. Shaw, and Anthony James Veal (New York: Palgrave Macmillan, 2006), 203.

8. Ibid., 204.

9. John E. Stapleford, *Bulls, Bears and Golden Calves: Applying Christian Ethics in Economics*, 2nd ed. (Downers Grove, IL: IVP Academic, 2009), 105–11.

10. Ibid., 107.

11. Ibid., 110.

12. Benjamin Kline Hunnicutt, *Free Time: The Forgotten American Dream* (Philadelphia: Temple University Press, 2013), ix.

13. Geoffrey Godbey, *Leisure and Leisure Services in the 21st Century: Toward Mid Century* (State College, PA: Venture, 2006), 183. See also Geoffrey Godbey, "Trends in Time for Leisure," in *Leisure Matters: The State and Future of Leisure Studies*, ed. Gordon Walker, David Scott, and Monika Stodolska (State College, PA: Venture, forthcoming).

14. Ibid.

15. Ibid., 187.

16. Ibid., 183.

17. Al Gini, *The Importance of Being Lazy* (New York: Routledge, 2003), 2–4.

18. Godbey, *Leisure and Leisure Services*, 180–87.

19. Tim Robinson, *Work, Leisure and the Environment: The Vicious Cycle of Overwork and Over Consumption* (Northampton, MA: Edward Elgar, 2006), 32.

20. Hunnicutt, *Free Time*, ix.

21. Mark Aguiar and Erik Hurst, *The Increase in Leisure Inequality, 1965–2005* (Washington, DC: AEI Press, 2009), 2.

22. Glenn J. Stalker, "A Widening Parental Leisure Gap: The Family as a Site for Late Modern Differentiation and Convergence in Leisure Time within Canada, the United Kingdom and the United States," *Canadian Journal of Sociology/Cahiers canadiens de sociologie* 36, no. 1 (2011): 25–58.

23. Canadian Index of Wellbeing, *How Are Canadians Really Doing?* The 2012 CIW Report (Waterloo, ON: Canadian Index of Wellbeing and University of Waterloo, 2012), 49–53.

24. Ibid., 51.

25. Godbey, *Leisure and Leisure Services*, 186.

26. Ibid.

27. Ibid., 202–4.

28. Charles Guignon and Kevin Aho, "Phenomenological Reflections on Work and Leisure in America," in *The Value of Time and Leisure in a World of Work*, ed. Mitchel R. Haney and A. David Kline (Lanham, MD: Lexington, 2010), 25.

29. John Robinson, "Are We There Yet? No, and Don't Hold Your Breath: The Family Vacation Is Fading Fast," *Sierra* (May/June 2008): 42.

30. Godbey, *Leisure and Leisure Services*.

31. Robinson, "Are We There Yet?," 40–43.

32. Ibid.

33. Godbey, *Leisure and Leisure Services*, 203.

34. Ibid., 203–4.

35. L. Morsch, *American Vacation Time Doesn't Add Up* (2005), cited in Godbey, *Leisure and Leisure Services*, 203.

36. Guignon and Aho, "Phenomenological Reflections," 26.

37. Stalker, "A Widening Parental Leisure Gap," 50.

38. Aguiar and Hurst, *Increase in Leisure Inequality*, 2–4.

39. Robinson and Godbey, *Time for Life*.

40. Canadian Index of Wellbeing, *How Are Canadians Really Doing?*, 51–53.

41. Robert Banks, *The Tyranny of Time: When 24 Hours Is Not Enough* (Downers Grove, IL: InterVarsity, 1983), 61.

42. Ibid., 40–73, 32.

43. J. I. Packer, *Keep in Step with the Spirit* (Old Tappan, NJ: Fleming H. Revell, 1984), 98.

44. Banks, *Tyranny of Time*, 32.

45. John de Graaf, ed., *Take Back Your Time: Fighting Overwork and Time Poverty in America* (San Francisco: Berrett-Koehler, 2003).

46. Karl Johnson, "From Sabbath to Weekend: Recreation, Sabbatarianism, and the Emergence of the Weekend" (PhD diss., Cornell University, 2011), 219.

47. Gordon J. Dahl, "Time, Work and Leisure Today," *The Christian Century* 88, no. 6 (February 10, 1971): 187.

48. Kenneth Roberts, *Leisure in Contemporary Society*, 2nd ed. (Wallingford, UK: CABI, 2006), 190.

49. Ibid., 192.

50. Ellis Cashmore, *And There Was Television* (London: Routledge, 2004).

51. Roberts, *Leisure in Contemporary Society*, 183.

52. Ibid.

53. Ibid., 197.

54. Ibid., 199.

55. Ibid., 203.

56. Ibid.

57. Ibid., 204.

58. Robert A. Stebbins, *Leisure and Consumption: Common Ground/Separate Worlds* (New York: Palgrave Macmillan, 2009), ix.

59. Hayden Ramsay, *Reclaiming Leisure: Art, Sport, and Philosophy* (New York: Palgrave Macmillan, 2005).

60. Ibid., 31.

61. Ibid., 32.

62. Ibid., 35, 38.

63. Ibid., 37.

64. Ibid., 38.

65. Gini, *Importance of Being Lazy*, 83.

66. Robinson and Godbey, *Time for Life*.

67. Gerald Fain, "Moral Leisure," in *Leisure and Ethics*, ed. Gerald Fain (Reston, VA: American Association for Leisure and Recreation, 1991), 7–30.

68. Ramsay, *Reclaiming Leisure*, 40.

69. Ibid., 5.

70. Graham Neville, *Free Time: Towards a Theology of Leisure* (Birmingham, UK: University of Birmingham Press, 2004), 69.

71. Ibid., 79.

72. Heather Mair, "What about the 'Rest of the Story'? Recreation on the Backs of 'Others,'" in *Speaking Up and Speaking Out: Working for Social and Environmental Justice through Parks, Recreation, and Leisure*, ed. Karen Paisley and Daniel Dustin (Urbana, IL: Sagamore, 2011), 117.

73. Ibid., 122.

74. Graham Miller et al., "Public Understanding of Sustainable Leisure and Tourism: A Research Report Completed for the Department for Environment, Food, and Rural Affairs" (London: University of Surrey, 2007), quoted in Mair, "What about the 'Rest of the Story'?," 120.

75. Mair, "What about the 'Rest of the Story'?," 121.

76. Daniel Scott, "Climate Change and Leisure: Impacts and Adaptation" (paper presented at the 10th World Leisure Congress, Quebec City, October 6–10, 2008).

77. Kelly Bricker, "Why Ride Roughshod over the Great Outdoors? The Problem with Motorized Recreation," in *Speaking Up and Speaking Out: Working for Social and Environmental Justice through Parks, Recreation, and Leisure*, ed. Karen Paisley and Daniel Dustin (Urbana, IL: Sagamore, 2011), 133.

78. Jennifer Fresque and Ryan Plummer, "Accounting for Consumption Related to Outdoor Recreation: An Application of Ecological Footprint Analysis," *Leisure/Loisir* 33, no. 2 (2009): 589–614.

79. Arne Naess, *Ecology, Community, and Lifestyle: Outline of an Ecosophy* (New York: Cambridge University Press, 1989), 181.

80. Mihaly Csikszentmihalyi, *Flow: The Psychology of Optimal Experience* (Toronto: Harper & Row, 1990), 2.

81. Elie Cohen-Gewerc and Robert A. Stebbins, "Conclusions," in *The Pivotal Role in Leisure Education: Finding Personal Fulfillment in This Century*, ed. Elie Cohen-Gewerc and Robert A. Stebbins (State College, PA: Venture, 2007), 169.

82. Neville, *Free Time*, 110.

83. Richard Winter, *Still Bored in a Culture of Entertainment: Rediscovering Passion and Wonder* (Downers Grove, IL: InterVarsity, 2002), 101.

84. Ibid.

85. Yankelovich Partners Market Research Study of Consumer Attitudes, as cited in ibid., 12.

86. Judson Gooding, "How to Cope with Boredom," *Reader's Digest* 108, no. 646 (February 1976): 51.

87. Rowan Williams, "You're Bored, Damned Bored," *The Sunday Times* (London), March 31, 2002, 3, quoted in Winter, *Still Bored in a Culture of Entertainment*, 13.

88. Bernice Kanner, "Hungry or Just Bored?," *American Demographics* 21, no. 1 (1999): 15.

89. Orrin Edgar Klapp, *Overload and Boredom: Essays on the Quality of Life in the Information Society* (New York: Greenwood, 1986), 20.

90. Patricia Meyer Spacks, *Boredom: The Literary History of a State of Mind* (Chicago: University of Chicago Press, 1995), 260.

91. Reinhard Kuhn, *The Demon of Noontide: Ennui in Western Literature* (Princeton: Princeton University Press, 1976), 331, 375.

92. Klapp, *Overload and Boredom*, 11–12.

93. Gregory Wolfe, "A Stranger and a Pilgrim," *Catholic World Report* (November 1991): 64, quoted in Steven Garber, *The Fabric of Faithfulness* (Downers Grove, IL: InterVarsity, 1996), 102.

94. Winter, *Still Bored in a Culture of Entertainment*, 32–44.

95. Mary Pipher, *The Shelter of Each Other: Rebuilding Our Families* (New York: Ballantine, 1996), 84, cited in Winter, *Still Bored in a Culture of Entertainment*, 34.

96. Robinson and Godbey, *Time for Life*, 124–26.

97. Gene Veith, "Boredom and the Law of Diminishing Returns," *AFA Journal* (January 1998): 20, quoted in Winter, *Still Bored in a Culture of Entertainment*, 44.

98. Susan M. Shaw and Karla Henderson, "Gender Analysis and Leisure Constraints: An Uneasy Alliance," in *Constraints to Leisure*, ed. Edgar L. Jackson (State College, PA: Venture, 2005), 23–34.

99. Godbey, *Leisure and Leisure Services*, 185.

100. Ibid.

101. Shaw and Henderson, "Gender Analysis and Leisure Constraints," 24.

102. Ibid.

103. Karla A. Henderson et al., *Both Gaps and Gains: Feminist Perspectives on Women's Leisure* (State College, PA: Venture, 1996), 196.

104. Tess Kay, "Having It All or Doing It All? The Construction of Women's Lifestyles in Time-Crunched Households," *Loisir et Société* 21, no. 2 (1998): 435–54.

105. Arlie Hochschild, *The Second Shift: Working Parents and the Revolution at Home* (New York: Viking, 1989).

106. Diana C. Parry, "Gender and Leisure," in *Leisure for Canadians*, ed. Ron McCarville and Kelly MacKay (State College, PA: Venture, 2007), 144.

107. Canadian Index of Wellbeing, *How Are Canadians Really Doing?*, 51.

108. Statistics Canada, *Women in Canada 2000: A Gender-based Statistical Report* (Ottawa: Canadian Ministry of Industry, 2000).

109. Neville, *Free Time*, 68.

110. Jennifer Mason, "'No Peace for the Wicked': Older Married Women and Leisure," in *Relative Freedoms: Women and Leisure*, ed. Erica Wimbush and Margaret Talbot (Milton Keynes, UK: Open University Press, 1988), 75–85.

111. Shaw and Henderson, "Gender Analysis and Leisure Constraints," 25.

112. Henderson et al., *Both Gaps and Gains*, 196.

113. Shaw and Henderson, "Gender Analysis and Leisure Constraints," 25.

114. Parry, "Gender and Leisure," 143–44.

115. Shaw and Henderson, "Gender Analysis and Leisure Constraints," 25.

116. Ibid.

117. Parry, "Gender and Leisure," 144.

118. Henderson et al., *Both Gaps and Gains*, 196.

119. Shaw and Henderson, "Gender Analysis and Leisure Constraints," 26.

120. Ibid.

121. Ibid.

122. Parry, "Gender and Leisure," 144.

123. Canadian Index of WellBeing, *How Are Canadians Really Doing? Highlights: Canadian Index of Wellbeing 1.0* (Waterloo, ON: Canadian Index of Wellbeing and University of Waterloo, 2011), 45.

124. Shaw and Henderson, "Gender Analysis and Leisure Constraints," 26–27.

125. Parry, "Gender and Leisure," 143.

126. Shaw and Henderson, "Gender Analysis and Leisure Constraints," 27.

127. Edgar L. Jackson, ed., *Leisure and the Quality of Life: Impacts on Social, Economic and Cultural Development—Hangzhou Consensus* (Hangzhou, China: Zheijiang University Press, 2006), 5.

128. Jearold W. Holland, *Black Recreation: A Historical Perspective* (Chicago: Burnham, 2004), 196.

129. Victoria W. Wolcott, *Race, Riots and Roller Coasters: The Struggle over Segregated Recreation in America* (Philadelphia: University of Pennsylvania Press, 2012), 232.

130. Valerie J. Freysinger and Othello Harris, "Race and Leisure," in *A Handbook of Leisure Studies*, ed. Chris Rojek, Susan M. Shaw, and Anthony James Veal (New York: Palgrave Macmillan, 2006), 258.

131. Ibid., 257–59.

132. Neville, *Free Time*, 65.

133. Ken Roberts, "Leisure: The Importance of Being Inconsequential," *Leisure Studies* 30, no. 1 (2011): 10.

134. Cohen-Gewerc and Stebbins, "Conclusions," 169.

135. Chris Rojek, "Deviant Leisure: The Dark Side of Free-Time Activity," *Leisure Studies: Prospects for the Twenty-First Century*, ed. Edgar L. Jackson and Thomas L. Burton (State College, PA: Venture, 1999), 81.

136. Ibid.

137. Ibid., 82.

138. Tony Blackshaw, *Routledge Handbook of Leisure Studies* (Oxford: Routledge, 2013), 293–372.

139. J. I. Packer, "Leisure and Life-Style: Leisure, Pleasure, and Treasure," in *God and Culture: Essays in Honour of Carl F. H. Henry*, ed. Donald A. Carson and John D. Woodbridge (Grand Rapids: Eerdmans, 1993), 365.

140. Mike W. Martin, "Balancing Work and Leisure," in *The Value of Time and Leisure in a World of Work*, ed. Mitchell R. Haney and A. David Kline (Toronto: Lexington, 2010), 13.

141. Ibid., 14.

142. Guignon and Aho, "Phenomenological Reflections," 26.

143. Ibid., 27.

144. Lam Thuy Vo, "What Americans Actually Do All Day Long, in 2 Graphics," National Public Radio, August 29, 2012, www.npr.org/blogs/money/2012/08/29/160244277/what-americans-actually-do-all-day-long-in-2-graphics.

145. Godbey, *Leisure and Leisure Services*, 190–92.

146. Ibid., 185.

147. Ibid.

148. Canadian Index of Wellbeing, *How Are Canadians Really Doing? Highlights: Canadian Index of Wellbeing 1.0*, 46.

149. Ibid.

150. Jiri Zuzanek, "Leisure and Time," in *A Handbook of Leisure Studies*, ed. Chris Rojek, Susan M. Shaw, and Anthony James Veal (New York: Palgrave Macmillan, 2006), 193.

151. James Kunstler, *The Geography of Nowhere: The Rise and Decline of America's Man-Made Landscape* (New York: Simon and Schuster, 1993), quoted in Godbey, *Leisure and Leisure Services*, 191.

152. Godbey, *Leisure and Leisure Services*, 191.

153. Ibid.

154. Ibid., 162–63.

155. Ibid., 154.

156. Ibid., 155.

157. Canadian Index of Wellbeing, *How Are Canadians Really Doing? The 2012 CIW Report*, 40–44.

158. David G. Myers, *The American Paradox: Spiritual Hunger in an Age of Plenty* (New Haven: Yale University Press, 2000), xi.

159. Hunnicutt, *Free Time*, x.

160. Martin Davies, "Another Way of Being: Leisure and the Possibility of Privacy," in *The Philosophy of Leisure*, ed. Cyril Barrett and Tom Winnifrith (London: Macmillan: 1989), 117.

161. Walker Percy, *Lost in the Cosmos: The Last Self-Help Book* (New York: Noonday, 1992), 70–71, as quoted in Winter, *Still Bored in a Culture of Entertainment*, 98.

162. Douglas Joblin, "Leisure and Spirituality: An Engaged and Responsible Pursuit of Freedom in Work, Play, and Worship," *Leisure/Loisir* 33, no. 1 (2009): 95–120.

163. Ibid., 103.

164. C. Forrest McDowell, "Wellness and Therapeutic Recreation: Challenge for Service," *Therapeutic Recreation Journal* 20, no. 2 (1986): 37.

165. Godbey, *Leisure and Leisure Services*, 79.

166. Mihaly Csikszentmihalyi, *The Evolving Self: A Psychology for the Third Millenium* (New York: HarperCollins, 1993), 240.

167. Godbey, *Leisure and Leisure Services*, 79.

168. Robinson and Godbey, *Time for Life*, 305.

169. John Kelly and Geoffrey Godbey, *Sociology of Leisure* (State College, PA: Venture, 1992), 508.

170. Ramsay, *Reclaiming Leisure*, 37.

171. Ibid., 1.

172. Staffan Linder, *The Harried Leisure Class* (New York: Columbia University Press, 1970), 101–2.

173. Walter Rauschenbusch, *Christianity and the Social Crisis* (New York: Harper & Row, 1907), 341.

174. Godbey, *Leisure and Leisure Services*, 184–85.

175. Robinson and Godbey, *Time for Life*.

176. Godbey, *Leisure and Leisure Services*, 186.

177. Margo Hilbrecht, "Leisure and the Changing Workplace" in *Leisure for Canadians*, 2nd ed., ed. Ron McCarville and Kelly MacKay (State College, PA: Venture, 2013), 99.

178. Andrew Heisz and Sébastien LaRochelle-Côté, *Summary of Work Hours Instability in Canada* (Catalogue No. 11F0019M1E, No. 279) (Ottawa: Statistics Canada, Business and Labour Market Analysis Division, 2006).

179. Hilbrecht, "Leisure and the Changing Workplace," 2nd ed., 103–4.

Chapter 3: The History of Classical Leisure

1. Joseph Owens, "Aristotle on Leisure," *Canadian Journal of Philosophy* 11, no. 4 (December 1981): 715.

2. Serena Arnold, "The Dilemma of Meaning," in *Recreation and Leisure: Issues in an Era of Change*, ed. Thomas L. Goodale and Peter A. Witt (State College, PA: Venture, 1980), 13.

3. Owens, "Aristotle on Leisure," 715.

4. Sebastian de Grazia, *Of Time, Work and Leisure* (New York: The Twentieth Century Fund, 1964), 12.

5. Arnold, "Dilemma of Meaning," 13.

6. Ernest Barker, *Church, State, and Study* (London: Methuen, 1930), 265–66.

7. Pierre Berton, *The Smug Minority* (Toronto: McClelland and Stewart, 1968), 57.

8. Owens, "Aristotle on Leisure," 713–14.

9. Thomas L. Goodale, "If Leisure Is to Matter," in *Recreation and Leisure: In An Era of Change*, ed. Thomas L. Goodale and Peter A. Witt (State College, PA: Venture, 1980), 38.

10. Benjamin Jowett, *The Politics of Aristotle*, vol. 1, *Introduction and Translation* (Oxford: Clarendon, 1885), cxliv.

11. Josef Pieper, *Leisure: The Basis of Culture* (New York: Random House, 1963), 21.

12. Aristotle, *Politics*, trans. Ernest Barker (London: Oxford University Press, 1960), 7.14, 7.3, 369–81, 393–97. These are the passages in which Aristotle refers to his concept of leisure as something frequently mentioned. The other passages are 7.15.1; 7.3.2, 377, 394.

13. Hermannus Bonitz, *Index Aristotelius* (Berlin: Akademie-Verlag, 1955), 741a20–50.

14. Owens, "Aristotle on Leisure," 715.

15. Justin Kaplan, ed., *The Pocket Aristotle*, trans. William David Ross (New York: Pocket Books, 1958), 336, quoted in Thomas L. Goodale, "If Leisure Is to Matter," 40.

16. Aristotle, *Politics*, 1137b, trans. Lindsay (Everyman Library), quoted in Will Durant, *Story of Civilization*, vol. 2, *The Life of Greece: Being a History of Greek Civilization from the Beginnings* (New York: Simon & Schuster, 1939), 533.

17. Goodale, "If Leisure Is to Matter," 40.

18. Aristotle, *The Nicomachean Ethics*, trans. Harris Rackham (Cambridge, MA: Harvard University Press, 1926), 10.7.6, 615.

19. Aristotle, *Politics*, trans. Barker, 8.3.3, 394.

20. John Gillies, *Aristotle's Ethics* (London: Routledge, 1886), 138, quoted in Goodale, "If Leisure Is to Matter," 40.

21. Aristotle, *Nicomachean Ethics* 10.6.6, 611.

22. Aristotle, *Politics*, trans. Barker, 8.3.3–4, 394–5.

23. Aristotle, *Nicomachean Ethics* 10.6.3, 609.

24. Ibid., 1.5, 12–17.

25. Owens, "Aristotle on Leisure," 716.

26. Ibid.

27. de Grazia, *Of Time, Work and Leisure*, 19.

28. Aristotle, *Politics*, trans. Barker, 4.6.6, 202.

29. Ibid., 2.9.5, 91–92.

30. Ibid., 2.9.2, 90.

31. de Grazia, *Of Time, Work and Leisure*, 14. Jay Shivers ("Leisure Constructs: A Conceptual Reference," *World Leisure and Recreation* 27, no. 1 [February 1985]: 25), disputes this interpretation of Aristotle.

32. Aristotle, *Politics*, trans. Barker, 7.15.1, 377.

33. de Grazia, *Of Time, Work and Leisure*, 15.

34. David A. Spence, *Towards a Theology of Leisure with Special Reference to Creativity* (Ottawa: Canadian Parks/Recreation Association, 1973), 7.

35. Ibid., 8.

36. Aristotle, *Politics*, trans. Rackham, 8.3.2, 394; cf. 7.14.22 and 15.1–2, 375–78.

37. Ibid., 8.3.6, 395.

38. John Newman, cited in de Grazia, *Of Time, Work and Leisure*, 19.

39. Aristotle, *Politics*, trans. Barker, 7.15.2, 377; 8.3.8, 394.

40. de Grazia, *Of Time, Work and Leisure*, 19.

41. Owens, "Aristotle on Leisure," 721–22.

42. Goodale, "If Leisure Is to Matter," 42.

43. Harold Henry Joachim, *Aristotle: The Nicomachean Ethics: A Commentary*, ed. David Arthur Rees (Oxford: Oxford University Press, 1951), 287.

44. Aristotle, *Politics*, trans. Barker, 7.9.4, 353.

45. Aristotle, *Politics* 7.1334a2, trans. Thomas Alan Sinclair, rev. ed. (New York: Penguin, 1981), 437.

46. Charles Sylvester, "Interpretation and Leisure Science: A Hermeneutical Example of Past and Present Oracles," *Journal of Leisure Research* 32, no. 1 (1990): 293.

47. Goodale, "If Leisure Is to Matter," 41.

48. Aristotle, *Nicomachean Ethics*, 10.7.6, 615.

49. Aristotle, *Politics*, 8.3.4, 395.

50. de Grazia, *Of Time, Work and Leisure*, 20.

51. Aristotle, *Nicomachean Ethics*, 10.8.8, 625.

52. Arnold, "Dilemma of Meaning," 12.

53. de Grazia, *Of Time, Work and Leisure*, 19–20.

54. Goodale, "If Leisure Is to Matter," 41.

55. John Ferguson, *Aristotle* (New York: Twayne, 1972), 138.

56. Owens, "Aristotle on Leisure," 723.

57. Robert A. Stebbins, "Serious Leisure: A Conceptual Statement," *Pacific Sociological Review* 25, no. 2 (1982): 268.

58. de Grazia, *Of Time, Work and Leisure*, 24.

59. Spence, *Towards a Theology of Leisure*, 12–13.

60. Jeffrey P. Crittenden, "Holy Leisure: A Life of Prayer, Contemplation and Celebration" (MTh thesis, St. Stephen's College, University of Alberta, 2001), 47–48.

61. Arnold, "Dilemma of Meaning," 13.

62. Augustine of Hippo, *The City of God*, trans. Marcus Dods (New York: Modern Library, 2000), 19.19, 168.

63. Graham Neville, *Free Time: Towards a Theology of Leisure* (Birmingham, UK: University of Birmingham Press, 2004), 12.

64. Augustine, *Exposition in Psalms* 69, 7; *In Ioann Evangel* 6, 25–26; *Tract in Ioann.* 124, 5, quoted in Paul Marshall, "Vocation, Work, and Jobs," in *Labour of Love: Essays on Work*, ed. Josina Van Nuis Zylstra (Toronto: Wedge, 1980), 7.

65. Neville, *Free Time*, 12.

66. Augustine, *City of God* 27.30.

67. Owens, "Aristotle on Leisure," 722.

68. Marshall, "Vocation, Work, and Jobs," 8.

69. Jean Leclercq, *The Love of Learning and the Desire for God: A Study of Monastic Culture* (New York: Fordham University Press, 1982), 69.

70. Ibid.

71. John Preston Dever, "Toward an Ethical Understanding of Leisure in a Technological Society" (PhD diss., Southern Baptist Theological Seminary, Louisville, 1968), 45, quoted in Harold D. Lehman, *In Praise of Leisure* (Kitchener, ON: Herald, 1974), 126.

Chapter 4: The History of Leisure as Activity

1. Kenneth Scott Latourette, *Christianity through the Ages* (New York: Harper & Row, 1965), 147–48.

2. C. S. Lewis, "De Descriptione Temporum," Inaugural Lecture from the Chair of Medieval and Renaissance Literature at Cambridge University, 1954, accessed September 19, 2013, http://www.eng.uc.edu/~dwschae/temporum.html.

3. David A. Spence, *Towards a Theology of Leisure with Special Reference to Creativity* (Ottawa: Canadian Parks/Recreation Association, 1973), 20.

4. Johan Huizinga, *Homo Ludens: A Study of the Play-Element in Culture* (Boston: Beacon, 1955), 180.

5. Thomas More, *Utopia* (London: Pelican, 1965), 76, quoted in Paul Marshall, "Vocation, Work, and Jobs," in *Labour of Love: Essays on Work*, ed. Josina Van Nuis Zylstra (Toronto: Wedge, 1980), 11.

6. Thomas Lupset, "A Treatise of Charity" (1533), quoted in Marshall, "Vocation, Work, and Jobs," 11.

7. Marshall, "Vocation, Work, and Jobs," 11.

8. Sebastian de Grazia, *Of Time, Work and Leisure* (New York: The Twentieth Century Fund, 1964), 44.

9. Thomas Starkey, *A Dialogue between Pole and Lupset* (London: Chatto and Windus, 1948), 25, quoted in Marshall, "Vocation, Work, and Jobs," 11.

10. Harold D. Lehman, *In Praise of Leisure* (Kitchener, ON: Herald, 1974), 127.

11. Paul Althaus, *The Ethics of Martin Luther*, trans. Robert C. Schultz (Philadelphia: Fortress, 1972), 39.

12. Lehman, *In Praise of Leisure*, 127.

13. Althaus, *Ethics of Martin Luther*, 101, 104.

14. Martin Luther, *Luther's Works*, vol. 53, ed. Ulrich S. Leupold (Philadelphia: Fortress, 1965), 279.

15. D. Martin Luther, *Luther's Werke* (Briefwechsel: Weimar, 1930–48), 5:317, quoted in Althaus, *Ethics of Martin Luther*, 104.

16. Althaus, *Ethics of Martin Luther*, 104.

17. Gordon Dahl, *Work, Play and Worship in a Leisure Oriented Society* (Minneapolis: Augsburg, 1972), 40.

18. Edward Vanderkloet, "Why Work Anyway," in *Labour of Love: Essays on Work*, ed. Josina Van Nuis Zylstra (Toronto: Wedge, 1980), 29.

19. Jay S. Shivers, *Leisure and Recreation Concepts: A Critical Analysis* (Toronto: Allyn and Bacon, 1981), 89.

20. Lehman, *In Praise of Leisure*, 12.

21. Charles Gregg Singer, *John Calvin: His Roots and Fruits* (Philadelphia: P&R, 1967), 65.

22. John Calvin, *Institutes of the Christian Religion*, trans. John Allan (London: 1813), 2.316; 3.14.9.

23. Georgia E. Harkness, *John Calvin: The Man and His Ethics* (Nashville: Abingdon, 1958), 163.

24. J. I. Packer, "Hot Tub Religion: Toward a Theology of Enjoyment," in *God's Plans for You* (Wheaton: Crossway, 2001), 59.

25. Lehman, *In Praise of Leisure*, 126.

26. William Haller, *The Rise of Puritanism* (Philadelphia: University of Pennsylvania Press, 1972), 123.

27. Richard Baxter, *A Christian Directory* (London, 1763), 274–77, quoted in Robert Banks, *The Tyranny of Time* (Downers Grove, IL: InterVarsity, 1983), 108.

28. Richard Rodgers, "A Garden of Spiritual Flowers," in *Two Elizabethan Diaries*, ed. Marshall M. Knappen (Gloucester, MA: Peter Smith, 1966), 88, quoted in Banks, *Tyranny of Time*, 108.

29. James T. Dennison Jr., *The Market Day of the Soul: The Puritan Doctrine of the Sabbath in England 1532–1760* (Lanham, MD: University Press of America, 1983), 113.

30. Haller, *Rise of Puritanism*, 123.

31. Dennison, *Market Day of the Soul*, 144.

32. Haller, *Rise of Puritanism*, 123.

33. Dennison, *Market Day of the Soul*, 88.

34. Ibid. Dennison cites Gilbert Ironside, *Seven Questions of the Sabbath Briefly Disputed, after the Manner of the Schools* (Oxford, 1637), 234.

35. Benjamin Colman, *The Government & Improvement of Mirth* (Boston, 1707), 29, quoted in Perry Miller and Thomas H. Johnson, *The Puritans*, rev. ed. (New York: Harper, 1963), 2:392.

36. Edmund S. Morgan, *The Puritan Dilemma: The Story of John Winthrop* (Boston: Little, Brown, 1958), 10.

37. Spence, *Towards a Theology of Leisure*, 26.

38. Karl E. Johnson, "Problematizing Puritan Play," *Leisure/Loisir* 33, no. 1 (2009): 31–54.

39. J. I. Packer, "Leisure and Life-Style: Leisure, Pleasure, and Treasure," in *God and Culture: Essays in Honour of Carl F. H. Henry*, ed. Donald A. Carson and John D. Woodbridge (Grand Rapids: Eerdmans, 1993), 366.

40. Johnson, "Problematizing Puritan Play."

41. Ibid., 50.

42. Leland Ryken, *Redeeming the Time: A Christian Approach to Work and Leisure* (Grand Rapids: Baker Books, 1995), 113–26; Leland Ryken, "The Puritan Ethic and Christian Leisure for Today," in *Christianity and Leisure: Issues in a Pluralistic Society*, rev. ed., ed. Paul Heintzman, Glen E. Van Andel, and Thomas L. Visker (Sioux Center, IA: Dordt College Press, 2006), 32–49.

43. Robert Lee, *Religion and Leisure in America* (New York: Abingdon, 1964), 170.

44. de Grazia, *Of Time, Work and Leisure*, 32.

45. Pardon E. Tillinghast, "Leisure: Old Patterns and New Problems," in *Planning for Diversity and Choice: Possible Futures and Their Relations to the Man-Controlled Environment*, ed. Stanford Anderson (Cambridge, MA: MIT Press, 1968), 147.

46. Ibid.

47. Banks, *Tyranny of Time*, 113.

48. Walter Kerr, *The Decline of Pleasure* (New York: Simon & Schuster, 1962), 39–40.

49. Spence, *Towards a Theology of Leisure*, 30.

50. Serena Arnold, "The Dilemma of Meaning," in *Recreation and Leisure: Issues in an Era of Change*, ed. Thomas L. Goodale and Peter A. Witt (State College, PA: Venture, 1980), 14.

51. Henry Pratt Fairchild, ed., *Dictionary of Sociology* (Totowa, NJ: Littlefield, Adams, 1976), 175.

52. Arnold, *Dilemma of Meaning*, 14.

Chapter 5: The Sabbath

1. Alan Richardson, *The Biblical Doctrine of Work* (London: SCM, 1952), 51.

2. Harold D. Lehman, *In Praise of Leisure* (Kitchener, ON: Herald, 1974), 134–36.

3. David A. Spence, *Towards a Theology of Leisure with Special Reference to Creativity* (Ottawa: Canadian Parks/Recreation Association, 1973), 57–66.

4. Lehman, *In Praise of Leisure*, 134–36; Arthur Holmes, *Contours of a World View* (Grand Rapids: Eerdmans, 1983), 229–30; Robert K. Johnston, *The Christian at Play* (Grand Rapids: Eerdmans, 1983), 88–95.

5. Holmes, *Contours of a World View*, 228–29.

6. Johnston, *Christian at Play*, 102–10.

7. Ibid., 110–19.

8. Gordon Dahl, *Work, Play and Worship in a Leisure-Oriented Society* (Minneapolis: Augsburg, 1972), 70–71.

9. Holmes, *Contours of a World View*, 230–31.

10. Karen M. Fox and Elizabeth Klaiber, "Listening for a Leisure Remix," *Leisure Sciences* 28, no. 5 (2006): 411–31.

11. Robert D. Crabtree, "Leisure in Ancient Israel" (PhD diss., Texas A&M University, 1982), 10.

12. Dain A. Trafton, "In Praise of Three Traditional Ideas of Leisure," in *Transitions to Leisure: Conceptual and Human Issues*, ed. Billy G. Gunter, Jay Stanley, and Robert St. Clair (Lanham, MD: University Press of America), 23–31.

13. Robert Gordis, "The Sabbath—Cornerstone and Capstone of Jewish Life," *Judaism* 31, no. 1 (Winter 1982): 6–11.

14. Fox and Klaiber, "Listening for a Leisure Remix."

15. Crabtree, "Leisure in Ancient Israel."

16. Ibid., 128.

17. Andrew T. Lincoln, "From Sabbath to Lord's Day: A Biblical and Theological Perspective," in *From Sabbath to Lord's Day: A Biblical, Historical and Theological Investigation*, ed. Donald A. Carson (Grand Rapids: Zondervan, 1982), 344.

18. Ibid.

19. Leland Ryken, Jim C. Wilhoit, and Tremper Longman III, eds., "Leisure," in *Dictionary of Biblical Imagery* (Downers Grove, IL: InterVarsity, 1998), 505.

20. William J. Dumbrell, *Covenant and Creation* (Exeter, UK: Paternoster, 1984), 32.

21. Abraham Joshua Heschel, *The Sabbath* (New York: Harper & Row, 1966), 14.

22. Victor P. Hamilton, "Shābat," in *Theological Wordbook of the Old Testament*, vol. 2, ed. Robert Laird Harris, Gleason Leonard Archer, and Bruce K. Waltke (Chicago: Moody, 1980), 902.

23. Hans Walter Wolff, "The Day of Rest in the Old Testament," *Lexington Theological Quarterly* 7, no. 3 (July 1972): 70.

24. Edward J. Young, "Sabbath," in *The New Bible Dictionary*, ed. James Dixon Douglas (Grand Rapids: Eerdmans, 1962), 1110.

25. Johnston, *Christian at Play*, 91, 95.

26. Young, "Sabbath," 1110.

27. Richardson, *Biblical Doctrine of Work*, 53–54.

28. Wolff, "Day of Rest in the Old Testament," 69.

29. Paul Stevens, *Seven Days of Faith* (Colorado Springs: NavPress, 2001), 214–15.

30. Claus Westermann, *Creation*, trans. John J. Scullion (Philadelphia: Fortress, 1974), 65.

31. Karl Barth, *Church Dogmatics* III/1, trans. J. W. Edwards, O. Bussey, and Harold Knight (Edinburgh: T&T Clark, 1958), 98.

32. Gnana Robinson, "The Idea of Rest in the Old Testament and the Search for the Basic Character of Sabbath," *Zeitschrift für die alttestamentliche Wissenschaft* 92, no. 1 (1980): 42.

33. Heschel, *The Sabbath*, 22–23.

34. Robinson, "Idea of Rest in the Old Testament," 39.

35. William J. Dumbrell, "A Sabbath Rest for the People of God," lecture given at Regent College, Vancouver, October 9, 1985.

36. Hamilton, "Shābat," 903.

37. Roger T. Beckwith and Wilfrid Stott, "The Biblical and Jewish Evidence," part 1 of *The Christian Sunday: A Biblical and Historical Study* (Grand Rapids: Baker, 1980), 2.

38. Wolff, "Day of Rest in the Old Testament," 70.

39. Ben Witherington III, *The Rest of Life: Rest, Play, Eating, Studying, Sex from a Kingdom Perspective* (Grand Rapids: Eerdmans, 2012), 5.

40. Beckwith and Stott, "Biblical and Jewish Evidence," 2.

41. G. Henry Waterman, "Sabbath," in *The Zondervan Pictorial Encyclopedia of the Bible*, vol. 5, ed. Merrill C. Tenney (Grand Rapids: Zondervan, 1975), 183.

42. Wolff, "Day of Rest in the Old Testament," 73.

43. Witherington, *Rest of Life*, 6.

44. Hamilton, "Shābat," 903.

45. Johnston, *Christian at Play*, 95.

46. Hamilton, "Shābat," 903.

47. Heschel, *The Sabbath*, 19–20. His quotation is from *Shibbole haleget*, chap. 126.

48. W. Gunther Plaut, "The Sabbath as Protest: Thoughts on Work and Leisure in the Automated Society," The B. G. Rudolph Lectures in Judaic Studies, Syracuse University, New York, April 1970, 10, quoted in Johnston, *The Christian at Play*, 90.

49. Dumbrell, *Covenant and Creation*, 35.

50. Ibid.

51. Heschel, *The Sabbath*, 19.

52. David Ehrenfeld and Philip J. Bentley, "Nature in the Jewish Tradition: The Source of Stewardship" (unpublished article).

53. Stevens, *Seven Days of Faith*, 222, 216.

54. Jürgen Moltmann, *God in Creation: An Ecological Doctrine of Creation*, trans. Margaret Kohl (London: SCM, 1985), 286.

55. Loren Wilkinson, "Garden-City-Sabbath: Hints toward a Theology of Culture" (unpublished paper, 1989), quoted in Stevens, *Seven Days of Faith*, 216.

56. Johnston, *Christian at Play*, 89.

57. Young, "Sabbath," 1110.

58. Dumbrell, *Covenant and Creation*, 123.

59. Johnston, *Christian at Play*, 90.

60. Ibid., 93.

61. Gerhard Hasel, "Health and Healing in the Old Testament," *Andrews University Seminary Studies* 21, no. 3 (Autumn 1983): 194.

62. Waterman, "Sabbath," 50.

63. Wolff, "Day of Rest in the Old Testament," 67.

64. Albrecht Alt, *Kleine Schriften zur Geschicte des Volkes Israel*, vol. 1 (Munich: C. H. Beck, 1953), 131n1, quoted in Wolff, "Day of Rest in the Old Testament," 67.

65. Beckwith and Stott, "Biblical and Jewish Evidence," 40, 16.

66. Johnston, *Christian at Play*, 95.

67. Lincoln, "From Sabbath to Lord's Day," 352.

68. W. Vischer, "Nehemiah," *Probleme Biblisher Theologie*, ed. Hans Wolter Wolff (Munich: Chr. Kaiser Verlag, 1971), 609, quoted in Wolff, "Day of Rest in the Old Testament," 73.

69. Young, "Sabbath," 1111.

70. Stevens, *Seven Days of Faith*, 215.

71. Ibid., 220.

72. Banks, *Tyranny of Time*, 185.

73. Stevens, *Seven Days of Faith*, 217.

74. Lincoln, "From Sabbath to Lord's Day," 403.

75. Roland Kenneth Harrison, "Heal," in *International Standard Bible Encyclopedia*, rev. ed., vol. 2, ed. Geoffrey W. Bromiley (Grand Rapids: Eerdmans, 1982), 642.

76. J. I. Packer, "Leisure and Life-Style: Leisure, Pleasure, and Treasure," in *God and Culture: Essays in Honour of Carl F. H. Henry*, ed. Donald A. Carson and John D. Woodbridge (Grand Rapids: Eerdmans, 1993), 363.

77. Richard Winter, *Still Bored in a Culture of Entertainment: Rediscovering Passion and Wonder* (Downers Grove, IL: InterVarsity, 2002), 127.

78. Hasel, "Health and Healing in the Old Testament," 194.

79. Philo, *De Specialibus Legibus* 2, quoted in Heschel, *The Sabbath*, 13–14.

80. Heschel, *The Sabbath*, 14.

81. Aristotle, *The Nicomachean Ethics* 10.6.6, trans. Harris Rackham (Cambridge, MA: Harvard University Press, 1926), 611.

82. Heschel, *The Sabbath*, 21, 31–30.

83. Ibid., 60.

Chapter 6: The Biblical Concept of Rest

1. Gordon Dahl, *Work, Play and Worship in a Leisure-Oriented Society* (Minneapolis: Augsburg, 1972), 136.

2. James Houston, "The Theology of Work," in *Looking at Lifestyles Professional Priorities—A Christian Perspective*, Proceedings from the Conference for Physicians and Dentists, Banff, May 2–8, 1981 (Vancouver: Christian Medical and Dental Society of Canada, 1981), 46.

3. Jeanne E. Sherrow, *It's About Time: A Look at Leisure, Lifestyle, and Christianity* (Grand Rapids: Zondervan, 1984), 95–96.

4. Bertha Cato, "Leisure and Jesus' Rest: Making the Connection," Leadership U website, December 28, 1998, http://www.leaderu.com/theology/leisure-rest.html.

5. William J. Dumbrell, *Covenant and Creation* (Exeter, UK: Paternoster, 1984), 35.

6. Gerhard von Rad, "There Remains Still a Rest for the People of God: An Investigation of a Biblical Conception," in *The Problem of the Hexateuch and Other Essays* (Edinburgh and London: Oliver & Boyd, 1966), 94.

7. Gordon Preece, "Re-Creation and Recreation in the Eighties," in *Faith Active in Love*, Proceedings of the 1980 Conference of the AFES Fellowship, ed. John Diesendorf (Sydney, Australia: AFES Graduate Fellowship, 1981), 77.

8. Leonard J. Coppes, "*Nûaḥ*," in *Theological Wordbook of the Old Testament*, vol. 2, ed. Robert Laird Harris, Gleason Leonard Archer, and Bruce K. Waltke (Chicago: Moody, 1980), 562.

9. Von Rad, "There Remains Still," 95.

10. Dumbrell, *Covenant and Creation*, 121–22.

11. Von Rad, "There Remains Still," 97–98.

12. Ibid., 98.

13. Donald A. Hagner, *Hebrews: A Good News Commentary* (New York: Harper & Row, 1983), 54.

14. Von Rad, "There Remains Still," 102.

15. Andrew T. Lincoln, "From Sabbath to Lord's Day: A Biblical and Theological Perspective," in *From Sabbath to Lord's Day: A Biblical, Historical and Theological Investigation*, ed. Donald A. Carson (Grand Rapids: Zondervan, 1982), 210–12.

16. Charles K. Barrett, "The Eschatology of the Epistle to the Hebrews," in *The Background of the New Testament and its Eschatology: Essays in Honour of C. H. Dodd*, ed. William David Davies and David Daube (Cambridge: Cambridge University Press, 1956), 381.

17. Hagner, *Hebrews*, 52.

18. Ibid., 50.

19. Lincoln, "From Sabbath to Lord's Day," 212.

20. Barrett, "Eschatology of the Epistle to the Hebrews," 372.

21. Lincoln, "From Sabbath to Lord's Day," 217.

22. Thomas Hewitt, *The Epistle to the Hebrews* (Grand Rapids: Eerdmans, 1960), 92.

23. Donald Guthrie, *Hebrews*, Tyndale New Testament Commentaries (Grand Rapids: Eerdmans, 1983), 113, 116.

24. Ibid., 114.

25. Jean Hering, *The Epistle to the Hebrews*, trans. Arthur W. Heathcote and Philip J. Allcock (London: Epworth, 1970), 32.

26. John Calvin, *The Epistle of Paul the Apostle to the Hebrews and the First and Second Epistle of St. Peter*, trans. William B. Johnston (Edinburgh: Oliver & Boyd, 1963), 49.

27. Lincoln, "From Sabbath to Lord's Day," 217.

28. Hagner, *Hebrews*, 52.

29. Ben Witherington III, *The Rest of Life: Rest, Play, Eating, Studying, Sex from a Kingdom Perspective* (Grand Rapids: Eerdmans, 2012), 37.

30. Robert Hensel and Colin Brown, "Rest," in *The New International Dictionary of New Testament Theology*, vol. 3, ed. Colin Brown (Grand Rapids: Zondervan, 1978), 256.

31. Hans Dieter Betz, "The Logion of the Easy Yoke and of Rest (Matt. 11:28–30)," *Journal of Biblical Literature* 86, no. 1 (1967): 10.

32. Ibid., 22.

33. Willoughby C. Allen, *The International Critical Commentary According to S. Matthew*, 3rd ed. (Edinburgh: T&T Clark, 1912), 124.

34. William Hendriksen, *Exposition of the Gospel according to Matthew*, New Testament Commentary (Grand Rapids: Baker, 1973), 503.

35. Randolph Vincent Greenwood Tasker, *The Gospel According to St. Matthew*, Tyndale New Testament Commentaries (London: The Tyndale Press, 1961), 121.

36. Theodore H. Robinson, *The Gospel of Matthew* (London: Hodder & Stoughton, 1928), 106.

37. John Calvin, *The Gospels* (Grand Rapids: Associated Publishers and Authors Inc., 1960), 227.

38. John Peter Lange, *A Commentary on the Holy Scriptures, vol. 1 of the New Testament: Containing a General Introduction and the Gospel according to Matthew*, trans. Philip Schaff (New York: Charles Scribner's Sons, 1884), 213; and Richard Charles Henry Lenski, *The Interpretation of St. Matthew's Gospel* (Minneapolis: Augsburg, 1964), 456.

39. Lenski, *St. Matthew's Gospel*, 102.

40. Hensel and Brown, "Rest," 256.

41. Eduard Schweizer, *The Good News according to Matthew*, trans. David E. Green (Atlanta: John Knox, 1975), 273.

42. David Hill, *The Gospel of Matthew* (London: Oliphants, 1972), 208.

43. Floyd V. Filson, *A Commentary on the Gospel according to St. Matthew* (London: Adam & Charles Black, 1960), 144.

44. William Robertson Nicoll, *St. Matthew*, The Expositor's Bible (New York: Funk & Wagnalls, 1900), 155.

45. Robinson, *Gospel of Matthew*, 105.

46. Filson, *Gospel according to St. Matthew*, 144.

47. Tasker, *Gospel according to St. Matthew*, 122.

48. Hensel and Brown, "Rest," 256.

49. Lenski, *St. Matthew's Gospel*, 259.

50. Hendriksen, *Exposition of the Gospel according to Matthew*, 504.

51. Henry Leopold Ellison, *Matthew* (London: Pickering & Inglis, 1969), 154.

52. Hendriksen, *Exposition of the Gospel according to Matthew*, 505–6.

53. Preece, "Re-creation and Recreation in the Eighties," 79.

54. Dahl, *Work, Play and Worship*, 99.

55. Sherrow, *It's About Time*, 114.

56. Cato, "Leisure and Jesus' Rest."

57. Francis Bregha, "Philosophy of Leisure: Unanswered Questions," *Recreation Research Review* 8, no. 1 (July 1980): 16.

58. Dahl, *Work, Play and Worship*, 71.

59. Leonard Doohan, *Leisure: A Spiritual Need* (Notre Dame, IN: Ave Maria, 1990), 97.

Chapter 7: Other Biblical Words and Themes Related to Leisure

1. Scott L. Harris, "Holy and Free, Part 6—Leisure," Grace Bible Church, Wappingers Falls, NY, August 24, 2003, accessed March 6, 2012, http://gracebibleny.org/holy_free_part_6_leisure.

2. Ibid.

3. Leland Ryken, *Redeeming the Time: A Christian Approach to Work and Leisure* (Grand Rapids: Baker Books, 1995), 168, 235.

4. Eric O. Springsted, "Leisure, The Basis of Culture," Georgetown Presbyterian Church, Washington, DC, July 19, 2009, accessed March 6, 2012, http://www.gtownpres.org.

5. Ibid.

6. Ibid.

7. Ibid.

8. R. T. Allen, "Leisure: The Purpose of Life," in *The Philosophy of Leisure*, ed. Cyril Barrett and Tom Winnifrith (London: Macmillan, 1989), 26; Francis J. Bregha, "Leisure and Freedom Re-examined," in *Recreation and Leisure: Issues in an Era of Change*, ed. Thomas L. Goodale and Peter A. Witt (State College, PA: Venture, 1980), 36; Margaret Hothem, "The Wonder of Leisure," in *Christianity and Leisure: Issues at the Millenium*, ed. Glen Van Andel and Paul Heintzman (Sioux Center, IA: Dordt College Press, forthcoming); Robert Lee, *Religion and Leisure in America: A Study in Four Dimensions* (New York: Abingdon, 1964), 260; Graham Neville, *Free Time: Towards a Theology of Leisure* (Birmingham, UK: University of Birmingham Press, 2004), 17, 147; Jay S. Shivers and Lee J. deLisle, *The Story of Leisure: Context, Concepts, and Current Controversy* (Champaign, IL: Human Kinetics, 1997), 31; Joseph Teaff, "Contemplative Leisure within Christian Spirituality,"

in *Christianity and Leisure: Issues in a Pluralistic Society*, rev. ed., ed. Paul Heintzman, Glen E. Van Andel, and Thomas L. Visker (Sioux Center, IA: Dordt College Press, 2006), 112–15.

9. Josef Pieper, *Leisure: The Basis of Culture* (New York: Random House, 1963), 19.

10. Arnold Albert Anderson, *The Book of Psalms*, vol. 1, *Psalms 1–72*, New Century Bible Commentary (Grand Rapids: Eerdmans, 1972); John Herbert Eaton, *Psalms: Introduction and Commentary* (London: SCM, 1967); Willem S. Prinsloo, "The Psalms," *Eerdmans Commentary on the Bible*, ed. James Douglas Grant Dunn and John William Rogerson (Grand Rapids: Eerdmans, 2003), 391.

11. Anderson, *Book of Psalms*.

12. Eaton, *Psalms*, 127.

13. John William Rogerson and John William McKay, *Psalms 1–50* (London: Cambridge University Press, 1977), 219.

14. Peter Craigie, *Psalms 1–50*, Word Biblical Commentary (Waco: Word, 1983); Prinsloo, "Psalms," 391.

15. Craigie, *Psalms 1–50*, 344.

16. Neville, *Free Time*, 17.

17. John J. Parsons, "Be Still and Know That I Am God: Surrender . . . God's Irrepressible Care of the World," Hebrews for Christians website, accessed July 1, 2013, http://www.hebrew4 christians.com/Meditations/Be_Still/be_still.html.

18. Samuel L. Terrien, *The Psalms: Strophic Structure and Theological Commentary* (Grand Rapids: Eerdmans, 2003), 374.

19. Craigie, *Psalms 1–50*, 345.

20. Charles Sylvester, "Interpretation and Leisure Science: A Hermeneutical Example of Past and Present Oracles," *Journal of Leisure Research* 32, no. 1 (1990): 292.

21. Pieper, *Leisure: The Basis of Culture*, 40–41.

22. Parsons, "Be Still and Know."

23. Pieper, *Leisure: The Basis of Culture*, 41.

24. Ibid.

25. Ben Witherington III, *The Rest of Life: Rest, Play, Eating, Studying, Sex from a Kingdom Perspective* (Grand Rapids: Eerdmans, 2012), 30–31, 38.

26. Pieper, *Leisure: The Basis of Culture*.

27. Leonard Doohan, *Leisure: A Spiritual Need* (Notre Dame, IN: Ave Maria, 1990).

28. Leland Ryken, Jim C. Wilhoit, and Tremper Longman III, eds., "Leisure," in *Dictionary of Biblical Imagery* (Downers Grove, IL: InterVarsity, 1998), 505–6.

29. Ibid., 505.

30. Craigie, *Psalms 1–50*, 345–46.

31. Ibid.

32. Pieper, *Leisure: The Basis of Culture*.

33. Lee, *Religion and Leisure*, 262.

34. Ryken, Wilhoit, and Longman, "Leisure," 505.

35. Elmer A. Martens, *God's Design: A Focus on Old Testament Theology* (Grand Rapids: Baker, 1981), 114–15.

36. Robert K. Johnston, *The Christian at Play* (Grand Rapids: Eerdmans, 1983), 112.

37. Martens, *God's Design*, 115.

38. Johnston, *Christian at Play*, 110.

39. Ryken, *Redeeming the Time*, 241.

40. Johnston, *Christian at Play*, 114.

41. Ibid., 116.

42. Ibid., 119.

43. Ryken, *Redeeming the Time*, 243.

44. C. S. Lewis, *Christian Reflections* (Grand Rapids: Eerdmans, 1967), 15.

45. Jeffrey P. Crittenden, "Holy Leisure: A Life of Prayer, Contemplation and Celebration" (MTh thesis, St. Stephen's College, University of Alberta, 2001), 70–71.

46. Johnston, *Christian at Play*, 115.

47. Crittenden, "Holy Leisure," 87.

48. Ibid., 88.

49. Ibid., 85.

50. Kenneth R. Ross, "You Did Not Dance: Reflections on a Theology of Recreation in the African Context," *Journal of Theology for Southern Africa* 82 (March 1993): 50.

51. Witherington, *Rest of Life*, 85.

52. Ibid., 86.

53. Ibid.

54. Ibid., 67.

55. Ibid., 69, 73.

56. J. I. Packer, "Leisure and Life-Style: Leisure, Pleasure, and Treasure," in *God and Culture: Essays in Honour of Carl F. H. Henry*, ed. Donald A. Carson and John D. Woodbridge (Grand Rapids: Eerdmans, 1993), 364.

57. Johnston, *Christian at Play*, 112.

58. Ibid., 113.

59. Witherington, *Rest of Life*, 61.

60. Ross, "You Did Not Dance," 47.

61. Johnston, *Christian at Play*, 116.

62. Witherington, *Rest of Life*, 85.

63. Ibid., 116–17.

64. Ibid., 117–18.

65. Ryken, *Redeeming the Time*, 242.

66. Johnston, *Christian at Play*, 117.

67. Ibid., 120.

68. Ibid.

69. I. Howard Marshall, *The Gospel of Luke: A Commentary on the Greek Text*, The New International Greek Testament Commentary (Grand Rapids: Eerdmans, 1978), 302.

70. Johnston, *Christian at Play*, 121.

71. Ibid., 122.

72. Karen M. Fox, "Does the Gospel of Luke Suggest a Christian-Judaic Form of Leisure in the Graeco-Roman World?," *Leisure/Loisir* 33, no. 1 (2009): 11–30.

73. Brendan J. Byrne, *The Hospitality of God: A Reading of Luke's Gospel* (Collegeville, MN: Liturgical Press, 2000), 4.

74. Fox, "A Christian-Judaic Form of Leisure," 25.

75. Ibid., 24.

76. Thomas Cahill, *Sailing the Wine-Dark Sea: Why the Greeks Matter* (New York: Doubleday, 2011), 86.

77. Fox, "A Christian-Judaic Form of Leisure," 22–23.

78. Ibid., 22.

Chapter 8: Work Today and in the Past

1. Robert D. Putnam, *Bowling Alone* (New York: Simon & Schuster, 2000), 91.

2. Ibid., 198.

3. Tim Kasser and Kirk Warren Brown, "On Time, Happiness, and Ecological Footprints," in *Take Back Your Time: Fighting Overwork and Time Poverty in America,* ed. John de Graaf (San Francisco: Berrett-Koehler, 2003), 109.

4. Gordon Dahl, *Work, Play and Worship in a Leisure-Oriented Society* (Minneapolis: Augsburg, 1972), 12.

5. Calvin Redekop, "The Promise of Work," *The Conrad Grebel Review* 1, no. 3 (Fall 1983): 2.

6. Ibid., 8–9.

7. Ibid., 2.

8. Ibid., 3.

9. Ibid., 6–7.

10. Everett Cherrington Hughes, *Men and Their Work* (Glencoe, IL: The Free Press, 1958), 7.

11. Redekop, "Promise of Work," 7.

12. Cicero, *De Officiis* 1, quoted in Robert L. Heilbroner, *The Economic Problem*, 2nd ed. (Englewood Cliffs, NJ: Prentice-Hall, 1970), 31.

13. Otto A. Piper, "The Meaning of Work," *Theology Today* 14, no. 2 (July 1957): 175.

14. Sebastian de Grazia, *Of Time, Work and Leisure* (New York: The Twentieth Century Fund, 1964), 26.

15. Don Fabun, *The Dynamics of Change* (Englewood Cliffs, NJ: Prentice-Hall, 1967), 14.

16. Edward Vanderkloet, "Why Work Anyway," in *Labour of Love: Essays on Work*, ed. Josina Van Nuis Zylstra (Toronto: Wedge, 1980), 22.

17. Ibid., 23.

18. Harvey Cox, *The Secular City* (London: SCM, 1965), 185.

19. Richard Henry Tawney, *Religion and the Rise of Capitalism* (London: John Murray, 1926), 92.

20. Dahl, *Work, Play and Worship*, 46.

21. Paul Marshall, "Vocation, Work, and Jobs," in *Labour of Love: Essays on Work*, ed. Josina Van Nuis Zylstra (Toronto: Wedge, 1980), 10.

22. Ibid., 12.

23. Ibid., 12–14.

24. Vanderkloet, "Why Work Anyway," 29.

25. Bob Goudzwaard, *Aid for the Overdeveloped West* (Toronto: Wedge, 1975), 30, 28.

26. Vanderkloet, "Why Work Anyway," 29.

27. Fabun, *Dynamics of Change*, 13.

28. Vanderkloet, "Why Work Anyway," 27.

29. Leland Ryken, *Work and Leisure in Christian Perspective* (Portland, OR: Multnomah, 1987), 87–92.

30. Ibid., 92.

31. Fabun, *Dynamics of Change*, 14.

32. *The Economist* 9, no. 401 (May 3, 1851): 474, quoted in Vanderkloet, "Why Work Anyway," 28.

33. Albert Rasmussen, *Christian Responsibility in Economic Life* (Philadelphia: Westminster, 1965), 62.

34. Ibid., 61.

35. Cox, *The Secular City*, 183.

36. Harry Elmer Brown, *Social Institutions* (New York: Prentice-Hall, 1942), citing Gus Dyer in a syndicated newspaper article (1939), 85, quoted in Harold D. Lehman, *In Praise of Leisure* (Kitchener, ON: Herald, 1974), 95–96.

37. Studs Terkel, *Working* (New York: Pantheon, 1974), ix.

38. Wayne Oates, *Confessions of a Workaholic* (New York: World, 1971), 12.

39. Aleksandr I. Solzhenitsyn, *The Gulag Archipelago* (New York: Harper & Row, 1973).

40. Dahl, *Work, Play and Worship*, 55.

41. Ibid., 53.

Chapter 9: The Biblical View of Work

1. Alan Richardson, *The Biblical Doctrine of Work* (London: SCM, 1952).

2. Ibid., 11.

3. Ibid., 11, 16, 19.

4. Ibid., 22.

5. Graham Dow, "What Place Does Work Have in God's Purpose?," *Anvil* 1, no. 2 (1984): 141.

6. Paul Marshall, "Vocation, Work, and Jobs," in *Labour of Love: Essays on Work*, ed. Josina Van Nuis Zylstra (Toronto: Wedge, 1980), 2.

7. Richardson, *Biblical Doctrine of Work*, 25–27.

8. Ibid., 25.

9. Ibid., 26.

10. Mark Geldard, "2001—A Factory Odyssey: Work, Theology and Industrial Revolution," *Anvil* 2, no. 1 (1985): 66.

11. John Stott, "Reclaiming the Biblical Doctrine of Work," *Christianity Today* 23, no. 15 (May 4, 1979): 36–37.

12. Ibid., 36.

13. Ibid., 37.

14. Dow, "What Place Does Work Have?," 141.

15. Stott, "Reclaiming the Biblical Doctrine of Work," 36.

16. Dow, "What Place Does Work Have?," 141.

17. Geldard, "2001—A Factory Odyssey," 63.

18. Derek Kidner, *Genesis* (London: Tyndale, 1967), 35.

19. Edward Vanderkloet, "Why Work Anyway," in *Labour of Love: Essays on Work*, ed. Josina Van Nuis Zylstra (Toronto: Wedge, 1980), 39.

20. Stott, "Reclaiming the Biblical Doctrine of Work," 36–37.

21. Dow, "What Place Does Work Have?," 142.

22. Stott, "Reclaiming the Biblical Doctrine of Work," 37.

23. Vanderkloet, "Why Work Anyway," 38.

24. Richardson, *Biblical Doctrine of Work*, 31.

25. Philip H. Towner, "Households and Household Codes," in *Dictionary of Paul and His Letters*, ed. Gerald F. Hawthorne, Ralph P. Martin, and Daniel G. Reid (Downers Grove, IL: InterVarsity, 1993), 418.

26. Richardson, *Biblical Doctrine of Work*, 39–40.

27. Marshall, "Vocation, Work and Jobs," 3.

28. Peter Nijkamp, "Socioethical Aspects of Labour," in *Labour of Love: Essays on Work*, 59.

29. Richardson, *Biblical Doctrine of Work*, 39.

30. Karla A. Henderson et al., *Introduction to Recreation and Leisure Services*, 8th ed. (State College, PA: Venture, 2001), 112.

31. Thomas Goodale and Geoffrey Godbey, *The Evolution of Leisure: Historical and Philosophical Perspectives* (State College, PA: Venture, 1988), 33.

32. Charles Sylvester, "The Western Idea of Work and Leisure: Traditions, Transformations, and the Future," in *Leisure Studies: Prospects for the 21st Century*, ed. Edgar L. Jackson and Thomas L. Burton (State College, PA: Venture, 1999), 24.

33. F. F. Bruce, "1 and 2 Thessalonians," in *The New Bible Commentary: Revised*, ed. Donald Guthrie and J. Alec Motyer (Grand Rapids: Eerdmans, 1970), 1154.

34. Ibid., 1155.

35. Ibid., 1162.

36. William Barclay, *The Daily Study Bible: The Letters to the Philippians, Colossians and Thessalonians* (Toronto: G. R. Welch Co., 1975), 182–83.

37. Barclay, *Daily Study Bible*; Bruce, "1 and 2 Thessalonians"; Kenneth Grayston, *The Letters of Paul to the Philippians and to the Thessalonians* (Cambridge: Cambridge University Press, 1967).

38. Herbert Tom Andrews, "I and II Thessalonians," in *A Commentary on the Bible*, ed. Arthur Samuel Peake (London: T. C. & E. C. Jack, Ltd., 1926), 876–80; Barclay, *Daily Study Bible*; Bruce, "1 and 2 Thessalonians"; Grayston, *Letters of Paul*; Matthew Henry, *Commentary on the Whole Bible*, ed. Leslie Frederic Church (Grand Rapids: Zondervan, 1961), 1884.

39. Grayston, *The Letters of Paul*; J. Terence Forestell, "The Letters to the Thessalonians," in *The Jerome Biblical Commentary*, ed. Raymond Edward Brown, Joseph Augustine Fitzmyer, and Roland Edmund Murphy (Englewood Cliffs, NJ: Prentice-Hall, 1968), 235.

40. John Stott, "Creative by Creation: Our Need for Work," *Christianity Today* 23, no. 17 (June 8, 1979): 33.

41. Denys Edward Hugh Whitely, *Thessalonians in the Revised Standard Version with Introduction and Commentary* (London: Oxford University Press, 1969), 109.

42. John Vernon McGee, *Thru the Bible*, vol. 5 (Nashville: Thomas Nelson, 1983), 421.

43. Marshall, "Vocation, Work, and Jobs," 3.

44. Jerry Falwell, *Listen America* (Garden City, NY: Doubleday, 1980), 77.

45. Robert K. Johnston, "'Confessions of a Workaholic': A Reappraisal of Qoheleth," *Catholic Biblical Quarterly* 38, no. 1 (January 1979): 21.

46. Robert K. Johnston, *The Christian at Play* (Grand Rapids: Eerdmans, 1983), 96.

47. Robert Gordis, *Koheleth—The Man and His World: A Study of Ecclesiastes* (New York: Schocken, 1968), 241.

48. Johnston, "'Confessions of a Workaholic,'" 18.

49. Micheal A. Eaton, *Ecclesiastes* (Downers Grove, IL: InterVarsity, 1983), 92.

50. Walter C. Kaiser Jr., *Ecclesiastes: Total Life* (Chicago: Moody, 1979), 72.

51. Eaton, *Ecclesiastes*, 93.

52. Derek Kidner, *A Time to Mourn and a Time to Dance: Ecclesiastes and the Way of the World* (Leicester, UK: Inter-Varsity, 1976), 46.

53. Ibid.

54. Eaton, *Ecclesiastes*, 93.

55. Kidner, *A Time to Mourn and a Time to Dance*, 47.

56. William S. LaSor, David A. Hubbard, and Fredric W. Bush, *Old Testament Survey* (Grand Rapids: Eerdmans, 1982), 589.

57. Eaton, *Ecclesiastes*, 65.

58. Louis Goldberg, *Ecclesiastes* (Grand Rapids: Zondervan, 1983), 46.

59. Eaton, *Ecclesiastes*, 65.

60. Ibid.

61. Ibid.

62. Ibid., 68.

63. Ibid., 74.

64. Richard Winter, *Still Bored in a Culture of Entertainment: Rediscovering Passion and Wonder* (Downers Grove, IL: InterVarsity, 2002), 117.

65. Roger N. Whybray, "Qoheleth, Preacher of Joy," *Journal for the Study of the Old Testament* 23 (July 1982): 87.

66. Ibid., 92.

67. Johnston, "'Confessions of a Workaholic,'" 14.

68. Frederick L. Moriarty, *Introducing the Old Testament* (Milwaukee: Bruce, 1960), 216.

69. Eaton, *Ecclesiastes*, 48.

70. Gordis, *Koheleth*, 131, 127.

71. Norbert Lohfink, *The Christian Meaning of the Old Testament* (Milwaukee: Bruce Publishing, 1968), 154.

72. Johnston, "'Confessions of a Workaholic,'" 18, 21. (Hebrew transliteration has been simplified.)

73. Ibid., 22.

74. Ibid., 22–23.

75. Walter Eichrodt, *Man in the Old Testament*, trans. K. and R. Gregor Smith (London: SCM, 1959), 33–34.

Chapter 10: A Critique of the Concepts of Leisure

1. Gordon Dahl, *Work, Play and Worship in a Leisure-Oriented Society* (Minneapolis: Augsburg, 1972), 61.

2. Ibid., 62.

3. Ibid.

4. Bennett M. Berger, "The Sociology of Leisure: Some Suggestions," in *Work and Leisure*, ed. Erwin O. Smigel (New Haven: College and University Press, 1963), 29.

5. Nelvin Vos, "To Take Life Leisurely," *Reformed Journal* 29, no. 5 (May 1979): 14–15.

6. Thorstein Veblen, *The Theory of the Leisure Class* (New York: Vanguard, 1912).

7. Ibid.

8. Robert Gordis, "The Sabbath—Cornerstone and Capstone of Jewish Life," *Judaism* 31, no. 1 (Winter 1982): 7.

9. Jeffrey P. Crittenden, "Holy Leisure: A Life of Prayer, Contemplation and Celebration" (MTh thesis, St. Stephen's College, University of Alberta, 2001), 82.

10. Graham Neville, *Free Time: Towards a Theology of Leisure* (Birmingham, UK: University of Birmingham Press, 2004), 6.

11. J. I. Packer, "Leisure and Life-Style: Leisure, Pleasure, and Treasure," in *God and Culture: Essays in Honour of Carl F. H. Henry*, ed. Donald A. Carson and John D. Woodbridge (Grand Rapids: Eerdmans, 1993), 368.

12. Ben Witherington, *The Rest of Life: Rest, Play, Eating, Studying, Sex from a Kingdom Perspective* (Grand Rapids: Eerdmans, 2012), 82.

13. Leonard Doohan, "The Spiritual Value of Leisure," *Spirituality Today* 31, no. 2 (1981): 162.

14. Isabella Csikszentmihalyi, "Flow in Historical Context: The Case of the Jesuits," in *Optimal Experience: Psychological Studies of Flow in Consciousness*, ed. Mihaly Csikszentmihalyi and Isabella S. Csikszentmihalyi (Cambridge: Cambridge University Press, 1988).

15. Ibid., 247.

16. Marcia Jean Carter, "The Flow Experience: An Integration of Spiritual and Leisure Well-Being," in *Christianity and Leisure: Issues at the Millenium*, ed. Glen Van Andel and Paul Heintzman (Sioux Center, IA: Dordt College Press, forthcoming).

17. Marcia Jean Carter, "Quality of Life in a Christian Community: Conceptual Investigation of Flow Experiences and HPERD Responsibilities," in *Christianity and Leisure: Issues at the Millenium*, ed. Glen Van Andel and Paul Heintzman (Sioux Center, IA: Dordt College Press, forthcoming).

18. Douglas A. Kleiber, "The Neglect of Relaxation," *Journal of Leisure Research* 32, no. 1 (2000): 82–86.

19. Lisa Feldman Barrett and James A. Russell, "The Structure of Current Affect: Controversies and Emerging Consensus," *Current Directions in Psychology* 8, no. 1 (1999): 10–14.

20. Kleiber, "Neglect of Relaxation."

21. Karla A. Henderson et al., *A Leisure of One's Own: A Feminist Perspective on Women's Leisure* (State College, PA: Venture, 1989), 13.

22. Susan M. Shaw, "Resistance," in *A Handbook of Leisure Studies*, ed. Chris Rojek, Susan M. Shaw, and Anthony James Veal (New York: Palgrave Macmillan, 2006), 534.

23. Ibid.

24. Crittenden, "Holy Leisure," 12.

25. Ibid., 24.

26. Ibid., 25.

27. Charles Sylvester, "Interpretation and Leisure Science: A Hermeneutical Example of Past and Present Oracles," *Journal of Leisure Research* 32, no. 1 (1990): 292–94.

28. Ibid., 293.

29. Chris Rojek, *The Labour of Leisure: The Culture of Free Time* (Los Angeles: Sage, 2010), 112.

30. Mihaly Csikszentmihalyi, *The Evolving Self: A Psychology for the Third Millenium* (New York: HarperCollins, 1993), 207.

31. Richard Winter, *Still Bored in a Culture of Entertainment: Rediscovering Passion and Wonder* (Downers Grove, IL: InterVarsity, 2002).

32. Patricia Meyer Spacks, *Boredom: The Literary History of a State of Mind* (Chicago: University of Chicago Press, 1995).

33. Winter, *Still Bored in a Culture of Entertainment*, 83.

34. Carl Rogers, *On Becoming a Person: A Therapist's View of Psychotherapy* (Boston: Houghton Mifflin, 1961), 23–24, emphasis in original, quoted in Winter, *Still Bored in a Culture of Entertainment*, 54.

35. Winter, *Still Bored in a Culture of Entertainment*, 85.

36. Ibid., 98.

37. Andrew Fellows, "The Self at the Dawn of the New Millenium," *Lev International: The International Newsletter of L'Abri Fellowship* (Summer 2000): 6, quoted in Winter, *Still Bored in a Culture of Entertainment*, 98.

38. Mihaly Csikszentmihalyi, *Flow: The Psychology of Optimal Experience* (Toronto: Harper & Row, 1990), 225, 227.

39. Winter, *Still Bored in a Culture of Entertainment*, 97.

40. Augustine, *Confessions*, trans. Joseph Green Pilkington, ed. Justin Lovill (London: The Folio Society, 1993), 13.

41. Blaise Pascal, *Pensées*, trans. Alban John Krailsheimer (Baltimore: Penguin, 1966), 75.

42. Pope John Paul II (1978–2005) and Giuseppe Acocella, *Centesimus Annus* (Vatican City: Edizioni Logos, 1991), 36.

43. J. I. Packer, "Hot Tub Religion: Toward a Theology of Enjoyment," in *God's Plans for You* (Wheaton: Crossway, 2001), 50.

44. Creath Davis, "Joy," in *Evangelical Dictionary of Theology*, 2nd ed., ed. Walter A. Elwell (Grand Rapids: Baker Academic, 2001), 636.

45. Packer, "Hot Tub Religion," 54–60.

46. Ibid., 71.

47. Tony Campolo, *The Kingdom of God Is a Party* (Dallas: Word, 1990), 132.

48. Paul C. Vitz, *Psychology as Religion: The Cult of Self-Worship*, 2nd ed. (Grand Rapids: Eerdmans, 1994), 139.

49. Ibid., 140.

50. Leland Ryken, *Redeeming the Time: A Christian Approach to Work and Leisure* (Grand Rapids: Baker Books, 1995), 134.

51. Neville, *Free Time*, 67.

52. Karla A. Henderson et al., *Both Gaps and Gains: Feminist Perspectives on Women's Leisure* (State College, PA: Venture, 1996), 46, 192.

53. Nicola Hoggard-Creegan, "Why We Still Need Feminist Theology: A Response to Craig Blomberg," in *Reconsidering Gender: Evangelical Perspectives*, ed. Myk Habets and Beulah Wood (Eugene, OR: Pickwick, 2011), 65.

54. John G. Stackhouse, *Finally Feminist: A Pragmatic Christian Understanding of Gender* (Grand Rapids: Baker Academic, 2005), 35–36.

55. Hoggard-Creegan, "Why We Still Need Feminist Theology," 65.

56. Chris Marshall, "Heads and Bodies: A Response to Immanuel Koks," in *Reconsidering Gender: Evangelical Perspectives*, ed. Myk Habets and Beulah Wood (Eugene, OR: Pickwick, 2011), 189.

57. Neville, *Free Time*, 69.

58. Hoggard-Creegan, "Why We Still Need Feminist Theology," 65.

59. Ibid., 70.

60. Henderson et al., *Both Gaps and Gains*.

61. Stackhouse, *Finally Feminist*, 93.

62. Crittenden, *Holy Leisure*, 71.

63. Ibid., 80.

64. Ibid., 70–72.
65. Ibid., 88.
66. Elaine Storkey, *What's Right with Feminism* (London: SPCK, 1985), 135.
67. Ibid., 135.
68. Ibid., 136.
69. Stackhouse, *Finally Feminist*, 85.
70. Storkey, *What's Right with Feminism*, 176.
71. Ibid., 177.
72. Packer, "Leisure and Life-Style," 362.
73. Jennifer Livengood, "The Role of Leisure in the Spirituality of New Paradigm Christians," *Leisure/Loisir* 33, no. 2 (2009): 408.
74. Dietrich Bonhoeffer, *Letters and Papers from Prison*, ed. Eberhard Bethge (New York: Macmillan, 1971), 193.
75. Ryken, *Redeeming the Time*, 237.
76. Ibid., 240.
77. Ibid., 238.
78. Neville, *Free Time*, 8.
79. Ibid., 76.
80. Ibid., 116.
81. James T. Dennison Jr., *The Market Day of the Soul: The Puritan Doctrine of the Sabbath in England 1532–1760* (Lanham, MD: University Press of America, 1983), 80.
82. Robert Lee, *Religion and Leisure in America* (New York: Abingdon, 1964), 170.
83. Dahl, *Work, Play and Worship*, 63.
84. David A. Spence, *Towards a Theology of Leisure with Special Reference to Creativity* (Ottawa: Canadian Parks/Recreation Association, 1973), 38, 39.
85. Robert Banks, *The Tyranny of Time: When 24 Hours Is Not Enough* (Downers Grove, IL: InterVarsity, 1983), 40–73.
86. Dahl, *Work, Play and Worship*, 64.
87. Conference on Christian Politics, Economics and Citizenship Commission Reports, vol. 5, "Leisure" (1924), 282, quoted in Neville, *Free Time*, 72.
88. Bernard J. Hahn, "Approaching Leisure Redemptively: Leisure Misunderstood," *Christian Renewal* 3, no. 19 (June 3, 1985): 15.
89. Neville, *Free Time*, 65.
90. James F. Murphy, *Concepts of Leisure: Philosophical Implications* (Englewood Cliffs, NJ: Prentice-Hall, 1974), 145–50.
91. Dahl, *Work, Play and Worship*, 80.
92. Elie Cohen-Gewerc and Robert A. Stebbins, conclusion to *The Pivotal Role in Leisure Education: Finding Personal Fulfillment in This Century*, ed. Elie Cohen-Gewerc and Robert A. Stebbins (State College, PA: Venture, 2007), 169.
93. Elie Cohen-Gewerc and Robert A. Stebbins, "The Idea of Leisure," in *The Pivotal Role in Leisure Education: Finding Personal Fulfillment in This Century*, ed. Elie Cohen-Gewerc and Robert A. Stebbins (State College, PA: Venture, 2007), 10.
94. Micheal A. Eaton, *Ecclesiastes* (Downers Grove, IL: InterVarsity, 1983), 68.
95. Francis Bregha, "Philosophy of Leisure: Unanswered Questions," *Recreation Research Review* 8, no. 1 (July 1980): 17.
96. Peter Kreeft, *Christianity for Modern Pagans: Pascal's Pensées Edited, Outlined and Explained* (San Francisco: Ignatius, 1993), 188.
97. Doohan, "Spiritual Value of Leisure," 164.
98. Dennis J. Billy, "The Call to Holy Rest," *New Blackfriars* 82, no. 962 (April 2001): 185.
99. Paul Heintzman, "Leisure Studies and Spirituality: A Christian Critique," *Journal of the Christian Society for Kinesiology and Leisure Studies* 1 (2010): 19–31.

100. Banks, *Tyranny of Time*, 208.

101. Dahl, *Work, Play and Worship*, 70–71.

102. Neville, *Free Time*, 106.

103. Packer, "Leisure and Life-Style," 362.

104. John Stott, *Decisive Issues Facing Christians Today* (Old Tappan, NJ: Fleming H. Revell, 1990), 180–81.

105. Robert A. Stebbins, *Serious Leisure* (New Brunswick, NJ: Transaction, 2007), 58, cited in Mike W. Martin, "Balancing Work and Leisure," in *The Value of Time and Leisure in a World of Work*, ed. Mitchell R. Haney and A. David Kline (Toronto: Lexington, 2010), 13.

106. Neville, *Free Time*, 8.

107. William Hubert Vanstone, *The Stature of Waiting* (London: Seabury, 1982), 113, quoted in Neville, *Free Time*, 8.

108. Chris Rojek, "Deviant Leisure: The Dark Side of Free-Time Activity," *Leisure Studies: Prospects for the Twenty-First Century*, ed. Edgar L. Jackson and Thomas L. Burton (State College, PA: Venture, 1999), 82.

109. Cohen-Gewerc and Stebbins, "Idea of Leisure," 10.

110. Michael F. Pond, "Investigating Climbing as a Spiritual Experience" (MSRS thesis, Ohio University, 2013).

111. Rachel Kraus, "They Danced in the Bible: Identity Integration among Christian Women Who Belly Dance," *Sociology of Religion* 71 (2010): 457–82.

112. Hayden Ramsay, *Reclaiming Leisure: Art, Sport, and Philosophy* (New York: Palgrave Macmillan, 2005), 24.

113. Robert A. Stebbins, "Leisure Reflections 11: Contemplation as Leisure and Non-Leisure," *LSA Newsletter* 73 (March 2006): 16–18.

114. Robert K. Johnston, *The Christian at Play* (Grand Rapids: Eerdmans, 1983), 83–85.

115. Ryken, *Redeeming the Time*, 85–86.

116. Josef Pieper, *Leisure: The Basis of Culture* (New York: Random House, 1963), 21.

117. Joseph Owens, "Aristotle on Leisure," *Canadian Journal of Philosophy* 11, no. 4 (December 1981): 723.

118. Ibid., 722–23.

119. Jean Leclercq, *The Love of Learning and the Desire for God: A Study of Monastic Culture* (New York: Image Doubleday, 1977), 67.

120. Owens, "Aristotle on Leisure," 722.

121. Pieper, *Leisure: The Basis of Culture*, 56.

122. Ibid., 40.

123. Ibid.

124. Ibid., 41.

125. Ibid., 42–43.

126. Johnston, *Christian at Play*, 130.

127. Neville, *Free Time*, 39.

128. Pieper, *Leisure: The Basis of Culture*, 40.

129. Thomas L. Goodale, "If Leisure Is to Matter," in *Recreation and Leisure: In An Era of Change*, ed. Thomas L. Goodale and Peter A. Witt, 3rd ed. (State College, PA: Venture, 1991), 42–43.

130. Pieper, *Leisure: The Basis of Culture*.

131. Leonard Doohan, *Leisure: A Spiritual Need* (Notre Dame, IN: Ave Maria, 1990).

132. Ryken, *Redeeming the Time*.

133. Neville, *Free Time*.

134. Jeanne E. Sherrow, *It's About Time: A Look at Leisure, Lifestyle, and Christianity* (Grand Rapids: Zondervan, 1984).

135. Gordon Dahl, "Whatever Happened to the Leisure Revolution," in *Christianity and Leisure: Issues in a Pluralistic Society*, rev. ed., ed. Paul Heintzman, Glen E. Van Andel, and Thomas L. Visker (Sioux Center, IA: Dordt College Press, 2006), 95.

136. Douglas Joblin, "Leisure and Spirituality: An Engaged and Responsible Pursuit of Freedom in Work, Play, and Worship," *Leisure/Loisir* 33, no. 1 (2009): 95–120.

137. Doohan, *Leisure: A Spiritual Need*, 97, 98, 100.

138. James Murphy, *Concepts of Leisure: Philosophical Implications* (Englewood Cliffs, NJ: Prentice Hall, 1974), 5.

139. Max Kaplan, "New Concepts of Leisure Today," in James Murphy, *Concepts of Leisure: Philosophical Implications* (Englewood Cliffs, NJ: Prentice Hall, 1974), 230–31.

140. Neville, *Free Time*, 43.

141. Spence, *Towards a Theology of Leisure*, 40.

142. Hayden Ramsay, "Reflective Leisure, Freedom and Identity," in *Contemporary Perspectives in Leisure: Meanings, Motives, and Lifelong Learning*, ed. Sam Elkington and Sean J. Gammon (New York: Routledge, 2014), 178.

Chapter 11: Leisure, Work, and Ethics

1. Kunio Odaka, "Work and Leisure: As Viewed by Japanese Industrial Workers" (paper presented to Sixth World Congress of Sociology, Evian, 1966), quoted in Stanley Parker, *Leisure and Work* (London: George Allen and Unwin, 1983), 81–82.

2. Robert K. Johnston, *The Christian at Play* (Grand Rapids: Eerdmans, 1983), 137–38.

3. Leland Ryken, *Redeeming the Time: A Christian Approach to Work and Leisure* (Grand Rapids: Baker Books, 1995), 287.

4. Margaret Mead, "The Pattern of Leisure in Contemporary American Culture," in *Mass Leisure*, ed. Eric Larrabee and Rolf Meyersohn (Glencoe, IL: Free Press, 1958), 10–12.

5. Pierre Berton, *The Smug Minority* (Toronto: McClelland and Stewart, 1968), 17.

6. James Houston, "The Theology of Work," in *Looking at Lifestyles Professional Priorities—A Christian Perspective*, Proceedings from the Conference for Physicians and Dentists, Banff, May 2–8, 1981 (Vancouver: Christian Medical and Dental Society of Canada, 1981), 41.

7. Jacques Ellul, *The Technological Society*, trans. John Wilkinson (New York: Random House, 1964), 399–400.

8. Paul Marshall, "Vocation, Work, and Jobs," in *Labour of Love: Essays on Work*, ed. Josina Van Nuis Zylstra (Toronto: Wedge, 1980).

9. Johnston, *Christian at Play*, 133.

10. Odaka, quoted in Parker, *Leisure and Work*, 82.

11. Johnston, *Christian at Play*, 134.

12. Arthur Holmes, *Contours of a World View* (Grand Rapids: Eerdmans, 1983), 228.

13. Oswald Chambers, *My Utmost for His Highest*, rev. ed. (Toronto: McClelland & Stewart), 218.

14. Nelvin Vos, "To Take Life Leisurely," *Reformed Journal* 29, no. 5 (May 1979): 15.

15. Robert Banks, *The Tyranny of Time: When 24 Hours Is Not Enough* (Downers Grove, IL: InterVarsity, 1983), 194.

16. Houston, "Theology of Work," 46–47.

17. William Still, *Rhythms of Rest and Work* (Aberdeen, Scotland: Gilcomston South Church, 1985).

18. Leonard Doohan, *Leisure: A Spiritual Need* (Notre Dame, IN: Ave Maria, 1990), 36.

19. Leonard Doohan, "The Spiritual Value of Leisure," *Spirituality Today* 31, no. 2 (1981): 165–66.

20. Graham Neville, *Free Time: Towards a Theology of Leisure* (Birmingham, UK: University of Birmingham Press, 2004), 42.

21. Ibid., 114.

22. Thomas Goodale and Geoffrey C. Godbey, *The Evolution of Leisure: Historical and Philosophical Perspectives* (State College, PA: Venture, 1988), 221.

23. Thomas Visker, "Play, Game and Sport in a Reformed, Biblical Worldview," in *Christianity and Leisure: Issues in a Pluralistic Society*, rev. ed., ed. Paul Heintzman, Glen E. Van Andel, and Thomas L. Visker (Sioux Center, IA: Dordt College Press, 2006), 173–92.

24. Goodale and Godbey, *Evolution of Leisure*.

25. Neville, *Free Time*, 41.

26. Ibid., 42.

27. Ron Johnson and Don McLean, "Leisure and the Development of Ethical Character: Changing Views of the North American Ideal," *Journal of Applied Recreation Research* 19, no. 2 (1994): 128–29.

28. Neville, *Free Time*, 79.

29. Glen E. Van Andel, "Redeeming Play: A Christian Perspective," in *Christianity and Leisure: Issues at the Millennium*, ed. Glen Van Andel and Paul Heintzman (Sioux Center, IA: Dordt College Press, forthcoming).

30. John Hick, "The Universality of the Golden Rule," in *Ethics, Religion and the Good Society: New Directions in a Pluralistic World*, ed. Joseph Runzo (Louisville: Westminster/John Knox, 1992), 155–66.

31. Neville, *Free Time*, 76, 65.

32. Ibid.

Chapter 12: Leisure and Spiritual Well-Being

1. Leonard Doohan, *Leisure: A Spiritual Need* (Notre Dame, IN: Ave Maria, 1990).

2. Barbara L. McDonald and Richard Schreyer, "Spiritual Benefits of Leisure Participation and Leisure Settings," in *Benefits of Leisure*, ed. Beverly L. Driver, Perry J. Brown, and George L. Peterson (State College, PA: Venture, 1991), 179–94.

3. Chris Schmidt, "The Lived Experience of the Spiritual Potential of Leisure," *Annals of Leisure Research* 9, no. 3 (2006): 177.

4. Paul Heintzman, "The Spiritual Benefits of Leisure," *Leisure/Loisir* 33, no. 1 (2009): 419–45.

5. Steven Hawks, "Spiritual Health: Definition and Theory," *Wellness Perspectives: Research, Theory and Practice* 10, no. 4 (1994): 3–13.

6. Heintzman, "Spiritual Benefits of Leisure," 428–37; Paul Heintzman, "Religion, Leisure and Spirituality," in *Leisure Matters: The State and Future of Leisure Studies*, ed. Gordon Walker, David Scott, and Monika Stodolska (State College, PA: Venture, forthcoming).

7. For example, Richard J. Foster, *Celebration of Discipline: The Path to Spiritual Growth* (San Francisco: Harper & Row, 1978).

8. Richard J. Foster and Emilie Griffin, eds., *Spiritual Classics* (New York: HarperSanFrancisco, 2000); Richard J. Foster and James B. Smith, eds., *Devotional Classics* (New York: HarperSanFrancisco, 1993).

9. Foster, *Celebration of Discipline*; Mark Harris, *Companions for Your Spiritual Journey: Discovering the Disciplines of the Saints* (Downers Grove, IL: InterVarsity, 1999).

10. Paul Heintzman, "Leisure and Spiritual Well-Being Relationships: A Qualitative Study," *Society and Leisure* 23, no. 1 (2000): 48–49.

11. Maria Anderegg et al., *"When Heaven and Earth Meet": A Qualitative Study on the Experience of Leisure and Spirituality among Mental Health Professionals* (Ottawa: St. Paul University, 2002), 221.

12. Ibid., 194.

13. Foster, *Celebration of Discipline*, 20–21.

14. Brother Lawrence, *The Practice of the Presence of God*, ed. John J. Delaney (New York: Image Doubleday, 1977), 47.

15. Jean Leclercq, *The Love of Learning and the Desire for God: A Study of Monastic Culture* (New York: Fordham University Press, 1982), 69.

16. Heintzman, "Leisure and Spiritual Well-Being Relationships," 45–46.

17. Christopher Schmidt and Donna E. Little, "The Spiritual Nature of Time and Space for Self: The Potential of Leisure to Engage the Human Soul," in *The Two Solitudes: Isolation or Impact? Book of Abstracts from the Eleventh Canadian Congress on Leisure Research*, ed. Tom Delamere, Carleigh Randall, and David Robinson (Nanaimo, BC: Department of Recreation and Tourism Management, Malaspina University-College, 2005), 546–49.

18. Anderegg et al., *"When Heaven and Earth Meet": A Qualitative Study*, 221.

19. Roman R. Williams, "Space for God: Lived Religion at Work, Home and Play," *Sociology of Religion* 71, no. 3 (2010): 257–79.

20. Doohan, *Leisure: A Spiritual Need*, 35.

21. Joseph Teaff, "Contemplative Leisure within Christian Spirituality," in *Christianity and Leisure: Issues in a Pluralistic Society*, rev. ed., ed. Paul Heintzman, Glen E. Van Andel, and Thomas L. Visker (Sioux Center, IA: Dordt College Press, 2006), 115.

22. Henri J. M. Nouwen, *Making All Things New: An Invitation to the Spiritual Life* (New York: Harper Collins, 1981), quoted in Foster and Smith, *Devotional Classics*, 95.

23. Heintzman, "Leisure and Spiritual Well-Being Relationships, 46–47."

24. Anderegg et al., *"When Heaven and Earth Meet": A Qualitative Study*, 174.

25. Foster, *Celebration of Discipline*, 164.

26. Don Postema, *Space for God: The Study and Practice of Prayer and Spirituality* (Grand Rapids: Bible Way, 1983), 60.

27. Doohan, *Leisure: A Spiritual Need*, 21.

28. Ibid., 57.

29. Neville, *Free Time*, 94.

30. Heintzman, "Leisure and Spiritual Well-Being Relationships, 51."

31. Rebecca Fox, "Enhancing Spiritual Experience in Adventure Programs," in *Adventure Programming*, ed. John C. Miles and Simon Priest (State College, PA: Venture, 1999), 459.

32. Christopher Schmidt and Donna E. Little, "Qualitative Insights into Leisure as a Spiritual Experience," *Journal of Leisure Research* 39, no. 2 (2007): 222–47.

33. Boris Vukonić, *Tourism and Religion*, trans. S. Matešić (New York: Elsevier, 1996).

34. Richard J. Foster, introduction to *Celtic Daily Prayer: Prayers and Readings from the Northumbria Community* (New York: Harper Collins, 2002), xi–xx.

35. Bradley P. Holt, *Thirsty for God: A Brief History of Christian Spirituality*, 2nd ed. (Minneapolis: Fortress, 2005), 208.

36. Paul Heintzman, "Nature-Based Recreation and Spirituality: A Complex Relationship," *Leisure Sciences* 32, no. 1 (2010): 72–89.

37. Jeffrey R. Behan, Merton T. Richards, and Martha E. Lee, "Effects of Tour Jeeps in a Wildland Setting on Non-motorized Recreationist Benefits," *Journal of Park and Recreation Administration* 19, no. 2 (2001): 1–19; Paul Heintzman, "The Role of Introspection and Spirituality in the Park Experience of Day Visitors to Ontario Provincial Parks," in *Managing Protected Areas in a Changing World*, ed. Soren Bondrup-Nielsen et al. (Wolfville, NS: Science and Management of Protected Areas Association, 2002), 992–1004; Paul Heintzman, "The Spiritual Dimension of Campers' Park Experience," *Managing Leisure* 17, no. 4 (2012): 291–310; Heintzman, "Nature-Based Recreation and Spirituality," 72–89.

38. L. Allison Stringer and Leo H. McAvoy, "The Need for Something Different: Spirituality and the Wilderness Adventure," *The Journal of Experiential Education* 15, no. 1 (1992): 18.

39. Laura M. Fredrickson and Dorothy H. Anderson, "A Qualitative Exploration of the Wilderness Experience as a Source of Spiritual Inspiration," *Journal of Environmental Psychology* 19, no. 1 (1999): 30–31.

40. Rebecca J. Fox, "Women, Nature and Spirituality: A Qualitative Study Exploring Women's Wilderness Experience," *Proceedings of ANZALS Conference 1997*, ed. David Rowe and Peter Brown (Newcastle: Australian and New Zealand Association for Leisure Studies and the Department of Leisure and Tourism Studies, University of Newcastle, 1997), 61–62.

41. Paul Heintzman, "Men's Wilderness Experience and Spirituality: A Qualitative Study," in *Proceedings of the 2006 Northeastern Recreation Research Symposium*, comp. Robert Burns and Karen Robinson (Gen. Tech. Rep. NRS-P-14) (Newton Square, PA: U.S. Department of Agriculture, Forest Services, Northern Research Station, 2007), 220–21.

42. Anderegg et al., *"When Heaven and Earth Meet"*: A Qualitative Study.

43. Jennifer Livengood, "The Role of Leisure in the Spirituality of New Paradigm Christians," *Leisure/Loisir* 33, no. 2 (2009): 405–7.

44. Heintzman, "Leisure and Spiritual Well-Being Relationships"; T. A. Loeffler, "A Photo Elicitation Study of the Meanings of Outdoor Adventure Experiences," *Journal of Leisure Research* 36, no. 4 (2004): 536–56; Al Ellard, Norma Polovitz Nickerson, and Robert Dvorak, "The Spiritual Dimension of the Montana Vacation Experience," *Leisure/Loisir* 33, no. 1 (2009): 269–89.

45. Ibid.

46. Heintzman, "Leisure and Spiritual Well-Being Relationships," 49.

47. Heintzman, "Men's Wilderness Experience and Spirituality," 218; Loeffler, "Photo Elicitation Study."

48. Heintzman, "Leisure and Spiritual Well-Being Relationships," 49.

49. Evelyn Underhill, *Practical Mysticism* (New York: Dutton, 1943), 90.

50. "Opening the Book of Nature," Book of Nature website, accessed November 15, 2010, http://www.bookofnature.org/library/ngb.html.

51. Ibid.

52. Ibid.

53. Ibid.

54. Stephen Kaplan, "The Restorative Benefits of Nature: Toward an Integrative Framework," *Journal of Environmental Psychology* 15, no. 3 (1995): 169–82.

55. Stringer and McAvoy, "The Need for Something Different," 17.

56. Heintzman, "Leisure and Spiritual Well-Being Relationships," 50.

57. Mary Sweatman and Paul Heintzman, "The Perceived Impact of Outdoor Residential Camp Experience on the Spirituality of Youth," *World Leisure Journal* 46, no. 1 (2004): 23–31.

58. Heintzman, "Men's Wilderness Experience and Spirituality," 220; Paul Heintzman, "Men's Wilderness Experience and Spirituality: Further Explorations," in *Proceedings of the 2007 Northeastern Recreation Research Symposium* (Gen. Tech. Rep. NRS-P-23), comp. Cherie LeBlanc and Christine Vogt (Newton Square, PA: U.S. Department of Agriculture, Forest Services, Northern Research Station, 2008), 58.

59. Ellard, Nickerson, and Dvorak, "Spiritual Dimension of the Montana Vacation Experience," 282–83.

60. Pierre Ouellette, Rachel Kaplan, and Stephen Kaplan, "The Monastery as a Restorative Environment," *Journal of Environmental Psychology* 25, no. 2 (2005): 178–88; Pierre Ouellette, Paul Heintzman, and Raymond Carette, "Les motivations et les effets d'une retraite faite par des personnes âgées dans un monastère bénédictin" ["The Motives and Effects of a Retreat Taken by Older People in a Benedictine Monastery"], in *The Two Solitudes: Isolation or Impact? Book of Abstracts from the Eleventh Canadian Congress on Leisure Research*, ed. Tom Delamere, Carleigh Randall, and David Robinson (Nanaimo, BC: Department of Recreation and Tourism Management, Malaspina University-College, 2005), 448–52.

61. Foster, *Celebration of Discipline*, 85.

62. Thomas H. Green, *A Vacation with the Lord: A Personal Directed Retreat Based on the Spiritual Exercises of Saint Ignatius Loyola* (Notre Dame, IN: Ave Maria, 1986).

63. Foster, *Celebration of Discipline*, 61.

64. Fox, "Women, Nature and Spirituality," 62.

65. Fredrickson and Anderson, "A Qualitative Exploration of the Wilderness Experience," 31–32.

66. Stringer and McAvoy, "Need for Something Different," 19.

67. Theresa G. Coble, Steve W. Selin, and Beth B. Erickson, "Hiking Alone: Understanding Fear, Negotiation Strategies, and Leisure Experience," *Journal of Leisure Research* 35, no. 1 (2003): 1–22.

68. Heintzman, "Spiritual Dimension of Camper's Park Experience," 300.

69. Sweatman and Heintzman, "Perceived Impact of Outdoor Residential Camp Experience," 26–27.

70. Heintzman, "Leisure and Spiritual Well-Being Relationships," 52–53.

71. Thomas Merton, ed. and trans., *The Wisdom of the Desert: Sayings from the Desert Fathers of the Fourth Century* (London: Sheldon, 1960), 30.

72. Andrew J. Bobilya, "Wilderness, Solitude, and Monastic Traditions," in *Exploring the Power of Solo, Silence, and Solitude*, ed. Clifford E. Knapp and Thomas E. Smith (Boulder, CO: Association for Experiential Education, 2005).

73. Foster and Griffin, *Spiritual Classics*, 149–50.

74. Ibid., 156.

75. Ibid., 95, 97.

76. Stringer and McAvoy, "Need for Something Different," 18.

77. Fox, "Women, Nature and Spirituality," 61.

78. Fredrickson and Anderson, "A Qualitative Exploration of Wilderness Experience," 29–30.

79. Heintzman, "Men's Wilderness Experience and Spirituality: Further Explorations," 56–57.

80. Heintzman, "Leisure and Spiritual Well-Being Relationships," 52–53.

81. Sweatman and Heintzman, "Perceived Impact of Outdoor Residential Camp Experience," 26–28.

82. Schmidt and Little, "Qualitative Insights into Leisure as a Spiritual Experience," 234.

83. Donna E. Little and Chris Schmidt, "Self, Wonder and God! The Spiritual Dimensions of Travel Experiences," *Tourism* 54, no. 2 (2006): 107–16.

84. R. Paul Stevens, "Friendship," in *The Complete Book of Everyday Christianity*, ed. Robert Banks and R. Paul Stevens (Downers Grove, IL: InterVarsity, 1997), 441.

85. Harris, *Companions for Your Spiritual Journey*, 96.

86. Ibid., 87.

87. Stevens, "Friendship," 441.

88. Stringer and McAvoy, "Need for Something Different," 18–19.

89. Fredrickson and Anderson, "A Qualitative Exploration of Wilderness Experience," 38.

90. Heintzman, "Men's Wilderness Experience: A Qualitative Study," 221.

91. Paul Heintzman, "Rowing, Sailing, Reading, Discussing, Praying: The Spiritual and Lifestyle Impact of an Experientially Based, Graduate, Environmental Education Course" (paper presented at the Trails to Sustainability Conference, Kananaskis, Alberta, May 2007); Paul E. Marsh, "Backcountry Adventure as Spiritual Development: A Means-end Study," *Journal of Experiential Education* 30, no. 3 (2008): 290–93.

92. Sweatman and Heintzman, "Perceived Impact of Outdoor Residential Camp Experience," 29–30.

93. Edward C. Sellner, "Soul Friendship in Early Celtic Monasticism," *Aisling Magazine* 17 (Samhain 1995), http://www.aislingmagazine.com/aislingmagazine/articles/TAM17/Friendship.html.

94. Ibid.

95. Dietrich Bonhoeffer, *Life Together* (New York: Harper & Row, 1952), 77–78.

Chapter 13: Leisure-Spiritual Coping

1. Leonard Doohan, *Leisure: A Spiritual Need* (Notre Dame, IN: Ave Maria, 1990), 15, 55.

2. Paul Heintzman, "Leisure-Spiritual Coping: A Model for Therapeutic Recreation and Leisure Services," *Therapeutic Recreation Journal* 42, no. 1 (2008): 56–73.

3. Terry Lynn Gall et al., "Understanding the Nature and Role of Spirituality in Relation to Coping and Health: A Conceptual Framework," *Canadian Psychology/Psychologie canadienne* 46, no. 2 (2005): 88–104.

4. Kenneth I. Pargament and June Hahn, "God and the Just World: Causal and Coping Attributions to God in Health Situations," *Journal for the Scientific Study of Religion* 25, no. 2 (1986): 193–207.

5. Bernard Spilka, Phillip Shaver, and Lee A. Kirkpatrick, "A General Attribution Theory for the Psychology of Religion," *Journal for the Scientific Study of Religion* 24, no. 1 (1985): 1–20.

6. Gall et al., "Nature and Role of Spirituality," 91.

7. Ibid.

8. Pargament and Hahn, "God and the Just World."

9. Gall et al., "Nature and Role of Spirituality," 91.

10. For example, see Yoshitika Iwasaki et al., "Social Exclusion and Resilience as Frameworks of Stress and Coping among Selected Non-dominant Groups," *International Journal of Mental Health Promotion* 7, no. 3 (2005): 4–17.

11. Gordon Willard Allport, *Pattern and Growth in Personality* (New York: Holt, Rinehart & Winston, 1961); Baldwin Ross Hergenhahn and Matthew Olson, *An Introduction to Theories of Personality*, 5th ed. (Upper Saddle River, NJ: Prentice Hall, 1991).

12. Gall et al., "Nature and Role of Spirituality," 92.

13. Crystal L. Park and Lawrence Cohen, "Religious and Non-religious Coping with the Death of a Friend," *Cognitive Therapy and Research* 17, no. 6 (1993): 561–77.

14. Kenneth I. Pargament et al., "God Help Me (II): The Relationship of Religious Orientations to Religious Coping with Negative Life Events," *Journal for the Scientific Study of Religion* 31, no. 4 (1992): 504–13.

15. Crystal Park, Lawrence H. Cohen, and Lisa Herb, "Intrinsic Religiousness and Religious Coping as Life Stress Moderators for Catholics versus Protestants," *Journal of Personality and Social Psychology* 59, no. 3 (1990): 562–74.

16. Gall et al., "Nature and Role of Spirituality," 94.

17. Ellen L. Idler, "Organizational Religiousness," in *Multidimensional Measurement of Religiousness/Spirituality for Use in Health Research*, Fetzer Institute/National Institute on Ageing Working Group (Kalamazoo, MI: Fetzer Institute, 1999), 75–79.

18. Jeffrey S. Levin, "Private Religious Practices," in *Multidimensional Measurement of Religiousness/Spirituality*, 39–42.

19. Jane Dyson, Mark Cobb, and Dawn Forman, "The Meaning of Spirituality: A Literature Review," *Journal of Advanced Nursing* 26, no. 6 (1997): 1183–88.

20. Chyrell D. Bellamy et al., "Relevance of Spirituality for People with Mental Illness Attending Consumer-centered Services," *Psychiatric Rehabilitation Journal* 30, no. 4 (2007): 287–94.

21. Iwasaki et al., "Social Exclusion and Resilience."

22. Paul Heintzman and Roger C. Mannell, "Spiritual Functions of Leisure and Spiritual Well-Being: Coping with Time Pressure," *Leisure Sciences* 25, nos. 2–3 (2003): 207–30.

23. Doohan, *Leisure: A Spiritual Need*; Richard J. Foster, *Celebration of Discipline: The Path to Spiritual Growth* (San Francisco: Harper & Row, 1978); Robert Lee, *Religion and Leisure in America* (New York: Abingdon, 1964).

24. Jiri Zuzanek and Roger Mannell, "Life-cycle Squeeze, Time Pressure, Daily Stress, and Leisure Participation: A Canadian Perspective," *Society and Leisure* 21, no. 2 (1998): 513–44.

25. Cynthia K. Chandler, Janice M. Holden, and Cheryl A. Kolander, "Counseling for Spiritual Wellness: Theory and Practice," *Journal of Counseling and Development* 71, no. 2 (1992): 168–75.

26. Josef Pieper, *Leisure: The Basis of Culture* (New York: Random House, 1963), 40–41.

27. Veda E. Ward, "Leisure: Spiritual Well-Being and Personal Power," *Spiritual Life* 45, no. 4 (1999): 231–36.

28. Paul Heintzman, "Leisure and Spiritual Well-Being Relationships: A Qualitative Study," *Society and Leisure* 23, no. 1 (2000): 46–47.

29. Carol A. Gosselink and Susan A. Myllykangas, "The Leisure Experiences of Older US Women Living with HIV/AIDS," *Health Care for Women International* 28, no. 1 (2007): 3–20.

30. Yoshi Iwasaki and Jamir Butcher, "Common Stress-Coping Methods Shared by Older Women and Men with Arthritis," *International Journal of Psychosocial Rehabilitation* 8 (2004): 179–208.

31. Yoshitaka Iwasaki, Jennifer Mactavish, and Kelly MacKay, "Building on Strengths and Resilience: Leisure as a Stress Survival Strategy," *British Journal of Guidance and Counselling* 33, no. 1 (2005): 81–100.

32. Martina Anderegg et al., *"When Heaven and Earth Meet": A Qualitative Study on the Experience of Leisure and Spirituality among Mental Health Professionals* (Ottawa: St. Paul University, 2002); Heintzman, "Leisure and Spiritual Well-Being Relationships," 45–46; Chris Schmidt and Donna Little, "The Spiritual Nature of Time and Space for Self: The Potential of Leisure to Engage the Human Soul," in *The Two Solitudes: Isolation or Impact? Book of Abstracts from the Eleventh Canadian Congress on Leisure Research*, ed. Tom Delamere, Carleigh Randall, and David Robinson (Nanaimo, BC: Department of Recreation and Tourism Management, Malaspina University-College, 2005), 546–49.

33. Soti Grafanaki et al., "Sources of Renewal: A Qualitative Study of the Experience and Role of Leisure in the Life of Counselors and Psychologists," *Counselling Psychology Quarterly* 18, no. 1 (2005): 31–40.

34. Dvora Luboshitzky and Lee Bennett Gaber, "Holidays and Celebrations as Spiritual Occupation," *Australian Occupational Therapy Journal* 48, no. 2 (2001): 66–74.

35. Margaret Diddams, Lisa Klein Surdyk, and Denise Daniels, "Rediscovering Models of Sabbath Keeping: Implications for Psychological Well-Being," *Journal of Psychology and Theology* 32, no. 1 (2004): 3–11.

36. Joyce M. Earickson, *"The Religious Practice of the Sabbath: A Framework for Psychological Health and Spiritual Well-Being"* (PhD diss., Alliant International University, San Diego, 2004).

37. Traci Lee, "Sabbath-keeping by Protestant Ministers: An Avenue of Meeting the Basic Psychological Needs and Mitigating Professional Burnout" (PhD diss., Seattle Pacific University, Seattle, 2003).

38. Matilda Burian Anhalt, "The Relationship between the Jewish Sabbath and Stress as a Function of Personality Type" (PhD diss., Hofstra University, New York, 1987).

39. Jane K. Boyd, "An Analysis of the Relationship between Sabbath Meaning and Leisure, Marital Intimacy and Marital Satisfaction Among Seventh-day Adventists" (PhD diss., Fuller Theological Seminary, Pasadena, CA, 1998).

40. Bianca Stern, "A Phenomenological Approach towards Understanding the Nature and Meaning of Engagement in Religious Ritual Activity: Perspectives from Persons with Dementia and Their Caregivers" (MSc thesis, University of Toronto, 2005).

41. Stephen Kaplan, "The Restorative Benefits of Nature: Toward an Integrative Framework," *Journal of Environmental Psychology* 15, no. 3 (1995): 169–82.

42. Pierre Ouellette, Rachel Kaplan, and Stephen Kaplan, "The Monastery as a Restorative Environment," *Journal of Environmental Psychology* 25, no. 2 (2005): 178–88; Pierre Ouellette, Paul Heintzman, and Raymond Carette, "Les motivations et les effets d'une retraite faite par des personnes âgées dans un monastère bénédictin" ["The Motives and Effects of a Retreat Taken by Older People in a Benedictine Monastery"] in *The Two Solitudes: Isolation or Impact? Book of Abstracts from the Eleventh Canadian Congress on Leisure Research*, ed. Tom Delamere, Carleigh Randall, and David Robinson (Nanaimo, BC: Department of Recreation and Tourism Management, Malaspina University-College, 2005), 448–52.

43. L. Allison Stringer and Leo H. McAvoy, "The Need for Something Different: Spirituality and the Wilderness Adventure," *The Journal of Experiential Education* 15, no. 1 (1992): 17.

44. Laura M. Fredrickson and Dorothy H. Anderson, "A Qualitative Exploration of the Wilderness Experience as a Source of Spiritual Inspiration," *Journal of Environmental Psychology* 19, no. 1 (1999): 30.

45. Barbara L. McDonald and Richard Schreyer, "Spiritual Benefits of Leisure Participation and Leisure Settings," in *Benefits of Leisure*, ed. Beverly L. Driver, Perry J. Brown, and George L. Peterson (State College, PA: Venture, 1991), 179–94.

46. Stringer and McAvoy, "Need for Something Different." 18–19; Fredrickson and Anderson, "A Qualitative Exploration of Wilderness Experience," 30–31.

47. Anita M. Unruh, Nancy Smith, and Cynthia Scammell, "The Occupation of Gardening in Life-Threatening Illness: A Qualitative Pilot Study," *Canadian Journal of Occupational Therapy* 67, no. 1 (2000): 70–77.

48. Mary Infantino, "Gardening: A Strategy for Health Promotion in Older Women," *Journal of the New York State Nurses Association* 35, no. 2 (2004–5): 10–17; Christine Milligan, Anthony Gatrell, and Amanda Bingley, "Cultivating Health: Therapeutic Landscapes and Older People in Northern England," *Social Science & Medicine* 58, no. 9 (2003): 1781–93.

49. Margaret A. Schneider and Roger C. Mannell, "Beacon in the Storm: An Exploration of the Spirituality and Faith of Parents Whose Children Have Cancer," *Issues in Comprehensive Pediatric Nursing* 29, no. 1 (2006): 3–24.

50. Fredrickson and Anderson, "A Qualitative Exploration of Wilderness Experience," 29.

51. Glen Van Andel and Paul Heintzman, "Christian Spirituality and Therapeutic Recreation," in *Philosophy of Therapeutic Recreation: Ideas and Issues*, vol. 2, ed. Charles Sylvester (Arlington, VA: National Recreation and Park Association, 1996), 71–85.

52. Gall et al., "Nature and Role of Spirituality," 95.

53. Schmidt and Little, "Spiritual Nature of Time and Space," 548.

54. Gosselink and Myllykangas, "Leisure Experiences of Older US Women Living with HIV/AIDS," 13–14.

55. Gall et al., "Nature and Role of Spirituality," 95.

56. Yoshitaka Iwasaki et al., "Voices from the Margins: Stress, Active Living, and Leisure as a Contributor to Coping with Stress," *Leisure Sciences* 28, no. 2 (2006): 163–80.

57. Yoshitaka Iwasaki and Judith Bartlett, "Stress-coping among Aboriginal Individuals with Diabetes in an Urban Canadian City: From Woundedness to Resilience," *Journal of Aboriginal Health* 3, no. 1 (2006): 15–25.

58. Gosselink and Myllykangas, "Leisure Experiences of Older US Women Living with HIV/AIDS."

59. Ibid., 16.

Epilogue: A Concise and Illustrated Theology of Leisure

1. *Waterwalker*, directed by Bill Mason (Ottawa: National Film Board of Canada and Imago, 1984).

2. Ibid.

3. Bill Mason, *Canoescapes* (North York, ON: Stoddart, 1995), 156.

4. James Raffan, *Fire in the Bones: Bill Mason and the Canadian Canoeing Tradition* (Toronto: Harper Collins, 1996), 265.

5. Gordon Preece, "Re-creation and Recreation in the Eighties," *Faith Active in Love*, Proceedings of the 1980 Conference of the AFES Fellowship, ed. John Diesendorf (Sydney: AFES Graduate Fellowship, 1981), 79.

6. Bill Mason, *Path of the Paddle* (Toronto: Van Nostrand Reinhold, 1980), 7.

7. Ibid., 59.

8. *Song of the Paddle*, directed by Bill Mason (Montreal: National Film Board of Canada, 1978).

9. Ken Buck, *Bill Mason: Wilderness Artist from Heart to Hand* (Surrey, BC: Rocky Mountain Books, 2005).

10. Chris Chapman, foreword to Bill Mason, *Canoescapes* (North York, ON: Stoddart, 1995), 8.

11. Ibid., 9.

12. Raffan, *Fire in the Bones*, 80.

13. Wilber Sutherland, "An Interview with Bill Mason," *Crux* 9, no. 4 (Summer 1972): 7.

14. Mason, *Canoescapes*, 10.

15. Mason, *Path of the Paddle*, 59.

16. Mason, *Canoescapes*, 52.

17. Sutherland, "Interview with Bill Mason," 14–15.

18. Mason, *Canoescapes*, 9.

19. Holmes Rolston III, "Creation and Recreation: Environmental Benefits and Human Leisure," in *Benefits of Leisure*, ed. Beverly L. Driver, Perry J. Brown, and George L. Peterson (State College, PA: Venture, 1991), 393.

20. Mason, *Path of the Paddle*, 192.

21. Bill Mason, *Song of the Paddle* (Toronto: Key Porter, 1988), 179.

22. Mason, *Path of the Paddle*, 194.

23. Arthur Holmes, *Contours of a World View* (Grand Rapids: Eerdmans, 1983).

24. Mason, *Path of the Paddle*, 194.

25. Ibid., 3.

26. Ibid., 59.

27. Raffan, *Fire in the Bones*, 228.

bibliography

Aguiar, Mark, and Erik Hurst. *The Increase in Leisure Inequality, 1965–2005*. Washington, DC: AEI, 2009.

Allen, R. T. "Leisure: The Purpose of Life." In *The Philosophy of Leisure*, edited by Cyril Barrett and Tom Winnifrith, 20–33. London: Macmillan, 1989.

Allen, Willoughby C. *The International Critical Commentary on the Gospel according to S. Matthew*. 3rd ed. Edinburgh: T&T Clark, 1912.

Allport, Gordon Willard. *Pattern and Growth in Personality*. New York: Holt, Rinehart & Winston, 1961.

Althaus, Paul. *The Ethics of Martin Luther*. Translated by Robert C. Schultz. Philadelphia: Fortress, 1965.

Anderegg, Martina, Frankie Cini, Magdalena Godula, Bruce MacKenzie, Deborah Pearson, Sandra Nason, and Sotiria Grafanaki. *"When Heaven and Earth Meet": A Qualitative Study on the Experience of Leisure and Spirituality among Mental Health Professionals*. Ottawa: St. Paul University, 2002.

Anderson, Arnold Albert. *The Book of Psalms*. Vol. 1, *Psalms 1–72*. New Century Bible Commentary. Grand Rapids: Eerdmans, 1972.

Andrews, Herbert Tom. "I and II Thessalonians." In *A Commentary on the Bible*, edited by Arthur Samuel Peake, 876–80. London: T. C. & E. C. Jack, Ltd., 1926.

Anhalt, Matilda Burian. "The Relationship between the Jewish Sabbath and Stress as a Function of Personality Type." PhD diss., Hofstra University, 1987.

Aristotle. *The Nicomachean Ethics*. Translated by Harris Rackham. Cambridge, MA: Harvard University Press, 1926.

———. *Politics*. Translated by Ernest Barker. London: Oxford University Press, 1960.

———. *Politics*. Translated by Thomas Alan Sinclair. Rev. ed. New York: Penguin, 1981.

Arnold, Serena. "The Dilemma of Meaning." In *Recreation and Leisure: Issues in an Era of Change*, edited by Thomas L. Goodale and Peter A. Witt, 5–18. State College, PA: Venture, 1980.

Augustine of Hippo. *The City of God.* Translated by Marcus Dods. New York: The Modern Library, 2000.

————. *The Confessions.* Translated by Joseph Green Pilkington. Edited by Justin Lovill. London: The Folio Society, 1993.

Ausubel, Jesse H., and Arnulf Grübler. "Working Less and Living Longer: Long-Term Trends in Working Time and Time Budgets." *Technological Forecasting and Social Change* 50, no. 3 (1995): 195–213.

Bacon, Anthony W. "Leisure and Research: A Critical Review of the Main Concepts Employed in Contemporary Research." *Society and Leisure* 4, no. 2 (1972): 83–92.

Banks, Robert. *The Tyranny of Time: When 24 Hours Is Not Enough.* Downers Grove, IL: InterVarsity, 1983.

Barclay, William. *The Daily Study Bible: The Letters to the Philippians, Colossians and Thessalonians.* Toronto: G. R. Welch Co., 1975.

Barker, Ernest. *Church, State and Study.* London: Methuen Ltd., 1930.

Barrett, Charles K. "The Eschatology of the Epistle to the Hebrews." In *The Background of the New Testament and Its Eschatology: Studies in Honour of C. H. Dodd*, edited by William David Davies and David Daube, 363–93. Cambridge: Cambridge University Press, 1956.

Barth, Karl. *Church Dogmatics* III/1. Translated by J. W. Edwards, O. Bussey, and Harold Knight. Edinburgh: T&T Clark, 1958.

Beatty, Joy, and William R. Torbert, "YIN AND YANG: The Relationship of Leisure and Work." In *Routledge Handbook of Leisure Studies*, edited by Tony Blackshaw, 468–79. New York: Routledge, 2013.

Beckwith, Roger T. "The Biblical and Jewish Evidence." In *The Christian Sunday: A Biblical and Historical Study*, part 1, edited by Roger T. Beckwith and Wilfrid Stott, 2–47. Grand Rapids: Baker, 1980.

Behan, Jeffrey R., Merton T. Richards, and Martha E. Lee. "Effects of Tour Jeeps in a Wildland Setting on Non-motorized Recreationist Benefits." *Journal of Park and Recreation Administration* 19, no. 2 (2001): 1–19.

Bellamy, Chyrell D., Nicole C. Jarrett, Orion Mowbray, Peter MacFarlane, Carol T. Mowbray, and Mark C. Holter. "Relevance of Spirituality for People with Mental Illness Attending Consumer-Centered Services." *Psychiatric Rehabilitation Journal* 30, no. 4 (2007): 287–94.

Berger, Bennett M. "The Sociology of Leisure: Some Suggestions." In *Work and Leisure*, edited by Erwin O. Smigel, 21–40. New Haven: College and University Press, 1963.

Berkers, Vera. "Religion, Spirituality and Leisure: A Relational Approach. The Experience of Religion and Spirituality of Dutch New Christians and New Spirituals during Leisure Activities." Master's thesis, Utrecht University, 2001.

Berton, Pierre. *The Smug Minority.* Toronto: McClelland and Stewart, 1968.

Betz, Hans Dieter. "The Logion of the Easy Yoke and of Rest (Matt. 11:28–30)." *Journal of Biblical Literature* 86, no. 1 (1967): 10–24.

Billy, Dennis J. "The Call to Holy Rest." *New Blackfriars* 82, no. 962 (April 2001): 182–87.

Blackshaw, Tony, ed. *Routledge Handbook of Leisure Studies.* Oxford: Routledge, 2013.

Bobilya, Andrew J. "Wilderness, Solitude, and Monastic Traditions." In *Exploring the Power of Solo, Silence, and Solitude*, edited by Clifford E. Knapp and Thomas E. Smith, 61–74. Boulder, CO: Association for Experiential Education, 2005.

Bonhoeffer, Dietrich. *Letters and Papers from Prison.* Edited by Eberhard Bethge. New York: Macmillan, 1971.

———. *Life Together.* New York: Harper & Row, 1952.

Bonitz, Hermannus. *Index Aristotelius.* Berlin: Akademie-Verlag, 1955.

Book of Nature. "Opening the Book of Nature." December 23, 2006. http://www.bookofnature.org/library/ngb.html.

Boyd, Jane K. "An Analysis of the Relationship between Sabbath Meaning and Leisure, Marital Intimacy and Marital Satisfaction among Seventh-Day Adventists." PhD diss., Fuller Theological Seminary, 1998.

Bregha, Francis J. "Leisure and Freedom Re-examined." In *Recreation and Leisure: Issues in an Era of Change*, edited by Thomas L. Goodale and Peter A. Witt, 30–37. State College, PA: Venture, 1980.

———. "Philosophy of Leisure: Unanswered Questions." *Recreation Research Review* 8, no. 1 (July 1980): 15–19.

Bricker, Kelly. "Why Ride Roughshod over the Great Outdoors? The Problem with Motorized Recreation." In *Speaking Up and Speaking Out: Working for Social and Environmental Justice through Parks, Recreation, and Leisure*, edited by Karen Paisley and Daniel Dustin, 125–34. Urbana, IL: Sagamore, 2011.

Bruce, F. F. "1 and 2 Thessalonians." In *The New Bible Commentary: Revised*, edited by Donald Guthrie and J. Alec Motyer, 1154–65. Grand Rapids: Eerdmans, 1970.

Buck, Ken. *Bill Mason: Wilderness Artist from Heart to Hand.* Surrey, BC: Rocky Mountain Books, 2005.

Byrne, Brendan J. *The Hospitality of God: A Reading of Luke's Gospel.* Collegeville, MN: Liturgical Press, 2000.

Cahill, Thomas. *Sailing the Wine-Dark Sea: Why the Greeks Matter.* New York: Doubleday, 2001.

Calvin, John. *The Epistle of Paul the Apostle to the Hebrews and the First and Second Epistle of St. Peter*. Translated by William B. Johnston. Edinburgh: Oliver & Boyd, 1963.

————. *The Gospels*. Grand Rapids: Associated Publishers and Authors, 1960.

————. *Institutes of the Christian Religion*. Translated by John Allan. London, 1813.

Campolo, Tony. *The Kingdom of God Is a Party*. Dallas: Word, 1990.

Canadian Index of Wellbeing. *How Are Canadians Really Doing? Highlights: Canadian Index of Wellbeing 1.0*. Waterloo, ON: Canadian Index of Wellbeing and University of Waterloo, 2011.

————. *How Are Canadians Really Doing?* The 2012 CIW Report. Waterloo, ON: Canadian Index of Wellbeing and University of Waterloo, 2012.

Carter, Marcia Jean. "The Flow Experience: An Integration of Spiritual and Leisure Well-Being." In *Christianity and Leisure: Issues at the Millenium*, edited by Glen Van Andel and Paul Heintzman. Sioux Center, IA: Dordt College Press, forthcoming.

————. "Quality of Life in a Christian Community: Conceptual Investigation of Flow Experiences and HPERD Responsibilities." In *Christianity and Leisure: Issues at the Millenium*, edited by Glen Van Andel and Paul Heintzman. Sioux Center, IA: Dordt College Press, forthcoming.

Cashmore, Ellis. *And There Was Television*. London: Routledge, 2004.

Cato, Bertha. "Leisure and Jesus' Rest: Making the Connection." Leadership U website. December 28, 1998. http://www.leaderu.com/theology/leisure-rest.html.

Chambers, Oswald. *My Utmost for His Highest*. Rev. ed. Toronto: McLelland & Stewart, 1947.

Chandler, Cynthia K., Janice M. Holden, and Cheryl A. Kolander. "Counseling for Spiritual Wellness: Theory and Practice." *Journal of Counseling and Development* 71, no. 2 (1992): 168–75.

Chapman, Chris. Foreword to *Canoescapes*, by Bill Mason, 8–9. North York, ON: Stoddart, 1995.

Coble, Theresa G., Steve W. Selin, and Beth B. Erickson. "Hiking Alone: Understanding Fear, Negotiation Strategies, and Leisure Experience." *Journal of Leisure Research* 35, no. 1 (2003): 1–22.

Cohen-Gewerc, Elie, and Robert A. Stebbins. Conclusion to *The Pivotal Role in Leisure Education: Finding Personal Fulfillment in This Century*, edited by Elie Cohen-Gewerc and Robert A. Stebbins, 153–72. State College, PA: Venture, 2007.

————. "The Idea of Leisure." In *The Pivotal Role in Leisure Education: Finding Personal Fulfillment in this Century*, edited by Elie Cohen-Gewerc and Robert A. Stebbins, 1–14. State College, PA: Venture, 2007.

Colloredo-Mansfeld, Rudi. *The Native Leisure Class: Consumption and Cultural Creativity in the Andes.* Chicago: University of Chicago Press, 1999.

Coppes, Leonard J. "Nûaḥ." In *Theological Wordbook of the Old Testament,* edited by Robert Laird Harris, Gleason Leonard Archer, and Bruce K. Waltke, 2:562. Chicago: Moody, 1980.

Cosgrove, Isobel, and Richard Jackson. *The Geography of Recreation and Leisure.* London: Hutchinson University Library, 1972.

Cox, Harvey. *The Secular City.* London: SCM, 1965.

Crabtree, Robert D. "Leisure in Ancient Israel." PhD diss., Texas A&M University, 1982.

Craigie, Peter C. *Psalms 1–50.* Word Biblical Commentary. Waco: Word, 1983.

Crittenden, Jeffrey P. "Holy Leisure: A Life of Prayer, Contemplation and Celebration." MTh thesis, St. Stephen's College, University of Alberta, 2001.

Csikszentmihalyi, Isabella. "Flow in Historical Context: The Case of the Jesuits." In *Optimal Experience: Psychological Studies of Flow in Consciousness,* edited by Mihaly Csikszentmihalyi and Isabella S. Csikszentmihalyi, 232–48. Cambridge: Cambridge University Press, 1988.

Csikszentmihalyi, Mihaly. *Beyond Boredom and Anxiety: The Experience of Play in Work and Games.* San Francisco: Jossey Bass, 1975.

———. *The Evolving Self: A Psychology for the Third Millennium.* New York: HarperCollins, 1993.

———. *Flow: The Psychology of Optimal Experience.* Toronto: Harper & Row, 1990.

Dahl, Gordon J. "Time, Work and Leisure Today." *The Christian Century* 88, no. 6 (February 1971): 185–89.

———. "Whatever Happened to the Leisure Revolution." In *Christianity and Leisure: Issues in a Pluralistic Society,* rev. ed., edited by Paul Heintzman, Glen E. Van Andel, and Thomas L. Visker, 85–97. Sioux Center, IA: Dordt College Press, 2006.

———. *Work, Play and Worship in a Leisure-Oriented Society.* Minneapolis: Augsburg, 1972.

Davies, Martin. "Another Way of Being: Leisure and the Possibility of Privacy." In *The Philosophy of Leisure,* edited by Cyril Barrett and Tom Winnifrith, 104–28. London: Macmillan, 1989.

Davis, Creath. "Joy." In *Evangelical Dictionary of Theology,* 2nd ed., edited by Walter A. Elwell, 636–37. Grand Rapids: Baker Academic, 2001.

de Graaf, John, ed. *Take Back Your Time: Fighting Overwork and Time Poverty in America.* San Francisco: Berrett-Koehler, 2003.

de Grazia, Sebastion. *Of Time, Work and Leisure.* New York: Twentieth Century Fund, 1962.

Dennison, James T., Jr. *The Market Day of the Soul: The Puritan Doctrine of the Sabbath in England, 1532–1760.* Lanham, MD: University Press of America, 1983.

Diddams, Margaret, Lisa K. Surdyk, and Denise Daniels. "Rediscovering Models of Sabbath Keeping: Implications for Psychological Well-Being." *Journal of Psychology and Theology* 32, no. 1 (2004): 3–11.

Doohan, Leonard. *Leisure: A Spiritual Need.* Notre Dame, IN: Ave Maria, 1990.

———. "The Spiritual Value of Leisure." *Spirituality Today* 31, no. 2 (1981): 157–67.

Dow, Graham. "What Place Does Work Have in God's Purpose?" *Anvil* 1, no. 2 (1984): 139–51.

Driver, Beverly L., Perry J. Brown, and George L. Peterson. "Research on Leisure Benefits: An Introduction to This Volume." In *Benefits of Leisure*, edited by Beverly L. Driver, Perry J. Brown, and George L. Peterson, 3–12. State College, PA: Venture, 1991.

Driver, Beverly L., and S. Ross Tocher. "Toward a Behavioral Interpretation of Recreational Engagements, with Implications for Planning." In *Elements of Outdoor Recreation Planning*, edited by Beverly Driver, 9–31. Ann Arbor: University of Michigan Press, 1970.

DuBay, Thomas. *The Evidential Power of Beauty: Science and Theology Meet.* San Francisco: Ignatius, 1999.

Dumazedier, Joffre. *Sociology of Leisure.* Translated by Marea A. McKenzie. New York: Elsevier, 1974.

———. *Toward a Society of Leisure.* Translated by Stewart E. McClure. New York: Free Press, 1967.

Dumbrell, William J. *Covenant and Creation.* Exeter, UK: Paternoster, 1984.

———. "A Sabbath Rest for the People of God." Lecture given at Regent College, Vancouver, October 9, 1985.

Durant, Will. *The Story of Civilization.* Vol. 2, *The Life of Greece.* New York: Simon & Schuster, 1939.

Dyson, Jane, Mark Cobb, and Dawn Forman. "The Meaning of Spirituality: A Literature Review." *Journal of Advanced Nursing* 26, no. 6 (1997): 1183–88.

Earickson, Joyce M. "The Religious Practice of the Sabbath: A Framework for Psychological Health and Spiritual Well-Being." PhD diss., Alliant International University, 2004.

Eaton, John Herbert. *Psalms: Introduction and Commentary.* London: SCM, 1967.

Eaton, Michael A. *Ecclesiastes.* Downers Grove, IL: InterVarsity, 1983.

Ehrenfeld, David, and Philip J. Bentley. "Nature in the Jewish Tradition: The Source of Stewardship." Unpublished paper.

Eichrodt, Walter. *Man in the Old Testament.* Translated by K. and R. Gregor Smith. London: SCM, 1959.

Ellard, Al, Norma Polovitz Nickerson, and Robert Dvorak. "The Spiritual Dimension of the Montana Vacation Experience." *Leisure/Loisir* 33, no. 1 (2009): 269–89.

Ellison, Henry Leopold. *Matthew.* London: Pickering & Inglis Ltd., 1969.

Ellul, Jacques. *The Technological Society.* Translated by John Wilkinson. New York: Random House, 1964.

Fabun, Don. *The Dynamics of Change.* Englewood Cliffs, NJ: Prentice Hall, 1967.

Fain, Gerald. "Moral Leisure." In *Leisure and Ethics,* edited by Gerald Fain, 7–30. Reston, VA: American Association for Leisure and Recreation, 1991.

Fairchild, Henry Pratt, ed. *Dictionary of Sociology.* Totowa, NJ: Littlefield, Adams, 1976.

Falwell, Jerry. *Listen America.* Garden City, NY: Doubleday, 1980.

Feldman Barrett, Lisa, and James A. Russell. "The Structure of Current Affect: Controversies and Emerging Consensus." *Current Directions in Psychology* 8, no. 1 (1999): 10–14.

Ferguson, John. *Aristotle.* New York: Twayne, 1972.

Filson, Floyd V. *A Commentary on the Gospel according to St. Matthew.* London: Adam & Charles Black, 1960.

Fitzgerald, Edward. "A Time for Play? I: The New Leisure." *Clergy Review* 59, no. 3 (1974): 283.

Forestell, J. Terence. "The Letters to the Thessalonians." In *The Jerome Biblical Commentary,* edited by Raymond Edward Brown, Joseph Augustine Fitzmyer, and Roland Edmund Murphy, 227–35. Englewood Cliffs, NJ: Prentice-Hall, 1968.

Foster, Richard J. *Celebration of Discipline: The Path to Spiritual Growth.* San Francisco: Harper & Row, 1978.

———. Introduction to *Celtic Daily Prayer: Prayers and Readings from the Northumbria Community*, xi–xx. New York: HarperCollins, 2002.

Foster, Richard J., and Emilie Griffin, eds. *Spiritual Classics.* New York: HarperSanFrancisco, 2000.

Foster, Richard J., and James B. Smith, eds. *Devotional Classics.* New York: HarperSanFrancisco, 1993.

Fox, Karen M. "Does the Gospel of Luke Suggest a Christian-Judaic Form of Leisure in the Graeco-Roman World?" *Leisure/Loisir* 33, no. 1 (2009): 11–30.

Fox, Karen M., and Elizabeth Klaiber. "Listening for a Leisure Remix." *Leisure Sciences* 28, no. 5 (2006): 411–30.

Fox, Rebecca. "Enhancing Spiritual Experience in Adventure Programs." In *Adventure Programming,* edited by John C. Miles and Simon Priest, 455–61. State College, PA: Venture, 1999.

———. "Women, Nature and Spirituality: A Qualitative Study Exploring Women's Wilderness Experience." In *Proceedings, ANZALS Conference 1997*, edited by David Rowe and Peter Brown, 59–64. Newcastle, NSW: Australian and New Zealand Association for Leisure Studies, and the Department of Leisure and Tourism Studies, University of Newcastle, 1997.

Fredrickson, Laura M., and Dorothy H. Anderson. "A Qualitative Exploration of the Wilderness Experience as a Source of Spiritual Inspiration." *Journal of Environmental Psychology* 19, no. 1 (1999): 21–39.

Fresque, Jennifer, and Ryan Plummer. "Accounting for Consumption Related to Outdoor Recreation: An Application of Ecological Footprint Analysis." *Leisure/Loisir* 33, no. 2 (2009): 589–614.

Freysinger, Valerie, and Othello Harris. "Race and Leisure." In *A Handbook of Leisure Studies,* edited by Chris Rojek, Susan M. Shaw, and Anthony James Veal, 250–70. New York: Palgrave Macmillan, 2006.

Freysinger, Valerie J., Susan M. Shaw, Karla A. Henderson, and M. Deborah Bialeschki, eds. *Leisure, Women and Gender.* State College, PA: Venture, 2013.

Gall, Terry Lynn, Claire Charbonneau, Neil Henry Clarke, Karen Grant, Anjali Joseph, and Lisa Shouldice. "Understanding the Nature and Role of Spirituality in Relation to Coping and Health: A Conceptual Framework." *Canadian Psychology/Psychologie canadienne* 46, no. 2 (2005): 88–104.

Gallant, Karen, Susan Arai, and Bryan Smale. "Celebrating, Challenging, and Re-Envisioning Serious Leisure." *Leisure/Loisir* 37, no. 2 (2013): 104.

Garber, Steven. *The Fabric of Faithfulness.* Downers Grove, IL: InterVarsity, 1996.

Geldard, Mark. "2001—A Factory Odyssey: Work Theology and Industrial Revolution." *Anvil* 2, no. 1 (1985): 55–73.

Gini, Al. *The Importance of Being Lazy.* New York: Routledge, 2003.

Godbey, Geoffrey. "Implications of Recreation and Leisure Research for Professionals." In *Understanding Leisure and Recreation: Mapping the Past, Charting the Future,* edited by Edgar L. Jackson and Thomas L. Burton, 613–28. State College, PA: Venture, 1989.

———. *Leisure and Leisure Services in the 21st Century: Toward Mid Century.* State College, PA: Venture, 2006.

———. "Trends in Time for Leisure." In *Leisure Matters: The State and Future of Leisure Studies,* edited by Gordon Walker, David Scott, and Monika Stodolska. State College, PA: Venture, forthcoming.

Goldberg, Louis. *Ecclesiastes.* Grand Rapids: Zondervan, 1983.

Goodale, Thomas L. "If Leisure Is to Matter." In *Recreation and Leisure: Issues in an Era of Change,* edited by Thomas L. Goodale and Peter A. Witt, 38–49. State College, PA: Venture, 1980.

———. "Legitimizing Leisure Anew." Paper presented at the 25th Anniversary of the Leisure Studies Department, University of Ottawa, May 14, 1994.

Goodale, Thomas, and Geoffrey Godbey. *The Evolution of Leisure: Historical and Philosophical Perspectives.* State College, PA: Venture, 1988.

Gooding, Judson. "How to Cope with Boredom." *Reader's Digest* 108, no. 646 (February 1976): 51–57.

Gordis, Robert. *Koheleth—The Man and His World: A Study of Ecclesiastes.* New York: Schocken, 1968.

———. "The Sabbath—Cornerstone and Capstone of Jewish Life." *Judaism* 31, no. 1 (1982): 6–11.

Gosselink, Carol A., and Susan A. Myllykangas. "The Leisure Experiences of Older U.S. Women Living with HIV/AIDS." *Health Care for Women International* 28, no. 1 (2007): 3–20.

Gourdzaard, Bob. *Aid for the Overdeveloped West.* Toronto: Wedge, 1975.

Grafanaki, Soti, Deborah Pearson, Frankie Cini, Magdalena Godula, Bruce McKenzie, Sandra Nason, and Martina Anderegg. "Sources of Renewal: A Qualitative Study of the Experience and Role of Leisure in the Life of Counselors and Psychologists." *Counselling Psychology Quarterly* 18, no. 1 (2005): 31–40.

Grayston, Kenneth. *The Letters of Paul to the Philippians and to the Thessalonians.* Cambridge: Cambridge University Press, 1967.

Green, Thomas H. *A Vacation with the Lord: A Personal, Directed Retreat Based on the Spiritual Exercises of Saint Ignatius Loyola.* Notre Dame, IN: Ave Maria, 1986.

Guignon, Charles, and Kevin Aho. "Phenomenological Reflections on Work and Leisure in America." In *The Value of Time and Leisure in a World of Work*, edited by Mitchell R. Haney and A. David Kline, 25–38. Lanham, MD: Lexington Books, 2010.

Guthrie, Donald. *Hebrews.* Tyndale New Testament Commentaries. Grand Rapids: Eerdmans, 1983.

Hagner, Donald A. *Hebrews. A Good News Commentary.* New York: Harper & Row, 1983.

Hahn, Bernard J. "Approaching Leisure Redemptively: Leisure Misunderstood." *Christian Renewal* 3, no. 19 (June 3, 1985): 6, 7, 15.

Haller, William. *The Rise of Puritanism.* Philadelphia: University of Pennsylvania Press, 1972.

Hamilton, Victor, P. "*Shābat.*" In *Theological Wordbook of the Old Testament*, edited by Robert Laird Harris, Gleason Leonard Archer, and Bruce K. Waltke, 2:902–3. Chicago: Moody, 1980.

Hansel, Tim. *When I Relax I Feel Guilty.* Elgin, IL: David C. Cook, 1979.

Harkness, Georgia E. *John Calvin: The Man and His Ethics.* Nashville: Abingdon, 1958.

Harris, Mark. *Companions for Your Spiritual Journey: Discovering the Disciplines of the Saints.* Downers Grove, IL: InterVarsity, 1999.

Harris, Scott. "Holy and Free, Part 6—Leisure." Grace Bible Church, Wappingers Falls, NY. August 24, 2003. http://gracebibleny.org/holy_free_part_6_leisure.

Harrison, Roland Kenneth. "Heal." In *The International Standard Bible Encyclopedia*, edited by Geoffrey Bromiley, 640–46. Grand Rapids: Eerdmans, 1982.

Hasel, Gerhard F. "Health and Healing in the Old Testament." *Andrews University Seminary Studies* 21, no. 3 (Autumn 1983): 191–202.

Hawks, Steven. "Spiritual Health: Definition and Theory." *Wellness Perspectives: Research, Theory and Practice* 10, no. 4 (1994): 3–13.

Hebert, L. Joseph, Jr. "Be Still and See: Leisure, Labor, and Human Dignity in Josef Pieper and Blessed John Paul II." *Logos: A Journal of Catholic Thought and Culture* 16, no. 2 (Spring 2013): 144–59.

Heilbroner, Robert L. *The Economic Problem.* 2nd ed. Englewood Cliffs, NJ: Prentice Hall, 1970.

Heintzman, Paul. "Defining Leisure." In *Leisure for Canadians*, 2nd ed., edited by Ron McCarville and Kelly MacKay, 3–14. State College, PA: Venture, 2013.

———. "Leisure and Spiritual Well-Being: A Social Scientific Exploration." PhD diss., University of Waterloo, 1997.

———. "Leisure and Spiritual Well-Being Relationships: A Qualitative Study." *Society and Leisure* 23, no. 1 (2000): 41–69.

———. "Leisure-Spiritual Coping: A Model for Therapeutic Recreation and Leisure Services." *Therapeutic Recreation Journal* 42, no. 1 (2008): 56–73.

———. "Leisure Studies and Spirituality: A Christian Critique." *Journal of the Christian Society for Kinesiology and Leisure Studies* 1 (2010): 19–31.

———. "Men's Wilderness Experience and Spirituality: A Qualitative Study." In *Proceedings of the 2006 Northeastern Recreation Research Symposium* (Gen. Tech. Rep. NRS-P-14), compiled by Robert Burns and Karen Robinson, 216–25. Newton Square, PA: U.S. Department of Agriculture, Forest Service, Northern Research Station, 2007.

———. "Men's Wilderness Experience and Spirituality: Further Explorations." In *Proceedings of the 2007 Northeastern Recreation Research Symposium* (Gen. Tech. Rep. NRS-P-23), compiled by Cherie LeBlanc and Christine Vogt, 55–59. Newton Square, PA: U.S. Department of Agriculture, Forest Service, Northern Research Station, 2008.

———. "Nature-based Recreation and Spirituality: A Complex Relationship." *Leisure Sciences* 32, no. 1 (2010): 72–89.

———. "Religion, Leisure and Spirituality." In *Leisure Matters: The State and Future of Leisure Studies*, edited by Gordon Walker, David Scott, and Monika Stodolska. State College, PA: Venture, forthcoming.

————. "The Role of Introspection and Spirituality in the Park Experience of Day Visitors to Ontario Provincial Parks." In *Managing Protected Areas in a Changing World*, edited by Soren Bondrup-Nielsen, Neil W. P. Munro, Gordon Nelson, J. H. Martin Willison, Tom B. Herman, and Paul Eagles, 992–1004. Wolfville, NS: Science and Management of Protected Areas Association, 2002.

————. "Rowing, Sailing, Reading, Discussing, Praying: The Spiritual and Lifestyle Impact of an Experientially Based, Graduate, Environmental Education Course." Paper presented at the Trails to Sustainability Conference, Kananaskis, AB, May 2007.

————. "The Spiritual Benefits of Leisure." *Leisure/Loisir* 33, no. 1 (2009): 419–45.

————. "The Spiritual Dimension of Campers' Park Experience." *Managing Leisure* 17, no. 4 (2012): 291–310.

Heintzman, Paul, and Roger C. Mannell. "Spiritual Functions of Leisure and Spiritual Well-Being: Coping with Time Pressure." *Leisure Sciences* 25, nos. 2–3 (2003): 207–30.

Heintzman, Paul, Glen E. Van Andel, and Thomas L. Visker, eds. *Christianity and Leisure: Issues in a Pluralistic Society*. Rev. ed. Sioux Center, IA: Dordt College Press, 2006.

Heisz, Andrew, and Sébastien Larochelle-Côté. *Summary of Work Hours Instability in Canada*. Catalogue No. 11F0019M1E, No. 279. Ottawa: Statistics Canada, Business and Labour Market Analysis Division, 2006.

Hemingway, John. "Lesiure [sic] and Civility: Reflections on a Greek Ideal." *Leisure Sciences* 10, no. 3 (1988): 179–91.

Henderson, Karla A., M. Deborah Bialeschki, John L. Hemingway, Jan S. Hodges, Beth D. Kivel, and H. Douglas Sessoms. *Introduction to Recreation and Leisure Services*. 8th ed. State College, PA: Venture, 2001.

Henderson, Karla A., M. Deborah Bialeschki, Susan M. Shaw, and Valerie J. Freysinger. *Both Gains and Gaps: Feminist Perspectives on Women's Leisure*. State College, PA: Venture, 1996.

————. *A Leisure of One's Own: A Feminist Perspective on Women's Leisure*. State College, PA: Venture, 1989.

Hendriksen, William. *Exposition of the Gospel according to Matthew*. Grand Rapids: Baker, 1973.

Henry, Matthew. *Commentary on the Whole Bible*. Edited by Leslie Frederic Church. Grand Rapids: Zondervan, 1961.

Hensel, Robert, and Colin Brown. "Rest." In *The New International Dictionary of New Testament Theology*, edited by Colin Brown, 254–58. Grand Rapids: Zondervan, 1978.

Hergenhahn, Baldwin Ross, and Matthew Olson. *An Introduction to Theories of Personality.* 5th ed. Upper Saddle River, NJ: Prentice Hall, 1991.

Hering, Jean. *The Epistle to the Hebrews.* Translated by Arthur W. Heathcote and Philip J. Allcock. London: Epworth, 1970.

Heschel, Abraham Joshua. *The Sabbath.* New York: Harper & Row, 1966.

Hewitt, Thomas. *The Epistle to the Hebrews.* Grand Rapids: Eerdmans, 1960.

Hick, John. "The Universality of the Golden Rule." In *Ethics, Religion and the Good Society: New Directions in a Pluralistic World,* edited by Joseph Runzon, 155–66. Louisville: Westminster/John Knox, 1992.

Hilbrecht, Margo. "Leisure and the Changing Workplace." In *Leisure for Canadians,* edited by Ron McCarville and Kelly MacKay, 83–91. State College, PA: Venture, 2007.

———. "Leisure and the Changing Workplace." In *Leisure for Canadians,* 2nd ed., edited by Ron McCarville and Kelly MacKay. State College, PA: Venture, 2013.

Hill, David. *The Gospel of Matthew.* London: Oliphants, 1972.

Hochschild, Arlie. *The Second Shift: Working Parents and the Revolution at Home.* New York: Viking, 1989.

Hoggard-Creegan, Nicola. "Why We Still Need Feminist Theology: A Response to Craig Blomberg." In *Reconsidering Gender: Evangelical Perspectives,* edited by Myk Habets and Beulah Wood, 63–74. Eugene, OR: Pickwick, 2011.

Holland, Jearold Winston. *Black Recreation: A Historical Perspective.* Chicago: Burnham, 2002.

Holmes, Arthur. *Contours of a World View.* Grand Rapids: Eerdmans, 1983.

Holt, Bradley P. *Thirsty for God: A Brief History of Christian Spirituality.* 2nd ed. Minneapolis: Fortress, 2005.

Hothem, Margaret. "The Integration of Christian Faith and Leisure: A Qualitative Study." EdD diss., Boston University, 1983.

———. "The Wonder of Leisure." In *Christianity and Leisure: Issues at the Millenium,* edited by Glen Van Andel and Paul Heintzman. Sioux Center, IA: Dordt College Press, forthcoming.

Houston, James. "The Theology of Work." In *Looking at Lifestyles Professional Priorities—A Christian Perspective.* Proceedings from A Conference for Physicians and Dentists. Banff, AB, May 2–8, 1981. Vancouver: Christian Medical and Dental Society of Canada, 1981.

Hughes, Everett Cherrington. *Men and Their Work.* Glencoe, IL: Free Press, 1958.

Huizinga, Johan. *Homo Ludens: A Study of the Play Element in Culture.* Boston: Beacon, 1955.

Hunnicutt, Benjamin Kline. *Free Time: The Forgotten American Dream.* Philadelphia: Temple University Press, 2013.

Ibrahim, Hilmi. "Leisure and Islam." In *Leisure and Ethics: Reflections on the Philosophy of Leisure*, edited by Gerald S. Fain, 203–20. Reston, VA: American Association for the Study of Leisure and Recreation in association with the American Alliance for Health, Physical Education, Recreation and Dance, 1991.

Idler, Ellen L. "Organizational Religiousness." In *Multidimensional Measurement of Religiousness/Spirituality for Use in Health Research*, edited by Fetzer Institute/National Institute on Ageing Working Group, 75–79. Kalamazoo, MI: Fetzer Institute, 1999.

Infantino, Mary. "Gardening: A Strategy for Health Promotion in Older Women." *Journal of the New York State Nurses Association* 35, no. 2 (2004–5): 10–17.

Iwasaki, Yoshi, and Jamir Butcher. "Common Stress-Coping Methods Shared by Older Women and Men with Arthritis." *International Journal of Psychosocial Rehabilitation* 8 (2004): 179–208.

Iwasaki, Yoshitaka, and Judith Bartlett. "Stress-Coping among Aboriginal Individuals with Diabetes in an Urban Canadian City: From Woundedness to Resilience." *Journal of Aboriginal Health* 3, no. 1 (2006): 15–25.

Iwasaki, Yoshitaka, Jennifer Mactavish, and Kelly MacKay. "Building on Strengths and Resilience: Leisure as a Stress Survival Strategy." *British Journal of Guidance and Counselling* 33, no. 1 (2005): 81–100.

Iwasaki, Yoshitaka, Judith Bartlett, Kelly MacKay, Jennifer Mactavish, and Janice Ristock. "Social Exclusion and Resilience as Frameworks of Stress and Coping among Selected Non-Dominant Groups." *International Journal of Mental Health Promotion* 7, no. 3 (2005): 4–17.

Iwasaki, Yoshitaka, Kelly J. MacKay, Jennifer B. Mactavish, Janice Ristock, and Judith Bartlett. "Voices from the Margins: Stress, Active Living, and Leisure as a Contributor to Coping with Stress." *Leisure Sciences* 28, no. 2 (2006): 163–80.

Jackson, Edgar Lionel. *Leisure and the Quality of Life: Impacts on Social, Economic and Cultural Development: Hangzhou Consensus: Invited Papers and Report of the Review Panel*. Hangzhou, China: Zhejiang University Press, 2006.

Joachim, Harold Henry. *Aristotle: The Nicomachean Ethics. A Commentary*, edited by David Arther Rees. Oxford: Oxford University Press, 1951.

Joblin, Douglas. "Leisure and Spirituality: An Engaged and Responsible Pursuit of Freedom in Work, Play, and Worship." *Leisure/Loisir* 33, no. 1 (2009): 95–120.

John Paul II, Pope, and Giuseppe Acocella. *Centesimus Annus*. Vatican City: Edizioni Logos, 1991.

Johnson, Karl. "From Sabbath to Weekend: Recreation, Sabbatarianism, and the Emergence of the Weekend." PhD diss., Cornell University, 2011.

———. "Problematizing Puritan Play." *Leisure/Loisir* 33, no. 1 (2009): 31–54.

Johnson, Ron, and Don McLean. "Leisure and the Development of Ethical Character: Changing Views of the North American Ideal." *Journal of Applied Recreation Research* 19, no. 2 (1994): 117–30.

Johnston, Robert K. *The Christian at Play.* Grand Rapids: Eerdmans, 1983.

———. "'Confessions of a Workaholic': A Reappraisal of Qoheleth." *Catholic Biblical Quarterly* 38, no. 1 (January 1976): 14–28.

Jowett, Benjamin, trans. Introduction to *The Politics of Aristotle.* Vol. 1. Oxford: Clarendon, 1885.

Kaiser, Walter C., Jr. *Ecclesiastes: Total Life.* Chicago: Moody, 1979.

Kanner, Bernice, "Hungry or Just Bored," *American Demographics* 21, no. 1 (1999): 15.

Kaplan, Max. "New Concepts of Leisure Today." In *Concepts of Leisure: Philosophical Implications*, edited by James F. Murphy, 229–36. Englewood Cliffs, NJ: Prentice-Hall, 1974.

Kaplan, Stephen. "The Restorative Benefits of Nature: Toward an Integrative Framework." *Journal of Environmental Psychology* 15, no. 3 (1995): 169–82.

Kashyap, Anand. "Leisure: An Indian Classical Perspective." *World Leisure and Recreation* 33, no. 2 (1991): 6–8.

Kasser, Tim, and Kirk Warren Brown. "On Time, Happiness, and Ecological Footprints." In *Take Back Your Time: Fighting Overwork and Time Poverty in America*, edited by John de Graaf, 107–12. San Francisco: Berrett-Koehler, 2003.

Kay, Tess. "Having It All or Doing It All? The Construction of Women's Lifestyles in Time-Crunched Households." *Leisure and Society/Loisir et Société* 21, no. 2 (1998): 435–54.

Kelly, John R. *Leisure.* 2nd ed. Englewood Cliffs, NJ: Prentice-Hall, 1990.

Kelly, John, and Geoffrey Godbey. *Sociology of Leisure.* State College, PA: Venture, 1992.

Kerr, Walter. *The Decline of Pleasure.* New York: Simon & Schuster, 1962.

Kidner, Derek. *Genesis.* London: Tyndale, 1967.

———. *A Time to Mourn, and a Time to Dance: Ecclesiastes and the Way of the World.* Leicester, UK: Inter-Varsity, 1976.

Klapp, Orrin E. *Overload and Boredom: Essays on the Quality of Life in the Information Society.* New York: Greenwood, 1986.

Kleiber, Douglas A. "The Neglect of Relaxation." *Journal of Leisure Research* 32, no. 1 (2000): 82–86.

Kleiber, Douglas A., Gordon J. Walker, and Roger C. Mannell. *A Social Psychology of Leisure.* 2nd ed. State College, PA: Venture, 2011.

Kraus, Rachel. "They Danced in the Bible: Identity Integration among Christian Women Who Belly Dance." *Sociology of Religion* 71, no. 4 (2010): 457–82.

Kraus, Richard. *Recreation and Leisure in Modern Society.* 3rd ed. Glenview, IL: Foresman, 1984.

Kuhn, Reinhard. *The Demon of Noontide: Ennui in Western Literature.* Princeton: Princeton University Press, 1976.

Lange, John Peter. *A Commentary on the Holy Scriptures,* vol. 1 of *The New Testament: Containing a General Introduction and the Gospel according to Matthew.* Translated by Philip Schaff. New York: Scribner, 1884.

LaSor, William Sanford, David Allan Hubbard, and Frederic William Bush. *Old Testament Survey.* Grand Rapids: Eerdmans, 1982.

Latourette, Kenneth Scott. *Christianity through the Ages.* New York: Harper & Row, 1965.

Lawrence, Brother. *The Practice of the Presence of God.* Edited by John J. Delaney. New York: Image Doubleday, 1977.

Leclercq, Jean. *The Love of Learning and the Desire for God: A Study of Monastic Culture.* New York: Fordham University Press, 1982.

———. "Otium Monasticum as a Context for Artistic Creativity." In *Monasticism and the Arts,* edited by Timothy G. Verdun, 63–69. Syracuse: Syracuse University Press, 1984.

Lee, Robert. *Religion and Leisure in America: A Study in Four Dimensions.* New York: Abingdon, 1964.

Lee, Traci. "Sabbath-keeping by Protestant Ministers: An Avenue of Meeting the Basic Psychological Needs and Mitigating Professional Burnout." PhD diss., Seattle Pacific University, 2003.

Lehman, Harold. *In Praise of Leisure.* Kitchener, ON: Herald, 1974.

Lenski, Richard Charles Henry. *The Interpretation of St. Matthew's Gospel.* Minneapolis: Augsburg, 1966.

Levin, J. "Private Religious Practices." In *Multidimensional Measurement of Religiousness/Spirituality for Use in Health Research,* edited by Fetzer Institute/National Institute on Ageing Working Group, 39–42. Kalamazoo, MI: Fetzer Institute, 1999.

Lewis, C. S. *Christian Reflections.* Grand Rapids: Eerdmans, 1967.

———. "De Descriptione Temporum." Inaugural Lecture from the Chair of Medieval and Renaissance Literature at Cambridge University. 1954. Accessed September 19, 2013. http://www.eng.uc.edu/~dwschae/temporum.html.

Lincoln, Andrew T. "From Sabbath to Lord's Day: A Biblical and Theological Perspective." In *From Sabbath to Lord's Day: A Biblical, Historical and Theological Investigation,* edited by Donald A. Carson, 343–412. Grand Rapids: Zondervan, 1982.

Linder, Staffan. *The Harried Leisure Class.* New York: Columbia University Press, 1970.

Little, Donna E., and Christopher Schmidt. "Self, Wonder and God! The Spiritual Dimensions of Travel Experiences." *Tourism* 54, no. 2 (2006): 107–16.

Livengood, Jennifer. "The Role of Leisure in the Spirituality of New Paradigm Christians." *Leisure/Loisir* 33, no. 2 (2009): 419–45.

Loeffler, T. A. "A Photo Elicitation Study of the Meanings of Outdoor Adventure Experiences." *Journal of Leisure Research* 36, no. 4 (2004): 536–56.

Lohfink, Norbert. *The Christian Meaning of the Old Testament.* Milwaukee: Bruce, 1968.

Luboshitzky, Dvora, and Lee Bennett Gaber. "Holidays and Celebrations as Spiritual Occupation." *Australian Occupational Therapy Journal* 48, no. 2 (2001): 66–74.

Luther, Martin. *Luther's Works.* Vol. 53. Edited by Ulrich S. Leupold. Philadelphia: Fortress, 1965.

Mair, Heather. "Civil Leisure? Exploring the Relationship between Leisure, Activism and Social Change." *Leisure/Loisir* 27, nos. 3–4 (2002): 213–37.

———. "What about the 'Rest of the Story'? Recreation on the Backs of 'Others.'" In *Speaking Up and Speaking Out: Working for Social and Environmental Justice through Parks, Recreation, and Leisure*, edited by Karen Paisley and Daniel Dustin, 117–23. Urbana, IL: Sagamore, 2011.

Mannell, Roger C., and Daniel J. Stynes, "A Retrospective: The Benefits of Leisure." In *Benefits of Leisure*, edited by Beverly L. Driver, Perry J. Brown, and George L. Peterson, 461–73. State College, PA: Venture, 1991.

Marsh, Paul E. "Backcountry Adventure as Spiritual Development: A Means-End Study." *Journal of Experiential Education* 30, no. 3 (2008): 290–93.

Marshall, Chris. "Heads and Bodies: A Response to Immanuel Koks." In *Reconsidering Gender: Evangelical Perspectives*, edited by Myk Habets and Beulah Wood, 188–95. Eugene, OR: Pickwick, 2011.

Marshall, I. Howard. *The Gospel of Luke: A Commentary on the Greek Text.* The New International Greek Testament Commentary. Grand Rapids: Eerdmans, 1978.

Marshall, Paul. "Vocation, Work, and Jobs." In *Labour of Love: Essays on Work*, edited by Josina Van Nuis Zylstra, 1–19. Toronto: Wedge, 1980.

Martens, Elmer A. *God's Design: A Focus on Old Testament Theology.* Grand Rapids: Baker, 1981.

Martin, Mike W. "Balancing Work and Leisure." In *The Value of Time and Leisure in a World of Work*, edited by Mitchell R. Haney and A. David Kline, 7–24. Toronto: Lexington, 2010.

Martin, William H., and Sandra Mason. "Leisure in an Islamic Context." *World Leisure* 46, no. 1 (2004): 4–13.

Maslow, Abraham H. *Toward a Psychology of Being.* 2nd ed. Toronto: Van Nos Reinhold, 1968.

Mason, Bill. *Canoescapes.* North York, ON: Stoddart, 1995.

———. *Path of the Paddle.* Toronto: Van Nostrand Reinhold, 1980.

———, director. *Song of the Paddle.* Montreal: National Film Board of Canada, 1978.

———. *Song of the Paddle.* Toronto: Key Porter Books, 1988.

————, producer and director. *Waterwalker*. Ottawa: National Film Board of Canada and Imago, 1984.

Mason, Jennifer. "'No Peace for the Wicked': Older Married Women and Leisure." In *Relative Freedoms: Women and Leisure*, edited by Erica Wimbush and Margaret Talbot, 75–85. Milton Keynes, UK: Open University Press, 1988.

McDonald, Barbara L., and Richard Schreyer. "Spiritual Benefits of Leisure Participation and Leisure Settings." In *Benefits of Leisure*, edited by Beverly L. Driver, J. Perry Brown, and George L. Peterson, 179–94. State College, PA: Venture, 1991.

McDonald, Daniel, and Leo McAvoy. "Native Americans and Leisure: State of the Research and Future Directions." *Journal of Leisure Research* 29, no. 2 (1997): 145–66.

McDowell, C. Forrest. "Wellness and Therapeutic Recreation: Challenge for Service." *Therapeutic Recreation Journal* 20, no. 2 (1986): 27–38.

McGee, John Vernon. *Thru the Bible*. Vol. 5. Nashville: Thomas Nelson, 1983.

Mead, Margaret. "The Pattern of Leisure in Contemporary American Culture." In *Mass Leisure*, edited by Eric Larrabee and Rolf Meyersohn. Glencoe, IL: Free Press, 1958.

Merton, Thomas, trans. *The Wisdom of the Desert: Sayings from the Desert Fathers of the Fourth Century*. London: Sheldon, 1960.

Miller, Perry, and Thomas H. Johnson. *The Puritans*. Rev. ed. New York: Harper, 1963.

Milligan, Christine, Anthony Gatrell, and Amanda Bingley. "Cultivating Health: Therapeutic Landscapes and Older People in Northern England." *Social Science & Medicine* 58, no. 9 (2003): 1781–93.

Moltmann, Jürgen. *God in Creation: An Ecological Doctrine of Creation*. Translated by Margaret Kohl. London: SCM, 1985.

Morgan, Edmund S. *The Puritan Dilemma: The Story of John Winthrop*. Boston: Little, Brown, 1958.

Moriarty, Frederick L. *Introducing the Old Testament*. Milwaukee: Bruce, 1960.

Mundy, Jean, and Linda Odum. *Leisure Education: Theory and Practice*. Toronto: John Wiley and Sons, 1979.

Murphy, James F. *Concepts of Leisure: Philosophical Implications*. Englewood Cliffs, NJ: Prentice Hall, 1974.

————. "A Rediscovery of the Spiritual Side of Leisure." *California Parks and Recreation* (December 1972/January 1973): 22–23.

Myers, David G. *The American Paradox: Spiritual Hunger in an Age of Plenty*. New Haven: Yale University Press, 2000.

Naess, Arne. *Ecology, Community, and Lifestyle: Outline of an Ecosophy*. New York: Cambridge University Press, 1989.

Neulinger, John. *The Psychology of Leisure*. Springfield, IL: Charles C. Thomas, 1981.

Neville, Graham. *Free Time: Towards a Theology of Leisure*. Birmingham, UK: University of Birmingham Press, 2004.

Nicoll, William Robertson. *St. Matthew*. The Expositor's Bible. New York: Funk & Wagnalls, 1900.

Nijkamp, Peter. "Socioethical Aspects of Labour." In *Labour of Love: Essays on Work*, edited by Josina Van Nuis Zylstra, 48–66. Toronto: Wedge, 1980.

Norden, Rudolph. *The Christian Encounters the New Leisure*. Saint Louis: Concordia, 1965.

Norris, Kathleen. *Acedia and Me: A Marriage, Monks, and a Writer's Life*. New York: Penguin, 2008.

Oates, Wayne. *Confessions of a Workaholic*. New York: World, 1971.

O'Rourke, James J. "Work, Leisure and Contemplation." *American Benedictine Review* 28, no. 4 (1977): 351–72.

Oswalt, John. *The Leisure Crisis: A Biblical Perspective on Guilt-Free Leisure*. Wheaton: Victor, 1987.

Ouellette, Pierre, Paul Heintzman, and Raymond Carette. "Les motivations et les effets d'une retraite faite par des personnes âgées dans un monastère bénédictin" ["The Motives and Effects of a Retreat Taken by Older People in a Benedictine Monastery"]. In *The Two Solitudes: Isolation or Impact?* Book of Abstracts from the Eleventh Canadian Congress on Leisure Research, edited by Tom Delamere, Carleigh Randall, and David Robinson, 448–52. Nanaimo, BC: Department of Recreation and Tourism Management, Malaspina University-College, 2005.

Ouellette, Pierre, Rachel Kaplan, and Stephen Kaplan. "The Monastery as a Restorative Environment." *Journal of Environmental Psychology* 25, no. 2 (2005): 178–88.

Owens, Joseph. "Aristotle on Leisure." *Canadian Journal of Philosophy* 11, no. 4 (December 1981): 713–24.

Packer, J. I. "Hot Tub Religion: Toward a Theology of Enjoyment." In *God's Plans for You*, 47–72. Wheaton: Crossway, 2001.

———. *Keep in Step with the Spirit*. Old Tappan, NJ: Fleming H. Revell, 1984.

———. "Leisure and Life-Style: Leisure, Pleasure, and Treasure." In *God and Culture: Essays in Honour of Carl F. H. Henry*, edited by Donald A. Carson and John D. Woodbridge, 356–68. Grand Rapids: Eerdmans, 1993.

Pargament, Kenneth I., and June Hahn. "God and the Just World: Causal and Coping Attributions to God in Health Situations." *Journal for the Scientific Study of Religion* 25, no. 2 (1986): 193–207.

Pargament, Kenneth I., Hannah Olsen, Barbara Reilly, Kathryn Falgout, David S. Ensing, and Kimberly Van Haitsma. "God Help Me (II): The Relationship of Religious Orientations to Religious Coping with Negative Life Events." *Journal for the Scientific Study of Religion* 31, no. 4 (1992): 504–13.

Park, Crystal L., and Lawrence Cohen. "Religious and Non-religious Coping with the Death of a Friend." *Cognitive Therapy and Research* 17, no. 6 (1993): 561–77.

Park, Crystal, Lawrence H. Cohen, and Lisa Herb. "Intrinsic Religiousness and Religious Coping as Life Stress Moderators for Catholics versus Protestants." *Journal of Personality and Social Psychology* 59, no. 3 (1990): 562–74.

Parker, Stanley. *Leisure and Work.* London: George Allen and Unwin, 1983.

———. *The Sociology of Leisure.* New York: International Publications, 1976.

The Parks and Recreation Federation of Ontario. *The Benefits of Parks and Recreation: A Catalogue.* North York, ON: The Parks and Recreation Federation of Ontario, 1992.

Parry, Diana C. "Gender and Leisure." In *Leisure for Canadians*, edited by Ronald E. McCarville and Kelly MacKay, 141–48. State College, PA: Venture, 2007.

Parsons, John J. "Be Still and Know That I Am God. Surrender: God's Irrepressible Care of the World." Hebrew for Christians website. Accessed June 2, 2008. http://www.hebrew4christians.com/Meditations/Be_Still/be_still.html.

Pascal, Blaise. *Pensées.* Translated by Alban John Krailsheimer. Baltimore: Penguin, 1966.

Percy, Walker. *Lost in the Cosmos: The Last Self-Help Book.* New York: Noonday, 1992.

Pieper, Josef. *Leisure: The Basis of Culture.* New York: Random House, 1963.

Piper, Otto A. "The Meaning of Work." *Theology Today* 14, no. 2 (July 1957): 174–94.

Pond, Michael F. "Investigating Climbing as a Spiritual Experience," M.S.R.S. thesis, Ohio University, 2013.

Postema, Don. *Space for God: The Study and Practice of Prayer and Spirituality.* Grand Rapids: Bible Way, 1983.

Preece, Gordon. "Re-creation and Recreation in the Eighties." In *Faith Active in Love.* Proceedings of the 1980 Conference of the A.F.E.S. Fellowship, edited by John Diesendorf. Sydney, Australia: A.F.E.S. Graduates Fellowship, 1981.

Prinsloo, Willem S. "Psalms." In *Eerdmans Commentary on the Bible*, edited by James Douglas, Grant Dunn, and John William Rogerson, 364–436. Grand Rapids: Eerdmans, 2003.

Putnam, Robert D. *Bowling Alone.* New York: Simon & Schuster, 2000.

Raffan, James. *Fire in the Bones: Bill Mason and the Canadian Canoeing Tradition.* Toronto: HarperCollins, 1996.

Ramsay, Hayden. *Reclaiming Leisure: Art, Sport, and Philosophy*. New York: Palgrave Macmillan, 2005.

Ramsay, Hayden. "Reflective Leisure, Freedom and Identity." In *Contemporary Perspectives in Leisure: Meanings, Motives, and Lifelong Learning*, edited by Sam Elkington and Sean J. Gammon. New York: Routledge, 2014.

Rasmussen, Albert. *Christian Responsibility in Economic Life*. Philadelphia: Westminster, 1965.

Rauschenbusch, Walter. *Christianity and the Social Crisis*. New York: Harper & Row, 1964.

Redekop, Calvin. "The Promise of Work." *Conrad Grebel Review* 1, no. 3 (Fall 1983): 1–19.

Reich, Charles. *The Greening of America*. New York: Random House, 1970.

Reid, Donald G., and Sue Welke. "Leisure and Traditional Culture in First Nations Communities." *Journal of Leisurability* 25, no. 1 (1998): 26–36.

Richardson, Alan. *The Biblical Doctrine of Work*. London: SCM, 1952.

Roberts, Kenneth. *Leisure*. London: Longman, 1970.

———. *Leisure in Contemporary Society*. 2nd ed. Wallingford, UK: CABI, 2006.

———. "Leisure: The Importance of Being Inconsequential." *Leisure Studies* 30, no. 1 (2011): 5–20.

Robinson, Gnana. "The Idea of Rest in the Old Testament and the Search for the Basic Character of Sabbath." *Zeitschrift für die alttestamentliche Wissenschaft* 92, no. 1 (1980): 32–42.

Robinson, John. "Are We There Yet? No, and Don't Hold Your Breath: The Family Vacation Is Fading Fast." *Sierra* (May/June 2008): 40–43.

Robinson, John P., and Geoffrey Godbey. *Time for Life: The Surprising Ways Americans Use Their Time*. University Park: Pennsylvania State University Press, 1997.

Robinson, Theodore H. *The Gospel of Matthew*. London: Hodder & Stoughton, 1928.

Robinson, Tim. *Work, Leisure and the Environment: The Vicious Cycle of Overwork and Over Consumption*. Northampton, MA: Edward Elgar, 2006.

Rogers, Carl. *On Becoming a Person: A Therapist's View of Psychotherapy*. Boston: Houghton Mifflin, 1961.

Rogerson, John William, and John William McKay. *Psalms 1–50*. Cambridge: Cambridge University Press, 1977.

Rojek, Chris. "Deviant Leisure: The Dark Side of Free-Time Activity." In *Leisure Studies: Prospects for the Twenty-First Century*, edited by Edgar L. Jackson and Thomas L. Burton, 81–95. State College, PA: Venture, 1999.

———. *The Labour of Leisure: The Culture of Free Time*. Los Angeles: Sage, 2010.

Rojek, Chris, Susan M. Shaw, and Anthony James Veal. Introduction to *A Handbook of Leisure Studies*, edited by Chris Rojek, Susan Shaw, and Anthony James Veal, 1–19. New York: Palgrave Macmillan, 2006.

Rolston, Holmes, III. "Creation and Recreation: Environmental Benefits and Human Leisure." In *Benefits of Leisure,* edited by Beverly L. Driver, Perry J. Brown, and George L. Peterson, 393–403. State College, PA: Venture, 1991.

Ross, Kenneth R. "You Did Not Dance: Reflections on a Theology of Recreation in the African Context." *Journal of Theology for Southern Africa* 82 (March 1993): 45–53.

Rybczynski, Witold. *Waiting for the Weekend*. New York: Viking, 1991.

Ryken, Leland. *Redeeming the Time: A Christian Approach to Work and Leisure*. Grand Rapids: Baker Books, 1995.

———. *Work and Leisure in Christian Perspective*. Portland, OR: Multnomah, 1987.

Ryken, Leland, Jim Wilhoit, and Tremper Longman III, eds. "Leisure." In *Dictionary of Biblical Imagery*, 505–6. Downers Grove, IL: InterVarsity, 1998.

Schmidt, Chris. "The Lived Experience of the Spiritual Potential of Leisure." *Annals of Leisure Research* 9, no. 3 (2006): 173–93.

Schmidt, Christopher, and Donna E. Little. "Qualitative Insights into Leisure as a Spiritual Experience." *Journal of Leisure Research* 39, no. 2 (2007): 222–47.

———. "The Spiritual Nature of Time and Space for Self: The Potential of Leisure to Engage the Human Soul." In *The Two Solitudes: Isolation or Impact? Book of Abstracts from the Eleventh Canadian Congress on Leisure Research*, edited by Tom Delamere, Carleigh Randall, and David Robinson, 546–49. Nanaimo, BC: Department of Recreation and Tourism Management, Malaspina University-College, 2005.

Schneider, Margaret A., and Roger C. Mannell, "Beacon in the Storm: An Exploration of the Spirituality and Faith of Parents Whose Children Have Cancer." *Issues in Comprehensive Pediatric Nursing* 29, no. 1 (2006): 3–24.

Schor, Juliet. "The (Even More) Overworked American." In *Take Back Your Time: Fighting Overwork and Time Poverty in America*, edited by John DeGraaf, 6–11. San Francisco: Berrett-Koehler, 2003.

———. "Overturning the Modernist Predictions: Recent Trends in Work and Leisure in the OECD." In *A Handbook of Leisure Studies*, edited by Chris Rojek, Susan M. Shaw, and Anthony James Veal, 203–15. New York: Palgrave Macmillan, 2006.

———. *The Overworked American: The Unexpected Decline of Leisure*. New York: Basic Books, 1991.

Schulz, John, and Christopher Auld. "A Social Psychological Investigation of the Relationship between Christianity and Contemporary Meanings of Leisure: An Australian Perspective." *Leisure/Loisir* 33, no. 1 (2009): 121–46.

Schweizer, Eduard. *The Good News according to Matthew.* Translated by David E. Green. Atlanta: Westminster John Knox, 1975.

Scott, Daniel. "Climate Change and Leisure: Impacts and Adaptation." Paper presented at the 10th World Leisure Congress, Quebec City, October 6–10, 2008.

Sellner, Edward C. "Soul Friendship in Early Celtic Monasticism—Part I." *Aisling Magazine* 17 (Samhain 1995). http://www.aislingmagazine.com/aisling magazine/articles/TAM17/Friendship.html.

Shaw, Susan M. "Conceptualizing Resistance: Women's Leisure as Political Practice." *Journal of Leisure Research* 33, no. 2 (2001): 186–201.

———. "Resistance." In *A Handbook of Leisure Studies*, edited by Chris Rojek, Susan M. Shaw, and Anthony James Veal, 533–45. New York: Palgrave Macmillan, 2006.

Shaw, Susan M., and Karla Henderson. "Gender Analysis and Leisure Constraints: An Uneasy Alliance." In *Constraints to Leisure*, edited by Edgar Lionel Jackson, 23–34. State College, PA: Venture, 2005.

Sherrow, Jeanne E. *It's About Time: A Look at Leisure, Lifestyle, and Christianity.* Grand Rapids: Zondervan, 1984.

Shivers, Jay. *Leisure and Recreation Concepts: A Critical Analysis.* Toronto: Allyn and Bacon, 1981.

———. "Leisure Constructs: A Conceptual Reference." *World Leisure & Recreation* 27, no. 1 (February 1985): 24–27.

Shivers, Jay S., and Lee J. DeLisle. *The Story of Leisure: Context, Concepts, and Current Controversy.* Champaign, IL: Human Kinetics, 1997.

Siddiqi, Maryam. "Ridiculously, Deliciously Conspicuous Consumption." *Financial Post*, December 20, 2003.

Singer, Charles Gregg. *John Calvin: His Roots and Fruits.* Philadelphia: P&R, 1967.

Solzhenitsyn, Aleksandr. *The Gulag Archipelago.* New York: Harper & Row, 1973.

Spacks, Patricia Meyer. *Boredom: The Literary History of a State of Mind.* Chicago: University of Chicago Press, 1995.

Spence, David. *Towards a Theology of Leisure with Special Reference to Creativity.* Ottawa: Canadian Parks/Recreation Association, 1973.

Spilka, Bernard, Phillip Shaver, and Lee A. Kirkpatrick. "A General Attribution Theory for the Psychology of Religion." *Journal for the Scientific Study of Religion* 24, no. 1 (1985): 1–20.

Springsted, Eric O. "Leisure, the Basis of Culture." Georgetown Presbyterian Church, Washington, DC. July 19, 2009. http://www.gtownpres.org.

Stackhouse, John G. *Finally Feminist: A Pragmatic Christian Understanding of Gender.* Grand Rapids: Baker Academic, 2005.

Stalker, Glenn J. "A Widening Parental Leisure Gap: The Family as a Site for Late Modern Differentiation and Convergence in Leisure Time within Canada, the United Kingdom and the United States." *Canadian Journal of Sociology/ Cahiers canadiens de sociologie* 36, no. 1 (2011): 25–58.

Stapleford, John E. *Bulls, Bears and Golden Calves: Applying Christian Ethics in Economics.* 2nd ed. Downers Grove, IL: IVP Academic, 2009.

Statistics Canada. *Women in Canada 2000: A Gender-Based Statistical Report.* Ottawa: Canadian Ministry of Industry, 2000.

Stebbins, Robert A. "Casual Leisure: A Conceptual Statement." *Leisure Studies* 16, no. 1 (1997): 17–25.

———. *The Idea of Leisure: First Principles.* New Brunswick, NJ: Transaction, 2012.

———. *Leisure and Consumption: Common Ground/Separate Worlds.* New York: Palgrave Macmillan, 2009.

———. "Leisure Reflections 11: Contemplation as Leisure and Non-Leisure." *LSA Newsletter* 73 (March 2006): 16–18.

———. "Project-Based Leisure: Theoretical Neglect of a Common Use of Free Time." *Leisure Studies* 24, no. 1 (2005): 1–11.

———. "Serious Leisure: A Conceptual Statement." *Pacific Sociological Review* 25, no. 2 (1982): 251–72.

———. "Serious Leisure." In *A Handbook of Leisure Studies*, edited by Chris Rojek, Susan M. Shaw, and Anthony James Veal, 448–56. New York: Palgrave Macmillan, 2006.

———. "Serious Leisure." In *Leisure Studies: Prospects for the Twenty-First Century*, edited by Edgar L. Jackson and Thomas L. Burton, 69–79. State College, PA: Venture, 1999.

Steere, Douglas V. "Contemplation and Leisure." *Humanitas* 8, no. 3 (1972): 287–306.

Stern, Bianca. "A Phenomenological Approach towards Understanding the Nature and Meaning of Engagement in Religious Ritual Activity: Perspectives from Persons with Dementia and Their Caregivers." MSc thesis, University of Toronto, 2005.

Stevens, Paul R. "Friendship." In *The Complete Book of Everyday Christianity: An A–Z Guide to Following Christ in Every Aspect of Life*, edited by Robert Banks and Paul R. Stevens, 435–42. Downers Grove, IL: InterVarsity, 1997.

———. *Seven Days of Faith.* Colorado Springs: NavPress, 2001.

Still, William. *Rhythms of Rest and Work.* 3rd ed. Aberdeen, Scotland: Gilcomston South Church, 1985.

Storkey, Elaine. *What's Right with Feminism.* London: SPCK, 1985.

Stott, John. "Creative by Creation: Our Need for Work." *Christianity Today* 23, no. 17 (June 8, 1979): 32–33.

———. *Decisive Issues Facing Christians Today.* Old Tappan, NJ: Fleming H. Revell, 1990.

———. "Reclaiming the Biblical Doctrine of Work." *Christianity Today* 23, no. 15 (May 4, 1979): 36–37.

Stringer, L. Allison, and Leo H. McAvoy. "The Need for Something Different: Spirituality and the Wilderness Adventure." *The Journal of Experiential Education* 15, no. 1 (1992): 13–21.

Sutherland, Wilbur. "An Interview with Bill Mason." *Crux* 9, no. 4 (Summer 1972): 6–17.

Sweatman, Mary, and Paul Heintzman, "The Perceived Impact of Outdoor Residential Camp Experience on the Spirituality of Youth." *World Leisure Journal* 46, no. 1 (2004): 23–31.

Sylvester, Charles. "Interpretation and Leisure Science: A Hermeneutical Example of Past and Present Oracles." *Journal of Leisure Research* 32, no. 1 (1990): 290–95.

———. "The Western Idea of Work and Leisure: Traditions, Transformations, and the Future." In *Leisure Studies: Prospects for the Twenty-First Century*, edited by Edgar L. Jackson and Thomas L. Burton, 17–33. State College, PA: Venture, 1999.

Tasker, Randolph Vincent Greenwood. *The Gospel according to St. Matthew*. The Tyndale New Testament Commentaries. London: Tyndale, 1961.

Tawney, Richard Henry. *Religion and the Rise of Capitalism*. London: John Murray, 1926.

Teaff, Joseph. "Contemplative Leisure within Christian Spirituality." In *Christianity and Leisure: Issues in a Pluralistic Society*, rev. ed., edited by Paul Heintzman, Glen E. Van Andel, and Thomas L. Visker, 112–15. Sioux Center, IA: Dordt College Press, 2006.

Terkel, Studs. *Working*. New York: Pantheon, 1974.

Terrien, Samuel L. *The Psalms: Strophic Structure and Theological Commentary*. Grand Rapids: Eerdmans, 2003.

Tillinghast, Pardon E. "Leisure: Old Patterns and New Problems." In *Planning for Diversity and Choice: Possible Futures and Their Relations to the Man-Controlled Environment*, edited by Stanford Anderson, 143–54. Cambridge, MA: MIT Press, 1968.

Toffler, Alvin. *Future Shock*. New York: Bantam, 1971.

Towner, Philip H. "Households and Household Codes." In *Dictionary of Paul and His Letters*, edited by Gerald F. Hawthorne, Ralph P. Martin, and Daniel G. Reid, 417–19. Downers Grove, IL: InterVarsity Press, 1993.

Trafton, Dain A. "In Praise of Three Traditional Ideas of Leisure." In *Transitions to Leisure: Conceptual and Human Issues*, edited by Billy G. Gunter, Jay Stanley, and Robert N. St. Clair, 23–31. Lanham, MD: University Press of America, 1985.

Trunfio, Margaret. "A Theological Perspective on the Ethics of Leisure." In *Leisure and Ethics: Reflections on the Philosophy of Leisure*, edited by Gerald Fain, 151–59. Reston, VA: American Association for Leisure and Recreation, 1991.

Tsai, Chiung-Tzu Lucetta. "A Reflection on Cultural Conflicts in Women's Leisure." *Leisure Sciences* 32, no. 4 (2010): 386–90.

———. "Research Note: The Influence of Confucianism on Women's Leisure in Taiwan." *Leisure Studies* 25, no. 4 (2006): 469–76.

———. "Women's Leisure, Leisurely Women? Feminist Perspectives on the Leisure Practice in Taiwan." *Asian Journal of Exercise and Sports Science* 5, no. 1 (2008): 39–47.

Underhill, Evelyn. *Practical Mysticism*. New York: Dutton, 1943.

Unruh, Anita M., Nancy Smith, and Cynthia Scammell. "The Occupation of Gardening in Life-Threatening Illness: A Qualitative Pilot Study." *Canadian Journal of Occupational Therapy* 67, no. 1 (2000): 70–77.

Van Andel, Glen E. "Redeeming Play: A Christian Perspective." In *Christianity and Leisure: Issues at the Millennium*. Sioux Center, IA: Dordt College Press, forthcoming.

Van Andel, Glen, and Paul Heintzman. "Christian Spirituality and Therapeutic Recreation." In *Philosophy of Therapeutic Recreation: Ideas and Issues*, edited by Charles Sylvester, 2:71–85. Arlington, VA: National Recreation and Park Association, 1996.

Vanderkloet, Edward. "Why Work Anyway." In *Labour of Love: Essays on Work*, edited by Josina Van Nuis Zylstra, 20–47. Toronto: Wedge, 1980.

Veblen, Thorstein. *The Theory of the Leisure Class*. New York: The New American Library, 1899/1953.

Visker, Thomas L. "Play, Game and Sport in a Reformed, Biblical Worldview." In *Christianity and Leisure: Issues in a Pluralistic Society*, rev. ed., edited by Paul Heintzman, Glen E. Van Andel, and Thomas L. Visker, 172–92. Sioux Center, IA: Dordt College Press, 2006.

Vitz, Paul Clayton. *Psychology as Religion: The Cult of Self-Worship*. 2nd ed. Grand Rapids: Eerdmans, 1994.

Vo, Lam Thuy. "What Americans Actually Do All Day Long, in 2 Graphics." National Public Radio. August 29, 2012. http://www.npr.org/blogs/money/2012/08/29/160244277/what-americans-actually-do-all-day-long-in-2-graphics.

Von Rad, Gerhard. "There Remains Still a Rest for the People of God: An Investigation of a Biblical Conception." In *The Problem of the Hexateuch and Other Essays*, 94–102. Edinburgh & London: Oliver & Boyd, 1966.

Vos, Nelvin. "To Take Life Leisurely." *Reformed Journal* 29, no. 5 (1979): 14–16.

Vukonić, Boris. *Tourism and Religion*. Translated by S. Matešić. New York: Elsevier, 1996.

Walker, Gordon J., and Jinyang Deng. "Comparing Leisure as Subjective Experience with the Chinese Experience of Rùmí." *Leisure/Loisir* 28, nos. 3–4 (2003–4): 245–76.

Wang, Jianyu, and L. Allison Stringer. "The Impact of Taoism on Chinese Leisure." *World Leisure* 42, no. 3 (2000): 33–41.

Ward, Veda E. "Leisure: Spiritual Well-Being and Personal Power." *Spiritual Life* 45, no. 4 (1999): 231–36.

Waterman, G. Henry. "Sabbath." In *The Zondervan Pictorial Encyclopedia of the Bible*, edited by Merrill C. Tenney, 5:181–89. Grand Rapids: Zondervan, 1975.

Westermann, Claus. *Creation*. Translated by John J. Scullion. Philadelphia: Fortress, 1974.

Whitely, Denys Edward Hugh. *Thessalonians in the Revised Standard Version with Introduction and Commentary*. London: Oxford University Press, 1969.

Whybray, Roger N. "Qoheleth, Preacher of Joy." *Journal for the Study of the Old Testament* 23 (July 1982): 87–98.

Williams, Roman R. "Space for God: Lived Religion at Work, Home and Play." *Sociology of Religion* 71, no. 3 (2010): 257–79.

Winter, Richard. *Still Bored in a Culture of Entertainment: Rediscovering Passion and Wonder*. Downers Grove, IL: InterVarsity, 2002.

Witherington, Ben, III. *The Rest of Life: Rest, Play, Eating, Studying, Sex from a Kingdom Perspective*. Grand Rapids: Eerdmans, 2012.

Wolcott, Victoria W. *Race, Riots and Roller Coasters: The Struggle over Segregated Recreation in America*. Philadelphia: University of Pennsylvania Press, 2012.

Wolff, Hans Walter. "The Day of Rest in the Old Testament." *Lexington Theology Quarterly* 7, no. 3 (July 1972): 65–76.

Wright, Gwen W. "Spirituality and Creative Leisure." *Pastoral Psychology* 32, no. 3 (1984): 192–203.

Young, Edward J. "Sabbath." In *The New Bible Dictionary*, edited by James Dixon Douglas, 1110–11. Grand Rapids: Eerdmans, 1962.

Zalatan, Antoine. "Work Utility and Disposable Time: The Canadian Evidence." *Leisure Studies* 3, no. 1 (1984): 89–96.

Zuzanek, Jiri. "Leisure and Time." In *A Handbook of Leisure Studies*, edited by Chris Rojek, Susan M. Shaw, and Anthony James Veal, 185–202. New York: Palgrave Macmillan, 2006.

Zuzanek, Jiri, and Roger Mannell. "Life-cycle Squeeze, Time Pressure, Daily Stress, and Leisure Participation: A Canadian Perspective." *Society and Leisure* 21, no. 2 (1998): 513–44.

index